Henry R. Luce, *Time*, and the American Crusade in Asia

Henry Robinson Luce (1898–1967) founded *Time*, *Life*, *Fortune*, and *Sports Illustrated*. Born in China to missionary parents, Luce was a kind of lay preacher, eager to mold the American mind and advance his ideological program of intervention, capitalism, democracy (when appropriate), and Christian activism. The most celebrated and influential editor of his day, Luce was also obsessed with the American mission in the world, and with China and East Asia. Luce tried to "sell" this mission to a sometimes reluctant public. A passionate anti-Communist interventionist, he also convinced Americans that the United States had perversely "lost" China to the Communists. A fervent advocate of the Vietnam intervention, Luce, the author of the "American Century," edited incoming correspondents' cables so that the magazines might conform to his ideas. For the first time, we see how Luce accomplished this. Using hitherto inaccessible or neglected sources, Robert E. Herzstein produces a gripping portrait of a great but tragic figure in American history.

Robert E. Herzstein is a Carolina Distinguished Professor of History at the University of South Carolina, where he teaches. He is the author of numerous books, including *Henry R. Luce: A Political Portrait of the Man Who Created the American Century*, *Waldheim: The Missing Years*, *Roosevelt and Hitler: Prelude to War*, *Adolf Hitler and the German Trauma*, and *The Nazis*. Professor Herzstein is also the author of numerous scholarly articles and the recipient of various awards and grants.

Also by the Author

Adolf Hitler and the German Trauma
The War That Hitler Won
The Nazis (Time-Life World War II Series)
When Nazi Dreams Come True
Waldheim: The Missing Years
Roosevelt and Hitler: Prelude to War
√ *Henry R. Luce: A Political Portrait of the Man*
Who Created the American Century

Henry R. Luce, *Time*, and the American Crusade in Asia

ROBERT E. HERZSTEIN

CAMBRIDGE
UNIVERSITY PRESS

CAMBRIDGE UNIVERSITY PRESS
Cambridge, New York, Melbourne, Madrid, Cape Town, Singapore, São Paulo

Cambridge University Press
40 West 20th Street, New York, NY 10011-4211, USA

www.cambridge.org
Information on this title: www.cambridge.org/9780521835770

First published 2005

Printed in the United States of America

A catalog record for this publication is available from the British Library.

Library of Congress Cataloging in Publication Data
Herzstein, Robert Edwin.
Henry R. Luce, *Time*, and the American crusade in Asia / Robert E. Herzstein.
p. cm.
Includes bibliographical references.
ISBN 0-521-83577-1
1. Luce, Henry Robinson, 1898–1967. 2. China – Foreign public opinion, American.
3. Asia – Foreign public opinion, American. 4. Public opinion – United States.
I. Title.
PN4874.L76H44 2005
070.5′092–dc22   2004021615

ISBN-13 978-0-521-83577-0 hardback
ISBN-10 0-521-83577-1 hardback

To Edward T. Chase, for three decades of wisdom,
criticism, inspiration, and friendship

Contents

Illustrations

Preface

To me, and to many other readers who grew into adulthood in the 1950s and the early 1960s, *Time* was much more than a magazine. It was required reading for middle-class Americans eager to learn about the world in which we lived. *Time*'s writing was often superb, and for many of us, the magazine presented a kind of unofficial but definitive version of America's righteous cause during the Cold War. *Time* also told fascinating stories; our high school history teachers boasted of reading it cover to cover, and in civics, we had to take weekly "*Time* quizzes," which filtered the news through Henry R. Luce's prism.

Most of us had never heard of Luce, but we realized that his newsmagazine was biased against the Democrats and in favor of Eisenhower. We detested the magazine's unrelenting attacks on liberal heroes like Adlai E. Stevenson, but we were all budding Cold Warriors, and if *Time* said that Ngo Dinh Diem of South Vietnam was a great man, most of us believed it. We read on, engrossed by the stories *Time* told, and above all, we accepted its version of world events. Luce's Red China was my Red China, and I took for granted the virtues of his global interventionism. It was only in the mid-1960s that the discrepancy between what *Time* said and what was actually happening in Vietnam badly eroded my faith – and that of many other Americans of my era – in Henry Luce's chosen instrument.

Memories of Luce's powerful journalism linger among people who were adult readers during the era of World War II and the early Cold War. The conservative William F. Buckley, Jr., who was a close friend of Clare Boothe Luce in her later years, recalls that "if it was in *Time*, it was important." In agreement, the liberal Arthur M. Schlesinger, Jr., who wrote for *Life* and *Fortune*, remembers the "Time Inc. ethos" as "powerful stuff in those days." Now, fifty years later, I return to those early decades of the Cold War. I will examine the ideology and impact of a man whose journalism helped to mold our history, although not so much as Luce would have liked or his enemies feared.

My aim is to probe the ways in which Luce tried to influence American foreign policy in regard to China and the Far East. I want to learn what Luce knew and then find out what he told his readers and friends among the political elites of the day. Then, when possible, I will comment upon his influence or lack of it. I will take three cases: China, Korea, and Vietnam.

In exploring these aspects of Henry Luce's journalism, I have made extensive use of a precious resource. This virtually unknown but massive collection was brought to my attention by Harvard librarians laboring in the stately Houghton Library. There, one finds large, dusty cartons containing a huge number of dispatches from *Time*'s correspondents. They seem to have been deposited there by Roy Larsen, Luce's longtime associate and the president of Time Inc. The documents are vaguely organized by date but are otherwise stored without reference to subject matter or authorship. So far as I can tell, none were destroyed, something that is not true of the copies perused by Time Inc.'s editors in New York. By examining those cables and then analyzing what Luce and the other editors then published, we can see through Time Inc.'s news filter. The results are sometimes disturbing, for what I found was a flawed journalism for which editor-in-chief Luce was primarily responsible.

One finds that Luce not only edited but also censored. His advocacy journalism, driven by hopes and prejudices and ideology, affected Time Inc.'s coverage. Objectivity, Luce believed, was often used as a cloak to hide indifference. As a result, there was an inverse ratio between Luce's passion about a subject and its objective treatment in *Time*.

I say this sadly, because Henry Luce was a man of powerful intellect and phenomenal energy, a patriot and a generous benefactor and patron of worthy causes. He was courageous, too, but often his journalism was misguided more than informative.

In this post–Cold War world we can move beyond the Communist-centered political debates that roiled this country fifty or thirty years ago. Perhaps we can now determine how Henry Robinson Luce affected our history during a long and bitter international conflict. Yet despite the demise of the Soviet Union and the abandonment of Marxism-Leninism by China, Luce's influence and mindset have hardly been laid to rest. As I write, the United States is involved in a massive project that seeks to convert Muslim Iraq into a democracy. Once again, the American nation-building mission is at work, in a different time but in ways defined by men like Woodrow Wilson and Henry R. Luce.

I want to thank many people for their kind assistance. Sadly, some who were so helpful in interviews have passed away, among them John Hersey, Allen Grover, Bob Sherrod, and Eliot Janeway. I learned much from them, and I treasure the memory of friendly but frank interviews.

Mr. Henry Luce III was kind enough to grant access to his father's papers at the Library of Congress before they were available to the public. I would also like to thank Mr. William F. Buckley, Jr., for allowing me to use his collected papers, which are accessible at Yale University; and Mr. David Halberstam, for permitting me to consult his papers, which are stored at Boston University.

To the historian researching the work and impact of Henry Luce, four collections stand out in importance: the papers of the Luces at the Library of Congress; the John Shaw Billings collection at the University of South Carolina; and the *Time* dispatches at Harvard University. In all cases, archivists and staff were courteous and helpful. In addition, the list of archival sources identified at the end of this book cites other collections essential to my work on Henry R. Luce.

I express my appreciation to the University of South Carolina for support from the office of Research and Productive Scholarship.

I would also like to thank individuals whose assistance went well beyond the call of duty. Among them are Elena Danielson and Carol Leadenham of the Hoover Institution, David J. Haight of the Eisenhower Library, Fred Bauman of the Library of Congress, and Dennis Bilger of the Truman Library.

I owe special debts of gratitude to Professor Ralph Levering of Davidson College; to Dr. Elizabeth Stewart; and to Professor Patrick J. Maney of the University of South Carolina for their suggestions, criticisms, and corrections.

A note on Chinese names and places: In most cases, I have used pinyin – for example, Zhou Enlai rather than Chou En-lai. In certain cases, I have put the older usage in parentheses (formerly Chou En-lai) after the first reference to an important figure. In other instances, however, the older form is so standard that I have retained it (Chiang Kai-shek, or KMT for Guomindang). Where I cite a document or comment where the older form occurs, I have of course retained the original usage – for example, "I arrived in Nanking today, November 25 ... "

Henry R. Luce, *Time*, and the American Crusade in Asia

Introduction

A little more than a century ago, Henry Robinson Luce was born to missionary parents in China. To the Reverend and Mrs. Henry W. Luce, it seemed like a happy coincidence that the little boy came into the world during the very time when America was acquiring an empire in the Pacific. The Luce family hero was Teddy Roosevelt, the symbol of the expansive America of that era. Henry R. Luce died at a time when Americans were fighting in another Asian war. A year before his death, Luce wrote, "I judge [Vietnam] to be a good thing rather than a bad thing – certainly an inescapable thing which is better to deal with than to try to escape from."[1]

Two forces shaped Henry Luce's character and worldview. One was Protestant Christianity; the other was a fervent faith in America's God-ordained global mission in Asia. As an adult, Luce used his vastly successful journalism as a kind of secular pulpit from which he preached the virtues of American engagement in Asia. Luce has been called the most influential private citizen in the America of his day. He controlled an enterprise that reached one-quarter or more of the American reading public. As the publisher of *Time*, *Life*, *Fortune*, and the *March of Time* film and radio documentaries, as a fervent Republican, philanthropist, and patron of the missionary cause, Henry R. Luce relentlessly lobbied for greater American involvement in the affairs of China and its neighbors. He operated at the center of a powerful network, one that encompassed the China lobby and other "Asia-firsters," members of Congress, philanthropists, business leaders, and people active in Hollywood and the arts. Luce was a prime supporter of the Christian educational mission in China, and during the war, his United China Relief was an influential part of the foreign aid effort. And as a journalist, Luce often enjoyed access to classified information. His sources were superb, especially among Republicans, and the written record, as amplified by interviews, allows us to reconstruct the networks within which he operated.

Henry R. Luce was the greatest journalistic innovator of his century and a dedicated patriot during some of the most turbulent times in our history. I have written with admiration about him, especially when looking at Luce's work before and during World War II.[2] Whether he was right or wrong at any given time, Luce was the most ardent and consistent interventionist of his day; he intended to make sure that politicians and the public thought the way *Time* told them to think. In 1953, John Shaw Billings, a close associate, said of his boss that he was "obsessed with the subject of foreign policy and his direct influence on it."[3] Billings added, "Nothing else interests him," and "he regards his position as 'unique' for exerting pressure – [with] Clare in Rome,* C. D. Jackson[†] in the White House and his magazines to press his points." Billings then concluded that Luce was uninterested in the daily operations of those magazines but believed that he was "molding the destiny of the U.S. in the world."

Luce's journalism educated – and sometimes miseducated – millions of people, bringing to them marvelous works of art and profound economic inquiries, along with snappy gossip and vivid personality portraits. His journalism damned enemies and lauded friends, in prose that could be snide and colorful – but also heroic and moving. The company's magazines (and sometimes, its newsreels and radio broadcasts) were a force in American culture, thanks in some measure to the vast prestige that accrued to the Luce publications in the wake of World War II. After all, this was the war that Henry Luce had foreseen as the final act precipitating the onset of American global hegemony. *Life* brilliantly covered the global conflict and moved millions with its pictures and words.

To Henry Luce, the American Century, which he had first prophesied in 1940, was a way station in humankind's attempt to build the City of God on earth. Humans, who were sinners, must fail, but try they must. Always, Luce had his eye upon America's opportunity, and he looked ahead to the time when Americans would make his better world. But after 1944 he discovered a new obstacle to the advent of the American Century. An unfashionably early anti-Communist increasingly suspicious of the Soviet ally, Luce resolved to block the rise of atheistic Communism in China and the lands adjacent to the Central Kingdom. To Luce, this contest pitted the true church against a Marxist, un-Chinese heresy. Americans, Luce insisted, could save China and, in the process, would save themselves. And thus occurred the most bitter experience of his lifetime. Unlike *Time*, the administration and the American public wanted no part of massive intervention in China's civil war; nor did they favor war against the entity that became "Red China." Luce, however, remained insistent. To him, America belonged in China, so when America failed to save China, Luce's anger knew few bounds.

To Luce, Asia, and not Europe, was the real prize. It was more populous, a veritable garden of souls, and, being underdeveloped, it was also subject to American influence. But to Luce's annoyance, most Americans were more

---

* Ambassador to Italy Clare Boothe Luce, Henry Luce's second wife.
† Charles Douglas Jackson, a senior executive and editor at Time Inc., served Eisenhower in 1953–1954 as an adviser on Cold War strategy.

interested in Europe than in Asia, even when the national interest seemed to mandate a more balanced view of the world. Even today, if you mention the Cold War, most Americans identify it as the great contest with the Soviet Union in Europe. But if Luce were here, he would probably remind us that very few Americans or citizens of North Atlantic Treaty Organization (NATO) countries died in the struggle against the Soviets. In fighting Communism in East Asia, by contrast, an estimated one hundred ten thousand Americans paid with their lives.

This book examines one man's attempt to involve the United States deeply in the battle against Communism in China and Korea and Vietnam. It is also the tale of a man who was indefatigable. Indeed, what Henry Luce first called "nation-making" in Vietnam became part of his controversial legacy. But behind the advocacy journalism, the ideological crusades, and the bitterness lurked a fascinating man, one who merits careful study. Luce's character, after all, contributed both to his greatness and to his defects.

Despite his cold, brusque demeanor, "Harry" Luce (he detested the name Henry) was more than the "thinking machine" described by his colleague John Billings. Inspired by a Christian sense of duty, Luce was also a complex, contradictory, and often suffering human being. For example, Luce had a poetic and nostalgic side that he concealed from most contemporaries and that would have astonished many of them. And there are other surprises in store for those who study Luce's life and work: A Presbyterian layman fascinated by theology, this Calvinist son of a missionary came close to converting to Roman Catholicism. A moralist and something of a work-obsessed prude, Luce committed adultery with guilty abandon and grew rich selling advertising space to liquor distillers. (In a moment of remorse, he suggested that his church try him for this transgression.) Possessed of fabled curiosity, Luce also had what *Life*'s Dan Longwell called "the faculty of not listening to anyone he didn't want to hear (or anything they said he disagreed with)."[4] Luce hated to fire anyone, but he abandoned the famous witness Whittaker Chambers at the lowest moment in the life of that *Time* senior editor.

When we examine Luce's media, it is fair to hold him responsible, because as editor-in-chief, he always claimed responsibility for *all* of their contents. To a remarkable extent, Time Inc.'s three great magazines more often than not reflected the views that Luce also expressed in memoranda, speeches, and diary notes. This was especially true in regard to issues in which Luce was passionately interested, among them the American commitment to "uplifting" – that is, modernizing and Christianizing – the people of China.

True, Luce's magazines spoke different languages: *Time* was the smart-alecky product of a union between an earnest college graduate and the fast-changing culture of the 1920s. *Fortune* was deeper and better researched, because it hoped to educate and influence the business elites, whose ignorance dismayed Luce. *Life* was America's magazine – friendly, diverse, easily accessible. All three publications conveyed the world as Henry Luce saw it to millions of Americans during difficult years. In the understated words of a *Life* managing editor, Ed Thompson, "We knew enough about what [Luce] didn't believe in to avoid direct contradiction of his views."[5] When Luce cared about an issue and made his views known, his magazines took his message to the American people.

With what results? At home, almost every major politician of the age courted Luce, and foreign heads of government were available. Luce was a major force within the Republican Party between 1940 and 1964. Yet Luce's impact upon Republican politics has been virtually ignored by historians, for two reasons. First, Henry Luce was a journalist who usually shunned personal publicity. (His second wife, Clare Boothe Luce, more than made up for her husband's reticence.) Second, Luce's papers, stored at the Library of Congress, have until recently been inaccessible to historians.* But these archival materials, along with various interviews and memoirs, now enable us to evaluate Luce's influence upon the Republican Party. Those documents show that Luce and the editors of *Fortune*, more than anyone else, created the presidential candidacy of Wendell L. Willkie. Without Luce and Time Inc., Dwight Eisenhower's decision to run, his nomination, and his election become more problematic.[†]

If historians have overlooked Luce as a player in Republican politics, his reputation as a man obsessed with China has never been challenged. In a bizarre tribute to Luce's alleged influence, a homesick Marine almost assassinated him right after the war: The would-be assassin blamed *Time* for making sure that he and some of his buddies were stationed in a land they wanted to abandon. But if Luce was so powerful, how did FDR and Truman win five straight elections? In 1948, Luce supported Senator Arthur Vandenberg for the Republican presidential nomination, and he crowned "President" Dewey before the election. And why did Luce, despite a media crusade that he waged for five years, fail to involve Americans more deeply in the Chinese civil war?

The answer lies in the fact of saliency: If an issue or cause did not engage the public's imagination, Americans generally allowed any administration to pursue its foreign policy without undue opposition. But if a problem engaged the public's imagination and if the administration seemed listless, that was another matter altogether. Large numbers of Americans favored assisting Britain in July 1940, but FDR failed to act until early September. Into the gap jumped Henry Luce and his media, and Roosevelt was happy to have the support of Time Inc.'s Republican bias. He ultimately did what Luce wanted him to do, though for his own reasons. When it came to aid for China in 1947, by contrast, the public was largely disengaged or opposed, and Luce failed to achieve very much. But later, when Communist triumphs fueled a growing aversion to the current administration, *Time*'s snarling question – "Who Lost China?" – mightily contributed to the national trauma of the McCarthy years.

---

* Luce's papers are now open to all.
† In 1964, when the Goldwaterites took over the GOP, Luce's influence was waning in a changed party, but by then he was ready to retire.

In examining Henry R. Luce's political use of his media, I will ask two questions: What information did Luce and his editors receive in regard to China and Vietnam? And what did they tell their thirty to forty million weekly readers?

In fact, there was a huge discrepancy between received facts and published articles. Newly available materials make it possible to explore this chasm and see how it widened year by year. A turning point in Luce's journalism came in 1945 and 1946, when instead of his benevolent American Century, there emerged a bipolar world of conflict. Luce's vision darkened, and he resolved to combat and if possible destroy the "cancer" – Communism – that had defaced or even derailed his American Century. Luce became bitter and frustrated, especially when America failed to save his China.

A 1946 encounter brings alive Harry Luce's suffering as he watched the decline of his Nationalist China. The scene took place in Nanjing, during the early stages of the civil war. A persistent detractor of the Nationalist regime, John Melby, was serving as a political officer at the U.S. embassy. Though new to China and only thirty-three years old, Melby had already concluded that "we were backing a dead horse."[6] He shared his opinion with Harry Luce, who felt wounded:

Those of you who criticize people like me for our stand in support of the Nationalists, you've got to remember that we were born here. This is all we've ever known. We had made a lifetime commitment to the advancement of Christianity in China. And now you're attacking us for it. You're asking us to say that all our lives have been wasted; they've been futile. They've been lived for nothing. That's a pretty tough thing to ask of anyone, isn't it?[7]

Unconvinced, John Melby replied, "Of course it is!" He added, "I'm still asking it of you. Because things have changed." But for Harry Luce, essential verities had *not* changed, not in 1946, not ever.

The gap between Luce's preconceptions and the realities of China and East Asia had widened into an abyss.

Fittingly, the story begins with Luce's triumphant return to China after World War II. Optimistic, even euphoric, Luce foresaw the day when Chiang's China, with our help, would enter the American Century.

PART ONE

FROM THE AMERICAN CENTURY TO THE COLD WAR, 1941–1946

Henry Luce and China

Prelude to an American Crusade

Soon after the second atomic bomb fell on Japan, Generalissimo Chiang Kai-shek decided to launch an offensive aimed at postwar American public opinion. Chiang was determined to counter the growing number of Americans who accused China's government of corruption and worse. As part of its campaign, Chiang's government invited Henry R. Luce, head of Time Inc., to visit China. In the words of the Chinese ambassador, the influential publisher's return to the land of his birth would be "of mutual benefit to China and the United States."[1] The Beijing *Chronicle* was more direct: Luce, the paper commented, published "articles on China which greatly influenced American public opinion in favor of China."[2]

Henry Robinson Luce (1898–1967) was the man who had cofounded the powerful newsweekly magazine called *Time*. His *Fortune* was the leading business magazine, and everyone read *Life*, America's weekly picture book. The *March of Time* newsreels were the best of their day. Henry Luce the would-be traveler, however, was aware of a potential problem. Harry S Truman detested *Time* for its Republican bias. As a result, a nervous State Department official decided to ask the White House about Luce's request for a revalidated passport. Much to Luce's relief, Truman's aide Charles Ross voiced no objections, perhaps because Chiang himself had invited Luce to China.[3]

Harry Luce, who was then forty-seven years old, left the United States on 29 September 1945 on a plane provided by General Robert B. McClure, head of the Chinese Combat Command. On 6 October, for the first time in more than four years, Luce saw the land where he had been born in 1898. After his plane landed near Chongqing, this devout son of Presbyterian missionaries attended church services at U.S. Army headquarters, once the site of a Methodist missionary compound. Luce was in a marvelous mood. American soldiers thanked Harry Luce for the "pony," or wartime overseas editions, of *Time*. Their gratitude moved Luce, but he most enjoyed his meetings with the men who ran China. Luce took tea with Nationalist financier Dr. H. H. "Daddy" Kung and dined with Chiang and his beautiful wife Mei-ling Soong, known to Americans as Madame Chiang.

Luce, the ever serious guest, discoursed with the Generalissimo on the nature of freedom. Chiang believed that freedom consisted of behaving in accord with one's nature, like a fish in water; he added that people sometimes needed to be told how to act. Luce overlooked the disturbing implication of his host's simile: Despite demands for liberalization, Chiang Kai-shek would not easily surrender his role of tutor to his people.[4] In the face of demands for land reform, democracy, and multiparty governance, he intended to stand firm. To Chiang, the most dire threat was the burgeoning Communist insurgency. Instead of liberalism, Chiang would face down the Reds with weapons and propaganda. Americans, he worried, did not understand the Chinese Communists. They were not, Chiang knew, "agrarian reformers," eager to bring democracy and reform to the impoverished millions. Because of American pressure he had to negotiate with the Marxists, but the Generalissimo knew that he could count on the support of Henry Robinson Luce and his powerful network of philanthropic and political contacts. They formed the heart of what would soon become known as the "China lobby."

The latest American-mediated attempt to reunite China had reached a dead end. The Communist delegation would soon return to its wartime base, in the remote northern outpost of Yan'an. At the farewell banquet for the Communist leader Mao Zedong (then known as Mao Tse-tung), Harry Luce found himself the only foreigner among the three hundred assembled guests. His hosts had seated him on the dais, near Mao, where Luce examined his heavy, peasantlike face and his "sloppy blue-denim garment." He noticed that when Mao spoke to the gathering, he started slowly and then engaged in a "full-voiced shout." Perhaps Mao needed to convey sincerity, for he was making an unlikely pledge to support "unity under Chiang Kai-shek." Later, Luce and Mao met face to face, and the Communist leader expressed surprise at seeing the American in Chongqing. He gazed at Luce, Luce wrote in his diary, "with an intense but not unfriendly curiosity." The two men had little to say, however, and Luce soon found himself listening to Mao's "polite grunts."

Luce also renewed his acquaintance with Zhou Enlai. The two men had first met in 1941, when Luce was gathering information about China's resistance to the Japanese invader. At that time, Zhou invited the Luces to dine with him at the Guangdong (then Kuang-tung) restaurant, in this same city of Chongqing.[5] Zhou traded on his famous charm, but he was wasting it on Harry Luce, who disliked that quality in men – and especially in a Communist. On 10 October, when the two men met at the banquet for Mao, Zhou complained to Luce about Time Inc.'s coverage of China. *Time*'s editor-in-chief responded heatedly and denounced the current "world-wide left-wing propaganda" campaign against Chiang. But Luce, who would soon be traveling to Communist-infested Shandong, nonetheless professed his interest in meeting rural Communists in the field. Zhou promised to oblige Luce, but Chiang Kai-shek would have viewed any such visit as apostasy. Luce never visited Yan'an, nor did he ever review Communist units in the field.

Luce's tour only underscored his lifelong isolation from the great masses of China's people. He had spent his boyhood in a missionary compound in Shandong province and had later attended a British-run school. In his relative isolation, Harry had followed in the footsteps of an earlier generation: "The missionaries," one historian has written, "made little attempt to understand what we might broadly call the social structure of Chinese life."[6] As Luce admitted when a young man, "I know nothing of their [Chinese] social life aside from the formal feasts & holidays."[7] In 1945 Luce still viewed China from the vantage point of a Christian missionary compound.[8] Though famous for his curiosity, Luce relegated journalistic inquiry to a distant second place, behind his moral commitment to Chiang's Nationalist cause. As Luce defined it, China was America's ward. Step by faltering step, China would enter a marvelous new age in which Christianity, modern science, and the American big brother would bring the blessings of liberty and salvation to 450 million Chinese. Chiang welcomed his American visitor in ways calculated to please him.

Wes Bailey, Luce's personal aide, did not think that "any foreign visitor" had been "so welcome in China since Marco Polo." Indeed, Chiang's government turned Luce's tour into one long celebration.[9] Everywhere Luce rejoiced in the smiling faces of cheering schoolchildren, self-important governors, decorated generals, deans of Christian colleges, Buddhist monks, and government-approved newspaper editors. He was unaware that the citizens and children who cheered him in October 1945 were really actors playing roles in Chiang's version of Potemkin's village.

Despite the pleas of at least one prominent Chinese liberal, Luce refused to pressure Chiang into embracing democratic reforms. Instead, he agreed that "lawless military activity of every sort" must first be vigorously suppressed.[10] The publisher had come to strengthen and celebrate China and not to criticize its leaders. He came not as a journalist, but as a pilgrim. Luce returned to his boyhood haunts in Shandong for the first time in thirteen years and then traveled to Beijing. There, Luce inspected his father's old campus at Yenching University, where the Reverend Luce had once served as vice-president. Luce's Christian conscience was gladdened. In Beijing, the mayor hosted a fabulous banquet in the publisher's honor, and Luce, who was usually a moderate drinker, emptied many a glass filled with a highly potent local beverage. True to form, he was up and about early the next morning, resuming his tour. Eventually, Luce boarded a U.S. Navy ship docked in the harbor at Tianjin and visited the nearby Marine headquarters, where the local people, he believed, rejoiced in the presence of one thousand U.S. Marines.

In Tianjin, a homesick, disturbed Marine decided that Luce's magazines were responsible for his postwar duty in China. For years, they had argued for intervention, for war, for what Luce had in 1941 called the "American Century."

One day, this Marine saw Harry Luce in the distance. After loading his M-1 rifle, the soldier took aim at the back of Luce's neck. Fortunately for his would-be victim, another Marine dissuaded his buddy from firing the weapon. Years later, Luce learned about the incident and thanked his benefactor for his "interference in changing the signals."[11]

Saved from an early death, Luce arrived in Qingdao, where he had passed many summers as a child. He again admired its "magnificent port" and swam in the blue Pacific, which had recently been stained with the blood of American soldiers. Luce dined aboard the USS *Alaska* in the light of a full moon and basked in the fullness of American power. At times, Luce seemed entranced, as when he wrote that "incredible military power" was "represented by the Stars and Stripes." He later recalled that evening off Qingdao as part of "an autumn so rare and bright [that it] makes the heart joyful." Luce had surrendered to a sentimental euphoria generated by his hosts. "Problems [in China] are terrific," Harry Luce admitted, but he quickly added that they were "by no means insoluble."[12] By late November 1945, Luce predicted, "crack government armies, mostly U.S.-equipped and U.S.-trained, will have arrived in North China." This reoccupation of China "by the Chinese with American aid is something . . . unique in history," he added. Yet some observers urged caution: *Time*'s Bill Gray warned against overestimating the firepower of Chiang's vaunted American-trained and -equipped divisions.[13] Luce ignored him.

In a telegram home, Harry Luce cabled that China needed only "three or four ships to carry coal from Manchuria to Shanghai to get the wheels of industry started there."[14] He would send a hundred American businessmen to China, where they could help to restart the economy. But Luce also favored dispatching ten missionaries to that garden of souls. All that was required, he believed, was what his father had called "Lucepower," but on a grand scale: more money, more missionaries, more technicians, more modern weapons, more ships. Luce's thoughts raced ahead to glorious projects, such as restoring Christian missions and colleges disrupted by the terrible war. A proud alumnus of Yale College, Luce intended to reactivate Yale-in-China, an educational program that dated back two generations. Luce also hoped to do even more for United China Relief, the highly successful private aid program that he had founded in 1940.

The United States, *Time* pontificated, had "gone too deeply into the China affair to duck all responsibility for what may ensue."[15] Congresswoman Clare Boothe Luce, Harry's second wife, captured his mood when she wrote that he had sent "a note of urgency concerning immediate aid for China" but seemed "cheerful about the long term chances of our friends there." She added, "How well Harry and his father built in this matter of our friendship and understanding with the Orient!"[16] Never was such confidence so misplaced. In fact, Henry Luce's Chinese acquaintances were members of a beleaguered elite. Many of them had converted to a religion alien to their compatriots. Luce had few if any recorded contacts with poor peasants or struggling urban workers, whose misery and aspirations offered Communism its chance. Even as a teenager, Luce had recognized the problem of his cultural isolation: "I have talked with our servants and a few others," he wrote, "but usually in such circumstances that *I* created the conversation – In other words I have never been in a Chinese 'crowd' using the word in the collegiate slang sense."[17] As a journalist, Luce failed to visit Communist-controlled regions, and he rarely conversed with peasants, radical students, underpaid civil servants, dissidents, or opposition politicians. Stubbornly, Luce continued to insist that Chiang spoke for the masses both men failed to understand.

Though personally immune to the seductions of luxury, Henry R. Luce took for granted a lifestyle alien to all but the wealthiest of Chinese. When Luce mused about spending the next summer in Qingdao, he spoke to an aide about his modest housing needs. The place "need not be swank," wrote Luce, but the house should include "three or four bedrooms, a living room, dining room and something to serve as a library or study." He added, "I presume there will be no great difficulty in getting adequate servants."[18] In fact, Luce would never rent that non-swank home on a China sea.

Sadly, Henry Luce was visiting a dying, mythical China that was the product of his own imagination and upbringing. He misjudged his hosts, but another factor also blinded him to Nationalist China's grim prospects. Luce worshipped American power and could not imagine that a country that had produced more than 299,000 military aircraft during World War II could fail in China. Long after history had played a terrible trick on Luce's China, he argued wistfully that if he and Major General Lemuel Shepherd, the Marine commander in Shandong, had made China policy in 1945, then "China would not now be Communist."[19]

China: The Challenge

For years Luce had agonized over his media's coverage of China. He wanted to inform Americans about the problems facing Chiang without undermining support for the Chinese leader. This was proving to be impossible. Theodore H. White, a young, ambitious, and increasingly radical *Time* correspondent, tried to warn Luce against making myths about China. Americans, he warned, would learn the truth about a corrupt regime and would turn against it. *Time*'s credibility, White added, would suffer. But Luce intended to stand by Chiang, and he had already made sure that White had been sent home, pending reassignment. Luce also wanted to rid himself of Teddy White's colleague, Annalee Jacoby.

Luce's meeting with Jacoby went badly; Luce sourly concluded, "We should not have allowed this situation to continue so long."[20] After that "painful" discussion, Luce laconically noted, "She returns tomorrow to U.S." Having rid himself of Jacoby, Luce noted, "We have a great opportunity here to offset much mediocre reporting and to develop journalistically new territory."[21] A crack young reporter named Bill Gray could help *Time*, but Luce wanted to make sure that he did not have a second Teddy White on his hands: Without a trace of irony, Luce told Gray that *Time* was nonpartisan – but supported

Chiang. He added that *Time* favored the liberal elements in China, *as long as they were loyal to Chiang's government.*[22] But signs of trouble could not be ignored or played down forever, and even Charlie Murphy, a pro-Chiang man, admitted that the Communist forces were "pressing tirelessly into north China."[23] His editors insisted that he find better news.

In the middle of November, *Life* published Murphy's long article "China Reborn."[24] This glowing account of the American redemption of China lived up to its title.[25] Charlie Murphy insisted that in the event of full civil war, Chiang's modern divisions would prevail. That test might come soon, for *Time* suddenly sounded an alarm about new Communist offensives launched from bases in Henan and Shanxi.[26] In November Zhou Enlai warned an American diplomat that the Communists did not want a civil war, but if forced to fight, they would prevail.[27] Soon after Henry Luce left China in that autumn of 1945, Bill Gray cabled, "We are confronted with the ugly fact of civil war."[28]

Luce responded by launching a campaign for the retention of American troops in China; *Life* praised the Marines, who had a "clear right and duty" to guard Chiang's railroad lines against possible Communist attacks.[29] "Unless something else turns up in the next one or two days," Luce told a senior editor, "this [China] is No. 1 subject for TIME this coming week." Certainly, much depended upon Truman's policy. The new president had taken office only in April, and Luce carefully monitored interesting news from Washington. "For the American government," cabled *Time*'s well-informed James Shepley, "the hour of decision on China had arrived this week."[30] America, Luce believed, should continue to train Chiang's divisions and assign U.S. military advisers to Chinese field units. Nor did Luce rule out the eventual deployment of American combat forces. In *Life*'s hyperbolic words, "We need regret nothing if we stick by our friends in Asia, the best friends now and the greatest friends-to-be a nation ever had."[31] The two years that followed World War II would sorely test this assumption.

A Troubled Marriage

In the Luce home, things were going poorly. Former congresswoman Luce was tiring of her brief career in the House of Representatives (she would refuse to run in 1946). Luce no longer spent much of the year in her luxurious Wardman Park suite in Washington. Instead, she came home to Harry in New York and Connecticut to an uncertain reception. Luce's infatuation with Clare Boothe had long since cooled; according to editorial director John Shaw Billings, the two sometimes seemed to "hate each other."[32] After Clare's much publicized conversion to Catholicism, Luce resented her scheme to have his first marriage annulled; nor did her health problems make things easier. She showed troublesome symptoms that ultimately necessitated a hysterectomy.[33] Company gossip C. D. Jackson related one scene in which Clare was in tears, lying on the floor, crying to Harry, "It's all because I couldn't give you a baby that you don't love me anymore." This was too much for Luce, who told her to get up and stop

1.1   The Luces in mid-century. (Library of Congress)

the nonsense. Clare retaliated by denying him sexual relations and even asked Jackson to find a woman for Harry. Nothing serious, of course, just a sexual outlet for a clumsy lover with a strong libido. C. D. Jackson, who thought Clare was a "bitch," did not wish to add pimping to his long list of accomplishments at Time Inc.

Seeking escape from Clare's melodramatic outbursts and inner coldness, and riddled by a guilt that he refused to confront, Harry Luce fell into affairs with anyone who wanted him. At one point in 1947, a woman Harry had evidently bedded in California refused to be fobbed off as a one-night stand. According to C. D. Jackson, "The little bitch really has Harry by the short hairs and every time she pulls 'em, it costs Harry another $100,000."[34] Luce was making long, private phone calls from his office, probably to lawyers. The unfortunate woman threatened suicide and had to be hospitalized.[35] (With his usual bile, John Shaw Billings observed, "Sex makes more damn fools out of more people than liquor.")[36] For a time, Luce was involved with Jean Dalrymple, a lively theatrical agent whom he had met during the war.[37] Luce's interest soon dissipated, however, and he started to complain that Jean would not let him go. "What a hypocrite [Luce] is," wrote John Shaw Billings, "preaching great Christian virtues and then practicing just the opposite!"[38] "How pretentious and hollow sound all his great morality and idealism," added the cruel Billings.[39]

Luce sometimes confided in Clare, who, unlike her errant husband, enjoyed analyzing such affairs. Ultimately, Clare, a new but fervent Catholic, made one thing clear: no divorce, no matter what the circumstances. Clare pledged herself to chastity – although sexual passion had long since departed from her marriage. (Feigning indifference, she wickedly wrote, "Lie where and with whom you can.") After this or that revealed affair, Harry's mumbled regrets and professions of love would leave Clare triumphant but unmoved; they lacked "substance" and follow-through, she declared. And in an amazing bit of irrationality that revealed how difficult she could be, Clare blamed her husband for *not* opposing her conversion to Catholicism in 1945–1946. She reasoned that his acceptance betokened indifference and, ultimately, a desire to divorce her. He could then argue, she believed, that "the Catholic Church broke up our marriage." Perversely, Clare Luce then thanked her husband, for however unworthy his motives, Harry had helped to guide her toward the path to salvation. One can sympathize with the beleaguered Harry Luce.

Clare Luce then decided that she and her errant husband were both "moral lepers." Yet she also admitted, "I have never had the courage or wisdom or patience to live well with you." She then bemoaned one's inability to enjoy a "happy sexual life, a *married* life with the partner of our choice."[40] But she added, "I would with the utmost joy die for you this or any other night." Most moving was Clare's admission, "I never loved another, except [for my late daughter Ann, killed in an auto accident in 1944], so deeply." But despite these sentiments, Luce's marriage was evolving into a rivalry and partnership, or what Clare called a friendship.[41] The crusade against global Communism would cement their alliance.

Always on stage but never satisfied with her performance, Clare Boothe Luce perplexed her contemporaries. The fault was not entirely her own. She once declared, "Thought has no sex," and she added, "Either one thinks, or does not think."[42] But a woman who skewered her enemies, including FDR, with dazzling relish, was bound to make enemies and endure pain. Later, bright, attractive women who were outspoken earned the plaudits of the media. But American culture in the 1940s was boldly sexist, and Clare Boothe Luce was something of a freak. She was widely admired, but she remained a freak nonetheless: After she gave an important if nasty speech on foreign policy, a House colleague rushed to congratulate her – for her beautiful legs. At Time Inc., Harry's colleagues gossiped about her; some called her a drunk, and others claimed that she had lost her mind.[43] But Luce himself treated her as his intellectual equal, and he never condescended to her. For this reason, their political and intellectual partnership survived both Clare's emotional storms and the dalliances of her strange, driven husband.

As their love cooled, the Luces found common ground in anti-Communist politics. Clare Luce had played small roles when Luce sketched out his wartime

1.2 Fund-raising for China: The Luces (center and right, with an unidentified guest) host a tea, 1947. (American Bureau for Medical Aid to China Papers, Rare Book and Manuscript Library, Columbia University)

ideas on the American Century and the reorganization of the world. After 1944, however, they coordinated their campaigns on behalf of Chiang and against Communism as these passions superseded earlier, more personal ones.

A Driven, Lonely Genius

Henry Luce's relationship with his colleagues mirrored his troubled marriage. Although he really loved Time Inc., the atmosphere around him lacked joy: "I never saw Harry happy," recalled longtime senior editor Dan Longwell.[44] Tom Matthews observed, "He never did anything for pleasure, or perhaps it would be fairer to say that the business of journalism was his only pleasure."[45] Eager to make history and influence events, Luce felt stimulated by challenges and crusades. "This is a wonderful world," he once blurted out, "and I wouldn't miss being in it for anything."[46] But when it came to dealing with human beings, the results were less ecstatic. Visitors and colleagues commented on Luce's "remarkable gaze" and upon his "total absorption of what's going on in a given moment."[47] John Billings observed that Luce seemed to feel "happily useful" only when he was on "large tours of inquiry, shooting through the firmament like an inquisitive comet."[48] Yet what absorbed Luce? Certainly not the personalities nor problems of the people around him. John Shaw Billings, for example, saw Luce as a "strange lonely fellow" who didn't "know how to have fun and rest."[49] Billings also noted, "There's no place he really wants to go and nobody he really wants to go with." Not content with that jab, Billings added, "I'm getting a little bored with being his father confessor, the only guy in the company who will listen to his long-winded stammering."[50] Writer Emmet Hughes recalled Luce as a "lonely man" but also a "clumsy, graceless man" who showed "no capacity for human relationships."[51] And Bea Grover, wife of a top Luce lieutenant, observed that Luce had "the worst natural bad manners I've ever seen."[52]

An anecdote enjoyed by generations of Time Incers (as Time Inc.'ers called themselves) laid bare this side of Luce. One morning, he entered an elevator before ascending to the thirty-third floor of the Time-Life Building at Rockefeller Plaza. Luce expected to be the sole passenger, the way he preferred it. Suddenly, however, a young woman joined him, whereupon the elevator operator shut the doors and the brief ascent began. Luce stood there, glumly staring at his shoes. His companion broke the awkward silence and asked the middle-aged man if he were ill. "I'm Henry Luce," he growled. "Well, that's nothing to be ashamed of," the employee supposedly answered.[53] To avoid such spontaneous contacts with impudent inferiors, Luce thereafter insisted upon riding up alone each morning. His aides put out the word that he liked to pray before beginning his long workday.

Luce's nervous energy and brusque questions meant that editors needed to be fast on their feet. They were there to answer a myriad of Henry Luce's queries, and woe to the man who tried to bluff his way through an incompetent response. Luce focused upon one subject at a time; the boss alone decided when to change the subject or terminate the conversation. Leaning forward in his chair, Luce would slap his knee, and that was the end of it.[54] He remained impossibly restless, whether pacing about his large, mahogany-paneled office or scrawling one of his famous penciled memos. Peculiar habits added to Luce's reputation as a difficult colleague. Often inarticulate, he relied heavily upon gestures and expressions, which only a "sound movie could capture."[55] (It was said that after years of being around Luce, associates unconsciously mimicked his nasal monotone and slight stammer.)

Behind all the quirks and the harsh voice lurked a formidable intellect, a trait that made Harry Luce even more feared. This, after all, was a man who called himself "more intelligent than 90% of the reading public" (never a braggart, Luce was being modest). No wonder that one close associate complained, "[Luce] hurts my feelings the way he never talks to me – as if he didn't consider me intelligent enough to be responsive."[56] "I suppose he's the nearest I'll ever come to associating with a genius in my time," recalled senior editor Dan Longwell, in a grudging compliment.[57] Senior associates often preferred to communicate with Luce through memoranda to avoid having their heads "snapped off."[58] Certainly, Luce's journalists and business managers did their very best work, for they feared doing anything less.

At times, Luce seemed to be oblivious of the sacrifices made by others on behalf of their common enterprise. Corinne Thrasher, Luce's long-serving

1.3 The Luces enjoying a new radio: Harry rarely relaxed. (Library of Congress)

personal secretary, remembered him as a cold man, and added, "I can't say I was fond of him."[59] One senior researcher who had imbibed a bit too much at a party once cried out, "Harry Luce is a pompous arrogant bastard" and then left in tears.[60] A typical lunch with his managing editors involved Luce doing all the talking and eating nothing, while his colleagues dined and said nothing.[61] When a luncheon companion spilled hot coffee all over himself, Luce kept talking "as if nothing had happened."[62] In fact, Luce's maddeningly cold, abrupt, and cerebral demeanor concealed a poetic, even childish, core, but few contemporaries saw it. However, another side of Luce did sometimes surface. [63] An editor who needed a loan for his child's education could turn to Luce, as long as the student had a good record. Luce also gave Time Inc. stock to valued colleagues and scrawled letters to them when they were ill.[64]

As he entered ripe middle age, Harry Luce was a tall and reasonably fit, balding man. He suffered from incipient hearing loss, a factor that did nothing to improve his sociability. He also showed signs of arthritis of the back and neck, and his eyesight revealed minor deterioration. Luce suffered from bad spinal discs and often exhibited the heavy cough typical of compulsive cigarette smokers.[65] (He smoked up to five packs a day.) Indeed, Luce lived surrounded by a yellow haze of stale smoke, so his eyeglasses were invariably clouded. And a man more sensitive to warning signs might have worried when a doctor diagnosed him as a victim of "chronic exhaustion." Luce, however, convinced himself that thanks to modern diet and medicine, he would outlive his father, who had survived into his early seventies.

Pain and physical fear met their master in Harry Luce. After a gall bladder operation, Luce was up the next day, dictating to his secretary.[66] For recreation, Luce would occasionally play golf (poorly) while wearing his usual silk socks; he ignored the painful blisters that soon covered his feet. Some of Luce's stoicism may have been theological in origin: This Christian admirer of martyred missionaries wondered why he had "much less than average amount of physical pain" in his life.[67] He then asked, "What is or may be the meaning of this fact?" Luce did not know, but his bravery may have served to compensate for his perceived lack of pain. Luce would fly through dangerous weather and brave a German blitzkrieg in 1940 and Japanese bombs in 1941. He was superstitious, however, especially about the evil power of the number thirteen.[68]

Power and Its Limits

Henry R. Luce headed a remarkably successful and influential enterprise. World War II and the incipient Cold War marked the onset of Time Inc.'s greatest era.

In 1945–1947 much of Luce's daily work still involved *Time*, the first and most influential of his magazines. The editor-in-chief was pleased with its formula, which he described as Associated Press plus interpretation. *Time*, Luce boasted, was "a practical, and, I think, a valuable and important proposition in the life of the U.S. people."[69] In part, the magazine's growing influence rested upon its appeal to an expanding pool of potential readers – educated Americans. Before *Time*'s time, fewer than 10 percent of college-age youth attended college or earned a diploma. By 1947 that figure had reached 31.2 percent and would climb higher.[70] This was the audience that Luce's editors had in mind when they convened each week. If there was an imagined reader, he was white, male, youngish, and upscale and probably lived in a town of middling size. College-educated themselves, the editor-in-chief, the managing editor, and their senior editors (for national affairs, foreign and international, business, etc.) ran *Time* for that young man and his extended family.

In 1947 Time Inc.'s publications claimed a monthly circulation of about 30.5 million. They contained 18,145 pages, 10,635 of which hawked advertised products to readers of the magazines. In this same year, *Life* became the first magazine to gross more than $100 million from readers and advertisers.[71] Henry Luce owned two hundred fifty thousand shares of Time Inc., worth at least $30 million, but John Shaw Billings knew that he was "not interested in money or power." Instead, Billings observed, "He gets his power through his magazines and prefers to be an editor rather than a publisher."[72] But profits did not always translate into influence. Henry Luce was hawking China to a nation controlled by Europe-firsters, and polls indicated that less than one-third of the public had a favorable impression of Chiang's government.[73] Like President Truman, many Americans felt that sending more aid to Chiang would be "pouring sand in a rat hole."[74] Luce, however, still hoped to overcome the public's indifference.

Two factors accounted for Luce's obsessive optimism. One stemmed from his early life as the self-consciously American child of missionaries to China. The other cause for hope lay in the amazing story of the most successful journalistic enterprise of the twentieth century.

From China to *Time*

Henry Robinson Luce's parents were Henry Winters Luce and the former Elizabeth Root.[75] Both were missionary educators who had grown up in Pennsylvania. In the autumn of 1897 the couple settled in Dengzhou, a seaport on the Shandong peninsula. Filth and degrading poverty greeted the Luces whenever they emerged from their walled missionary compound. Like other missionaries of the era, the Luces hoped to convert the heathens while bringing the wonders of modern hygiene and science to a benighted nation. Harry quickly mastered Chinese, taught the New Testament and other subjects to eager students, and baptized them. The pregnant Elizabeth remained active in YMCA work through the winter.[76] On 3 April 1898 she gave birth to Henry Robinson Luce, the first of four children. In this same year, the United States acquired an empire stretching from the Philippines to Puerto Rico. American expansion stimulated much interest in China: Writers and business executives reported that four hundred million Chinese would soon offer a vast market to American exporters. American businessmen, in Luce's view, would help to bring modern roads and railroads, colleges, schools, dams, and canals to poverty-stricken China.[77] The Luces were therefore looking forward to a happy, productive life in an American-protected, modernizing China.

The Luce family prospered, and three more children – Emmavail, Elizabeth, and Sheldon – joined "Small Boy Luce" at the breakfast table. Harry, however, stood out, even at so tender an age. An intensely curious lad, young Luce seemed eager to skip from the cradle to maturity. At the age of three, Harry was attending religious services; and even before he enrolled in school, the child would ask his mother to write down his dictated "sermons."[78] To Harry, "Onward, Christian Soldiers" was not merely an anthem; it was an admonition. Fail we mortals must, but the race was to the quick; woe to him who gave up.

The Reverend Luce knew how to charm and persuade potential benefactors, as Nettie Fowler McCormick discovered. This enormously wealthy widow had inherited the fortune of Cyrus Hall McCormick, inventor of the famous reaper. Thanks to her friend the persistent Reverend Luce, McCormick donated a fortune – $40,000 – to the Christian colleges in Shandong.[79] And through her, the Reverend Luce met John D. Rockefeller, Jr., "Mr. Junior," who promptly demonstrated his own generosity.[80] Mrs. McCormick quickly came to admire the bright Harry, who handled himself like a little adult. His brain, Mrs. McCormick observed, worked like a "system of wheels."* As his father

---

* Young Harry Luce faced a severe challenge at the age of eight. After undergoing a tonsillectomy, he experienced a traumatic reaction when the anesthetic wore off too quickly; henceforth, Harry Luce stammered. Many boys with this affliction might have avoided public speaking, but Harry

put it, Harry was the smartest of children – with the possible exception of his sister Elizabeth.*

But these trips were mere interludes, and until Harry Luce was a teenager, a missionary compound in China was home. This prolonged separation from the United States engendered the exaggerated nationalism that would mark his career. As a boy in Weixian, Luce loved to celebrate the Fourth of July, and he would brook no insult to America.[81] When Luce attended the British China Inland Mission School in Yantai, he engaged in a fistfight with a "little British bastard who had insulted" America. Luce never forgot the slight – nor the appropriate American response. By 1912, when he was thirteen, it was time for the Luces to send Harry "home" to complete his education. Young Luce toured Europe and then arrived in America. By this time, he had learned some important lessons: Capitalism was part of the natural order of things; America was a source of bounty; and China must be uplifted by Americans.[82]

In the autumn of 1914 Harry Luce arrived in Lakeville, Connecticut, where he attended the elite Hotchkiss School.[83] Clad in what his Chinese tailor regarded as an "American-style" suit, Luce quickly acquired a nickname he despised: "Chink." Repelled by racial bigotry, Luce would always favor equal treatment for Chinese – and for American Negroes, as African Americans were then called. Hard-working, aloof, and not a "fun" type of person, Luce, one of his masters at Hotchkiss commented, could "sling the religious bull without appearing foolish."[84] And to young Luce, religious fervor sometimes turned politics and war into moral crusades. When war erupted in Europe in the summer of 1914, Harry Luce immediately decided that the democracies – Britain and France – were fighting for a just cause. More remarkably, by 1915 Luce prophesied "America's leadership of the world at the close of the European war."[85] He favored American engagement in "every international difficulty." He also wanted to help "the lame, the halt, and the blind among nations." The war, along with America's imminent global hegemony, made Luce's choice of career an easy one: Americans, he believed, would have to be informed about the world they were called upon to lead. Harry concluded, therefore, that he could be "of the greatest service in journalistic work" and in that way "come nearest to the heart of the world."[86] Luce arrived in New Haven in 1916, where he was quickly invited to serve on the board of the *Yale Daily News*.[87]

Harry Luce was a slim young man, six feet in height, with blue-gray eyes and reddish-brown hair. Photographs invariably display his serious demeanor; indeed, Luce became a familiar fixture around Yale, as he walked across the campus with his brow furrowed in thought. There was, however, another side to Luce. He was a great salesman and showed a knack for making lots of money

---

would later insist on joining debating societies. Eventually, he stammered less in public than in private, thanks to the faith that inspired his will.

* Throughout her long life, Elizabeth (later "Beth" Moore) displayed the charm her older brother sorely lacked.

by hawking advertising for the *Yale Daily News*.[88] But the Great War obsessed Harry, and after Woodrow Wilson asked for a declaration of war in early April 1917, Luce volunteered for service in the Reserve Officer Training Corps.[89] So did his good friend Brit Hadden, whom Luce had known since their days together in a Greek class at Hotchkiss.

The phrase "opposites attract" applied to Luce and Briton Hadden. A Brooklyn boy, Hadden was brash, witty, personable, funny, and sports-crazy. But Brit was also very bright, and the boys quickly became buddies whose academic pursuits soon yielded to military service.[90] After rising to the rank of sergeant in the ROTC, Luce and Hadden, along with the rest of their Yale artillery unit, shipped out to Camp Jackson near Columbia, South Carolina.[91] In the hot summer of 1918 the two men were commissioned second lieutenants in the field artillery. The young officers soon departed for service with the Seventh Training Battery at Camp Zachary Taylor, near Louisville.

Harry Luce was mustered out and returned to Yale College, where he found himself tapped by the elite, secretive Skull & Bones Society. He then graduated "most brilliant" in the class of 1920. (The far more popular Brit Hadden was voted "most likely to succeed.")[92] Harry Luce and classmate Morehead Patterson made a tour of England, Wales, and Scotland and then settled into lodgings at Christ Church College, Oxford. Luce admired his host nation, but he also conducted himself like a young American heir inspecting an expected legacy.[93] In August 1921 Luce found work as a stringer for Ben Hecht, a popular columnist with the *Chicago Daily News*.[94] But Hecht quickly decided that Luce was "much *too* naive" and concluded that he was "not going anywhere." Harry and Brit Hadden then relocated to Baltimore, where they both found menial reporting jobs at the *News*. Luce worked there until February 1922, but he and Hadden devoted their most intense hours to the formulation of a journalism appropriate to a new era.

Terrible new weapons had defaced the battlefields and seas of the world, and war had raged in the skies. Four great empires in Europe and Asia had collapsed; millions of people had died; a vast American army had won the greatest war in history; and the United States was supreme in industry and in the financial markets of the world. Communists had seized power in Russia, and this disruptive force would soon be joined by Fascism in Italy and the obscure National Socialist movement in Germany. The wireless had been invented, and radio was on the verge of becoming a national craze. The automobile industry enjoyed an enormous boom, and, like radio, new roads would knit the country closer together. Women were voting in all elections, smoked in public, and wore outrageously short skirts. Typewriters had changed the workplace and vastly increased the number of jobs available in white-collar and service industries – especially to women. But rapid change created a backlash: This same society outlawed liquor and fought over whether humans had descended from an apelike creature.

Brit and Harry hoped to explain this rapidly changing world to the educated middle class. What they found in newspapers and periodicals did not fit the bill. In their search for an appropriate formula, Hadden and Luce came up with the idea of a "newsmagazine" that told a story in each article. Their proposed publication, consisting of twenty or thirty pages, would be an easy and dramatic read. It would offer the country a national medium, comparable in its modernity to paved highways, automobiles, and radio. Reared in the values of the American, Christian middle class, Luce and Hadden were on the prowl for the one million college graduates who might read a paper that was modern – but also patriotic and respectful of religion. This was the vision that inspired *Time: The Weekly Newsmagazine*.

In pursuit of their goal, the young men moved to New York City early in 1922. Sitting in their modest office in an old, nondescript building on Manhattan's East 17th Street, Brit and Harry cut, pasted, edited, and, above all, rewrote articles and wire service reports. The new magazine, Harry Luce noted, would not appeal to "flat earth" types, but he admitted to being "biased in favor of God, the Republican party, and free enterprise."[95] Enlivened by Brit's flair for language and Luce's earnest curiosity, *Time* personified a unique philosophy of journalism. Luce insisted that his facts be accurate, and hence the reference books and researchers that were soon fixtures at *Time*. But Harry equated the search for objectivity with worship of the "stuffed dummy of impartiality." In Luce's view, the editor must reveal his core values to his readers. Having done that, it was his job to weigh both sides in a debate against those values, and *then tell his readers which argument had carried the day*. This formula – applied by writers who knew how to generate readable copy – would give *Time* much of its flair and influence. The formula could also rob *Time* of credibility.

Finally, the great day arrived: The first issue of *Time* was dated March 3, 1923. Hadden did most of the editing, and Luce and Roy Larsen ran the business side. At the office, Luce's rivalry with his partner masked a trust that survived Brit's sarcasm and his binges. Indeed, the magazine owed a lot to Hadden's ability to bring *Time*'s characters to life: People were "wild-eyed" or "long-whiskered" or "swarthy." Hadden also invented and popularized new words such as *socialite*, *tycoon*, and *cinemactor*.[96] By 1928 circulation was pushing two hundred thousand, and Luce's company – now called Time Inc. – reported a profit of $400,000.[97] Newspaper editors and reporters, however, despised the upstart magazine as a scissors-and-paste job. Byron Price, a newspaperman, derided *Time*'s ability to "make harmless facts appear as startling disclosures."[98] Perhaps, but the formula appealed to an audience that comprised upscale readers. Fewer than one out of five American workers earned more than $5,000 a year; among *Time* subscribers, that figure reached three out of five.[99]

Marketing manager Roy Larsen realized that radio offered new opportunities for Time Inc. In his quest for new readers, Larsen broadcast *Pop Question Game*, which served to gain publicity for *Time*.[100] Later, Larsen branched out into movies and became the originator of the *March of Time*, the premier newsreel of its day. These were happy, exciting years for Harry Luce. They were fulfilling personally, too. Late in 1923 Luce wed Lila Hotz, with whom he had two sons: Henry III and Peter Paul. But much of the time, the marriage proved to be a sidebar to Harry Luce's obsession with *Time*'s proposed sister magazine.

In 1929 Luce was hoping to publish a magazine devoted to the world of business enterprise. Hadden opposed the plan, but sadly, tragedy struck Brit in the middle of the debate. He contracted *streptococcus viridans*, or blood poisoning. Although Luce and others donated blood on a regular basis, it was to no avail. Henry R. Luce would never again be so close to any colleague. Still, Brit Hadden's death left him in a position to acquire his late partner's stock in Time Inc. Luce, who was in his early thirties, was soon a millionaire.[101] "I was poor once," Luce later mused, "and I saw no merit in it, if it can honestly be avoided."[102] But could Time Inc. survive both the loss of Brit Hadden and the collapse of the economy? Surely, people told Harry Luce, this Depression had written finis to any plan for a new business magazine. But Luce demurred. Displaying his uncanny ability to plumb the needs of potential readers, Luce insisted upon proceeding with *Fortune*. He was soon pouring huge sums into the most elaborate business magazine ever seen.

Luce hoped that *Fortune* would educate the emerging meritocracy.[103] Capitalists would have to come to terms with trade unionism and with the expanding role of government during hard times.[104] Harry Luce could pay top dollar and hire the best talent, men like Ralph M. ("Mac") Ingersoll and Russell Wheeler Davenport and the gifted poet Archibald MacLeish.[105] And no one would contribute more to *Fortune* than the great photographer Margaret Bourke-White.[106] In its early days, *Fortune*'s circulation stood at thirty thousand; nine years later it was well over one hundred thousand, and this during the bleakest decade in the history of *Fortune*'s subject – U.S. capitalism.

Time Inc.'s stock earned $4.11 per share in 1931, when *Time*'s circulation topped three hundred thousand (a year later it passed four hundred thousand). The company was awash in cash, for its readers could stay the course: More than one-third of *Time*'s subscribers still earned more than $10,000 a year, which in 1932 represented a fabulous sum.[107]

Discovering Chiang and Russian Communism

While millions of Americans sought any kind of work, Harry Luce could afford to take a long-postponed trip around the world. Accompanied by his brother-in-law, the Reverend Leslie R. Severinghaus, Luce returned to China. The wobbly empire of his boyhood had yielded to a republic run by military men, prime among them Chiang Kai-shek. To Luce's satisfaction, a number of the leaders of the ruling Guomindang party, including the Methodist Chiang, were converts to Christianity. Chiang's brother-in-law T. V. Soong, a prominent banker, flew to Shanghai to meet with Luce.[108] He knew something about Luce's growing reputation, for one of Soong's sisters (Mei-ling) had been a classmate of Beth Luce Moore at Wellesley College. Another of the Soong sisters had married Sun Yat-sen, the republican revolutionary, and a third had wed H. H. ("Daddy") Kung, a rich man who was allegedly descended from Confucius. Eager to stimulate American support for Chiang, Soong lobbied Luce on behalf of the beleaguered Guomindang regime.

Just before Luce's arrival, the Japanese army had completed its conquest of Manchuria. Meanwhile, Chiang was engaged in desperate "anti-bandit" campaigns against the Communists, who were strong in impoverished rural areas. T. V. Soong, however, assured a receptive Harry Luce that Chiang was on the verge of annihilating the Communists. He would then unite China and ward off further Japanese depredations. Soong had an easy sell, for Henry Luce, who was known for his insatiable curiosity, could also avoid seeing things that might undermine his faith. In fact, the Soongs and the Kungs were enmeshed in a web of kleptocracy and nepotism, but Luce tended to dismiss the allegations against them. Chiang was wary of Westerners, had created a secret police apparatus, and had fostered party youth organizations that some observers (not Luce) compared to the *Hitler-Jugend* or the Fascist *Avanguardisti*. In addition, Luce showed little interest in the strength or appeal of the Communists. By contrast, he overestimated the impact of Christianity upon Chinese society.[109] To Luce, Chiang and other Christian Chinese leaders were the instruments at hand. With American help, they would modernize and Christianize their ancient country. Henry Luce concluded a lifelong pact with the Guomindang.

Luce and Severinghaus left China and rode the Trans-Siberian Railway through the Soviet Union. Lingering in Luce's mind was an old animosity: As early as 1919, he had decided that if the United States did not intervene soon in Russia, "bolshevism" would "undermine the civilization of the world."[110] But the war ended, and Luce would have to deal with Communism in other ways, at a later time. In Russia, Henry Luce learned about the terrible famines caused by Joseph Stalin's collectivization of agriculture. Indeed, Luce found the whole Soviet system appalling, dirty, repressive, inhuman, even perverted. As he crossed into Poland, hardly a paragon of modern progress, Luce felt liberated.

After Luce returned home, indelible images remained with him: He acquired a lifelong loathing of the practices of Communism in Russia. He had also reinforced some enduring ideas about China. He never forgot boyhood memories of the small church in Weixian, "packed with people who come not for the glory of it, nor the fashion of it, nor the gain of it, but who come, simple in garb and heart, who come for the love of it."[111] But political images seized his imagination, too. As early as 1915, Luce, then seventeen, had decided that China had never "understood or embraced democracy as an ideal." Luce believed that the ancient nation first needed to find "law and order & courage"; then and only then could China secure the liberties that Americans valued.[112]

Luce never reordered his Chinese priorities. For the next thirty-five years, they would dominate much of Time Inc.'s published words and films about China.

Infatuation

Although he disliked giving direct orders, Henry Luce tended to dominate his rapidly expanding enterprise. Recalled one colleague, "I spent twenty years arguing with Henry Luce" – but everyone knew who was boss.[113] Another editor observed to Luce, "You *are* TIME, LIFE and FORTUNE."[114] But for those who survived his gruff manner, Henry Luce was a generous employer, one who offered medical insurance to his workers when such paternalism was almost unknown. Successful editors could become eligible for various bonuses, along with the occasional gift of Time Inc. stock from Harry Luce himself. (They later formed what was known as the Senior Group.) And who could argue with Luce's awe-inspiring string of successes? But Time Inc. was becoming an important part of American culture, so its critics were growing more vociferous. For a time, the radical Dwight Macdonald had worked for *Fortune*. Eventually, however, both Macdonald and Luce had had enough of one another. Soon Macdonald said, "[*Time*] gives us something to do with our minds when we aren't thinking."[115] And in 1937, Macdonald also concluded, "An organization which puts ideas into 30,000,000 heads is a powerful little gadget to be under the control of a single individual, even the most brilliant member of Yale '20." But Henry Luce would soon realize that his "powerful little gadgets" might serve as instruments that furthered his political and foreign policy goals.

The three years that followed his return from China were busy ones in Henry R. Luce's life. On the home front, his marriage bored him, for the romantic, poetic, and socially adept Lila had failed to "melt the glacier" that Harry seemed to carry around on his shoulders. Indeed, these two people were very different – a romantic socialite and a repressed workaholic locked in marriage.[116] At this vulnerable point in his life Harry Luce met Clare Boothe, a bright, beautiful young divorcée who had made a career for herself in magazine journalism. She had become an associate editor at *Vogue* magazine and then managing editor of *Vanity Fair*. Clare Boothe also had some ideas about publishing a new kind of picture magazine. Hidden from view, however, was a darker side of this woman.[117] As she later confessed to Luce, she was a "badly burnt child [and hence] . . . so afraid of happiness." Certainly, marriage had provided no solution: In 1923 Clare Boothe had wed George T. "Teddy" Brokaw, a wealthy, middle-aged socialite and abusive drunk. The miserable union produced a daughter, Ann, in 1924, but George became increasingly impossible and would eventually be institutionalized.

Clare Boothe was ambitious, manipulative, and clever. She later claimed or received credit for a variety of *bons mots*, from "age before beauty," to "no good deed goes unpunished."[118] Clare also became adept at manipulating powerful men, including her lover, stock market speculator Bernard M. Baruch. But her life was a long first act that never culminated in a satisfactory denouement. Clare Luce's memoirs, which might have been fascinating, at least as fiction and wit, never appeared. Indeed, Boothe's most substantial creation was her public persona – witty, acerbic, bright, beautiful.

This was the woman who decided in the early 1930s that she wanted Henry Robinson Luce, the celebrated editor of *Time* and *Fortune*.[119] They had met a few times, and Clare had once interviewed Harry for her magazine. Then, at a party where they had a chance encounter, Luce asked Clare to accompany him down to the lobby. Clearly, she had dazzled the young tycoon, for he abruptly posed the question that changed his life. "Do you know," Luce asked, "that you are the great love of my life?"[120] Luce crushed Lila when he bluntly asked her for a divorce, although he lamely promised that after he was free, he would be a better father than ever. Nevertheless, she agreed. After the legally mandated year of separation was up, Lila Luce filed for divorce in Reno on grounds of "cruelty."* A court granted her request on 5 October 1935. Seven weeks later, Luce married Boothe, and the newlyweds enjoyed a long honeymoon in Cuba.[121]

At Time Inc., Luce's colleagues resented Clare as an interloper. *Time*'s John Billings, for example, despised Clare, writing of her, "What an actress! Every move a dramatic gesture." He always feared that Clare was "up to tricks" and called her "a horrid woman – and no professional."[122] One of the fears gnawing away at his colleagues was unfounded, because Harry Luce would never give Clare control of the company he called "my life." Nor would she edit his future picture magazine.

Making use of breakthroughs in photography, Henry Luce and Dan Longwell soon sketched out a plan for a sensational new magazine.[123]

FDR, Hitler, and the Jews

Life, as they imagined it, would reflect Luce's insatiable curiosity about the world. The magazine would entertain by providing the best photos of celebrities, politicians, pretty girls, and cute animals. It would also preach and elevate by celebrating great art and the Christian faith. Presiding over the experiment was John Shaw Billings of *Time*, soon to be the managing editor of *Life*.[124] Billings, a courtly South Carolinian of good pedigree, had attended Harvard. He joined Time Inc. in 1928 and quickly rose to the post of national affairs editor. Later, Billings became the magazine's managing editor. At *Life*, Billings's brilliant editorship made the new (1936) picture magazine a staple of American life.

Luce had insisted that this magazine be big and that it be as cheap (ten cents) as *Fortune* was expensive.[125] *Life* was the great publishing phenomenon of its time, and within a few years, 15 percent of the population, or an estimated seventeen million people, read or looked at *Life* each week. Indeed, the magazine became the "television" of the pre-TV era. Like its successor, *Life* featured

---

* The first Mrs. Luce, who lived to be one hundred years old and died in 1999, concluded that Clare was "beautiful, brilliant, glamorous" but also "immoral" and "ruthless." The W. A. Swanberg collection, 18, interviews [Allen Grover]; and correspondence between HRL and Lila H. Luce, ibid., 17.

a wide array of "channels" – some in color – that offered contents ranging from the weighty to the trite. The magazine would soon have an impact upon politics. Certainly, the current president, though a Democrat and a liberal, was ideally suited to the needs of the magazine's photographers – and readers.

After meeting FDR in the White House early in 1933, Harry Luce had blurted out, "My God! What a man!"[126] In 1933 and 1934 Luce generally supported the laws and regulations enacted by FDR's New Deal. But his honeymoon with the president did not endure. FDR was soon assaulting the privileged few as parasites even as Harry Luce entered the *Social Register* and accumulated great wealth. Luce perceived Roosevelt's swing to the left in 1935 as a prelude to collectivism, and he feared that FDR's relief programs would turn America into a "nation of handouts." But by this time, a more pernicious figure than Roosevelt was distracting Harry Luce and changing his view of the world. Ironically, the new dictator of Germany would one day push Luce into an alliance of convenience with a president he had come to despise.

The rise of Adolf Hitler profoundly challenged the kind of social anti-Semitism harbored by the men who ran Time Inc. "During the recess after mid-years," a defensive Henry Luce wrote from Yale in 1918, "I may go up with a Jew to his home on the corner of Exeter & Beacon Streets, Boston!" Harry quickly reassured his parents, however, noting, "It's old Ep Herman, an old Hotchkiss fellow, not at all offensive, & absolutely loyal to our old set."[127] But old stereotypes sometimes surfaced in uglier ways. Under foreign news editor Laird Goldsborough, *Time* went out of its way to identify Jews who were criminals, Communists, and reprobates.[128] But by 1934 Luce, prodded by Archibald MacLeish at *Fortune*, had begun to rethink the implications of anti-Semitism. *Fortune*'s subsequent articles represented a pioneering if flawed examination of American attitudes toward Jews.[129] Other factors were at work, too: *Time* had long angered Jewish readers, but as Jews advanced in American life, they formed a significant segment of the Luce readership. In addition, the Anglo-Saxon Ivy Leaguers who had founded *Time* were now joined on the staff by talented Jews who had fled Nazi Germany. The photographer Alfred "Eisie" Eisenstadt, for example, helped to make *Life* a success.[130]

In the mid-1930s, Luce had begun to return to his internationalist roots, but he remained wary of moving too far ahead of his isolationist readers.[131] To clarify his thinking, Luce decided to see Europe firsthand, so he toured Central Europe between 11 May and 20 June 1938.[132] Hitler, Luce concluded, was aggressive, popular, and dangerous.[133] *Time* bemoaned the fate of the trapped Jews, but Luce's publications did not advocate substantial Jewish immigration into America until *after* the Holocaust had decimated European Jewry. In 1938–1945, Luce concentrated on the Nazi threat to the West and the United States, and not the Jewish plight. And he did so with increasing urgency. Laird Goldsborough finally received a permanent "sabbatical."[134] *Time* savaged "Man of the Year" Adolf Hitler and condemned Neville Chamberlain for having promised peace with honor at Munich – and having "achieved neither."[135] At an important dinner with senior editors early in 1939, Luce finally revealed that he would use *Time*'s power for a political purpose if he thought "the Republic was in danger."[136]

Time's Interventionism

Luce's flagship magazine was the product of a formula that had evolved over fifteen years. Editors and staffers constantly studied the rush of cables arriving from Washington and other venues. Each Thursday, the top editors convened and assigned stories to their writers and researchers. Cables, interviews, clippings from the morgue, and other data were all grist for *Time*'s research-and-write mill. The editors then reviewed progress and problems on Saturday. Sunday was particularly rough, for on that day editors read the submitted drafts and then edited, discarded, or resubmitted them to staffers for reworking. Edited pieces were supposed to be in good shape by Monday morning; final copy had to be ready by late Monday night.

The "book" was then teletyped to printers in Chicago, Philadelphia, and Los Angeles. (In Chicago, the press run began as early as 6 A.M. Tuesday.) Only on the rarest of occasions would a print run be stopped in order to make last-minute alterations. So to harried editorial workers at *Time*, Tuesday and Wednesday elicited the sarcastic farewell, "Have a nice weekend!" Copies of the new *Time* were on sale at Grand Central Terminal by Wednesday evening and were delivered to everyone else on Thursday or Friday. The latest *Time* was both a first look at contemporary history and a summary of recent news – as filtered through the lens provided by Henry R. Luce and his senior editors. In 1936 Luce sold six hundred forty-one thousand copies each week, and by the spring of 1940 that number had reached seven hundred fifty thousand. Where local newspapers were weak or one-sided, *Time* was ever more influential, as in Washington and Chicago, where the *Times-Herald* and the *Tribune* were ardently isolationist. *Time*, Luce believed, was a national institution that might offer leadership when it was most needed.

The crisis in Europe made Luce receptive to a rapprochement with Roosevelt. The Luces and the Roosevelts had met three or four times in the past, but their chemistry was poor to nonexistent. Luce lunched again with FDR on 10 May 1939, but the event also went badly.[137] The earnest Presbyterian felt ill at ease with the gaudy Episcopalian, and Luce had long since turned against the New Deal. For his part, the President hated *Time*, which had embarrassed him more than once. Roosevelt's forced attempts at intimacy only riled Luce, for the affable president called him "Henry," a name "Harry" Luce despised. Worse still, Roosevelt's foreign policy evasions annoyed Luce, who tried to elicit a blunt statement announcing America's interest in stopping Germany. But Hitler, history would soon prove, had a knack for uniting the most disparate of foes.

In 1939 Henry Luce's media launched a massive campaign on behalf of American rearmament, an important decision in the light of the magazine's large Republican readership.[138] The GOP, of course, contained the loudest isolationists, who often opposed the very measures – rearmament and intervention – that

Luce advocated. So when war came on 1 September, Luce insisted that his publications trumpet the virtues of massive American rearmament. General George C. Marshall, the new chief of staff of the Army, appreciated Luce's attitude, for he understood how Time Inc. could help him as he worked to rebuild America's defenses. Time was of the essence. Poland had fallen, and Soviet Russia was friendly with Nazi Germany. Hitler might be preparing to strike in the West, and Mussolini seemed poised to join him.

Early in 1940, Clare Luce left for Europe, where she intended to gather material for a book. Writing to Harry, she warned, "The curtain is about to go up on the greatest show the world has ever seen."[139] In April, Harry rushed to join Clare.[140] At this juncture, Maurice "Tex" Moore, Time Inc.'s lead counsel and husband to Harry Luce's sister Beth, gave Luce advice that confirmed his own hunch: "America," Moore telegraphed Luce, "still asleep having bad dreams desperately needs clarion voice disclosing utter lack preparedness particularly vital industries your leadership urgent."[141] Clare Luce added, "If you have anything to say, now is the time to say it." Thereafter, Henry Luce resolved to awaken what *Time* would call the "martial spirit." Luce's messianic globalism grated on some nerves: "He's too busy saving the nation to pay any attention to his magazines," groused *Life*'s John Billings.[142] Yes, Luce wanted to alert the nation and save the world, but Henry Luce still believed that America's greatest test would come in the Far East.

2

Learning to Market Chiang's China

On 10 May 1940 the Luces were in Brussels as the guests of U.S. ambassador John Cudahy. Before dawn, a maid who recalled a prior invasion knocked on their door yelling, "The Germans are back!" The Luces soon fled to a France verging on panic, and then they hurried back to the United States. (Luce prophetically joked about returning with the U.S. Army.)[1] Luce quickly assembled and harangued his editors, demanding that they beat the drums for rapid mobilization. He took to the radio, urging that Americans lead a crusade for justice and decency. But Americans wanted to stand aside, for only 7 percent favored war. At this juncture, Luce decided to speak to the president, and late in the morning of 1 June, FDR met with him.[2] FDR did most of the talking, and Luce felt that the president was treating him like a Yale "sub-freshman."[3] Of course, FDR knew that Harry Luce was heavily involved in the presidential campaign of Wendell L. Willkie.

Just before the war, *Fortune* had discovered the political potential inherent in this charismatic businessman. As packaged by Luce's magazine, Willkie was progressive and internationalist. *Fortune*'s Russell W. Davenport became his campaign manager, and Luce crafted Willkie's foreign policy proposals. Indeed, it was widely rumored that Luce would be Willkie's secretary of state. When the European crisis weakened the Republican isolationist establishment, Willkie won his party's presidential nomination. This miracle, Luce hoped, would be topped by a greater one in November. But while Luce worked to displace Roosevelt, he was also a key figure in the Century Group. This New York–based coterie of powerful internationalists favored all-out aid for Britain and was eager to work with the president on its behalf.

The Century Group gained access to the public through the Luce media, which campaigned for U.S. access to air and naval bases in Newfoundland, Trinidad, Brazil, and Bermuda.[4] Luce and his magazines also advocated the dispatch of American warships to the Royal Navy.[5] In late July, the Luces were overnight guests at the White House. After dinner and the showing of *The Ramparts We Watch*, an interventionist film produced by Time Inc., Henry

Luce finally received his private audience with the president.[6] He proposed that Britain lease bases to the United States in return for the dispatch of overage destroyers to the Royal Navy.[7] Early in September, FDR finally announced the signing of agreements effectively exchanging American destroyers for British bases. Roosevelt also deluded himself (perhaps with Luce's encouragement) into believing that Time Inc. might support him in his quest for a third term. Naturally, the White House reacted badly when Time Inc. refused to alter its pro-Willkie bias.[8] But Roosevelt had other reasons for his anger: In 1940 *Life* called the president's supporters "third termites." Earlier, the Luce empire had branded the recent downturn "the Roosevelt Recession." At times, the Time Inc. media even alluded to the president's physical infirmity.

This year (1940) bore witness both to Henry Luce's power and to its limits. When Time Inc.'s magazines and movies articulated a single, coherently orchestrated message, the polls tended to move in their direction – when Americans felt that a crisis loomed and they looked in vain to Washington for leadership. When FDR acted decisively – the transfer of the destroyers and the acquisition of bases, then conscription – the public was relieved, and the Willkie balloon quickly deflated.[9] Luce, however, was a graceless loser, angrily declaring that he wanted "nothing more done for Britain on the personal and exclusive authority of Franklin D. Roosevelt."[10] He later argued that Roosevelt had in effect lied the country into war. The president "as much as admitted that to me in private conversation," Luce would claim.[11]

After Roosevelt's reelection, payback time arrived for seventeen years of accumulated bile. Back in 1923, six months after *Time* first appeared, FDR had told Harry Luce that his magazine had "made statements in regard to events which are not wholly fact." Then FDR condemned the very tricks that would make the magazine a great success: *Time*'s misuse of "qualifying words" and its distortions through omission.[12] After the 1940 election, Roosevelt again attacked Luce and his publications, often on the pettiest of grounds. And on a later occasion, the president castigated *Time* for printing a "disgusting lie" that furthered "Nazi propaganda against the United States."[13]

China: The Ultimate Test

In the winter of 1940–1941 Henry Luce drafted his great essay on the future of America.[14] There would either be an "American Century," Luce concluded, or the world would witness the demise of a civilization suffering a "gigantic and rotten death." Convinced that an American-led alliance would win the war, Luce foresaw a postwar world run by the United States.[15] Americans would teach the ignorant, feed the hungry, and bring the blessings of liberty under the rule of law to two billion people.[16] Luce refused to concede that domination might engender imperialism; he wanted to uplift, and not exploit. "The American Century" provoked almost five thousand letters to *Life*, many of them thoughtful, others anguished in tone. Isolationists were outraged, and interventionists were inspired. But American public opinion was moving in the direction of intervention, for the interventionists' arguments rested upon an attractive premise: America was a great nation that could accomplish marvelous things in the world.

To Luce, the ultimate test of the American Century remained China. Even as German troops goosestepped into Paris, Harry Luce insisted that the Pacific problem was "far more important even than speedy aid to the Allies."[17] But unfortunately, as Clare Luce observed, Americans would "never have the same interest in China and its problems" as they had in Europe's.[18] Most Americans were of European descent, and Asia was much more distant than Europe. For some years, even the Luce media had not adequately covered the Japanese threat to Chiang's China. This deficit suddenly disappeared in 1937, when Japanese forces again attacked China, and Chiang Kai-shek, supported by the Communists, fought back. At this point he emerged as *Time*'s "disinterested patriot" leading his people in resistance to aggression.[19] Luce's Chinese were virtuous victims, whereas *Life*'s Japanese soldiers were predatory cockroaches, "superbly adapted to getting along on almost nothing."[20] Luce used scare tactics, too. *Fortune* displayed striking maps depicting Japan as an expansionist power and described it as an industrial competitor in a world of shrinking markets.[21]

Time Inc.'s campaign for China faced an immediate challenge: The U.S. supplied Japan with strategic materials such as scrap metal and high-octane fuel, and no less than 56 percent of Japan's "essential war materials" were of American origin. An American embargo, *Life* concluded, would quickly bring Japan to heel. This was dangerous thinking, the product of racist arrogance leavened by complacency.

Harry Luce's labor of love was the promotion of the Christian cause in China. Here he carried on the work of his father, who had helped to raise money for the construction of Yenching University in Beijing. The elder Luce served that institution as vice-president until his retirement in 1928 and then worked to create the Associated Boards for the Christian Colleges in China (ABCCC).[22] Founded in 1932, ABCCC represented thirteen educational institutions, for which it acted as a central source of funding. In support of his father's work, Henry R. Luce donated many thousands of dollars to the boards; he was the driving force behind their success. Calling upon his far-flung network – missionaries, philanthropists, China hands, and Christian churches in the United States – Luce worked wonders.

In 1939 and 1940, Henry Luce worked to found United China Relief (UCR), which funneled private money to worthy causes in beleaguered China. From early 1941 onward, UCR was a vast success, for Luce's fund-raising lists constantly grew. Politicians and Hollywood producers who knew what *Life* could do for their careers or their movies were eager to help. In 1941 alone, UCR raised about $4 million, an enormous sum; ultimately, the organization solicited a remarkable $47 million for China.[23] And while philanthropist Luce sought to raise money through UCR, publisher Luce was selling "fighting free China" to his millions of readers. In this endeavor, a young man named Theodore Harold White was making major contributions.

Chiang or the Communists?

Twenty-five years old, Teddy White was *Time*'s man in Chongqing, China's remote wartime capital. He was a short, bright, intense young man, a product of Boston's lower-middle-class Jewish community. He attended the Latin School, where his good work merited a scholarship to Harvard College. Too poor to live in Cambridge, White commuted from Dorchester to Harvard Square almost every day until his graduation in 1938. At Harvard, the man who changed Teddy White's life was his "surrogate father," a tall, impressive historian named John King Fairbank.[24] In a sense, White majored in Fairbank, whom he later described as "the first person, in a way, who really cared about me."[25] Indeed, it was this professor who inspired White's lifelong interest in China.[26] Fairbank long remembered Teddy White as "a not very tall bundle of energy with a world-wide imagination and eloquence to go with it."[27]

While Teddy White was preparing to graduate in 1938, Professor Fairbank gently pushed him in the direction of a career in journalism. By covering China's struggle for survival, Fairbank reasoned, Teddy would strike a blow against militarism and fascism. After some months had passed, White made his way to the wartime capital of Chongqing, where he went to work for Hollington "Holly" Tong.[28] White's job was to portray China's prospects in the rosiest of colors.[29] In a young American named John Hersey, White found a friend who shared his anguish at China's fate. A graduate of Yale, tall, athletic, and sophisticated, Hersey had gone to work for *Time* a couple of years earlier, and he had access to Harry Luce. Johnny Hersey realized that White could provide *Time* with something it lacked: firsthand reports on China.[30] White soon resigned from his job at Tong's agency and went to work full-time for Time Inc.[31]

A tireless traveler who endured many hardships in his quest for information, White wrote fact-crammed letters that conveyed the sights and smells of China. But Teddy White was already beginning to deviate from the Luce line. He did not think that the Nationalist regime, even with American help, could wage real war. And by 1941, White had come to admire Mao Zedong's Chinese Communist Party (CCP). Though not a Communist himself, White believed in the so-called United Front, in which all Chinese would fight side by side against Japan. He quickly learned, however, that Chiang viewed the Reds as his main enemy. He was saving his best troops for the struggle against them; in the shorter run, Chiang had concluded, America would defeat Japan. When Chiang provoked the Communists by attacking elements of their New Fourth Army early in 1941, White was appalled. But on 10 February, *Time* found Mao's army guilty of aggression. Chiang, the magazine explained, had merely "prevented internal disorder by disarming and disbanding" troublemakers.[32] *Time* concluded by ascribing Free China's plight to the Japanese blockade or to the paltry amount

2.1   Chiang Kai-shek, a Luce hero, in a happy moment. (Library of Congress)

of American aid. Teddy White's relations with New York were about to enter a troubled phase.

Ironically, Luce's father could have given his famous son a few insights into Communist China's appeal to many Chinese. In 1940, as part of his teaching curriculum, the Reverend Luce wrote "Brief Outline of the History of Chinese Communism."[33] In his notes, the seventy-one-year-old educator described the Communists as men who advocated a program of democracy and land reform. This was naïve, but no more inaccurate than Chiang's term "bandits." There is no evidence that Luce senior discussed his "Outline" with Harry; in any event, Luce junior tended to brush off unwelcome truths (or half-truths) about China. White was still unaware of this, so he was eager to expose *Time*'s editor-in-chief to the grim realities of wartime China. Luce had not been to the land of his birth in almost nine years, so in the spring of 1941, Harry and Clare booked passage on Pan American World Airways.

Since his boyhood days, Henry R. Luce had been searching for a providential Chinese leader, one fit to join "Hannibal, Caesar, Napoleon, Wellington, Lincoln."[34] A moment forever dear to Luce arrived in this spring of 1941, when a "slim wraithlike figure in khaki" received him.[35] The Chiangs and the Luces then exchanged gifts and discussed common concerns, after which the American hero-worshipper departed in a state of enchantment. The Chiangs,

Harry Luce insisted, would be remembered "for centuries and centuries." Luce was willing to urge reforms upon Chiang, but only in a respectful, cautious, and highly discreet manner.

Chiang had learned something important: He could ignore Luce's advice without forfeiting his support.

Oblivious of danger and discomfort, Harry and Clare flew on to remote Xi'an, to see the war front for themselves.[36] More than ever, the Luces came away convinced that the United States was morally bound to join China in this great struggle. In pursuit of his goal of a Sino-American alliance, Luce greatly exaggerated China's military prowess. He refused to accept more conventional accounts, which described the Japanese as bogged down in a vast, inhospitable land. But Luce had not been tricked; rather, what he saw confirmed what he already believed.[37] (Clare Luce, by contrast, admitted to harboring "a confusion" in her own mind about China.) If Luce had his way, *Time* would do for heroic China what Edward R. Murrow's reports on CBS radio had done for burning London under siege by the Nazi air blitz ("London can take it!").

Teddy White

It was in Chongqing that Harry Luce first met Teddy White. In White, he discovered a bubbling fountain of knowledge; for the moment, political differences dissipated. Luce was in a euphoric state as the two men traveled about town in a hired rickshaw. Luce could not ask enough questions, as one demand tripped over the previous one.[38] The editor-in-chief immersed himself in the "sheer joy and sorrow of the subject" – China. Discussing China with Harry Luce was, Teddy White later remembered, a "god-dam inspiring experience." White had acquired a new hero, one fit to stand alongside Professor John King Fairbank.[39]

On 20 May the Luce party, with White in tow, flew to Hong Kong before island-hopping eastward. On the way back, the Luces met with General Douglas MacArthur, the imperious marshal of the Philippine army, whose stern Roman profile was made for *Life* magazine. Better still, MacArthur was an Asia-firster whose ideas greatly pleased *Time*'s proprietor.[40] The general was also happy to cooperate with Clare Luce, who thereafter became a kind of volunteer publicist for him. Back at the Luce estate near Greenwich, Connecticut, White sometimes argued Chinese politics with his host, but the energetic young Jew and the middle-aged son of missionaries got along famously. Then Teddy headed back to China. While White labored on in Chongqing, Luce continued to propagandize for Chiang at home.

Despite his crowded work schedule, Henry Luce delivered a large number of speeches on behalf of his holy cause; rarely did he stammer when celebrating China's resistance. (Luce liked to quote Madame Chiang, his favorite first lady, who was asking Americans, "Why don't you wake up? Don't you know the world's on fire?")[41] *Cue* magazine saluted Luce for "his farseeing efforts to turn the eyes of the American people across the Pacific as well as the Atlantic."[42] As for the source of Luce's virtues, *Cue* shrewdly added that he combined "insatiable ambition with a genuine instinct for self effacement and a hard core of Presbyterian conscience."[43]

"Negotiations Have Gone Sour"

On the home front, Henry Luce continued to battle for intervention in the war. He bankrolled and staffed the Council for Democracy, a propaganda organization that collaborated with the Roosevelt administration. *Life*, meanwhile, continued to show Americans how their armed forces were preparing for war, and Dan Longwell boasted that "if the U.S. Government didn't have Life Magazine, it would have to invent it."[44] "[We] must," he added, "attempt to be the big educator of the kind of world [in which] we are evidently going to live." "It is indeed gratifying," General Marshall told *Life*, "to have the cooperation and assistance of your great magazine in building up the defenses of our nation."[45] Assistant Secretary of the Navy James V. Forrestal used Luce's "American Century" as a guide to the new world order that America would forge.[46]

Like his friend Madame Chiang, Henry Luce believed that America would soon have to face "the issue of war or dishonor in the Pacific."[47] In the middle of November, *Time*'s Bob Sherrod came away from a briefing by General Marshall convinced that Japan would attack soon.[48] *Time* lamented the fact that "the people of the U.S. remained unaware of the battle of the Pacific now underway." Time Inc., however, was hardly free of blame for this widespread apathy: *Life* had called General MacArthur's Corregidor fortress in the Philippines the "Gibraltar of the Pacific."[49] *Time*'s Bob Sherrod wrote that the American base at Pearl Harbor was safe.[50] Luce himself viewed the Japanese as a peculiar people, savagely aggressive and anti-Western but not up to fighting a major Western power like America.[51] But he had his moments of doubt, although he quickly suppressed them: During his trip to the Far East, Luce had visited the American naval base at Pearl Harbor, where he spoke with the Navy's commanding officer, Admiral Husband E. Kimmel. Kimmel warned against "biting off more than we can chew"; his lack of confidence upset Luce.[52] Although *Time* boasted in early December that "every man was at battle stations" in this "last act of the drama," that was pure propaganda.[53] More accurately, John Billings wrote in his diary, "Jap negotiations have gone sour – there's no telling what will happen next."[54]

On Sunday afternoon, 7 December, the Luces were entertaining guests at their estate near Greenwich. Suddenly, Clare Luce tapped her glass and demanded the attention of the assemblage. She then jolted the "appeasers" and "isolationists" among her friends with the grim news: The Japanese had bombed Pearl Harbor. Henry Luce rushed to Rockefeller Plaza, where his editors were already gathered. At some point in the late afternoon or early evening of 7 December, Luce momentarily left his agitated colleagues to speak on the telephone with his ailing father. Later that night the Reverend Henry W. Luce died in his sleep at the age of seventy-two. The next day, when his colleagues sought to console him, Harry brushed them off. "He lived long enough," Luce responded, "to know that we were on the same side as the Chinese."[55]

A "Staunch and Devoted" Friend of China

Harry Luce later described *Life*'s wartime editors as the "real historians of the day."[56] But the pictures told the most dramatic stories, and *Life*'s photographers were so ubiquitous on the war fronts that editor Ed Thompson called a military secret "something known only to the high command, the enemy and *Life* magazine."[57] *Life* expanded to a huge 156 pages, and four million Americans bought it each week.[58] "Big Red" was crammed with advertisements and promises of future consumer wonders, from larger refrigerators to something called television, all of which would be available after the victory. *Life* raised American morale in the cities and on the farms across the land, and on far-off islands in the Pacific. Men and women in uniform passed dog-eared copies from hand to hand; they far preferred *Life* to its blander rivals. Indeed, this was *Life*'s heroic time; never had journalism better served a nation fighting what President Roosevelt called "a war for survival." But Harry was not thinking defensively. He wanted to remake the world.

"If ever a nation had a mission," wrote Henry Luce, "that nation is America." Americans abroad, *Time* therefore decided, would need to export the "simple truths" learned "on the Kansas plains."[59] Luce added, "I want America to be different – always – to have a purpose – until all men are free." Presiding over this globalist era without equal would be Luce's God, worshiped anew by all people.[60] Luce offered one of his several visions of the future in a wartime memorandum bearing the grandiose title "Reorganization of the World." (His colleague Allen Grover aptly referred to the document as "Harry's idea of what might be done if human beings just had the wit to do it.") This globalist messianism had appeared, then faded during the tragic interlude of the Wilson presidency. Luce, Wilson's greatest disciple, would help to make it a permanent feature of American life.

After visiting England in 1942, Henry Luce decided that it could survive and even prosper – but only as the junior partner in an American alliance.[61] But to Luce, China remained the great challenge to the American global mission. If America failed China, he warned, then "we fail totally."[62] But to his dismay, the United States was paying little attention to the war in China. There, General Joseph W. Stilwell – commanding general of U.S. Army forces in the China-Burma-India theater and Chiang's chief of staff – was off to a rocky start.

Stilwell had arrived in theater during the late winter of 1942. From the beginning, he faced disaster. Stilwell and his ragtag Allied army hoped to hold Burma and then resupply China.[63] With defeat staring him in the face, Stilwell was increasingly disgusted by Chongqing's cesspools of intrigue and duplicity.[64] As his contempt for the Generalissimo mounted, Stilwell became increasingly

2.2   Generalissimo Chiang (left) with General Claire Lee Chennault during World
War II. (Library of Congress)

impressed by the fighting potential of the Communist forces serving under
the command of Mao Zedong. This flirtation frightened Chiang, who soon
embraced Colonel Claire Chennault as a fellow critic of Stilwell's misguided
strategy.[65] Chennault had commanded the prewar Flying Tigers, a group of volunteers whose P-40 fighters had harassed Japanese forces in China. Chennault,
who now headed the Fourteenth Army Air Force, insisted that his aircraft, if
properly supplied, could achieve a victory on the cheap. To Chiang, Chennault's
formula had the virtue of rendering Stilwell superfluous. Marshall, however,
and through him Roosevelt, had confidence in Stilwell. Though filled with
these unresolved tensions, the unstable Chiang–Stilwell–Chennault triumvirate
endured. To Harry Luce's dismay, however, China played a tertiary role in
Washington's strategy: Europe and the Pacific theater came first.[66] By contrast,
Luce fantasized that China, fighting alone, was winning a battle "for the entire
world."[67]

Luce's Chinese allies naturally praised him for demanding that the United
States do more for China. Writing to Luce, the Chinese foreign minister gushed,
"It is indeed the supreme good fortune of China that, at this crisis in her
national life, she has found in you and your family such staunch and devoted friends."[68] Luce was creating a legend: Chiang was the selfless ally,
uniting his country in the war against a "savage and perverted race." The

postwar Guomindang, Luce wrongly predicted, would preside over the "renaissance of a great Chinese civilization." In pursuit of this chimera, Time Inc.'s New York editors routinely explained away, altered, or dismissed uncongenial copy.

Luce's United China Relief published and distributed an avalanche of friendly materials about China, much of it aimed at schools and young people.[69] Thanks in some measure to Luce's propaganda mill, hundreds of millions of dollars in grants and loans soon flowed into the coffers of Chiang and his Washington operatives.[70] The polls affirmed the efficacy of Luce's work: When asked to describe images of the Chinese, Americans chose terms such as *honest, hardworking, brave,* and *religious* – precisely the four virtues most commonly ascribed to Chinese by a statistical count of phrases used by the Luce network.[71] (Luce's Chinese were American Presbyterians in the making.) Indeed, the polls showed that more than half of surveyed Americans now favored a permanent postwar alliance with China.[72] But how much of this support was based upon misinformation and delusion?

"I'm convinced," Teddy White cabled, "that the Time Inc. publications are among the greatest legend builders in the world." In a warning aimed at his boss, White added, "The less legends we create in this war, the better Time Inc. is going to look after it's all over."[73] By virtually ignoring the Communists and standing by Chiang, White added, both Luce and the U.S. government were misleading Americans. Convinced that Mao's Communists commanded an effective army of five hundred thousand men, White thought that America might yet mediate the grave situation "if a lot of our fascist-minded countrymen" didn't "fuck things up."[74]

At times, Luce did worry that his convictions about China might conflict with his obligation to *Time*'s readers. As a result, he sometimes tried to appease critics of Chiang while remaining loyal to the Great Man of China. In November 1943, Luce cabled T. V. Soong, warning, "Recent reports from experts regarding conditions in China are very unfavorable."[75] In fact, FDR mused that Chiang might be a spent force. He thought that America might need to "look for some other man or group of men to carry on."[76] But Luce resorted to a stratagem that would have a long and inglorious life: His editors at *Time* quietly called for various reforms (fight corruption and inflation, be more democratic) but refused to make aid to China contingent upon their implementation.[77]

Allied with Luce in this new propaganda campaign for Chiang was Dr. Walter Judd, a Republican representative from Minnesota. Judd had spent many years laboring in China as a medical missionary, and he had emerged a fervent anti-Communist. Judd now praised Henry Luce, who had "been so right, as our Government [had] been so wrong, on the most important issue of the Twentieth Century – the nature, the objective, and methods, and the strength of the Communist drive for world conquest."[78] "Both America and China are fortunate," Dr. Judd wrote to Luce, "to have at the head of such important opinion forming organs, a person with your background and firsthand knowledge."[79]

The Luces and Judd were charter members of what would later be called the "China lobby."

Early in 1944, Luce again tried to appease Chiang's critics. *Life*, he decided, would publish White's proposed article about China's wartime debacle. Of course, Luce and Billings would make sure that criticisms of the Guomindang were laced with appeals for more American support. So early in 1944, White drafted and redrafted an article for *Life*, but his work ran into trouble with censors at the State and War Departments – and at Time Inc.[80] After much haggling, *Life* (1 May 1944) imparted some of Teddy White's jarring opinions to its readers.[81] Yet Luce suppressed White's demand for a virtual abandonment of Chiang, whom *Life* praised to the skies.[82] Moreover, in the same issue *Life* editorially labeled hapless China "a great potential force for freedom and democracy in Asia." In Chongqing, Chiang's press-watchers breathed a sigh of relief. Once again, Harry Luce had come through for them.

While Teddy White's article was on the newsstands, military events in China betokened imminent disaster.[83] China, alone among the Allies, was losing World War II. To Teddy White and like-minded friends, Chiang's decline made the Communists all the more attractive. His former mentor, John Fairbank, who now headed the Office of War Information in Chongqing, admitted that "Yan'an glowed in the distance."[84] By contrast, the Generalissimo was fighting for his political life, thanks to the incompetence and corruption of the Nationalist regime. But as far as Henry Luce was concerned, China's misery could be ascribed to "the stress and strain of China's primary task and great achievement: her resistance to Japan."[85] Luce had begun to perceive the campaign against Chiang as part of a broader conspiracy. Its culprits included the Communists and certain members of the press, including his own Teddy White. Luce sometimes thought that Teddy was a Communist and soon decided to shunt him aside. In fact, as the Red Army smashed the Wehrmacht in Russia, Luce was becoming increasingly concerned about the Marxist postwar menace.

Whittaker Chambers

Luce's magazines had for two years and more applauded America's love affair with the "heroic Soviet ally." *Life*'s famous March 1943 cover story on Stalin's Russia contained lots of pro-Soviet fluff.[86] In 1943 and 1944, however, Luce's magazines would change their line, thanks in some measure to certain staffers at Time Inc. Of Luce's mentors, Willi Schlamm and Whittaker Chambers were the most influential. Schlamm, a onetime activist in Austria's Communist Party, knew a great deal about European Communism and the Soviet system.[87] After he went to work for Time Inc., Schlamm fought the pro-Soviet activists who tried to dominate the Time Inc. chapter of the Newspaper Guild.[88] Schlamm's colorful anecdotes about Red perfidy guaranteed his access to Luce, who worried about the guild.[89] Clare Luce also discovered Willi Schlamm's virtues and later told him, "You are a sort of father confessor to me."[90] But of Luce's tutors on the Communist issue, Whittaker Chambers was by far the most important. Squat and unprepossessing and always rumpled, Chambers was also a determined ideologue with firm convictions and enormous talent.

Whittaker Chambers had for many years lived a life filled with intrigue, tragedy, shame, and partial redemption. Chambers's family history revealed a past replete with alcoholism, insanity, and suicide, and his bisexuality exacerbated what was already a considerable measure of self-loathing. At an early age, Chambers undertook a long, anguishing spiritual journey. Branding the civilization that had produced him socially unjust and decadent, he cleansed himself by joining the Communist Party.[91] "I was a better Communist than Stalin," he once bragged.[92] In the mid-1930s, Chambers worked in the underground party as a courier for an espionage ring active in Washington. Then change came, and he found a new kind of inner peace in his strong marriage to the former Esther Shemitz.[93] Now the father of two children, Chambers had grown weary of the duplicity, the cynicism, the shadowy life in service to lies. He broke with the Communist Party early in 1938, but for ten years thereafter, Chambers feared assassination at the hands of his erstwhile comrades.[94] A paranoid who knew great truths, Chambers was eager to educate the American public.

In April 1939 Whittaker Chambers joined the staff of *Time* magazine. His status was a modest one – he reviewed books – but soon, his catchy and passionate prose drew attention. Chambers devoted most of his formidable energy to the exposure of the Communist conspiracy.[95] For this opportunity at *Time*, he remained forever grateful to Luce, with whom he shared a "common religious concern."[96] ("God bless you, Harry," was a familiar salutation.) Only the battle between Christians and Communists counted, Chambers taught; everything else was a skirmish. But Chambers's growing credibility with Luce owed something to a prophecy: As early as 1941, he had warned Americans against mistaking Chinese Communists for liberals.[97] Patiently, Chambers explained that Communists were orchestrating the assault on Chiang Kai-shek by Teddy White and his allies; this thesis made sense to Luce.

The many liberals and leftists working at *Time* counterattacked and drove Chambers out of the local chapter of the Newspaper Guild. But Chambers had his admirers and acolytes, too. Among them were two influential correspondents – Samuel Welles and Fred Gruin – as well as a young office boy named Henry A. Grunwald. As a result, *Time* was growing increasingly wary of the Russian ally. Worried, Soviet ambassador Andrei Gromyko asked a Time Incer, "Who makes the policy on Russia for TIME Inc. magazines?"[98] The answer, of course, was Luce, who in the summer of 1944 decided that Whit Chambers would edit foreign news.[99] Chambers was elated.[100] He could attack Communism on all fronts, because most people "seemed to know little about the forces that were shaping the history of their time."[101] With the Red Army pouring into Eastern Europe and with China in turmoil, there was much to be done. Before the war, the national affairs desk was the road to the top; now, thanks to America's new global role, foreign news could also bring prestige and advancement.[102]

On Fridays, Chambers would take the train to New York, lock himself in his office, and ensconce himself on a dilapidated couch. Smoking endless numbers of cigarettes, Chambers scribbled away for the better part of three days, writing and editing. Finally, the black coffee was gone, and Monday morning dawned. The next issue of *Time* would invariably reflect his interpretation of Communism and its dupes. Chambers tripled the size of the Foreign News section and made certain that no Soviet or Communist perfidy escaped mention. His prose was sometimes melodramatic, maudlin, heavy-handed; but it was also gripping, and his words rang with deep conviction.[103]

In 1944, *Time*'s Red Army was still heroic and the Russians were certainly allies; but they no longer possessed the virtues of a friend or partner. And in Luce's eyes, the situation in China only augmented Chambers's credibility. Years later, after a personal break with Luce, Chambers still praised "*Time*, and specifically Henry R. Luce" for first telling Americans the truth about Communism.[104]

Inside Red China

As the Red Army marched into Eastern Europe, the Japanese launched new offensives against Free China. Cruelly, the Communist journalist and China hand Agnes Smedley rejoiced, "The regime which *Time*, *Life*, and *Fortune* have chosen to champion is crumbling."[105] In Chongqing, a defiant Chiang barely survived FDR's demand that he place Joseph Stilwell in command of all Allied armies in China. Chiang also whined, "Americans want me to be a slave... [and] they treat me as if I were a thief!"[106] Patrick Hurley, the latest special emissary to China, warned President Roosevelt, "If you sustain Stilwell in this controversy, you will lose Chiang Kai-shek and possibly you will lose China with him."[107] (Talk about "losing" China had surfaced; the phrase would enjoy a long history.) A bitter Stilwell left China, to be replaced by General Albert C. Wedemeyer. At first, Wedemeyer, a gifted staff officer, expressed contempt for the corrupt Chinese leadership.[108] Wedemeyer even told Marshall, "Self-sacrifice and patriotism are unknown quantities among the [Chinese] educated and privileged classes."[109] But General Wedemeyer quickly fell into line with U.S. policy.[110] The contrast between Wedemeyer's public statements (patriotic China growing stronger) and his private views (corrupt leadership becoming weaker) reflected the contradictions confusing American policymakers.

Soon after Stilwell left China, Teddy White finally visited the Communist-controlled border regions. Gripped by enthusiasm, he found himself in a new world, one that was "remote, inaccessible, awe inspiring."[111] The Communists, White believed, had "unlocked the key to Chinese history."[112] Dazzled by what he wanted to see, White played down an unpleasant truth: Yan'an was a crude military base set "amid illiterate peasants and brutish soldiers," where, in the words of one scholar, "intellectuals were easily singled out for humiliating sessions of self-criticism and were turned into exemplary targets during the terrifying purges of 1942–1944."[113] Nevertheless, a hopeful Teddy White longed for the day when the United States would replace the Soviets as Yan'an's patron. After emerging from their isolation, the Communists might, he thought, evolve along more liberal lines.

White's information about Yan'an arrived just as *Time* was preparing to do a controversial cover on Stilwell's recall.[114] In New York, Fred Gruin, assisted by Harry Luce and Whittaker Chambers, concocted *Time*'s version of events: Their final product condemned Stilwell and even praised Chiang for having ruled "high-handedly in order to safeguard the last vestiges of democratic principles in China."[115] Citing *Time*, Japanese propagandists happily described the Stilwell clash as a sign of Allied disorder.[116] When White belatedly read *Time*'s Stilwell issue, he called it "the worst bit of journalism I have ever seen in America."[117] White then expressed his sentiments in a crude metaphor. "With bricks," he wrote, "you can build a temple to god, or you can make a brick shithouse. And in [Luce's] China stories he used most of the facts his correspondents sent to build a brick shithouse." White found the fumes in Luce's gaudy defecatorium ever more noxious, and he was slowly stumbling toward the exit.[118] But the lower-middle-class Jewish kid from Dorchester would not easily toss aside the rewards of being Luce's man in Chongqing: prestige, access to sources, good pay, the friendship of the powerful Harry Luce. So White made a few concessions, and the two men again argued back and forth. They were wasting their time. Luce later growled that he "should have fired him immediately, but it was difficult at that time to get good men."[119]

Though angry and hurt, Luce realized that Teddy White's impressions of remote, heroic Yan'an would fascinate *Life*'s readers. The editor-in-chief took care to see that the resulting article did not attack Chiang, and White's "Inside Red China" appeared in the 18 December 1944 issue of *Life*. There, White depicted the Communist leaders as revolutionaries committed to a Marxist vision of the world, but his conclusion was controversial: "In victory," White warned, "[the Communists] will remember who were friends and who stood coldly aloof." Teddy White realized that Luce had given him a consolation prize.[120] In a bitter rebuke, *Life* soon indicted its own list of culprits in China's tragedy: (1) *American* troublemakers, (2) *Americans* who cheated China out of overdue assistance, (3) *Americans* who threatened to use lend-lease to pressure Chiang, and (4) *American* journalists (like White), some of whom were Communists or pro-Communist.[121] China was indeed America's to "lose."

Prodded by John King Fairbank, who despised Luce and his alibis for Chiang, Teddy White moaned, "I'm not a Communist, not a Luce-man, not a pen-prostitute." On a personal level, White's heroes had revealed either feet of impure clay (Chiang) or had departed in frustration (Stilwell). So White boldly resolved in February 1945 that he would "never write about China for [Time Inc.] again," nor allow it to "use my name to cover their policy."[122] Henry Luce was thinking along the same lines; his mood grew darker with each report of Soviet victories.

By late 1944 the steady Soviet advance into Poland and southeastern Europe had come to obsess Harry Luce, who denounced FDR's acquiescence as "despicable stuff."[123] Almost a year before Winston Churchill spoke of an "iron curtain," *Time* was drawing an eight-hundred-mile line bisecting Europe. On the home front, Luce's line hardened, too. For years, his media had ridiculed hamhanded Congressional inquiries into Communist subversion in America. By 1945, however, after persuading himself that the newly created House Committee on Un-American Activities (HUAC) would act responsibly, Luce endorsed it.[124] He also helped to win over important moderates, including Governor Raymond Baldwin of Connecticut.[125] In backing HUAC, Luce was moving away from the United Front, that alliance of convenience between liberals and leftists engendered by the war against Hitler and Japan.

In China, Patrick Hurley, Roosevelt's latest ambassador, failed to unite the two feuding Chinese factions.[126] For this debacle he blamed both the Communists and his own liberal advisers – John Paton Davies, Jr., and Jack Service in particular.[127] In fact, Chiang and Mao could not tolerate one another, except during rare moments of exceptional outside danger. Even now, when Japan occupied much of their country, the two remained wary and uncooperative. Both offered frequent professions of their faith in democracy, but neither side understood, much less accepted, democracy as Americans defined the term. Chiang, however, would survive, and not because of his military ability. The Japanese were running out of steam, and abundant U.S. supplies were finally flowing into China.[128] *Time* smugly insisted that the Generalissimo was moving in the right direction.[129] After reviewing the magazine's errors, Teddy White concluded that *Time*'s prestige among U.S. military personnel in theater had hit an "all-time low."[130]

Like other knowledgeable observers in his extended family, Luce had heard rumors about FDR's declining health.[131] But when he learned of Roosevelt's death on 12 April, Luce, like many other Americans, expressed disbelief. For a moment, Luce was unable to respond, but when he did, the old bitterness resurfaced. Luce would go on for hours about the man who had kept him, "wholly without moral justification, physically isolated from the global war." Indeed, through a series of vindictive memos and asides, FDR had prevented Luce from visiting the Pacific theater – or China. Later, Luce bitterly cracked, "I think it is my duty to go on hating him."[132] Harry Truman, he believed, might be an improvement. *Time* correspondents Frank McNaughton and Eddie Lockett enjoyed good access to the new president, and Truman's private comments about the Russians sounded like a repudiation of FDR's Yalta policy.[133] That policy, which was predicated upon cooperation with the Soviet ally even at the expense of Chiang's China, had always troubled Luce, and more so with the passage of time. So he quickly expressed his confidence in Truman's "character and ability."[134] But in regard to China, Luce had no clue as to the new president's intentions. The president had none either, because Roosevelt had kept him in the dark. But of one thing Luce was certain: Pro-Communists were conniving to undermine U.S. support for Chiang Kai-shek.

Clashing Visions of the Postwar World

Amerasia was a journal dedicated to examining contemporary American and Soviet policy in East Asia. The publication, which had a small circulation, was run by leftists and Communists who opposed U.S. support for the "feudal" regime misgoverning China. In the spring of 1945, the Federal Bureau of Investigation concluded that the editors of *Amerasia* were receiving and publishing classified government documents leaked by Foreign Service officer John Service, among others. After several indictments were handed down, two of the *Amerasia* defendants pleaded guilty and paid modest fines; two other targets were exonerated.[135] Luce concluded that the *Amerasia* business pointed to treachery; the strangely passive reaction of the Truman administration diminished his enthusiasm for the new president. To Luce, moreover, the *Amerasia* scandal revealed how journalists of the Teddy White type had colluded with pro-Communist diplomats in smearing Chiang. But other sources told a different story; Luce was free to accept or reject their conclusions.

An unsigned and impeccably anti-Communist source known to Luce – probably dating from the early summer of 1945 – freely acknowledged that "the Chinese Communist movement" had provided "individuals, especially the laborers and peasants, with greater economic opportunities than the Kuomintang [*sic*] Nationalists provide."[136] Other sources confirmed this analysis. *Newsweek*, *Time*'s upstart imitator, had in Robert Shaplen and Harold Isaacs two crack correspondents who saw through Chiang's propaganda. Unlike Teddy White's *Time*, their magazine published what they wrote. *Newsweek*, for example, insisted that China remained oppressed by a "semi-medieval tyranny."[137] Until the 1960s, *Newsweek* lacked *Time*'s readership and influence, but anti-Luce experts confirmed at least some of *Newsweek*'s China reportage. Owen Lattimore, a specialist on the frontier peoples of China and central Asia, had served as an adviser to Chiang. Now, in memoranda to President Truman, Lattimore accurately predicted that the Guomindang regime was preparing to unleash a civil war. His advisers, Lattimore added, had told the Generalissimo, "Henry Luce, Walter Judd, etc., have guessed the trend correctly."[138] *Time*, of course, stood by Chiang, who moaned that too often the American press was ignoring "our efforts to correct ... shortcomings."[139] In June 1945 the Generalissimo himself thanked *Time*'s editor-in-chief for his "fair presentation" of the situation in China.

Clare Boothe Luce had been elected to Congress from Connecticut in 1942, and she proved controversial – and adept at capturing headlines. Hostile to the New Deal Democrats and to FDR, Luce was narrowly reelected in 1944. Then, in a series of powerful radio addresses delivered during the first half of 1945, Representative Luce virtually declared war on Soviet Russia.[140] Through her speeches, franking privileges, and radio commentaries, Clare Boothe Luce's words reached millions of Americans. The Hearst newspapers praised Luce, and pro-Chiang activist Alfred Kohlberg called her the "American Winston Churchill."[141] In response, American Communists called Luce a "courtesan," a "strip teaser and a Hitlerite"; and *Pravda* labeled Clare Boothe Luce a fascist.[142] But polls showed that almost two out of five Americans now questioned Russia's desire to work with the West.[143]

Clare Luce's assault on Russia coincided with the first phase of Henry Luce's long-postponed visit to the Pacific theater of war.[144] General MacArthur himself invited Luce, so in late May 1945 he flew westward. But before leaving, Luce and his adviser Raymond Buell decided to sketch out a foreign policy for postwar America.[145] These Luce–Buell proposals anticipated the postwar foreign policy that the United States would adopt in 1945–1949:

1. Unless Russia behaved, lend-lease aid must be halted.
2. A large American army should be permanently stationed in Europe.
3. The West must merge its three German zones of occupation into a new state, and America should take the lead in rebuilding Italy and France.

But the most explosive part of the Luce–Buell analysis concerned Japan. Thanks to wartime patriotism, as well as reports of documented Japanese atrocities, American anti-"Jap" fervor was reaching its high point. Many Americans, the historian John Dower has written, were gripped by a frenzied anti-Japanese racism that he calls "exterminationist." (*Life* sometimes contributed to this phenomenon.)[146] Even after newsreels showed Americans some of what the Nazis had done to human beings in their concentration camps, four out of five Americans saw the "Japs" as "more cruel" than the Germans. Yet Henry Luce was ready to buck this tide.*

In 1945 Luce foresaw the creation of a permanent U.S. defense perimeter in the western Pacific, one running from Alaska and Okinawa through the Philippines. He looked ahead to the time when Japan would cooperate in rebuilding the vast region that ran along that perimeter. Luce hoped to end the war with Japan on a basis short of "unconditional surrender." If peace came *before* the Russians entered the Pacific war and invaded Manchuria, Luce reasoned, then the Soviet Union could not challenge America for supremacy in East Asia. In the Luce–Buell scenario, Japan would subsequently be demilitarized under Allied (i.e., American) supervision, and the Japanese people would be allowed to decide the fate of Emperor Hirohito. Japan would be guaranteed access to Southeast Asian markets, and ultimately, a reformed Japan would enter the world of capitalism, democracy, and free trade – the American Century. Luce's stunning analysis, however, made for very bad politics. As he might have put it, it's good to stay ahead of your readers, but not too far ahead.[147] Luce was voicing a heresy, so instead of launching a self-destructive press campaign, he decided to visit the Pacific and then try some personal diplomacy.[148]

---

* Henry Luce had already expressed doubts about the security threat posed by Japanese Americans. In the summer of 1943 he approached J. Edgar Hoover to secure the FBI director's appraisal of Japanese American loyalty. But the suspicious Hoover mistrusted Luce and did not wish to touch this volatile issue. L. B. Nichols, memorandum for Mr. Tolson, 14 July 1943 (FOIA).

3

Bitter Victory

His inspection of the war theater in the late spring of 1945 filled Henry Luce with pride in the U.S. commanders, especially General MacArthur, with whom he spent four hours.[1] Luce returned convinced that the U.S. frontier now stretched from Manila to Okinawa, and it would "never be moved back from there." But his grand tour also intensified Luce's hostility to the doctrine of unconditional surrender, which the Allies had embraced early in 1943. In addition to lost American lives, Luce was convinced that *twenty million* Japanese might die if the war continued for another year.

Upon his return, Luce heard that some administration officials agreed that Japan might surrender – if Emperor Hirohito remained head of state. On 6 July Harry Luce met with the president, but Truman made sure that this encounter remained a courtesy call.[2] Undeterred, Luce returned to Washington on 11 July, when he met individually with more than one-third of the U.S. senators.[3] Arguing that the Japanese forces were weaker than ever, Luce called for negotiations. But Truman remained intransigent, the war continued, and by late July informed observers knew that the Soviets would soon enter the conflict. (John Hersey, who later become the celebrated author of *Hiroshima*, resigned on this same day, 11 July.)[4] Luce, who was already concerned about the Soviet presence in Germany and Eastern Europe, now worried about a Russian incursion into north China.

As Time Inc. prepared to hire lots of new talent, *Time*'s attitude toward Russia sometimes undermined the company's recruitment of editorial personnel.[5] One prospect – Harrison Salisbury, United Press's man in Moscow – rejected *Time*'s offer because, he said, "I don't think I'd be happy here." Eric Hodgins summed up the reason for Salisbury's refusal: "Russian policy."[6] Although his magazines were careful to intone occasional pieties about postwar cooperation, Harry Luce was unhappily preparing for a bipolar world.[7] He had not foreseen this development when he wrote "The American Century" back in 1941. "The trouble is," Luce would later comment, "history just took the American Century clean away from me."[8] Hints of the coming bipolar world began to appear in Luce's media.[9] But a fortuitous event might, some thought, bring about a change in *Time*'s ever harsher anti-Soviet tone.

One Monday morning in August 1945, Whittaker Chambers suffered a heart attack while on his way to New York. John Osborne replaced him as foreign news editor, but by this time the erstwhile dissident had embraced Chambers's anti-Soviet beliefs. Although *Time*'s literary quality now lacked the Chambers flair, its foreign news coverage followed the same hard line.[10] In the words of Archibald MacLeish, "Mr. Luce's boys" were busily searching for a Soviet conspirator under every bed in the world.[11]

The stunning atomic attack on Hiroshima on 6 August took everyone by surprise and rendered moot Teddy White's plan to show Luce Chiang's failed war effort. Luce, however, now saw a way of ending the war without Russian participation. On 8 August, the publisher, accompanied by Joseph Kennedy, called on Archbishop Francis Spellman of New York. The two men, Spellman noted in his diary, "came to see me to ask if I would ask President Truman for five or six days' truce to give Japan a chance to surrender."[12] There would be no respite, however, and the next day an American bomb incinerated Nagasaki. Still, Japan refused to surrender, even after Russia entered the war.

In the middle of August, Japan finally capitulated to the Allies, and the Japanese did indeed retain their emperor. If this concession had been offered in May or June, Luce always believed, many lives might have been saved – and Russia would not now be overrunning Manchuria. A few years later, Harry Luce still insisted, "If, instead of our doctrine of 'unconditional surrender,' we had all along made our conditions clear, I have little doubt that the war with Japan would have ended soon without the bomb explosion which so jarred the Christian conscience."[13] But in 1953, when Luce started to lecture Harry Truman on the "feeling of possible peace" that had existed in the spring of 1945, the former president snapped, "Nothing to it."[14]

In victory, Henry Luce was terribly proud of both his company and his country. "Dan, we've fought a wonderful war," he told editor Longwell.[15] Luce and his senior editors celebrated at a victory luncheon, replete with cocktails and champagne.[16] There was much to celebrate, in addition to the victory over Nazi Germany and Imperial Japan. By 1945, more than thirty million people read or scanned one of Henry Luce's publications every week. Sixty-three percent of the men in the U.S. armed forces named *Life* their favorite magazine; *Collier's* ran a poor second, with 28 percent of the vote.[17] The war brought *Life* an influx of new readers, and five million people now bought the magazine. *Time*'s circulation passed the one million mark. Eight thousand movie houses screened the *March of Time*, and eight million people listened to the radio version. Revenues poured in, even though it cost far more to run advertisements in the Luce magazines than in its blander and weaker competitors, the *Saturday Evening Post*, *Look*, and *Collier's*.[18] By the end of the war, Time Inc. employed about two thousand people, and its gross income had risen to more than $74 million.[19] But Luce rarely relaxed; he could never rest on his laurels, and China, he believed, was America's unfinished business.

An Ambiguous Victory

Luce was sure that with enough U.S. aid, China would make the transition to peace, democracy, and material progress. China, he insisted, had fought Japan for eight long years, and its postwar challenges paled in comparison to that ordeal. *Fortune* gently pushed Chiang in the direction of negotiations and reform but concluded, "If the present is the harbinger of the future and if U.S. aid is quick enough and great enough, the morrow may take care of itself."[20] But Teddy White again interrupted these reveries when he posed several troubling questions: Would the Red Army stay in Manchuria? How would millions of Chinese refugees return to their shattered homes? Could the regime deal with inflation and the destruction left in the wake of a vicious aggression? How much would the Americans help? Above all, could Chiang and Mao reach agreement, or would a war between the Guomindang and the Communists involve Americans in a new and futile bloodbath? These were vital questions, for late in August Chinese Communists killed their first American soldier. John Birch, a captain and intelligence officer attached to the 14th Air Force, was allegedly working to prevent clashes between the opposed Chinese armies. In fact, he led a small communications unit assigned to a Nationalist military detachment, and the Communists dismissed his efforts as those of a spy. They ambushed and brutally killed Birch and several Chinese companions on 25 August 1945.

At this time, the dogged Henry Luce insisted that his publications adopt a more positive view of China's future.[21] He growled that Teddy White was "an ardent sympathizer with the Chinese Communists" – a truth distorted by Luce's exaggeration.[22] In response, White passionately condemned the "filth of [Chiang's] government" and the "squalor of his past career."[23] Luce summoned White to New York; he wanted him out of China and perhaps out of *Time*. Meanwhile, *Time* and *Life* and *Fortune* insisted that Chiang really wanted to create a multiparty democratic regime with a coalition government, something he had never done – and would never do.[24] On the surface, moreover, Chiang Kai-shek appeared to be in a strong position: He was an Allied leader who had stayed on the winning side. But the Red Army quickly took the offensive in Manchuria and in north China.[25] Communist guerrillas severed rail lines essential to economic reconstruction and national unity. Other units seized Japanese warehouses filled with weapons and ammunition. The Soviets also made things rough for the Nationalists in Manchuria. They refused to let U.S. personnel land at the port of Yantai in Shandong; nor could the Chinese government gain access to the port of Lüda.[26]

Luce underestimated Mao's cunning and strength, while trusting Stalin's commitment to the new Sino-Soviet treaty of friendship. Soviet aid to China, Luce noted, would henceforth be channeled through Chiang's government. Though concerned about the looting in Manchuria, he insisted that Stalin stood "morally bound to withdraw his Red Army from Manchuria on or about November 15."[27] Stalin, *Life* concluded, was "pulling the rug from under the Chinese Communists."[28] In October, *Time*'s Washington staff added, "The

Chinese Communists pose no major threat to Chiang Kai-shek and won't unless they receive outside aid, such as arms which the Russians have taken from conquered Jap forces."²⁹ *Life* decided that "the present prospects of China [represented] a vindication of American policy in Asia." The previous week, wrote *Time*, "the ancient land of China" had been "bright with hope."³⁰

On 18 September Teddy White began his long trip home. In New York, he found a preoccupied Harry Luce, who was eager to leave for China. The two men decided that White would take six months off, during which time he and Annalee Jacoby intended to complete their book on wartime China. Both White and Luce sensed that these clumsy waltzes were useless, for the delightful music had long since faded away. White had a story to tell, but Harry Luce had a sermon to preach, and one calling undercut the other. White wanted to give the United Front one more chance; Luce, like Chiang, mistrusted it. Backed by other Time-Life hard-liners, Luce intended to mobilize his China network and fight back against Teddy White and all the other left-wing prophets of negativism.

From Hurley to Marshall

In the autumn, Henry Luce returned "home" to Chiang's China for the first time since 1941. What he saw exhilarated him. Yet he never visited the Communists in their peasant strongholds; and meetings with Mao and Zhou left him angry and unimpressed. Luce vowed to work ever harder on behalf of American intervention in China. But President Truman had no intention of committing U.S. troops to the looming civil war in China.³¹ And Truman, unlike Luce, wanted to keep China out of the headlines. The GIs, he knew, wanted to come home, find a job, start a family, and maybe enjoy some of the consumers' paradise promised by *Life* since 1936.³² *Time*, by contrast, endorsed the retention of a four-million-strong U.S. Army, standing guard alongside a Navy of 558,000 sailors and thirty-six aircraft carriers.³³ But the magazine was too far ahead of its readers: Neither the public nor the administration would support such a force – until at least 1948.

In late November 1945, Ambassador Patrick J. Hurley suddenly resigned, blaming disloyal left-wing embassy personnel for the failure of his mediation attempts. (In Tokyo, the Foreign Service officers pilloried by Hurley celebrated his resignation by breaking out a rare bottle of good bourbon.)³⁴ Speaking to the National Press Club, Hurley sputtered, "I am opposed to being leaked on by the career men in the State Department."³⁵ After denouncing unnamed Americans for "belittling the Nationalists and praising the Communists," General Claire L. Chennault lauded Hurley for "placing the issue of American foreign policy in China squarely before the American people."³⁶ Informed of the ambassador's move by press secretary Charlie Ross, President Harry Truman could only growl, "Why, the old son of a bitch!"³⁷ But Truman quickly sensed political danger, for the Hurley resignation had energized the China bloc. But before Luce and his allies could exploit the situation, the wily politician in the White

House named General George C. Marshall his special representative in China. The president charged Marshall with effecting a cease-fire. Marshall was then to bring about the "unification of China by peaceful, democratic methods."[38] Perhaps Marshall realized that winning World War II had been an easier task.

Truman made it clear that a China wracked by civil war would not be worthy of American economic or military aid. However, as China moved toward peace, political pluralism, and unification, more aid would be forthcoming.[39] But was this policy of reconciliation realistic? Although Mao Zedong often spoke of "peace, democracy, and unity," he explained his real aims to his comrades: "This roundabout road will help the Party mature in various ways...and help us thereafter to realize a New Democratic China."[40] Hurley's bumbling, blustery testimony before a Senate committee further undermined Chiang's cause. Even the former ambassador admitted, "I took a terrific beating not only in the public press but from my friends who believed that I had made charges...which I had not upheld."[41] Tom Connally, the powerful chairman of the Senate Foreign Relations Committee, denounced the idea of waging "a full-scale war on the side of Chiang Kai-shek's corrupt and reactionary government."[42] Connally gloated, "Pat's fiasco did not confer any credit upon him" and cruelly added, "All we had to do was let him rave." *Time* admitted as much, too.[43] So a dejected but still feisty Hurley returned to New Mexico, where he repeatedly embarrassed himself in failed attempts to win a seat in the U.S. Senate. When Hurley later tried to peddle his memoirs, John Billings of Time Inc. dismissed him as "an old bag of wind."[44]

Undeterred by Hurley's self-demolition, Henry Luce and his senior editors intensified their campaign on behalf of Chiang Kai-shek. Luce himself gave a series of speeches, including an important one at the influential Council on Foreign Relations.[45] At a black tie dinner on 6 December, Luce told of a land that was trying "to recreate herself along Western lines." Chiang himself, Luce assured his audience, was "a great and genuine patriot" who wanted peace. (In fact, like Mao, Chiang wanted peace on his own terms.) Then, with one eye on the Democratic administration, Luce described the leaders of the ruling Guomindang as "somewhat farther to the 'left' than the New Deal." This opportunistic statement was totally inaccurate, but in a second bow to the administration, Luce was careful to align himself with the China "policy of [Secretary of State] Byrnes, Truman, and Marshall." Henry Luce still refused to worry very much about the Chinese Communists. Although they could disrupt the economic reconstruction of China, he decided that they could not take "many cities." In remarkable denial, Luce would grant only that China might see the emergence of a "real pro-Communist movement three or four years hence if the government does not produce a solution for the current social economic ills." In fact, China would be Communist in three years.

Henry Luce joined the national chorus celebrating the Marshall mission.[46] *Time* hoped that with Marshall's imminent arrival in Chongqing, U.S. loans and military advisers would pour into China. Luce foresaw peace and justice triumphing in northeast Asia if the United States would exercise "sufficient intelligence and will."[47] But Marshall's task was made more difficult by a basic contradiction: He was to mediate, but America was not neutral, for a "united China," led by Chiang and sustained by American aid, would be used to block further Soviet inroads into East Asia.[48] The remaining American troops would assist Chiang, *even if* the Generalissimo "failed to make reasonable concessions."[49] In addition, important Chinese did not share Truman's goals. The Guomindang rightist leader Chen Lifu, director of the Central Executive Committee's Organization Department, believed that the Americans didn't know the Communists very well, so they would likely "be fooled by the Communists."[50] In Chen's view, "When we learn that the loss outweighs the gain, it will be too late to lament."[51] Chiang himself agreed, for he feared that in the end, the mission would have "a harmful influence on major events."[52] Among the Communists, too, there were doubters. "Our central task now," wrote Zhou Enlai, "is the struggle against Chiang Kai-shek." It would be a mistake, however, to judge the Marshall mission purely in policy terms, for it represented Truman's political attempt to buy time.[53] The maneuver worked even though Marshall failed.

The public relations surrounding the Marshall mission was a Time Inc. operation. During the crucial early phase of his stay in China, Marshall relied heavily upon the services of James Shepley, who had joined *Time* in 1942.[54] Shepley was clearly a future star at Time Inc. He was sometimes a temperamental and often a difficult colleague, but his ambition, fortified by a first-rate mind, enabled him to survive and prosper.[55] Late in 1945 Luce released Jim Shepley at Marshall's personal request, and for almost three months, Shepley was the general's man in Washington. Marshall later thanked Luce for Shepley's "invaluable assistance," and the journalist also received a letter of commendation from Secretary Byrnes.[56] A savvy and hard-driving man, Jim Shepley handled the press, wrote statements for Marshall, and even acted as an occasional liaison between the special envoy and his commander-in-chief. But Shepley always intended to return to Time Inc., and so he proved to be an invaluable source of high-level leaks to *Time* and Luce.[57] Once, Jim Shepley begged *Time*'s home office, "Please do not disclose that we have been reading Marshall's dispatches which are sent EYES ONLY to the Prex [president] and Secretary of State or we won't read any more."[58] But Jim Shepley was not the only Time Incer serving Marshall and China. Through most of 1946, *Time*'s John Robinson Beal worked on Chiang Kai-shek's staff as a personal adviser, and served as an informal liaison between Chiang and Luce. According to Teddy White, Beal was paid the princely sum of $25,000 per year, with a house and servants thrown in.[59]

To the great surprise of cynical observers, General Marshall quickly arranged a cease-fire between the Communists and the government.[60] Bipartisan truce teams, dispatched and supervised by Marshall's executive headquarters, would enforce the provisions of the armistice. As foreseen by General Marshall, a Political Consultative Conference (PCC) would then hasten the day when a coalition government and a united army would govern one China. At the moment, press aide James Shepley noted, General Marshall was working for a "coalition government," and he was making progress.[61] Marshall spoke about being "very good friends" with Zhou Enlai. The prospects for peace and unity improved further on 25 February, when the Communists and the Nationalists agreed to mandate the integration of their respective armies.[62] Once political and military unity was a fact, Shepley added, American aid would flow freely into the new, democratic China. With a settlement in sight, Harry Luce launched powerful humanitarian appeals on behalf of fifty million homeless Chinese, many of whom were starving.[63]

If the planned coalition failed, however, General Marshall predicted that China "would be easy prey for the Soviet."[64] But the optimism of the early mission was infectious. Henry Luce expressed gratitude to Marshall for what he had been "able to do in China," and *Time* even accepted the imminent participation of "the leaders of the various parties of society" – meaning the Communists, among others – in China's government.[65] It was in this spirit that Luce late in March met with Marshall, who had returned to the United States for a few weeks of rest and consultation. Meanwhile, *Time*'s New York office was busy preparing a highly favorable cover story about the general.[66] Henry Luce boarded a train for Washington, where he lunched with the general late in March.[67] Luce would have proudly displayed the current issue of *Time*, with its handsome picture of Marshall on its cover.

Just under the surface, however, lurked unresolved problems: The Communists were agitating for the immediate creation of a provisional coalition government.[68] Moreover, as Luce had commented to Marshall, "The realities of the [Manchurian] situation may be even worse than anticipated." And when the Soviets finally withdrew from Manchuria, the Chinese Communists, to *Time*'s dismay, quickly overran much of the region.[69] Marshall, meanwhile, had lost some of his luster. Chiang himself, who ultimately sat through sixty meetings with Marshall, worried that the general seemed to be "deeply influenced by the Communists."[70] Madame Chiang tried a softer approach. Writing to Marshall, she warned the general that the Communist negotiator Zhou Enlai had grown more "elusive," and she hoped that the Americans would pressure him.[71] Meanwhile, Chiang was poised to fight for Manchuria, and the Communists were calling him a dictator.[72] Writing to his deputy from the United States, an alarmed Marshall insisted, "You will have to force an agreement quickly regarding entry of [truce] teams into Manchuria...We cannot delay any longer."[73] But the United Front was collapsing elsewhere, too. Why should it revive in China?

The Soviet Ally as Enemy

From Iran and Turkey to Eastern Europe and Germany, new antagonisms divided the wartime alliance; Luce blamed the Soviets for its breakdown. He wanted to change the uncertain national mood so that Americans and their government would take the offensive against Soviet totalitarianism. In so doing,

Luce intended to make use of Catholics and liberals, of social democrats and Republicans. Ultimately, Luce's message in 1946 paved the way for the national consensus of 1948.

In its quest for an appropriate strategy, *Time*'s Washington bureau became familiar with the policy analysis offered by a little-known diplomat and historian named George Frost Kennan. Currently assigned to the U.S. embassy in Moscow, he had never embraced the popular wartime concept of a benevolent Soviet ally. Early in 1946, Kennan cabled home his "long telegram," which recommended firmness but also a willingness to negotiate, with infinite patience fortified by an abiding faith in the West's long-term spiritual and economic superiority. *Time*'s Sam Welles, a Princeton graduate who had joined Time Inc. in 1938, gained access to the secret Kennan telegram soon after it arrived at the State Department, and by April *Time* was making discreet use of it. Almost a year before Truman adopted a version of the "containment" policy, Time Inc. was popularizing Kennan's strategy.

In heightening public awareness of the Soviet threat, the Luce media also placed an increasing emphasis upon appeals to Catholic anti-Communism. Here Clare Boothe Luce's religious conversion played an important role. In 1944 Clare's daughter Ann Brokaw, her only child and Harry's stepdaughter, had been killed in an automobile accident. Clare Luce, a nominal Episcopalian, found consolation in the Catholic Church, and when she visited Rome with a congressional committee, she twice met with Pope Pius XII. Now she sought instruction in the Catholic faith from Father Fulton J. Sheen.[74] Faith alone, Sheen taught, could bring real fulfillment. Clare Luce's baptism, perhaps the most famous of its day, took place in St. Patrick's Cathedral in New York on 16 February 1946.[75] Father Sheen would later recount how "many times this morning during Mass and Holy Hour I said 'Clare.'" The date 16 February, the anniversary of her baptism, became a blessed date on Father Sheen's calendar. A "father always has a favorite child," he wrote, adding, "You are mine, Clare!"[76] Critics of Clare Luce would ridicule her as "Fulton's folly," but in Father Sheen, Clare Luce found faith and friendship.

Despite her pending retirement from the Congress in January 1947, Clare Luce still craved publicity and controversy, and Communism offered her a new foil. As the Soviets grew more threatening in Europe and China, Father Sheen's views found their way into Clare Luce's speeches and statements. Indeed, words written in 1944 now struck many admirers as prophetic: From China to the United States, Sheen had declared, Communism challenged the true faith in a battle for the allegiance of humankind. The priest wanted to wage a holy crusade against the "pinks" and "fellow travelers" who were "trying to impose upon America the very scum which Russia rejected."[77] Paraphrasing Sheen, Clare Luce declared that Communism was "an attack on the Western concept of man as a child of God, a creature with a sovereign soul." Time Inc. agreed, and it fostered Sheen's career as a public figure. Long before he became a star on American television, Sheen enjoyed a favorable press in the Luce media. He was, according to *Time*, dark and very handsome, and endowed with deep-set eyes, strong features, an intense gaze, and a mellifluous voice.

Although she insisted that war was not inevitable, Clare Luce, like Sheen, warned that a failure by the West to profess faith in Christ was "Soviet Russia's greatest hope of Communizing the world."[78] Her bold call for international control of nuclear weapons (1945) now yielded to a demand that the United States retain the Bomb and its secrets, at least until peace was secured. Anyone, Luce declared, who favored a Russian arms control plan "probably ought to be impeached as a traitor."[79]

The heroic Soviet ally of 1942 was now the enemy of the Luces. Could Americans be made to agree?

Forging an Anti-Communist Consensus

Clare Luce constantly lobbied for stories favorable to the church. Often, Harry complied, for the Catholic hierarchy's militant anti-Communism appealed to him. Although Luce never converted ("An ample road to salvation was marked out for me in childhood"), Clare's Catholicism nurtured his alliance with New York's Cardinal Francis Spellman.[80] Spellman, like Luce and Father Sheen, advocated an aggressive defense against the Communist threat. "If China goes Communist," the cardinal asked, "where will we be?" *Life*'s lavish, two-part portrait of the new cardinal sealed the union between militant anti-Communist Catholics and the Presbyterian who used Time Inc. as his pulpit. Often, Luce wondered why mainline Protestant churches seemed more reluctant to defy the Communists. The Protestant Federal Council of Churches, for example, annoyed him by refusing to endorse the retention of U.S. bases abroad.[81] But in his drive to create a national consensus, Henry Luce found at least one reliable Protestant of impeccable anti-Communist credentials.

Time Inc. had introduced John Foster Dulles, the son of a Presbyterian minister, to its readers during the 1944 campaign. An international lawyer and prominent Presbyterian layman, Dulles often professed his belief in applying Christian principles to political questions. (Others saw him as a sanctimonious power player whose ambition was cloaked in piety.) When the Republican party, egged on by Governor Dewey and his adviser Dulles, finally embraced the idea of a postwar international organization, Luce felt vindicated.[82] From 1944 onward, Luce made sure that his editors made Dulles look as pure as the driven snow.[83] Grateful for Luce's support, Dulles was careful to make sure that his views on China echoed those of Time Inc. Typical was the time when he asked Luce whether Luce thought Dulles had presented the China policy "fairly and effectively."[84] But Dulles knew the answer to his own question, because his comments on the Far East were vintage Henry Luce. As Luce later admitted, *Life* soon "chose [Dulles] to express" certain ideas, which "very much coincided with the general ideas that we had here."[85]

John Foster Dulles's heavily edited essay was called "Thoughts on Soviet Foreign Policy and What to Do about It."[86] Dulles's Soviet Union (the "inner zone") was protected by a belt of satellite states (the "middle zone"). Neverthe-less, Moscow was intolerant, militarist, and incapable of envisioning peaceful coexistence with an "outer zone" of liberal, Christian states. To the detriment of the West, this outer zone was ravaged by postwar problems, and hence Dulles warned of a coming *Pax Sovietica*. Twice in twenty-five years, he reminded his readers, American leaders had failed to deter aggression by "not making ap-parent, in time, our devotion to our ideals." And recently, Dulles charged, the country had "bartered away to the Soviet Union, the rights of weak nations, [such] as China and Poland." But then Dulles conjured up a nostrum sure to win Luce's support. Like Luce, Dulles insisted that American ideals were both religious and civil in nature, and if "hardheaded, competent persons" – presumably men like Luce and Dulles – took charge in the West and especially in America, then the Soviet plot would be foiled, and the Soviet Union itself might change. Luce liked what he read, and on 15 March 1946, he insisted that Time Inc.'s senior editors adopt the Dulles approach to Russia in their magazines.[87] Through a contract with *Reader's Digest*, a condensed version of the Dulles–Luce line would gain access to millions of people throughout the world.

Luce invariably linked foreign policy goals to domestic politics. In 1946 he feared that Truman's weakness might play into the hands of those liberals and leftists who were coalescing around Commerce Secretary Henry A. Wallace. Ea-ger to maintain the wartime alliance with Russia, these people were, in Luce's eyes, "appeasers." At war's end there were about seventy-three thousand Com-munists in the United States and its armed forces, along with many more fel-low travelers and sympathizers. Although the Communist Party of the U.S.A. (CPUSA) contained many well-intentioned people, it was a wholly owned and controlled subsidiary of the Soviet Union and its intelligence apparatus.[88] Luce was eager to expose the American Communist Party as a Soviet front and thereby pry its liberal allies out of its embrace.[89] His goals coincided with those of Professor Arthur M. Schlesinger, Jr., a talented young Harvard historian.

An advocate of anti-Communist liberalism, Schlesinger sought to engage the Wallaceites in a public debate. The professor knew that if one wanted to reach a huge audience, *Life* offered a unique medium. "The Time Inc. ethos was powerful stuff in those days," Schlesinger later recalled. "The U.S. Com-munist Party" appeared in *Life* in July 1946.[90] Citing example after exam-ple, Schlesinger showed how Moscow played the ventriloquist to the CPUSA's dummy. He alerted the labor movement, civil rights activists, and "Hollywood intellectuals" to Communist machinations. Schlesinger was particularly hard on the influential Independent Citizens' Committee of the Arts, Sciences and Professions, or ICCASP, which he correctly labeled a Communist front.[91] Luce and Billings were happy with Schlesinger's product, but in one sense, their choice backfired: Arthur Schlesinger, Jr., had used *Life* to lay the polemical ground-work for the *Democratic* anti-Communist coalition that in 1948 defeated not only the Wallaceites but also Luce's beloved Republicans.

"I do not," rasped Harry Luce in September 1946, "want any Commu-nist sympathizers working for TIME INC."[92] Although Time Inc. refrained

from launching the kind of broad witch-hunt that soon disfigured other orga-
nizations, many of Luce's employees grew fearful, and some left the company.
This tougher anti-Communist line coincided with *Time*'s growing doubts about
Marshall's mediation mission.

Incipient Civil War

George Marshall had returned to China on 18 April 1946, and he soon found
that the euphoria engendered by the January truce had dissipated.[93] Speaking
on background to *Time*, General Albert Wedemeyer declared that Marshall's
mission was "impossible of accomplishment at this time."[94] The two rival
Chinese armies hated each other too much, Wedemeyer explained, and they
would both resist integration. He went on to blame Marshall for the imminent withdrawal of more American troops. The China theater shut down on
1 May, and two days later Jim Shepley told New York that the pullout had
deprived Marshall of any means of bringing "effective pressure" to bear on the
Communists.[95] Only about twenty-five thousand sailors and Marines remained
in China by June 1946, and within six months, that figure would decrease to
twelve thousand. Luce's memory of the days when the Stars and Stripes flew over
towns in Shandong would long endure, but the men who hoisted those colors
were coming home. In May, Mao's Eighth Route Army occupied Changchun,
the capital of Manchuria.[96] Jim Shepley reported that "if Communist acceptance [of a compromise] could not be obtained, the chances of the unification
were slim."[97]

Richard Lauterbach, cabling from Shanghai, warned *Time* that "die-hards"
around Chiang wanted him to settle scores with the Communists. Any other
course, they cautioned, amounted to "slow suicide." Disgusted by what he
saw, Lauterbach decided to write a book dedicated to exposing the Guomindang's "ruthlessness, greed, and corruption."[98] Luce and his court were not
amused, and the lengthy manuscript that became *Danger from the East* cost
Dick Lauterbach his career at Time Inc. This outcome was not surprising, given
Time's China coverage. The magazine glorified ultra-rightists such as Dai Li, a
deceased Chinese official whom Teddy White had called (with some hyperbole)
the "Chinese Himmler."[99]

A frustrated George Marshall warned that the inflamed mood on both sides
"seriously" worsened the situation and could "lead to results that would be
disastrous for the people of China."[100] Marshall, according to Fred Gruin of
Time, "felt that his mediation was being used as a cloak for a policy of force,"
presumably by Chiang. Actually, the general wished a plague on both houses:
"Publicly," Marshall complained, "you communists attack me as untrustwor-
thy," but "privately, you trust me with your case before the Government."[101]
From President Truman, however, came a terse response: "Keep trying."

Chiang, who had flown to Manchuria, was busily encouraging the Nationalist forces driving on Harbin and Jilin. On 1 June, *Time*'s Bill Gray cabled home a
devastating report. Although the government was making military gains in the

north, its offensive betokened the doom of hopes for, in Gray's words, "peaceful agreement and political compromise."[102] He added that Chiang's government maintained itself by force alone; it would be voted out of office in a landslide – if it permitted a free election. Unless liberals took over and changed things, Gray added, the Communists would win. If the United States could not bring about reform, Gray mused, perhaps it should abandon China. What would Luce do with this information? A story citing Bill Gray's name did appear in *Time*, and Luce admitted that it was too bad "the Government chaps haven't done better."[103] Yet *Time*, using tested techniques, again managed to eviscerate Gray's reporting. The magazine acknowledged the corruption and then blamed the Communists, and paltry American aid, for Chiang's plight. But the old technique was not working, and readers often came away convinced that China was a losing proposition, best avoided by Americans.

White Leaves and Marshall Fails

While Teddy White worked on his long-planned book about wartime China, he led a shadowy existence at Time Inc. He had already flunked Harry Luce's loyalty test: No matter what the salary, White made clear, he would not take an assignment if it conflicted with his own desires. John King Fairbank again needled his former student: "Why the hell don't you cut loose from Henry [Luce] and get out from under the stigma of being kept by a guy who is on the wrong side?" Luce, Fairbank charged, had "prostituted the truth and his own staff for policy purposes."[104] Fairbank had already called White a whore; now he was demoted to equine status in Luce's "stable." But Fairbank was a tenured member of the Harvard faculty, whereas White had no way of knowing whether his book on China would sell. So he remained in Time Inc.'s stable. But late in June, Luce finally told White, "You will be more likely to find the kind of career you have envisioned for yourself outside of TIME INC." White sadly agreed that the "finest of feasts must come to an end."[105] However, one last scene needed to be played out.

As China veered toward civil war, Teddy White, as agreed, permitted Luce to scan the manuscript of *Thunder Out of China*. The book recounted China's wartime horrors, pilloried the Chiang regime, and expressed admiration for its liberal and Communist enemies. *Thunder Out of China* also advocated the dispatch of massive amounts of aid to a coalition government capable of uniting China. But sadly, White's Chinese liberals lacked "an army, a political machine, roots in any social class."[106] The Communists, by contrast, knew how to mobilize the alienated peasantry.[107] White admired Marshall for restoring America's position as "nonpartisan in China's internal dispute."[108] His optimism was badly out of date, however, for George Marshall had already failed in China.

Although Marshall cobbled together a brief truce in Manchuria in the middle of June, a frustrated Chiang Kai-shek warned him that "it would be his "final effort at doing business with the communists...all-out war would be preferable."[109] Marshall, Chiang commented in his journal, "completely disregards the life and death struggle of China and my historical mission toward our country."[110] The Generalissimo launched a new offensive in central China and justified it by stating that Marshall's efforts had "seemingly proved unavailing." Then two of China's bolder reformers fell victim to Chiang's secret police. In August, Truman upbraided Chiang for allowing reactionary elements to triumph, and he came close to blaming him for the murder of those Chinese liberals in Kunming.[111]

From Harry Luce's viewpoint, there was a bright spot amid all the gloom. Back in April, Luce had asked that Jack Beal pass a message to General Marshall. Luce hoped that Marshall would include Dr. John Leighton Stuart in his party when he returned to China. Luce assured the general that he would enjoy conversing with this seventy-year-old China hand, who was a "person of importance and influence in China as well as here." Stuart had served for many years as president of Harvard-Yenching University in Beijing, where he worked with the Reverend Henry W. Luce. Harry Luce hoped that Stuart, a defender of Chiang's regime, would influence Marshall. The general's plane lacked the necessary space, however, and Marshall turned down Luce's request.[112] Undeterred, Stuart finally arrived in Shanghai and soon met the general, who came to respect the elderly, China-born missionary as a man of integrity and wisdom. Marshall recommended that John Leighton Stuart be named ambassador to China.[113]

Rightist elements in China were at first dubious about Stuart: Both Chen Lifu and Chiang Kai-shek felt that left-wing students and alumni from Yenching University would control Leighton Stuart, their former president.[114] The retired educator was taken aback by the challenge, but his love for China prevailed. President Truman nominated him on 4 July. Confirmation followed a week later, and on 19 July 1946 Stuart presented his credentials to the Chinese government. His tenure would be a troubled one. Given Leighton Stuart's advanced age, poor health, and less than forceful personality, the new ambassador was unlikely to make trouble, nor would he greatly influence events.

Although Ed Lockett of *Time* blandly reported that Stuart would work for "peace and coalition," Luce thought – and hoped – otherwise.[115] Writing to his ally James Forrestal, the publisher noted, "China will be a tough pull – tougher than I think it had to be – but, as you say, we have no choice but to pull or push as hard as we can."[116] Perhaps the appointment of Dr. Stuart, he thought, would make the "pull" a bit easier. Stuart recalled, "My hope was that by giving [Chiang] outright military aid, especially in the form of technical advice, we could enable the National Government to recover and hold a certain area north of the Yangtse River, and to give to its population a sense of political and economic security while introducing the needed reforms."[117] But his tenure would not be an easy one, for Stuart personified the American mission at a time of growing Chinese xenophobia and nationalism.[118] Long an admirer of Chiang Kai-shek, Stuart was perplexed and indignant when left-wing Chinese students protested against American support for a regime they accused of fomenting a bloody civil war.

On 29 July 1946, Communist forces operating near Beijing opened fire on incoming Nationalist troops, and the dead included three U.S. Marines.[119] Zhou denied that the Communists were responsible for these fatalities, but he clearly wanted the United States out of China.[120] Though discouraged, Marshall would not give up, and he continued to put pressure on Chiang and the hard-liners around him. The State Department placed an embargo upon export licenses for U.S. arms and munitions destined for China. The date of the embargo coincided with the death of those three Marines killed by Communist troops near Beijing. To Luce, the Truman administration was trying to force Chiang into the kind of coalition government that had turned Poland into a Soviet pawn.

The American Mission Endures

At home, dedicated private citizens, foremost among them Harry Luce, were again trying to raise millions of dollars for the war-damaged Christian colleges and other worthy causes in China. Luce – and hence his editors – was therefore cautious about knocking George Marshall's troubled mission, especially after the general agreed to serve as honorary chairman of Luce's United China Relief (soon renamed United Service to China).[121] Luce donated generously to UCR, as he had before, and once again he drafted Time Inc. executives for work on behalf of this beloved cause.[122] As an active Yale alumnus, Luce was particularly interested in the Campaign to Rebuild Yale-in-China, which he chaired. "Yali's" campus in Changsha had been wrecked during the war, but by the end of 1947 Luce had raised almost $200,000 for its reconstruction.[123] Overall, American contributors now covered 70 percent of the overhead expenses incurred by all Chinese universities.[124]

In this endeavor, Henry P. Van Dusen, the president-elect of the Union Theological Seminary and chairman of the Associated Boards of the Christian Colleges, had been a longtime Luce ally.[125] When Van Dusen prepared to visit China in 1946, Luce gladly wrote Marshall a letter of introduction. Marshall agreed to see Van Dusen, who also spent some pleasant hours with Dr. Stuart. The Luce network in China was running smoothly, but "Pitt" Van Dusen brought home grim news. At a lunch with senior editors at Time Inc., Van Dusen expressed doubts about the so-called reforms instituted by Chiang. The Chinese economy was hopeless, Van Dusen added, and no one could restore it while the Communists wrecked communications networks.[126] Van Dusen then offered his luncheon hosts a small ray of hope: Stuart favored providing the Chinese government with U.S. military assistance.[127] *Life* took heart. Once again, Americans should – and could – save China.

4

China on the Brink

What Role for America?

In September 1946 Henry Luce journeyed to San Francisco to attend a dinner honoring Protestant missionaries active in Asia.[1] If Luce was ever happy, it was at that banquet, where he eloquently saluted the American Christians who were working to save his China.

Luce delivered a long, moving sermon on faith, love, and God. He reflected upon Calvin Mateer, a pioneering missionary who had made the arduous 166-day trip to China in the middle of the preceding century. Mateer's story gave Luce hope, for such missionaries offered living proof that faith can overcome a hostile world.[2] But as he looked at his audience, Henry Luce also feared for the sorry fate of Christian missionaries in a Communist China. The San Francisco dinner reinforced Luce's commitment to Chiang's aggressive strategy.

As Chiang began his bid for victory, a major figure in his military apparatus easily secured Luce's support. Former war minister General He Yingqin visited Time Inc., where Luce hosted a lunch for him. Considered one of the more reactionary militarists in Chiang's entourage, He defied Marshall and forthrightly professed his faith in the Nationalist drive against the Reds.[3] And a few weeks later, Luce hosted a small dinner party honoring Zhang Qun, governor of Sichuan province. In its aftermath, *Time* predicted that unless the United States supported the Nanking government, China would perforce "pass into the Russian orbit."[4] If this happened, *Time* warned, the American frontier would be pushed back to the Mariana Islands. At first, as the government's armies made gains, Luce grew more confident.[5] Yet public opinion was troubling him. The growing chorus of Chiang's critics included many readers of *Time* and numerous influential Americans. This trend worried Luce, who wanted to protect his company from charges of bias and bad reporting.

Torn between blind loyalty to Chiang and the interests of Time Inc., Henry Luce found himself involved in an unpleasant encounter with Charles J. V. Murphy, a senior and very self-assured correspondent. After returning from China, Murphy had drafted a four-part article for *Life*, and, in September, an edited two-part version was ready for publication. Because his articles reflected

Luce's view that Chiang Kai-shek was "a truly great man," Murphy expected quick approval.[6] But Murphy had virtually declared war on the Chinese Communists and, by implication, on Marshall's mediation mission. Luce did not disagree, but he had qualms about the advisability of going ahead with the Murphy articles.[7] He was eager to remain on good terms with Marshall, and he was concerned about the many readers who complained of Time Inc.'s noisome pro-Chiang bias. At such times, Luce groused, "I don't like to be identified with that Far East thing.... Because I was born in China, they wanted to make a Chinaman out of me."[8] As Luce liked to say, stay ahead of your readers – but not too far ahead.

Luce's hesitation angered Charlie Murphy, especially when the editor-in-chief maintained that it was "time to get off the hook with Chiang."[9] Luce was proud of his China coverage, but he also recognized that in most of the mainstream press, China was a sidebar story.[10] But in no sense was Luce turning his back on "that Far East thing"; he was merely pulling in his horns and preparing for new offensives. Luce later regretted his timorous behavior, calling it "my worst mistake."[11] This was hardly the case.

Alfred Kohlberg versus the IPR

The Institute of Pacific Relations (IPR) was an organization dedicated to increasing mutual understanding among the diverse peoples living around the Pacific Basin.[12] The institute contained six national councils, of which the American (AIPR) was the most prominent. From time to time, the IPR convened international conferences, and the organization also funded scholarly research, sponsored the publication of books and journals, and produced pamphlets for the general public. Time Inc.'s editors and researchers often exploited the institute's collections and reference staff. In the 1930s, Luce had begun to make modest donations to the IPR, although he later increased those sums to $7,376.01.[13] Edward C.(Ned) Carter, the IPR's energetic secretary general, was not bashful about asking Harry Luce for more money.[14] Luce himself pledged $7,500 to the IPR, to be paid over a three-year period.[15] Throughout the war, Luce served on the AIPR's board of trustees.[16]

Ned Carter's pet project was Pacific House, a new, spacious headquarters that would replace the IPR's cramped building on 52nd Street.[17] Discussions about buying and renovating an old brownstone on 79th Street dragged on through the war, but Luce refused to commit himself. His resistance only spurred Carter on, and by 1945 the unrealistic secretary was asking an increasingly hesitant Luce for $50,000.[18] But while Harry Luce continued to work with Ned Carter, albeit on his own terms, another, more suspicious member of the institute was busy amassing evidence against the IPR.

A short, bald, energetic man, Alfred Kohlberg had been born in San Francisco in 1887, and attended the University of California. When visiting China in 1916, he laid the groundwork for a highly profitable business.

Kohlberg bought linen in Ireland and shipped it to his factories in China, where contractors provided the cheap labor supplied by local women. Kohlberg then exported their high-quality textile products.[19] He prided himself on his gaudy yellow stationery, which hawked imported silks, laces, linens, and gloves. Things went well, although Kohlberg's alleged habit of passing off Chinese products as "Irish crochet lace" elicited two cease-and-desist orders from the Federal Trade Commission. On the eve of World War II, Kohlberg's business was grossing $1.5 million a year.

Alfred Kohlberg was a supporter of the Guomindang, and he became a vehement critic of Chiang's enemies, especially the Communists. He claimed to have uncovered a global Communist conspiracy dating back to 1928; Kohlberg intended to prevent it from overthrowing Chiang.[20] He aggressively defended the Chinese government and army against the charges of corruption that were rampant by 1943. During the war, Kohlberg served as chairman of the American Bureau for Medical Aid to China (ABMAC), which was part of the aid network coordinated and funded by United China Relief. With more than thirty million Chinese suffering from debilitating diseases, China's blood banks lacked funds, and other Chinese medical relief operations failed to operate efficiently.[21] In the spring of 1943, therefore, ABMAC authorized an inquiry, and Kohlberg soon found that large amounts of vital medical supplies were rotting away in warehouses or had surfaced for sale on the black market. The investigator, however, insisted that Chiang's minions were not to blame. Instead, Kohlberg accused Dwight Edwards, China field director for UCR, of opposing the Chinese government. He later implied that Luce's UCR was prey to Communist machinations.

When Kohlberg returned to the United States, his campaign to expose Edwards as incompetent and pro-Communist won the support of Chiang's officials.[22] The UCR's executive committee decided to establish a three-man special committee of inquiry, consisting of James G. Blaine, Paul G. Hoffman, and Henry R. Luce.[23] The committee heard from Kohlberg on 29 February 1944 during a meeting that lasted three hours.[24] Luce, like his colleagues, was predisposed to support Edwards, a Princeton alumnus (1904) from the American heartland and a man who had taught the Chinese language to a generation of American missionaries.[25] Edwards, the Luce committee concluded, had not undermined UCR's support of ABMAC's programs, although it recommended that ABMAC's disbursement procedures be reformed.[26] This outcome angered Kohlberg, who later insisted that UCR was knowingly aiding the Communists.[27] Alfred Kohlberg's techniques would later become standard operating procedure: Make a charge of pro-Communist activity; if it did not stick, make another one, repeat it, document it, and spread it around. Something would find its mark, because Americans were growing more suspicious of their one-time Soviet ally. Kohlberg remained on the prowl, eager to destroy critics of Chiang Kai-shek.[28]

Kohlberg worked especially hard to discredit the Institute of Pacific Relations, which he viewed as the subversive fount of anti-Chiang activity. Day after day, Kohlberg trudged up to the public library at Fifth Avenue and 42nd Street and then took the elevator to the vast reading rooms on the third floor. There, he pored through a select few of the publications sponsored by the Institute of Pacific Relations. Indeed, Kohlberg based his research on 33 articles and reviews, 3 pamphlets, and one book. (During the time in question, the IPR had sponsored the publication of 1,961 articles and book reviews, and 384 books and pamphlets.)[29] The IPR's writers, Kohlberg concluded, were nice to Chiang's regime from 1937 to 1939; more critical of it from 1939 until June 1941; very friendly to the Guomindang until the battle of Stalingrad; and once again hostile from February 1943 to the present.[30] This pattern, he argued, followed the Soviet line, and proved that the Communists were running the IPR. "I think," he confided to Congressman Walter Judd, "I have found the well of misunderstanding between Americans and Chinese."[31] Kohlberg added, "I soon saw that the center of the [Communist] conspiracy was the Institute of Pacific Relations, to which I had contributed time and money."[32]

Late in 1944, Alfred Kohlberg, who had served on the American IPR's board, privately published an eighty-eight-page brochure detailing his charges. He demanded that Executive Secretary Ned Carter purge his staff of Communists.[33] Carter angrily dismissed Kohlberg's charges as nonsense, but he would have to respond. The IPR depended heavily upon corporate funding and needed support from anti-Communist Republicans like Harry Luce and the Rockefellers.[34] Throughout the stormy year, Carter collected testimonials from a wide array of eminent Americans interested in Asia. Academic supporters included John King Fairbank of Harvard, but also David Rowe, director of Chinese, Japanese, and Russian studies at Yale.[35] But Kohlberg counterattacked, cracking that the United States was fighting a war to prevent Japan from conquering China – so that it could hand China over to Russia.[36] Walter Judd placed this kind of material in the *Congressional Record*.

Ned Carter and a colleague met with Kohlberg on 2 February 1945, but they failed to appease him.[37] Angrily rejecting their proffer, Kohlberg went to court. The judge delayed the IPR's annual meeting until 15 May. Kohlberg then extracted a promise from the executive committee to provide the IPR's members with "any communication which Mr. Kohlberg wishes to send," as long as it was not libelous. All 1,785 members would also receive Kohlberg's request for their proxy votes. The IPR, of course, also sought proxies for its position and candidates; the battle was joined.[38] On 11 May the court rejected Kohlberg's appeal for another delay, and the IPR's membership convened four days later.[39] Support for Kohlberg was negligible. But resistance only stimulated the inquisitor, who busily launched new attacks on alleged Communists.[40] He also warned major sponsors against funding the discredited IPR.[41] Here Kohlberg made some progress, for doubts about the IPR's ideology soon troubled the Rockefeller Foundation, the Henry Luce Foundation, and Time Inc.

Henry Luce's concerns about Carter and the American Council of the IPR dated all the way back to the summer of 1941. After the Nazis had invaded the

Soviet Union, Ned Carter became a leader of Russian War Relief, and he asked that Americans donate money to pay for medical aid destined for Russia.[42] Harry Luce angrily responded, "The people of America have been totally cut off from the people of Russia by the despicable tyranny of J. Stalin & Co." Luce believed deeply in the "generous impulses of private charity" and did not wish to see them debased and misused "for a propaganda effort for the Stalin regime." If "power politics" dictated that aid be sent to Russia, Luce added, then let the U.S. government do it. But a year later, Carter could still tell Luce, "The masses in China and the masses in Russia have been organized so that they are an immense military as well as a great psychological asset."[43] It was clear to Luce that Ned Carter admired the Yan'an revolution and looked forward to warm – perhaps too warm – postwar relations with the Soviet Union.

In the winter of 1942–1943, Luce asked that his aide Douglas Auchincloss look into the politics of the IPR. The young man did not find anything unduly troubling about the Institute except for an allegation made by Eliot Janeway, a Luce adviser. A tough, blunt-spoken self-promoter with good access to high sources, Janeway knew how to tantalize Harry Luce with gossipy information. Early in 1943, Janeway told Auchincloss that the IPR was "manipulated by a group of dubious Communists and near-Communists" who were "intriguing madly behind a good front of respectable research men." Carter, he added, was a stooge.[44] But Carter had worked with Harry for years; the two men belonged to some of the same prestigious clubs and shared a few friends in common. So Luce waffled in regard to Kohlberg's "massive document" exposing the IPR, and he commented that he did not expect to read it "in any foreseeable future." Kohlberg, however, found new ammunition in the Communist *Daily Worker*, which cited a pro-Yan'an petition signed by twenty-one Americans. Among them were IPR stalwarts like Frederick V. Field, Mrs. Edward C. Carter, Laurence Salisbury, and Mrs. Edgar Snow.[45] Kohlberg made sure that all this material reached potential allies, including Clare Boothe Luce, his "American Winston Churchill."[46]

Henry Luce remained a member of the AIPR and was even a vice-chairman of its board.[47] But when Carter badgered him for more money, Luce warned that he no longer had much time for the IPR. Although he disliked dismissing old allies, neither could Luce tolerate losers in the ideological wars. Just as he had distanced himself from Laird Goldsborough in 1938 and Wendell Willkie in 1944, so Luce turned his back on Ned Carter in 1946. He could hardly do otherwise when Carter admitted that he was "not particularly anxious to have my sons, Bill and John, go through another war fighting the Russians on the plains of Manchuria."[48] Ultimately, Luce was prepared to fight Russia over China. Carter was not, so Kohlberg and his allies opened a second front. Using their franking privileges, Representatives Luce and Judd disseminated a new flood of pro-Chiang literature.[49]

In 1946, along with scores of allies, the Luces signed "The Manchurian Manifesto," which advocated ending disinterested American mediation in

China.[50] From this alliance emerged Alfred Kohlberg's American China Policy Association (ACPA), which he hoped would counter the allegedly leftist IPR.[51] Kohlberg paid most of ACPA's costs and printed and distributed its literature. He proudly reported to Chiang Kai-shek later in the year, "I have been very busy in our campaign to attempt to re-educate America about China, for unfortunately America has been completely confused by the barrage of Communist propaganda that has poured out over us for the past three years."[52] Kohlberg was hitting his mark, thanks to the changing political climate. Encouraged, he began publishing a magazine called *Plain Talk*, which Clare Boothe Luce distributed to people like James Forrestal and Douglas MacArthur.[53] (Like the others, Forrestal agreed that the "Russian question" was *the* question of our day, even of our century.")[54]

The Institute of Pacific Relations had flourished during the war, when it celebrated the alliance with Russia, but by 1946 much of American opinion had turned against the united front. Some frightened IPR officers wanted to appease Kohlberg, but Fred Field, whose presence on its staff would cause the IPR much grief, successfully insisted that the organization oppose "red-baiting" by pro-fascists.[55] Frederick Vanderbilt Field was a wealthy Communist who may have been active in the party's underground in the late 1930s. He had helped to found the journal *Amerasia*, and later, Fred Field wrote about China for *The Communist*, official organ of the CPUSA.[56] Henry Luce knew Field slightly, thanks to their occasional encounters at board meetings. Prodded by Field and others, the institute stood fast in the face of Kohlberg's assault, and at a long meeting on 6 August, Carter and his tormenter found no common ground.[57] At the end of their encounter, Kohlberg even threatened Carter: Carter's compassion for the Russian people, Kohlberg declared, had "warped his political outlook and . . . this Carter would eventually regret."[58] But even if Ned Carter had changed his tune, Kohlberg would have been hard to please. Here was a man, after all, who accused Ambassador Leighton Stuart, a former Christian missionary, of being too tolerant of the Communists.[59] And although he was a Jew, Kohlberg denounced critics of John Rankin, the anti-Semitic congressman from Mississippi, as un-Americans who had "joined the *Daily Worker*."[60] Later, Kohlberg would ask the hapless Ned Carter whether the IPR planned to publish Harry Luce's comments on China instead of wasting "paper and ink on the pontifications of the young 'preposterous ignoramuses' (not my phrase) who write about China for you."[61]

In a condescending note, Kohlberg warned Luce, "We must think hard if the 'American Century' is to come about." In a letter, he suggested that Harry read a fantasy by Kohlberg called "My Dream of World History."[62] Allegedly composed before Yalta, the piece portrayed a terrifying Communist triumph throughout the world. For the first time, Luce responded to Kohlberg in a friendly manner, denying that he considered Kohlberg's charges against the IPR "discredited."[63] Indeed, when he wrote to Ned Carter in the summer of 1946, Luce echoed one of Kohlberg's chief tenets. He would be "considerably relieved" said Luce, if he could discover "any really critical material which the

[IPR] has published on Soviet or Communist policies and activities." Carter evaded the challenge and called Kohlberg "a very shrewd businessman" (i.e., a Jew) but also a "crackpot" given to "sophomoric outpourings."[64] Carter displayed a tenuous grasp of his situation when he asked whether Harry Luce would like to buy the Doris Duke mansion on Fifth Avenue – and donate it to the IPR for use as its long-awaited Pacific House. Such a generous gesture, Carter added, "might be a great credit both to you and the IPR."[65] Luce ignored the suggestion.

During this same summer (1946) Henry Luce decided to find out whether Kohlberg's charges had merit. He turned his inquiry over to a young assistant named Boyce P. Price, who had served as Franklin Roosevelt's daily military briefer. Assisted by Professor Arthur Schlesinger, Jr., Price read through some of the IPR's vast output, and in late August his report landed on Harry Luce's desk.[66] "Communist Influence in the Publications of the Institute of Pacific Relations" exposed a few fellow travelers, one certain Communist (Field), and two other possible Reds. Carter, Price believed, was gullible, whereas Owen Lattimore was sympathetic to Russia. But the Price memorandum failed to substantiate Kohlberg's main charge, that the IPR had slavishly followed the Soviet line on China from 1937 to 1944. Nevertheless, Price thought that the IPR had shown undue sympathy for the Chinese Communists, and he pointed out that Owen Lattimore had defended Stalin's purge trials. The truth, Price concluded, lay somewhere between Alfred Kohlberg's fulminations and Ned Carter's defensiveness. Henry Luce decided that at best, the Carter crowd was irresponsible, gullible, and incorrigible. At worst, it was serving America's next global enemy.

Days after he received the Price report, Luce wrote a letter that he said "should have been written several years ago." "In so far as I.P.R. has taken a 'line,'" he told Ned Carter, "it is a line with which I disagree considerably." After admitting that few IPR publications endorsed Communist positions, Luce explained that some were "far closer to Communist presuppositions and policy than my convictions allow me to be." And in words that recalled the crusading Luce of 1917 (against the "Huns"), 1919 (the Bolsheviks), and 1941 (the Nazis and the Japanese), Harry said, "With regard to world-wide Communism, the time for me [to take a stand] was yesterday." But Luce added that if the IPR was "prepared to face fully the issue presented by Communism," then he would remain on its board.

A shaken Ned Carter replied with a letter four and a half pages in length.[67] Defensive yet defiant, he rejected Luce's charges. But Carter also worried about an imminent court date, and he begged Luce to refrain from giving "aid or comfort to Kohlberg by identifying" himself with him. In a clumsy move, Carter warned that if Luce ignored this sage advice, his reputation would suffer.[68] Perhaps, but Luce thought that a continued association with the IPR could hurt Time Inc. even more. Carter urgently sought an audience with Luce, but the breach was irreparable. The American IPR's executive committee continued to resist change. Like a broken record, the Institute's biennial report insisted that its critics were trying to "force the Institute to abandon its impartial, critical treatment of Far Eastern questions in the case of China."[69] Carter, who displayed a tin ear when confronted with obvious disharmonies, had made another blunder if he wanted to regain Harry Luce's allegiance.

Civil War

In China, General Marshall again warned Chiang Kai-shek, "You can't win with the people against you."[70] The government's strategy, Marshall added, would lead to the domination of China by the Communist enemy.[71] But Chiang was adamant. He defiantly demanded that the Communists withdraw from areas where they threatened the peace and obstructed communications. For their part, the Communists resented the Americans for aiding Chiang's armies; to mollify them, the United States refused to grant export licenses for combat equipment already purchased by the Chinese government. As a result, Chiang privately complained, "Marshall's concessions to the Communists only hurt both China and the United States."[72] At other times, the mercurial Chiang believed that Marshall was "no longer sympathetic toward the Communists." He also hoped that the United States would fully back the government of China if it sought to "find a military solution to this [Communist] problem."[73] But a poll showed that only 6 percent of the American public was willing to offer open-ended assistance to Chiang Kai-shek.[74]

U.S. mediation efforts lay in tatters.[75] In the autumn, Nationalist drives threatened the Communist stronghold of Zhangjiakou, and on 10 October 1946 Chiang's army took the town. In vain, Marshall wearily warned that Chiang could not proceed with civil war and political democratization at the same time.[76] But Marshall had also tired of Communist duplicity. Clearly, Zhou Enlai wanted the Americans out of China, without being blamed for Marshall's failure. "The core task of the final phase of the negotiations," Zhou believed, was a "struggle to expose 'all of the Chiang Kai-shek and U.S. frauds.' "[77] In Japan, a cynical administrator likened Marshall to an eighteen-year-old virgin "moralizing with two gangsters aged forty." And in another metaphor, the same critic added that American fumbling in China also reminded him of a rich man's son who had fallen into "the clutches of an old prostitute."[78] *Time* recounted new fictions about Chiang's victorious armies and again condemned Mao for rejecting democracy.[79] Other figures sympathetic to Chiang joined *Time*'s chorus; they too would become part of what famously became the China lobby.[80] General Wedemeyer praised Chiang as "a real Christian gentleman" who had demonstrated "high moral purpose" and a strong commitment to democracy.[81] Freda Utley played an important part in this campaign, too.[82]

Like Whittaker Chambers, the British-born Utley had been a Communist, and after her break with the party she too felt persecuted: "My anti-communist views," she complained, "have made things extremely difficult for me these past years."[83] Her work soon attracted the interest of Representative Clare Luce, who used Utleyisms when attacking unnamed American journalists and officials.[84] Luce also brought Utley to the attention of editors employed by national news organizations, including Scripps-Howard.[85] When in 1947 Freda Utley published a provocative book on the China crisis, Clare Luce's stunning blurb declared, "This remarkable and exciting book is essential reading." In response, Utley tried to use Luce as her entrée into the lucrative world of *Life*. She did so unaware that its editors were suspicious of anyone who boasted that Clare had read a proposed article and was "enthusiastic" about it.[86] On one occasion, an editor told Utley that her piece was not "strong or meaty enough ... to displace one of the other Chinese subjects" that the magazine had in hand.[87] Ever suspicious, Utley believed that a "communist sympathiser" must have blocked her way at Time Inc.[88]

"Yes, I am angry and embittered," Utley admitted, but she then decided that Luce could make amends by "doing something" for her in the magazine – an offer that Luce declined. (His response, Utley told Walter Judd, "is very unsatisfactory but there is nothing I can do about it.")[89] Yet Utley herself was dishonest in ways that would have annoyed Harry Luce. She had once written in a draft that the Chinese Communists were "less subservient to Moscow than the artificially created Communist parties of Europe and America."[90] And after the war, Utley admitted that Chiang did "squeeze the peasants" and that he remained dependent upon "the corrupt, the reactionary and the ignorant." But these words would have offended the China lobby, so Utley excised them.[91]

A Visit to China

Given Chiang's weakness, the China lobby could best advance his cause by linking China's fate to a global struggle against Communism.[92] Yet the patriots who made this case, Luce complained, were treated as if their advocacy was "some sort of bottled chop-suey that we were trying to sneak through the Pure Food laws."[93] He hoped that political changes in Washington would alter the situation for the better. Congressional and state elections loomed in November, and popular discontent with Truman did not bode well for the Democrats. So given all its other problems, the Truman White House worked to avoid a divisive partisan debate over its failed China policy. For this reason, in a surprise move, the administration invited the head of Time Inc. to visit China. Luce also received an invitation from his friend General MacArthur, SCAP (Supreme Commander for the Allied Powers) proconsul in Tokyo. Accompanied by senior Time Incers Robert T. Elson and Roy Alexander, Luce flew to China in General Carl "Tooey" Spaatz's plane. Assistant Secretary of War Stuart Symington provided the luxurious aircraft, which contained five beds, an office, a bar, and a lounge. The trip cost the taxpayers dearly, a fact Luce was urged to keep secret.[94]

The Luce party landed near Shanghai on 26 October, and a large delegation greeted the distinguished American visitor. In its ranks were the mayor of Shanghai, as well as Jack Beal, T. V. Soong, Bill Gray, and a high official from the Ministry of Information. In Nanjing, Soong gave a dinner in honor of Ambassador Leighton Stuart and Luce, and Chiang's doomed elite was certainly in good form.* The Soongs served shark and crab, shrimp, chicken, sweet ham, and other delicacies. Madame Soong wore a black velvet dress, which set off jade dinner rings on each hand, along with many other jewels, among them a "pin that looked as if it were carved from jade, with a border of diamonds." China's fading elite remained capable of the grand gesture, but the men who had brought China close to ruin still resisted the reforms that might have staved off their doom.

At dinners with Luce, Jack Beal recalled, the intense guest dominated the conversation, as he had at all the Chinese functions Beal had attended with him.[95] When Luce did listen, he nodded in approval as the Soongs gave their view of the world. T. V. Soong leaked "secret" military reports to Luce, and they were replete with optimistic prognostications about the various war fronts. Chiang's brother-in-law, H. H. Kung, confirmed Soong's analysis. Military victories, Kung claimed, foreshadowed a Guomindang decision to "terminate tutelage" and inaugurate an era of constitutional government.[96] But was this optimism justified? A meeting with Zhou Enlai confused Luce, for Zhou spoke like a man who "expected soon to be in control of China." Luce's momentary confusion did not last long, however, thanks to Leighton Stuart. "You know, Harry," the ambassador explained, "these Communists don't *think* like Chinese."[97] Luce agreed with him, and they concluded that the *real* Chinese would prevail. It was no wonder that Chiang's enemies in the dissident press attacked Henry Luce as a "propaganda minister" who never "came in contact with the common people."[98]

One pleasant day in Nanjing, Luce joined the Chiangs, General Marshall, and Mrs. Marshall on the Generalissimo's private train. It was Chiang's birthday, and the group celebrated the occasion on a houseboat moored in a large lake. Then, on the slow train back to Nanjing, Luce had a private talk with General Marshall. The general said little about the situation in China; instead, he delivered a "long and earnest exhortation on the necessity for universal military service in the U.S."[99] Back in Nanjing, Luce again met with Marshall for a briefing on China. According to Luce, Marshall was still determined to "get the Communists and the government together," whereas Leighton Stuart wanted "to give active assistance, especially in the way of military advice, to the National Government, in the expectation that the needed reforms would be undertaken."[100] General Marshall, however, thought that such aid would only harden Chiang's intransigence.[101] Harry Luce found it ironic but sad that Dr. Stuart, the man of the cloth, favored military action, whereas Marshall, the soldier was "unwilling to use the sword."

---

* Earlier in the year, Madame Soong had fallen ill. To cheer her up, T. V. chartered a plane, which made a long and very expensive flight to Connecticut. There, the pilot loaded some dogwood on board and took the precious cargo back to Nanjing, all because Madame Soong loved its tender blossoms.

In fact, Leighton Stuart was not an effective ambassador. He might have been the "greatest of modern American missionaries, the symbol" of everything that had been "best and fruitful in a century of Christian endeavor in China," but Stuart was also ill, "gentle [and] self-effacing." Sadly, the current situation demanded strength and authority.[102] When he recommended military assistance, for example, Stuart was at a disadvantage, for he lacked technical expertise. Neglected by Washington, spied upon by Chiang's agents, Leighton Stuart would disappoint Harry Luce. But as always, Luce refused to give up on China.

With Chiang apparently gaining the upper hand on the battlefield, he would, Luce believed, be able to proceed with his own political and constitutional "settlement." Americans would be impressed and presumably would rally to the Nationalist cause. As Harry Luce was packing his bags for the return voyage, the *Central Daily News* paid tribute to his optimism about China, which was "hopeful and with good prospect." The newspaper noted on 9 November that Luce planned to revisit the country in the summer of 1947.[103] But while Luce enjoyed his reveries, Communist troops entered Yantai, where "Small Boy Luce" had once attended the British Inland Mission School.

Henry Luce would never return to the Chinese mainland.

Thunder Out of China

Back in the United States, Theodore White was sitting in an office in the Time-Life Building, chatting with Arthur Schlesinger, Jr., when the phone rang. An elated White soon learned that the Book-of-the-Month Club had chosen *Thunder Out of China* as its main selection. An extraordinary four hundred fifty thousand copies would be sold by November, and for the moment, White's financial worries were over.[104] Teddy White was all over the radio and the lecture circuit, and Chiang's growing army of critics now had a Bible from which they cited chapter and verse. White's reputation and sales only grew when Americans learned that Chiang's censors had immediately banned *Thunder Out of China*. Not even *Time*'s lengthy review hurt the book, although it was worthy of the magazine's reputation for subtle distortion.[105] *Time* praised the "basic validity" of a book that told how the *Chinese people* had "fought and suffered for freedom." In fact, White and Jacoby had portrayed a China in which the people had barely survived the corrupt incompetence of the doomed *Chiang regime*.

For the next several years, White and Luce worked in vain to forget each other.[106] Freed from his financial dependence upon Harry Luce, White once again enjoyed the confidence of John King Fairbank.[107] Both men saw the Chinese Communist revolution as a force spawned by social discontent and peasant nationalism.[108] The Democratic administration, Luce feared, would listen to such people. On the other side, Teddy White never underestimated Harry Luce's abilities as a propagandist. He worried that the publisher – widely regarded as a China expert – would return to New York and extol Chiang's commitment to democracy. Hence, White warned Ned Carter, "You should not be caught flat-footed on any statement you make to Harry when he returns."[109] He added that the recent "elections" to Chiang's National Assembly were "false and vicious." But Luce and his editors proceeded to cheer China's alleged march toward democracy.[110]

Luce and White were both right and wrong about China. Like many other Americans then and now, they overestimated America's ability to change China, although White had grown more cautious since the Stilwell debacle. Luce knew something important, for he realized that Yan'an was both anti-American and totalitarian; but he failed to confront the rot and oppression that were subverting Chiang's regime. White understood that Chiang's military successes late in 1946 represented the death rattle of a weak regime. But White overreacted when he put Chiang in a dictators' league populated by the likes of Hitler and Stalin. And Teddy White overlooked a troublesome prospect: Chiang was indeed a fading authoritarian, but Mao would be a far worse totalitarian.

Uneasy Optimism

Energized by his visit to the land of his birth, Henry Luce resolved to help the embattled Chinese government. Addressing a group of advertising executives in New York City on 18 November 1946, he demanded a more "courageous" and "vigorous" foreign policy in Asia.[111] Stirred by Chiang's illusory victories and his purported endorsement of constitutional government, Luce also drew inspiration from his old dream of a vast Asian market.* *Time* again insisted that Nationalist military victories betokened China's reunification.[112] If so, Chiang would have to succeed with very little American help. Only twenty-nine thousand U.S. troops remained in China late in the autumn of 1946, and neither the American people nor President Truman would stand for the dispatch of an expeditionary force to a distant, troubled country.

Even as Henry Luce was calling for more vigorous American intervention in Asia, General Zhou Enlai paid his final visit to General Marshall. The encounter was a purely formal one, and Zhou flew back to Yan'an. Early in December, he proposed that troops on both sides return to the positions they held on 13 January 1946, and the Communists also endorsed the formation of an interim coalition government.[113] Nothing came of Zhou's proposals. On 18 December President Truman expressed his "deep regret" that China had not been able to "achieve unity by peaceful methods."[114] He also boasted that fewer than twelve thousand American troops remained in China, and he promised to bring more of them home in the near future.[115] In retaliation, *Time* found a new whipping boy.

---

* The ad men listening to Luce had imbibed a few drinks and expected a short, anecdotal speech about *Life*'s advertising revenues. But Luce rambled on for perhaps two hours, and when he finally finished his speech, cheers echoed through the hall. Then a large number of ad executives rushed to the men's room.

According to the Washington bureau, John Carter Vincent, who ran the East Asia desk at the State Department, influenced "the China policy and its execution to an appreciable degree."[116] *Time* decided that Vincent was a Yan'an sympathizer, as was Dean Acheson, the power behind the throne at Foggy Bottom.[117] Alfred Kohlberg found further proof of Vincent's malfeasance when he looked into Henry Luce's wartime exclusion from China. Luce, he claimed, intended to investigate Teddy White's leftist reportage, but to protect White, Vincent had refused Luce a passport. Dean Acheson called this charge "false in the extreme," which it was.[118] Kohlberg, however, believed in the buckshot theory of truth: Keep firing, and some lucky shell would find its target. As a result, Senator Styles Bridges was able to stall Vincent's most recent appointment for six months. The globalization of the anti-Communist struggle had infused John Carter Vincent's critics with renewed energy. Luce's media served as their institutional memory, so Vincent's future was clouded. Henceforth, Luce would view him as an American who was losing our China.

PART TWO

LUCE AND THE "LOSS" OF CHINA, 1947–1951

5

Cold War Strategy

Allies and Enemies in the Battle for China

On 6 January 1947, President Truman announced the recall of General Marshall, who soon replaced James Byrnes as secretary of state. Graciously, or perhaps from a sense of relief, Chiang Kai-shek accompanied Marshall to the airfield outside Nanjing.[1] In his personal statement, Marshall criticized the Communists' vituperative propaganda, but he also attacked "a dominant group of reactionaries" in Chiang's government. Then, in its most vivid attack to date, *Life* assailed Marshall's idea of a coalition government as "stupidity." The magazine also called for "all-out support to the government of Chiang Kai-shek."[2] Privately, Luce threatened to "blow the whistle" on Marshall's failures in China, but most of the time, Luce restrained himself.[3] Because Marshall was now secretary of state, Luce needed Marshall's support for his diverse philanthropic enterprises in China. Marshall, however, believed that Luce had been "'taken for a ride' in China, where he got all mixed up in 'personal relationships.'"[4] As if to prove the point, Chiang Kai-shek bestowed the Special Cravat of the Auspicious Star upon his friend Henry Luce. Luce could not affect the China policy pursued by Marshall, but he could help to drive the Republican Party into all-out opposition to Truman's anti-Chiang bias. And that was no small thing, given the looming Republican victory in 1948.

Euphoria and Suffering

Luce had for months anticipated the twenty-first annual institute of the Cleveland Council on World Affairs, for in a way, the conference was a tribute to his influence. It was thanks to Luce's friendly pressure that luminaries like James F. Byrnes, James V. Forrestal, and Arthur Vandenberg attended the meeting. Cohosted by *Time*, the gathering opened amid pomp and ceremony on 9 January 1947.[5] The immense audience in Cleveland, plus a national radio hook-up, encouraged Luce. The institute, Luce hoped, would showcase the bipartisan foreign policy crafted by Vandenberg and Byrnes, but Luce also hoped to secure support for the dispatch of significant aid to Chiang.

In language that owed much to Luce, Navy Secretary James V. Forrestal stressed American leadership in the world. And more than ten thousand people had crowded into the Municipal Auditorium by the time Luce introduced outgoing Secretary of State James F. Byrnes. He praised the South Carolinian for coinventing (with Senator Vandenberg) a new, "magnificent partnership."[6] Byrnes then paid a moving tribute to Arthur Vandenberg, who repaid him by advocating support for Chiang in his struggle against Communism. Ambassador Wellington Koo, in a bitter address that pleased Luce, bemoaned the betrayal of China by its American ally at Yalta. He also insisted against all evidence that China was "squarely on the road to democracy."[7] Francis Cardinal Spellman lauded America as a multiethnic land of hope, and Henry P. Van Dusen called for the creation of a global community based upon an all-unifying "world Christian movement." American globalism, anti-Communism, Christian redemption: Luce was in his element. He would not have been disappointed to learn that Gus Hall, the leader of the local Communist Party, attacked the Cleveland meeting as the work of a man promoting "his Hitlerite dream of world conquest."[8]

Harry and Clare Luce hosted a farewell reception in his spacious suite, but thereafter the pleasantries between the pair ended. Few of Luce's guests would have guessed that the second Mrs. Luce, who occupied an adjoining suite, had recently thrown a tantrum. Clare wanted to talk to Harry, but when she knocked on his locked door, he told her to go away; he was busy. Undeterred, she banged away at the door and then loudly threatened to pack and leave, all in front of a distraught maid, and all to no avail.[9]

Harry Luce returned to Rockefeller Plaza, but he took little pleasure in the good press engendered by his Cleveland conference. Indeed, part of Luce's ongoing misery stemmed from his success: If the leaders of the nation paid homage to *Time* in Cleveland, why had Luce failed to help China more? A frustrated boss argued with *Time*'s Jim Shepley, who insisted that the suppression of the Communists would require *two million* American troops. Luce waved aside such objections, raving on about Chiang's American-trained "Alpha" divisions. Give them U.S. logistical support, Luce argued, plus enough ammunition, and they would prevail over the Communists. Shepley countered by pointing to Manchuria and north China, where the Communists had already defeated some of those same divisions. Barely a month after Luce's World Affairs Institute triumph, editorial director Billings described Luce as "suffering visibly over China."[10] He added, "China and its treatment in the magazines cause [Luce] untold personal anguish."

Only nine thousand Marines remained in China, and most of them were slated to return home soon. At this juncture, *Time* argued that America faced three choices in China: Withdraw completely from the China imbroglio; drift along; or aid Chiang while he instituted reforms.[11] *Time* clearly favored the third course.[12] But despite all the efforts of the China lobby, Secretary Marshall refused to involve the United States more deeply in China.[13] In response, Luce "became very, very bitter" and called the new secretary of state a man who had "failed miserably in China."[14] Indeed, Luce argued, George Marshall didn't "give a tooting damn about China."[15] Jim Shepley demurred and insisted that if Chiang instituted democratization, he would receive "all-out support from George Marshall."[16] But two weeks later, Shepley learned that the State Department would merely recommend the appropriation of limited financial aid.[17] In fact, the withdrawal of the Soviets from Manchuria and the growing crisis in Europe had diminished American interest in the Chinese morass.[18] In a moment of candor, even *Life* admitted that the American people would not "prop up a regime incapable of reforming itself."[19]

Why else were Americans so loath to support Chiang's government? One answer came in the late winter of 1947 from *Time*'s Bill Gray: Under Japanese rule, the island called Formosa (the Chinese Taiwan) had made substantial economic progress, but the postwar Guomindang administration of the brutal governor General Chen Yi acted like a military kleptocracy looting a conquered province. When the Formosans revolted in 1947, the government responded by massacring thousands of them. There were scenes of killings and even castrations right across the way from the American consulate in Taipei. Bill Gray cabled fact-filled dispatches to New York; but for weeks *Time* virtually ignored the Formosa troubles. (Luce the journalist was overly sensitive to criticism from Nationalist officials like T. V. Soong and did not wish to offend them.) But in April, *Time* finally blamed the Chen regime for firing on demonstrators and for killing three to four thousand people. (Gray knew that the true figure was much higher.)[20] Then, with a straight face, *Time* cited the governor's conclusion: "I expect to take about five years to re-educate the people so they will be more happy with the Chinese administration."

A similar optimism prevailed at Rockefeller Plaza. *Time*, for example, thought that the recent Nationalist seizure of Yan'an, the longtime Communist capital, would "strengthen confidence in Chiang's ultimate victory."[21] The defiant rhetoric coming out of Nanjing was encouraging: General Chen Cheng, chief of staff of Chiang's army, boasted at a press conference that "within six months" the army would be able to "wipe the Communists out."[22] Meanwhile, the intensification of the crisis in Europe might also redound to the benefit of Chiang and his American supporters.

New Offensives Against Communism

President Truman spoke of global confrontation when he pitted freedom against Communism in Greece and Turkey. This Truman Doctrine was all to the good, as far as Henry Luce was concerned. Unfortunately, Truman had mentioned only Greece and Turkey, and not China, so Luce unleashed James Burnham on *Life*'s public. A former Trotskyite who had moved sharply to the right, Burnham would later discover the managerial class remaking American capitalism.[23]

Now, in his soon-to-be-published book *The Struggle for the World*, Burnham argued that World War III was already in progress, and he called for nothing less than American "world control."[24] If the United States had to become a "tyrant" to save the world, then so be it. America, Burnham argued, must prepare to win a nuclear war, and Communism at home must be suppressed. Burnham's world of steel was Luce's American Century stripped of its faith, humanity, and generosity.

Life did not buy the whole message, because James Burnham emphasized power at the expense of freedom; and he was a bit too belligerent for some of Luce's editors.[25] But for weeks Harry Luce walked around his editorial offices sounding like Burnham's echo chamber.[26] *Time* now campaigned for a drastic upward revision of the defense budget and endorsed universal military training.[27] *Life* decided that the United States possessed a third-rate air force and could put only two hundred thousand combat-ready soldiers in the field "in case of emergency."[28] The magazine also devoted much space to the need for bomb shelters capable of withstanding atomic attacks: This plan became a Luce obsession for the next fifteen years.[29] The Cold War had arrived, and John Billings could boast with some justification that Time Inc. was "America's most effective publishing enemy of Communism."[30] As if to confirm this diagnosis, the Soviets, like the Nazis and the Fascists before them, blocked the distribution of Luce's magazines in their sphere of influence.[31]

Luce now banished the term "American Century" from his vocabulary; once a man of hope, he had become the great prophet of confrontation.[32]

In an atmosphere of growing tension and fear, any organization Luce suspected of neutrality or undue leftism was in trouble. Time Inc. was not spared, and a "wild and emotional" Henry Luce schemed to purge Communists who worked there.[33] His operatives discovered seventeen suspects and intended to monitor them closely. Time Inc. even sent a researcher to the Communist Jefferson School near Union Square to learn about its indoctrination techniques.[34] Luce wanted to hire a Red-busting private detective, but Billings talked him out of a move that might disrupt the company.[35] Although Billings felt "like a member of Gestapo in secret session," he concluded that he and his colleagues "were all too mild and sweet for the role."[36] Perhaps, but one woman found herself unemployed because her husband was deputy editor of the *Daily Worker*.[37] A leftist named Leon Sversky (dubbed "subversky" and a "crypto Communist" by his detractors) resigned under pressure. John Hersey was gone, Teddy White had left, and Dick Lauterbach would soon be out the door. John Billings gloated, "Gradually we clean up our own dirty background."[38] Group journalism, a hallmark of *Time*, would be banished too, some said because it sounded too collectivist – or even Communist.[39]

A Break with the IPR

In his search for scapegoats in the war against Chinese Communism, Harry Luce took aim at the Institute of Pacific Relations. Here he did not labor alone, for Congressman Walter Judd was agitating for an investigation of its alleged un-American activities.[40] Executive Secretary Ned Carter's financial woes mounted each day. *Time* donated only $1,500 to the IPR in 1946, a 40 percent decrease from the prior year. Luce refused to make a personal contribution. And even though he was vice-chairman of the board of the American IPR, Luce did not attend any meetings in 1946. Carter noted, "Because of expected pressure in 1947, [Luce] asked that he not be nominated for the new board." But if Luce went out the door, he might be followed by other business leaders, such as Paul Gray Hoffman, president of the Studebaker Corporation.[41] An anguished Carter thought about resigning as executive vice-chairman before his term ended in 1949.[42] Some troubled members of the IPR even called for a purge of Communist staffer Fred Field, but most felt that dismissing him signaled a cave-in to Alfred Kohlberg.[43] Still, it was not easy to explain away Field's presence at AIPR headquarters.[44] True, he was personable, generous, rich, and diligent – but Field had attacked "American imperialism in China," which he accused of supporting "feudalism, gangsterism and corruption against [the Communist struggle for] democracy and unity and peoples' welfare."[45]

In March the indefatigable Kohlberg was busy preparing for the upcoming general meeting of the AIPR, where he hoped to secure the appointment of a friendly committee tasked with investigating his charges. After reading Kohlberg's proxy form, Clare Luce sent a note to her husband. "Oughtn't you do something," she asked, "about resigning (or busting) I.P.R.?"[46] Luce then called in the discreet Allen Grover and asked him to discuss matters with Ned Carter.

Grover, a suave socialite, spent two days with the IPR people, but Carter again refused to investigate or condemn suspect research sponsored by the IPR. Nor, Grover told Luce, would Carter "get rid of his close associate, Freddie Field, a known Communist." So Grover recommended that until the IPR reformed itself, Luce have nothing more to do with it. He did, however, suggest that *Time* continue to pay something to the IPR, because *Time* staffers "used them constantly for reference." Grover made his recommendations right before Kohlberg launched his assault at the AIPR's 22 April 1947 meeting. Alleged Communist infiltration was the sole issue at hand, and the national media covered the event. The debate itself was a calm one; Kohlberg spoke softly but with great conviction. The usual charges and rebuttals flew back and forth, and Carter dismissed Kohlberg as a "zealot" who fostered "hysteria." When it came to the votes, Kohlberg could produce only 66 proxies, whereas the executive committee received 1,163.[47] As far as the mainstream press was concerned, the IPR had been cleared, and Teddy White congratulated Carter. Even Clare Luce felt that Kohlberg had misfired.[48] She did, however, find consolation in the fact that she had "repeatedly urged Harry to look into the I.P.R. *very* closely."[49]

Kohlberg angrily resigned from the IPR and demanded that the House Un-American Activities Committee investigate it.[50] His charges grew wilder, and Kohlberg soon claimed that Carter was a Communist.[51] Supporting his appeal was the head of the China Information Service in New York City, who told Luce's assistant that the IPR "had done as much damage to China as the U.S. Congress."[52] When a misguided agency of the Chinese government planned to bestow a medal on Carter, Clare Luce joined with Kohlberg in counterattacking: "Mr. Carter," Kohlberg wrote, "is the head of a conspiracy which has developed in this country to destroy the Government of the Republic of China." In a conversation with the foreign minister of China, Clare Luce declared that awarding the medal to Ned Carter would be "a direct slap in the face" to the Luces.[53] Carter did not receive his elusive award.

On 23 July 1947 Freddie Field finally announced that he would leave the AIPR's board and its executive committee. Ned Carter, worn out by the struggle, considered early retirement, and mounting financial woes plagued the IPR. (Carter blamed Henry Luce "and his crowd" for much of the institute's misery.)[54] Wary of more financial damage, the IPR reached out to Chiang's supporters, but hesitantly and to little effect. The lobby had discredited the IPR, but it still could not force the Truman administration to change its China policy. Most Americans, as well as their government, wished to avoid involving the United States more deeply in China. How could it be otherwise when even *Time* told stories like this one? A hunchbacked Communist judge had executed an old woman who had shared some water with Chiang's troops. When the Nationalists returned, "a heavy, short-bladed sickle, used to harvest wheat, was fashioned into an executioner's tool." *Time* approved of the bloody denouement: "While fellow informers watched, Hunchback Chen's head was hacked off."[55] *Time*, which could not resist a good anecdote, had thus provided American skeptics with one more reason for avoiding immersion in China's bloodbath.

China Abandoned?

Arrogant, rigid, and remarkably ignorant of important facts, Chiang Kai-shek resolutely marched toward disaster. Almost as if he were imitating the defeated Japanese, Chiang fought to hold the big cities, thereby exposing his long lines of communication to enemy forces based in remote rural areas of his vast country. Oppressed peasants were tired of the government's rapacious tax collectors, and they resented a system of conscription that gobbled up their sons while sparing children of the rich and the well connected. In the cities, students blamed foreigners for many of China's ills.[56] Suffering from a ruinous inflation – one U.S. dollar was now worth 14,000 Chinese dollars – students, whether Marxist or not, felt that nothing could be worse than the present regime.[57] Everywhere, there was war weariness, fear of the secret police, and a total lack of idealism and self-sacrifice. Chiang promoted associates on the basis of loyalty and repaid them by tolerating widespread corruption.[58] By contrast, many Chinese saw the Communists as relatively incorruptible nationalists, people who would stand up to foreigners, whether Russian or American.[59]

Time consoled its readers with the "certainty" that Chiang would not surrender.[60] There was another reason for optimism: The 1946 arms embargo was lifted, and later, 130 million rounds of ammunition would be released to China.[61] (Unfortunately, many of those bullets could not be used in Chiang's rifles.) But if the United States would not help the government of China buy the arms that it needed, repeal of the embargo would prove to be a hollow act. In Washington, "Europe first" still prevailed. In June 1947 Marshall received an honorary degree at Harvard University, where he called for the massive outlay of funds for Europe. He did not mention China. But even if Truman were to change his mind and extend generous credits to China, it was unlikely that a budget-conscious Congress would vote them.[62]

In response to Truman's opposition, the Luce media played the Russian card, arguing that the Soviets were poised to dismember and exploit China from Xinjiang to Inner Mongolia.[63] *Time* also claimed – but could not prove – that Soviet aircraft and artillery accounted for Chiang's Manchurian debacle.[64] An angry Harry Luce continued to bemoan the "mistakes of policy and the tragic failures of American efforts in China."[65] And *Life* cracked, "It makes no sense to oppose Russian infiltration in Greece, Turkey and Iran . . . , while we actively maneuver to increase Russian penetration of China."[66] This comment ignored the fact that for various reasons, the situation in those other countries was on a smaller scale and hence manageable.

The Battle for Aid to China

If the United States refused to provide adequate aid to China, then Henry Luce the philanthropist intended to make good on at least part of America's shameful default. His fund-raising philosophy was simple: "When to raise the money? Now. How? Ask for it."[67] In this effort, his restraint in regard to personal attacks on Marshall paid dividends in May, when Luce sought the endorsement of the secretary of state. Yes, he could use Marshall's name, and he was soon telling potential donors to the Christian colleges or United Service to China (USC) that General Marshall believed that it was "vital that the greatest possible support be given to American-sponsored institutions in China."[68] During these tough postwar years, Luce was Yale-in-China's major backer. Yali's center in Changsha – Mao's birthplace – had suffered greatly during the war, and Luce needed to raise $200,000 for its reconstruction. Working with Secretary of Commerce W. Averell Harriman, a fellow alumnus, he acquired the funds within a year. Unfortunately, as Chiang faltered, it became harder to secure such funds. "Does it make sense," asked one reluctant donor, "to give money today to anything in China where it is possible that the Communists, instead of the Japs, next time may destroy the installations?"[69] In the face of such pessimism, Luce fell back upon a favorite analogy: "Again, as in 1937 against Japan," claimed United Service to China, "China is the ally of America in our stupendous struggle."[70] As always, Luce drew upon old corporate and personal ties. He and his wife sponsored fund-raising events at the Waldorf and supported USC through their personal appeals.[71]

In June 1947 Harry Luce made a sentimental journey to Scranton, Pennsylvania, where he visited the Friendship House, a charitable institution supported by his grandparents in the late nineteenth century.[72] In his public comments, the publisher blamed America for failing to provide China with badly needed foreign aid. Had we acted, Luce continued, Chinese liberals would

5.1   Republican alliances and China politics: Clare Boothe Luce with House minority
leader (and sometime Speaker) Joseph W. Martin, Jr. (Martin Papers, Stonehill College)

today be on the verge of victory. Then came a chilling conclusion, almost a
threat. "Some day, some how," Luce promised, "we've got to go back there
and put the situation in order." He added, "I pray god it may not be necessary to do so with force of arms." But what if Americans refused to intervene?
At grim times like these, Luce wondered whether he would "ever grow up
and cease to be disappointed in what was intended to be so great and good a
country."[73] He was referring not to China, but to his own America.

On 9 July 1947, Chiang's deteriorating military situation provoked a new
Truman directive. Lieutenant General Albert C. Wedemeyer would go to China
on a fact-finding mission. Accompanied by appropriate experts, Wedemeyer,
special representative of the president, was ordered to see whether the Chinese
government presented "satisfactory evidence of effective measures looking

towards Chinese recovery." If Wedemeyer so determined, then Truman was prepared to "consider assistance in a program of rehabilitation."[74] A day after Wedemeyer's appointment, Luce ordered that his mission receive prominent coverage at Time Inc.[75] *Time* quickly decided that the general "was on the way to see what could be done to retrieve the losses that followed from five-star General Marshall's indecisive decision."[76]

Harry Luce had for the fifth time (Stilwell in 1942, Chennault in 1943, Wedemeyer himself in 1944, and Marshall in 1945) found an American who would be the agent of China's salvation.

Wedemeyer and Bullitt

Albert Wedemeyer was a talented – some said brilliant – staff officer. When it came to politics and foreign policy, however, he was often adrift, and his

5.2 General Albert C. Wedemeyer replaced General Stilwell in China late in 1944. (Hoover Institution Archives, Stanford University)

impressions were contradictory. In verbose letters to Luce, Wedemeyer railed on about the Chinese government's "incompetence" and "corrupt practices," and he found "apathy and lethargy in many quarters."[77] At a dinner hosted by Ambassador Stuart, Wedemeyer publicly upbraided high Chinese officials for failing to address China's problems.[78] Wedemeyer even engaged in some blunt conversations with Chiang himself.[79] In Shanghai, at an off-the-record press conference, Wedemeyer called for a "new representative body that will truly represent the farmers." He also argued that the Chinese Communists were "not real adherents of Kremlinism or Communism," although he still opposed sharing power with them.[80] (He was right about Kremlinism but wrong about Mao's Communism.) The Generalissimo was furious, but he also needed to maintain his ties to Wedemeyer, who might open the foreign aid spigot.

In the late summer, Wedemeyer and his colleagues stayed in Hawaii on their way home. Working day and night on his final report, Wedemeyer nonetheless found the time to write a long letter to Luce. He bemoaned the terrible quality of China's fighting forces, where officers treated their men like dogs. Conditions, the general declared, "have reverted right back to the conditions that existed when I took over in China in September 1944."[81] Even the vaunted "Alpha divisions," in which Luce placed so much faith, were discredited.[82] Billions in aid and "shiploads of material" would be of no avail, Wedemeyer concluded, unless the Chinese government reformed itself and regained the confidence of its people.

The letter disturbed Luce, who was soon telling his editors that Marshall had needled Wedemeyer into saying nasty things about the Chinese. Tersely, *Time* noted only that Wedemeyer had called for reforms and an end to corruption.[83] But the United States, the magazine added, should not judge China by "standards of political morality higher than those applied to Greece, Turkey or Russia – to whom the U.S. gave billions without inquiring whether their officers were competent and politically pure."[84] Luce was desperate to find out what Wedemeyer's report contained, and he even met with the general at the Waldorf, where the envoy parried his aggressive questions.[85] Nevertheless, Luce had reason to be optimistic.

Thanks to Clare Luce, Wedemeyer had carefully studied James Burnham's *Struggle for the World* and had brought the book to the attention of the faculty of the National War College.[86] China, according to Wedemeyer, was part of this struggle, and he wanted Washington to snatch Manchuria away from the Chinese Communists. "My eyes were fixed on America," Wedemeyer wrote, for in his view the fate of China depended upon U.S. foreign policy.[87] In his proposal, a five-power, U.N.-sponsored guardianship would take over northeastern China. Such a mandate, however, would have required Chinese, American, and Soviet approval, so ultimately the Wedemeyer plan went nowhere. On the crucial issue of aid, Wedemeyer came down on the side of Chiang Kai-shek. Though surrounded by discredited cliques and selfish patrons who stored their assets abroad, the Generalissimo, Wedemeyer concluded, was trying to advance the cause of democracy. Above all, Chiang was anti-Communist.

Instead of demanding reforms as a prerequisite to aid, Wedemeyer recommended the near-term dispatch of "American advisors...in specified military and economic field."[88] And in conversations with the Joint Chiefs, Albert Wedemeyer recommended sending ten thousand American advisers to China.[89] The United States, if he had his way, could soon be involved in an Asian civil war.

General Wedemeyer was the first responsible official to advocate involving American ground troops – though only as advisers – in an Asian war against Communism. To his dismay, however, the administration wished to steer clear of military involvement in China. Marshall, Wedemeyer claimed, "virtually told me that if I had any hopes of advancing to the Chief of Staff's job, my report did not enhance that possibility."[90] But Wedemeyer would not alter his conclusions; as a result, the administration decided to block publication of the Wedemeyer report. Clare Boothe Luce, the incoming president of Alfred Kohlberg's American China Policy Association, demanded that the government release Wedemeyer's elusive recommendations.[91] For the rest of his life, Wedemeyer insisted that "had munitions been given in appropriate quantities to mainland China in 1947–48, and had Manchuria and Korea been temporarily placed under the aegis of the U.N., the spread of Communism might never have occurred in the Far East."[92] To the China lobby, the conspiracy to silence Wedemeyer had cost America dearly. Herbert Hoover, for example, later told the general that the "last chance to save China was when your report of 1947 was suppressed and its recommendations repudiated."[93] Henry Luce, who had placed much faith in General Wedemeyer, was disappointed, but he quickly fell back upon a favorite adage: "The remaining heathen are likelier to be attracted by our certitude than convinced by our arguments."[94] In 1947 Luce found the man who would broadcast his sermon to the American people.

Life's "special correspondent" was former diplomat William Christian Bullitt, whom Henry R. Luce had known since prewar days. Fiercely anti-Communist, Bullitt displayed another virtue dear to editor-in-chief Luce: He blamed FDR and other New Deal Democrats for Stalin's political victories in Europe and Asia. Luce's associates saw William Bullitt as a relentless self-promoter ("in to brag some more," wrote Billings), but the boss demurred: "Yes, yes – I know some people think he's a shit," Harry declared, but he retained Bullitt as a consultant and author.[95] In 1947 Time Inc. paid him the princely sum of $13,000 for inspecting troubled China.[96] Luce knew that Bullitt would propose plans acceptable to the China lobby. The fact that he lacked regional expertise was of no concern to Luce.

Life hoped to publish Bullitt's piece in the autumn of 1947.[97] Editorial Director Billings thought that Bullitt's draft pieces on China were "superficial & mediocre," but Luce brushed aside his criticisms.[98] In October *Life*'s full-page advertisement in the *New York Times* asked, "CAN CHINA BE KEPT OUT OF THE HANDS OF STALIN?" Alfred Kohlberg hailed the appearance of Bullitt's "magnificent article," seeing it as a weapon to be used against the allegedly pro-Chinese Communist bias of much of the American press.[99] "If China falls into the hands of Stalin," Bullitt wrote in *Life*, "all Asia, including Japan, sooner or later will fall into his hands."[100] Bullitt's "Report on China" expressed fear of a time when a Soviet-dominated China would wage war against the United States. "Report on China" did acknowledge the need for military reforms in China, and Bullitt endorsed conscripting the sons of the rich and other egalitarian measures.[101] He proposed granting China $75 million in immediate currency stabilization credits, with an equal amount to follow in the near future. The generous ex-ambassador also proposed giving Chiang $600 million for other purposes over a three-year period. All told, Bullitt's recommendations added up to at least $1.35 *billion* in aid for China. But because China's infrastructure was weak or shattered by war and it lacked trained cadres at all levels, Americans would have to administer that assistance. Where would that lead? If Bullitt had his way, Americans would train and equip the ten new Chinese divisions needed for the liberation of Manchuria. *Time* followed suit, and its two-page "editorial" spread echoed Bullitt's recommendations down to the most minute detail.[102]

Chiang critic Laurence Salisbury feared that "Bullit's [*sic*] favorable report will be spread through out the country by Life-time [*sic*] incorporated."[103] He was right, and Luce's network made ample use of Bullitt's "Report on China."[104] A tireless and determined William Bullitt testified before Congress, debated Chiang's critics on the radio, and spoke to any audience that would have him. He took credit for the fact that Republicans on the Hill favored "immediate and adequate aid."[105] With hyperbole worthy of Harry Luce's wartime paeans to China's heroism, Bullitt gravely predicted, "The independence of the U.S. will not live a generation longer than the independence of China."[106] Trapped in his apocalyptic vision, Bullitt lost sight of a grave danger: To manipulate China like a pawn in a foreigner's game of geopolitics could lead to disaster for those who played it. The Japanese had already discovered this, and the American people wanted no part of Bullitt's massive interventionist scheme.

On 27 October 1947 the United States agreed to provide China with $30 million worth of food, medicines, and other nonmilitary American supplies, but this belated and minimal assistance did nothing to reverse Nationalist China's decline.[107] *Time* dryly described the scope of the catastrophe: Manchuria was 93 percent lost, as was 70 percent of north China. In a new tone of urgency, the newsmagazine warned that "history was passing the eleventh hour, and . . . only Washington could stop the clock."[108] "How," *Life* asked in exasperation, "could an administration that is frankly dedicated to the 'containment' of totalitarian aggression have so long ignored the war in China?"[109] But this question masked a weak argument. Shattered Western Europe lacked capital, but it possessed the infrastructure, managers, engineers, political elites, entrepreneurs, and skilled labor needed for reconstruction. China did not. Undeterred, Luce labored on. His crusade disturbed the IPR's

Laurence Salisbury, who wrote that Luce's influence through the magazines was "a force to be reckoned with." He concluded, "Even though our authorities regard aid to Chiang as throwing money away and a mistake, this betrayal of the public interest would be more than repaid by Luce support in the elections."[110]

Luce would never support Truman, but he did have useful contacts in the administration. In September, Assistant Secretary of State William Benton (A. B., Yale 1921), who knew Luce well, argued that offering positions to Harry and Clare would be politically "astute."[111] But Truman detested the Luces, especially Clare, who had made a disparaging comment about Mrs. Bess Truman during the nasty 1944 campaign. In any case, the only job Harry Luce wanted in government was the one Marshall held. Nothing came of Benton's idea, but within the administration, officials like Harry B. Price continued to court Luce. Deputy director of the China office of the Economic Cooperation Administration (ECA), Price was an expert on China's current problems.[112] China, Price observed, badly needed reform, because it lacked "an efficient, competent and honest civil service." Time was of the essence, Price added, because the postwar UN-sponsored relief programs were being terminated. He therefore suggested that the Chinese government issue an invitation "for extensive American participation in the practical implementation" of a new aid program involving food, petroleum, and other goods intended to lead to "increased production." Five to ten thousand Americans would administer the aid program, and if China agreed to these terms, military aid (Price provided no specifics) would be forthcoming. China would presumably carry out extensive political, social, and agrarian reforms.

In a bid for support, Harry Price leaked one of his confidential memoranda to Henry Luce. Luce, however, disliked the idea of making military assistance contingent upon social and political reform. In any event, George Marshall was not prepared to provide China with thousands of American experts and a blank check. Still, Marshall tried to mollify Luce. He made sure that his former aide, Jim Shepley of *Time*, learned that the administration was considering overall aid worth $1.5 billion, to be doled out over an indeterminate number of years. William Bullitt's sources, however, contradicted Shepley. Only $18 million worth of foodstuffs would be made immediately available to China under Public Law 84. Bullitt added that the administration might support $300 million in assistance in 1948, or seventy-five cents for each Chinese.[113] Marshall's recommendation became public on 12 November, and it amounted to $300 million over two years.[114] But even if Congress agreed, the aid would not start to flow until 1 April 1948, and most of the assistance – which did not include military hardware – would not reach China until 1949. Cynics saw this delay as intentional.[115] *Time* agreed and pronounced the China aid plan "too little, too late."[116]

When Marshall reported to the House Committee on Foreign Affairs, he spoke in terms of $60 million in near-term aid, and again he refused further military assistance. *Time*'s Frank McNaughton promptly denounced the Marshall proposal as "niggardly." In fact, Luce's efforts on behalf of aid to China seemed to be bearing some small fruit. *Time*'s Bob Elson saw a "gleam of hope" when the administration considered issuing export licenses for arms, munitions, and airplanes bound for China. "It was not much, but it was a start," insisted Elson.[117] Although the polled public held Chiang in scant regard, it would soon favor supplying China with "more military supplies, goods, and money."[118] If Chiang could hold out until the Republicans regained the White House, Luce believed, all might end well. But once again, Europe took center stage.

Ill Omens

In February 1948 a Soviet-instigated coup toppled the democratic government of Czechoslovakia. In the middle of the crisis, two of Luce's senior editors returned from Washington with even more troubling news. War, they said, might come in two years, and according to *Time*'s sources in the army, the deflated postwar American military establishment would soon need to field an army of sixty divisions.[119] Secretary of National Defense James Forrestal, a man sure to receive a sympathetic hearing at Rockefeller Plaza, proposed building an armed force of 1.734 million troops, backed up by a seventy-group Air Force. Forrestal also wanted to conscript 3.6 million men aged nineteen to twenty-five.[120] Luce and Billings compared this world of 1948 to that of 1938. *Time* ominously prophesied, "Either this is the American century or the Soviet century."[121] The magazine insisted that "the world now looked to the U.S. for hope and leadership," to a *Pax Americana* molded by the "heart, the wisdom and the power of the U.S."[122]

Some of *Time*'s sources thought that the Soviets might have the Bomb in a very few years, and John Billings worried about a Russian sneak attack on Detroit or Chicago.[123] In a blood-curdling warning, *Time* mused, "Ten years from now a divided, stunned and defeated U.S. may be trying to adjust itself to a Communist-ruled world."[124] Luce accurately predicted that Communism would "still do much evil in the world, a terrible cancer destined to destroy millions of people before it is destroyed."[125] From time to time, he pondered the morality of launching a "preventive" atomic war. But a moment later, Luce foresaw the end of the long crisis that had begun in 1914. Then would come a new golden age, when "throughout the world, and not least in China," there would be "large groups of men and women leading lives of clearer purpose and measured confidence."[126] American optimism usually triumphed over Luce's darker moods.

In the midst of crises in Europe, *Fortune* again reminded Americans of their stake in Asia. America, the magazine argued, faced a choice: Either let all of Asia fall to "the messianic nationalism of Russian Communism," or win the support of the continent as an "ally in its battle for basic liberties."[127] In Luce's view, the good America of Theodore Roosevelt, Henry Winters Luce,

Leighton Stuart, and Colonel Henry L. Stimson had saved China from imperialist partition and Japanese aggression. Luce had always admired Stimson as a "great American."[128] After he returned from China in 1946, Luce conferred with Stimson, who found Luce stimulating. Luce complained that Truman and Marshall had placed the Communist faction on a par with the legitimate government of China. Fortunately, however, Chiang was winning his war, and he would probably emerge victorious in a few months. But Luce was worried about men like the State Department's John Carter Vincent, who opposed giving China "any help until everything in China is hunky-dory."[129] The aged, painfully ill Henry Stimson captured the spirit of Luce's message in a single sentence. "Luce," Stimson wrote, "seemed to think that to get the Chinese and the Communists together, except by the road of conquest by the Nationalists, was an impossible task."[130]

A year later, after Luce had learned that Stimson was writing his memoirs in collaboration with McGeorge Bundy, he quickly moved to secure first serial rights for *Life*.[131] The *Ladies' Home Journal* had already gotten to Stimson, however, so Luce was doubly disappointed. Stimson's account of China as a wartime ally could have been written by Stilwell. In Stimson's article, Chiang emerged as an authoritarian incompetent, and Luce reacted like a man who had been stabbed in the back. He came close to calling Stimson a Judas or a Brutus. "I cannot think," Luce complained, "of any utterance which ever hurt me so much as your recent statement about Chiang-Kai-shek and China."[132] Avoiding the proprieties, Luce accused the ill old man of having acted "carelessly and irresponsibly."

Fearing the impact of the Luce letter upon his health, Stimson's aide withheld it from him pending some rest and relaxation.[133] Luce seems to have met with Bundy and suggested that Stimson retract his unkind comments about Chiang. To Luce's dismay, however, Stimson, in his response of 31 March, recounted Chiang's wartime failures, expressed confidence in George Marshall, and refused to retract anything.[134] Stimson tactfully expressed great admiration for "the spirit which animates your interest in this terribly difficult problem."[135] But he would not join Luce in the China lobby's campaign.

Luce's displeasure might have turned to rage had he known about Stimson's role in Teddy White's latest project. The ex-Time Incer was editing *The Stilwell Papers*, a devastating portrait of "Peanut" (Chiang) and the alleged incompetents and crooks staffing the Chinese high command during World War II.[136] And none other than Henry Stimson was supplying that reprobate White with copies of secret wartime correspondence between Stilwell and the War Department. White's sad but funny book would cause the China lobby more anguish.

The China Lobby at Work

Early in 1948 Chiang suffered more defeats. In a sad letter to George Marshall, Madame Chiang herself admitted, "We all are...even a little more tired and worn than during those [war] years." Stoically, however, she insisted, "We must struggle on" in the battle against "totalitarians."[137] Senator Robert A. Taft (Republican of Ohio) insisted, "The Far East is ultimately even more important to our future peace than is Europe."[138] In fact, the prospects for substantial aid to China had suddenly improved. Truman wanted to exclude China from election-year politics – and he would pay a price to do so. Pressured by *Time*, the Luce network, the China bloc in the House, and the *New York Times*, President Truman ultimately agreed to support a bill granting China $570,000,000 in aid through 30 June 1949.[139] Chinese officials, however, complained to friendly senators, for the proposed aid would do nothing for China's armies, nor would it assist its government in its losing war against inflation. *Time* (8 March 1948) sarcastically observed that Chiang had finally received some technical help from the United States – a "brand-new set of American false teeth."

The decline in Chiang's fortunes put more pressure on Truman, who seemed adrift when asked about America's China policy.[140] In *Life*'s harsh words, America's policy in China was, in effect, "pro-Communist," and Congress must change that.[141] In their quest for more aid, Luce's correspondents relied heavily upon former Flying Tiger chief Claire Chennault. Still flamboyant but partly deaf, the leathery old soldier testified that China was "the key to world peace." He suggested that the U.S. immediately dispatch munitions, military person-nel, and economic assistance worth perhaps $1.5 billion. While the Luce media beat the drums for this kind of military aid, *Time* rarely exposed the finan-cial interests that expected to benefit from such aid. William J. Goodwin, for example, was a registered lobbyist working for Chiang, and he spent a lot of money entertaining U.S. senators interested in helping China.[142] Pirnie, Lee & Company, a neighbor of Luce's at Rockefeller Center, heavily lobbied Senators Styles Bridges and Henry Cabot Lodge for aid that could be used to pay for Pirnie's proposed reconstruction projects in China.[143]

Claire Chennault was a modern American missionary with wings, one who fervently believed in Chiang, in China, in the American calling in Asia. More at home in China than in America, Chennault had in 1947 married Anna Chan, daughter of Dr. Y. W. Chan, Chiang's former consul in San Francisco. There was, however, a financial motive behind Chennault's relentless lobbying. Along with Whiting Willauer, a wartime associate of T. V. Soong at China Defense Supplies, Chennault ran the lucrative China Air Transport (CAT). Anna Chan had served CAT as its public relations representative, and she too became an elo-quent spokesperson for the Nationalists. The airline ferried supplies to besieged garrisons, evacuated soldiers and officials, and engaged in other activities of an export-import nature. In fact, CAT enjoyed a virtual monopoly on air trans-port within Nationalist China. Its profits were enormous, especially because Chennault and his partners had acquired their U.S.-made planes for a frac-tion of their original cost. Pilots who might make $300 a month in the United States earned $2,400 (almost tax-free) working for CAT. Any additional aid granted China would further enrich Willauer and Chennault, as well as their chief Washington contact, New Dealer turned fixer Thomas "Tommy the Cork" Corcoran.[144] Chennault's company faced ruin if the Communists won. *Time*'s

5.3   China lobby stalwarts: Anna Chennault, Thomas Corcoran, and Claire Chennault in the mid-1950s. (Library of Congress)

readership remained ignorant of this and related facts about the China lobby, because the magazine's Washington correspondents knew better than to cable such information to the home office.

When Senator Vandenberg's growing skepticism about Chiang's chances for survival surfaced, Luce and his editors quickly brought the senator back on board. Vandenberg harbored presidential ambitions, and in the words of the Chinese ambassador, the senator was soon "as good as gold" on China policy.[145] Vandenberg made sure that the new Economic Cooperation Administration, not the anti-Chiang State Department, administered the China aid program.[146] Indeed, Luce could take further comfort from the fact that his good friend Paul Gray Hoffman, *Fortune*'s favorite industrialist, would be the ECA administrator. After more negotiations and delays, the requisite legislation became law in June. Its final price tag came to $400 million, a figure that included $125 million for any purchases (i.e., arms and munitions) that the Chinese government might desire.

The man in charge of monitoring ECA-supported reconstruction projects in China was Charles L. Stillman. A vice-president of Time Inc., Stillman had experience in fund-raising for China and had been active in the Far East-American Council of Commerce and Industry.[147] A financial wizard who had done much

to make Time Inc. rich, Stillman could be counted upon to provide the administration – and Luce – with a candid survey of his subject. Stillman mistrusted Chinese government officials, who reported that aid money had disappeared "mys-
teriously in transit." The war, combined with China's administrative lethargy,
made ECA's proposed $60 million investment in industrial projects a dubious
proposition, at best.[148]

According to *Time*'s Jim Shepley, Ambassador Stuart had warned the State
Department, "The days of the Chiang government are numbered."[149] It now
took 380 million Chinese "dollars" to buy one U.S. dollar. Thirty million
refugees were soon fleeing southward, where they added to the general misery. By 1948 the whole country was sick of war. The news from the battlefronts
in China remained grim. Americans might support the dispatch of limited aid
to Chiang, but if things deteriorated further, both Truman and the public would
view China as "a veritable rat hole down which we fruitlessly pour American
money."[150]

Some of these unpleasant facts did survive *Time*'s editorial scalpel; most did
not. In fact, Harry Luce, who anticipated a Republican sweep in November,
had regained some of his old optimism.[151]

6

Losing China

The Hunt for Culprits Intensifies

Henry Luce and the men who edited Time Inc.'s publications lacked a realistic framework for understanding the ongoing agony of Nationalist China.

Often ignored were unpleasant facts: Chiang's vast China lacked a viable industrial and transportation infrastructure; it had airplanes but no aviation, and foreign aid was often mismanaged or stolen. Nationalist armies sheltered numerous corrupt generals and a much larger number of hungry, lice-infested, dirty, poorly trained recruits. To millions of Chinese, modernization had come to mean foreign influence and exploitation. In the countryside, only the wealthy landowners supported the Guomindang, for they profited from the regime. To poor farmers, the Nationalists were a horde of tax collectors and conscription agents. Chiang's failures offered Mao Zedong his chance.

When they entered communities populated by bitter, exploited villagers, the Communists mobilized the peasants. Using force, propaganda, and social reform as tools, Mao's cadres whipped their subjects into a fighting force of high morale and purpose. Their armies then waged sporadic war against the Japanese and now, all-out war against Chiang. (The U.S. policy of rebuilding Japan only strengthened the nationalist appeal of the Chinese Communists, as even *Time* once acknowledged.)[1] But Marxism-Leninism, even in its Maoist form, was not the key to Communist triumphs. More important was the fact that the CCP was mobilizing the modern (or modernizing) ideal known as nationalism. The Communists were creating the vanguard, not of the proletariat, but of a totalitarian nation-state. In 1948 a few wise observers in the State Department even predicted that Communism might be more successful in East Asia than in Europe.[2]

In the face of defeat, Luce and his editors consoled themselves with an old illusion: Americans would bring about China's salvation. In this, the agent of the miracle would be a Republican victory. Like many Republicans, Luce convinced himself that the 1948 Republican convention was preparing to "name a president."[3] He dreamed about updating his "American Century" after the natural proprietors of the nation resumed their rightful places in Washington.[4]

Governor Thomas E. Dewey of New York was the clear front-runner.[5] Luce and Dewey were not really close; it took years before the publisher addressed the coldly efficient governor as "Tom." Nevertheless, Luce watched Dewey's evolving foreign policy with satisfaction. The governor and his adviser John Foster Dulles knew that the road to Luce's heart ran through China, and by the autumn of 1947, Dewey's statements on the Far East read like copy edited by Time Inc.'s wordsmiths. Invoking a nostrum favored by Life's William Bullitt, Dewey proposed sending General MacArthur to Nanjing.[6] And at Columbia University, the governor endorsed a vague but highly expensive aid program for China. After one address, Harry Luce complimented the governor about his "insistence" that Asia was "part of the world" they lived in.[7] Dewey quickly thanked Luce and expressed pleasure that Luce had found the China references "agreeable" with his views. At his very first post-convention press conference, candidate Dewey promised to send China more money, along with military advisers.[8]

John Foster Dulles was a frequent contributor to Life, and he would certainly become Dewey's secretary of state. Dulles, Luce liked to say, was like old brandy. You had to swish it around for a time and then savor its full bouquet and flavor.[9] In 1948, Luce showed his appreciation by paying Dulles $2,000 for "research." (Kip Finch, Luce's alert assistant, naïvely wondered whether this donation should be considered "political.")[10] Certainly, Luce's money was a down payment on future services rendered – to America and to China. After Dewey was nominated, Time Inc. treated readers to a four-month-long prospectus on the incoming Dewey administration.[11] Now it was time for Luce's media to savage the Democrats, and they did so with relish.

Time had buried the New Deal coalition as early as 1946; in the spring of 1948, the magazine referred to the "desperate straits" in which the Democratic Party found itself.[12] The far left had bolted, and in Frank McNaughton's view, Progressive candidate Henry A. Wallace "would hold the lunatic fringe and the pacifists and the commies, regardless of how wild he gets."[13] At one point during the Progressives' convention, Will Rogers, Jr., denounced the "imperialism" of the American Century – a crack that amused Luce, who was watching the convention on John Shaw Billings's new television set.[14] Henry Wallace, Luce realized, could hurt Truman, of whom Luce had long since tired.* As for Truman, Clare Luce had insulted Mrs. Truman during the 1944 campaign, and Truman regularly excoriated "Time and Life and the scandal press."[15] The president called Time Inc. "too damn big," and he regularly reviled the "Loose" publications. Years later, Truman told Luce, "You must have trouble sleeping at night."[16]

---

* Despite Luce's aversion to Henry Wallace's foreign policy concepts, the two men shared a common faith in America and later became friendly. Soon after Wallace's death, Luce wrote in an unpublished memoir, "A good man, an American idealist, and unvainglorious, Henry Wallace went with good cheer from [the] limelight into obscurity." Luce's admiration is ironic in view of the fact that Clare Luce's ridicule (1943) hurt Wallace politically.

As was his habit, Luce sometimes ignored unpleasant omens: In late June, a Truman crony informed a skeptical *Time* correspondent that the president would "make the damndest campaign you ever saw or heard."[17] True to this promise, Truman relentlessly attacked the "do-nothing Eightieth Congress" and invoked the specter of another Republican depression, especially in rural areas. Truman, *Time*'s Win Booth reported, was drawing unexpectedly large crowds.[18] But Clare Luce, after having privately predicted a Truman victory, gloated about the president's imminent defeat.[19] *Life* looked forward to the day when President Dewey "would throw our influence, our money and our military and economic advice into the scales against increasing Russian infiltration and spoliation [in China]."[20] Indeed, China's salvation would come none too soon.

Harry Luce might ignore unwelcome news, but he could not plead ignorance. His sister, Beth Moore, served as an adviser to the ECA's China mission, headed by Roger Lapham. Knowing that Moore was a confidante of her powerful brother, Lapham "divulged to her some of the things" Lapham "couldn't very well say" at official meetings.[21] Lapham had just told President Truman that the "military and economic situations in China were bad," and he spoke bluntly to Mrs. Moore.[22] And Harry Price, deputy director of the ECA's China office, wrote that barring massive American military intervention (airmen, field advisers, and the like), China would disappear behind the Iron Curtain.[23]

1948: A Political Delusion

In his enthusiasm for Dewey, Luce overlooked facts that militated in favor of Truman's election.

The administration was building a strong anti-Soviet bulwark in Germany and Western Europe. West Berlin was a flash point, but the U.S.-sponsored airlift had been able to supply the needs of that blockaded city. The China aid package made it harder for the opposition to attack Truman, especially given that the Far East engaged the attention of few Americans. Above all, the country was becoming prosperous. The great strikes of 1946 were history, and since the passage of the Taft-Hartley Act in 1947, big labor had lost some of its power. Many families were moving to new suburbs, buying little houses, dreaming about that first, snowy black-and-white television set (eight hundred thousand units were produced in 1948). In 1948, builders put up 1.25 million homes, a figure that dwarfed those of all years to date. In another first for many working and lower-middle-class families, men in their twenties and thirties were attending college under the GI bill. Price controls were mostly gone, and a record number of people (5.2 million) were buying the new cars and trucks made in factories that had turned out tanks three years before. In fact, the American economy was producing an astounding 50 percent of all the world's manufactured goods.[24] Farmers were doing well, too, but they worried about damage to price supports that might be inflicted upon them by the "do-nothing" Republican Congress. The era of prosperity foreseen by Luce in 1941 had dawned, but sadly for him, its sun shone brightly on Truman and the Democrats.

Readers of *Time*, *Life*, and *Fortune* learned about these trends in the same magazines that told them why Dewey would win.

Americans, Luce prayed, would once again have a chance to save China and thereby redeem the promise of the Open Door. But the election demonstrated the limits of Luce's power, and its results were a further blow to his allies in China. In Beijing, pro-Dewey crowds monitored the election returns posted by the U.S. Information Service and then went home dejected.[25] With Dewey, the Republican Congress also went down to crushing defeat. A bitter Harry Luce felt that the voters should have relieved "the Democratic Party of the vast responsibilities for which it was ill-fitted."[26] When *Life* lamely called itself one more victim of a mass illusion, an angry reader correctly observed, "You did your level best to CREATE that illusion."[27] In the aftermath of the election, *Time* endured an avalanche of criticism. Professors at Dartmouth College and Iowa State University now used *Time* to illustrate the kinds of bias that good journalists should avoid.[28]

Losing China

President Truman had decided to pull the U.S. Navy out of Qingdao, where Harry Luce had passed idyllic summers as a boy. In the autumn, the Communists took Chiang's last remaining strongholds in the northeast, and their armies soon prepared to drive on Beijing. Signs of collapse were everywhere. Defeated generals fled south, saving themselves as well as their gold bars and concubines. All of Shandong, Small Boy Luce's provincial birthplace, had fallen. *Life* finally wrote about the "beginning of the end of Chiang Kai-shek's China" when the Nationalists lost four hundred thousand more troops in their failed battle for Manchuria.[29] In sadness, *Life* mourned the passing of the China that Americans had "known, befriended, neglected, deplored."[30] Evoking "red hordes pressing down toward the Yangtze," America's magazine prepared its readers for the line that Luce would adopt toward "Red China": Mao Zedong's China, *Life* insisted, would be a Soviet satellite.[31] Meanwhile, Harry Luce's friend ECA administrator Paul Hoffman suspended the funding of reconstruction projects in China.[32] And in a statement that *Time* called a "kick in the teeth to the tottering Nationalist government and a boost, in effect, to the Communists," Hoffman mused about aiding a new, non-Communist but post-Chiang government.[33]

In Washington, the Chinese embassy claimed that little more than $2 million in new military aid had reached China, whereas the White House insisted that more than $88 million had been authorized for shipment to China.[34] But *Time*'s Frank McNaughton wrote, "It's a goddam lousy performance." The administration, Senator Bridges said, had "virtually sold China down the river to the Communists."[35] Venting its despair, *Time* admitted that nothing except some kind of very expensive American military intervention could save China.[36] But Luce felt compelled to press on, for he could not believe that Americans would abandon his China. *Time* ominously invoked the "loss of China," popularizing a phrase that it, along with Patrick Hurley, had first employed in 1944. The magazine soon became the prosecutor indicting those guilty of losing China, all of whom were Americans.[37] Its list of gravediggers included Stilwell; FDR and his courtiers who had met at Yalta; the wartime military leaders who decided not to land U.S. forces in Formosa or on the China coast; the mainly Democratic politicians who provided China with inadequate aid after the fall of Japan; Marshall, for his attempt at coalition government in China; and the foreign policy "experts" like John Carter Vincent, who had decided upon the U.S. arms embargo to China.[38] New conspiracy theories arose and would soon be cited as fact in the Luce media. Perhaps their most striking example was "How We Won the War and Lost the Peace," a bitter *Life* article by William C. Bullitt.[39] American blunders, Bullitt insisted, meant that Russia would "be able to mobilize the manpower and industrial strength of China and Japan for its ultimate assault on the United States." Wrong on all three counts, Bullitt's article nonetheless was hailed as prophecy by true believers in Chiang's cause.

It was ironic that the attacks on Luce's alleged influence were increasing precisely when the cause most dear to him was on the verge of defeat. Eric Sevareid of CBS, for example, proclaimed that Luce had won "in his fight for military aid for China" and attacked *Life*'s campaign on behalf of Chiang. The *China Weekly Review*, which appeared in Shanghai, published long letters denouncing Luce for alienating the mass of China's people.[40] The English-language *Shanghai Evening Post*, which was left of center but non-Communist, attacked *Life* for declaring war on Communist China. How, asked its editors, could Americans remain in China if the United States refused to engage in colloquy with the apparent winners?[41]

"Barring miracles," *Time* finally admitted, "Chiang Kai-shek was beaten."[42] Still, Luce refused to give up. He contacted Chiang, suggesting that the Generalissimo take personal command of the armies committed to defending the line of the Yangtze. Luce also advised forming a non-Communist coalition government.[43] But Chiang ignored this wise if belated proposal, for he wanted supplies and money from the United States, and not political advice from his chief American propagandist. Like Luce, Senator Styles Bridges still hoped to work a "miracle," so he sent an investigative team to China. The panel included former *Time* White House correspondent Eddie Lockett, who was now working for Tom Corcoran's lucrative lobbying operations.[44] The Bridges team returned to advocate the dispatch of MacArthur to China, *the deployment of U.S. combat advisers at the tactical level*, and the shipment of vast amounts of money to Chiang. *Time* agreed, even arguing that China's need for immediate aid justified calling Congress into special session.[45] Truman, however, ignored all these suggestions.[46] The administration had concluded that *Japan*, and not China, was the best anchor for U.S. power in the Far East.

There was no chance that China would receive the $3 billion it requested. At the U.S. embassy in Nanjing, personnel hurriedly prepared to evacuate the city. Embassy officials burned documents and abandoned fourteen thousand phonograph records but salvaged their supply of American beer.[47] Communist armies were soon besieging Beijing, where Chiang's sorry troops, *Time* reported, surrendered 276,000 weapons without a fight.[48] Another American official added that much American weaponry was never used, and "much that was used was either wasted or simply lost and abandoned to the Communists as the Communists came forward."[49]

A desperate visit to the United States by Madame Chiang contrasted sharply with her halcyon tour in 1943, which Henry Luce had orchestrated before audiences of cheering Americans. Now she was a supplicant holding no trump cards. Upon her arrival, Madame Chiang avoided the cameras for fear of further antagonizing an unfriendly administration.[50] Treated politely by a sympathetic but noncommittal secretary of state, Madame Chiang waited ten days for a meaningless audience with President Truman.[51] Madame Chiang's handlers consulted Henry Luce about her next move, but here too the results were disappointing. Luce, burned by Chiang's defeats and Truman's victory, scotched the rumor that attributed Madame's visit to his invitation. Writing to an assistant, a grumpy Luce declared, "I have no 'reaction' to the visit except to wish her well in her efforts." Ominously, Luce added, "I may or may not agree with what she says or how she says it."[52] Luce would soldier on for China aid, but he disliked losers and did not want to hurt Time Inc. by aligning himself too closely with a failed emissary. So when Luce was asked whether Madame Chiang should outflank the president and appeal directly to the American people, he advised her against such a futile move. Madame Chiang took Luce's advice because "she considered Mr. and Mrs. Luce to be China's special friends."[53] *Time*'s Manfred Gottfried contrasted the general misery in China with the figure of Madame Chiang, dressed "in a padded gown that looked as if it had come from Bergdorf Goodman."[54] Allen Griffin cruelly called her a "dramatic female" who belonged in a curio shop.[55]

Nationalist China was finished, Truman privately declared, and Secretary of State George Marshall agreed. The U.S. government could say so, and thereby "deliver the knock out blow," or it could "play along with the existing government and keep facts from the American people."[56] If the administration took the latter course, Marshall added, it would "be accused later of playing into the hands of the Communists." Marshall and Truman did "play along" with Chiang, they did conceal the facts, and they would indeed be blamed for losing China. Only later would Luce admit that "perhaps even a majority" of the Chinese welcomed the Red triumph "because it meant order."[57] In 1948, however, Luce spared *Time*'s readers such confusing truths.

Supporting Chambers

In 1948 Luce had endorsed two losers – Dewey and Chiang – and during these last months of 1948 a third disaster threatened to further tarnish *Time*'s reputation. With Cold War tensions rising, many *Time*-haters – unrepentant isolationists, liberals, Red-hunters – were gloating over the exposed presence of a former Communist in Henry Luce's court. The reprobate was Whittaker Chambers, who had taught Luce much about Communism.

A severe heart attack in August 1945 ended Chambers's reign at foreign news, but *Time* continued to bear his imprint. Chambers's salary rose to $21,000 a year for part-time work, and he wrote important cover stories. Chambers was also heavily involved in *Life*'s lavish *Picture History of Western Man*, which became a great success.[58] One notable effort involved an important *Time* essay devoted to Rebecca West's *The Meaning of Treason*. Treason, Chambers argued, was a "sin against the spirit," one that occurs when a person abandons God. He wrote as if he had experienced that torment, and many others, but his readers could not have known why.[59] Within a year, however, Whittaker Chambers would be bearing public witness.

Explosive testimony was reviving public interest in the discredited House Committee on Un-American Activities. Elizabeth Bentley, a middle-aged former Communist, swore that she had served as a courier for a Communist cell in Washington, D.C.[60] Investigators knew that Chambers might be able to substantiate some of Bentley's rather bold charges, but he was a reluctant witness. Why, Chambers wondered, should he jeopardize his family and himself? Soon, however, a HUAC subpoena left him with no choice. On the plus side, Chambers would be testifying before a body dominated by friendly Republicans: Karl Mundt of South Dakota and Richard M. Nixon of California. Still, Chambers remained conflicted and reluctant; all the years of secrecy and lies had left their mark. And betraying a Communist he had served and admired – and possibly loved – did not come easily to Chambers.

Chambers assumed that his public appearance, and the furor it would cause, would mark the end of his career at *Time*. He feared for his family's economic security, but in fact Luce was highly supportive. He had coffee with Chambers, who offered to resign. "Nonsense," replied Luce, "testifying is a simple patriotic duty."[61] So the self-described "short, squat, solitary figure" would spend months and more "trudging through the impersonal halls of public buildings," determined to tell his story.[62] On 3 August 1948 Whittaker Chambers entered the House hearing room on Capitol Hill. He exposed as an alleged Communist Alger Hiss, currently the president of the Carnegie Endowment for International Peace, and formerly a middle-ranking State Department official. Time Inc. had a special interest in the case. Chambers was its employee, and throughout his public career, Hiss had been a minor star in the Luce publications. Slim, youthful, and handsome, the Alger Hiss of the early postwar years looked like the kind of man who would be welcomed into the inner circle by *Time* – and he was: "In a class by himself [at San Francisco] was young, handsome Alger Hiss," wrote *Time*, adding that "the able Secretary General" was "relaxed and alert amid innumerable annoyances."[63] *Life* featured a famous photo of Hiss returning from San Francisco, replete with the heavily secured, precious Charter of the United Nations.* This same Alger Hiss, Chambers repeated, was a member of a Communist ring operating in Washington in the 1930s.

---

* Priscilla Hobson, better known as "Prossy" Hiss, had long before served Henry Luce as an office manager, chief researcher, and special assistant. She married Alger Hiss in 1928. Sterling, "The Luce Empire," p.15.

As far as Chambers knew, Hiss had never broken with the CPUSA, and this, in *Time*'s words, was a "shocker."[64] But Hiss denied knowing Chambers "so far as I am aware" and insisted upon refuting the charges. Given to depression and a sense of martyrdom, Chambers wandered about like a doomed man. He kept poison handy in case the world rejected his truths. At Time Inc., John Billings worried about the outcome, for Hiss seemed strong, personable, and decent, whereas Whit appeared to be conspiratorial, and perhaps unconvincing.[65] Luce observed that the Hiss-Chambers case had been "a pain and an embarrassment," and "[our] confirmed enemies, [Walter] Winchell, [Westbrook] Pegler, the Chicago Tribune, continue to beat hell out of us."[66] Indeed, Hearst's Pegler, a popular columnist, published a long, nasty, hilarious spoof in which he called the "backslid Bolshevik" Chambers a "fat-faced, vapid senior editor of Time Magazine, New York smear sheet of Fuey Pi-yu (in Chinese: Henry Luce)."[67] Walter Winchell was also at his smarmy best, as he avenged himself on the magazine that had tormented his idol FDR. "Gee Whittaker!" he scribbled, "Time Marxes on."[68] How, he later asked, could you get the Reds out of the State Department if you could not rid Time Inc. of them?[69] Defensively, Luce muttered that although Yale had "produced the liberal suckers," Harvard had turned out more Communists.[70]

Representative Richard M. Nixon, an ambitious young California Republican, aided by committee investigator Robert Stripling, decided to probe further.[71] Nixon, who detested Hiss for his arrogant demeanor, found Chambers convincing. Invariably appearing without counsel, his witness struck Nixon as an honest man. On 16 August Hiss began to waver, and he admitted that the photographs of Chambers showed a vaguely familiar face. But who was it? When pressed, Hiss still denied knowing Chambers, either by his real name or by his underground alias, "Carl." Finally, Hiss decided that he might have known the man under yet another name, "George Crosley."[72] The problem was that no one outside the Hiss camp could ever recall having heard the name George Crosley.[73]

Abandoning Chambers

At Time Inc., John Billings sensed that the tide was turning in Whit Chambers's favor. Luce and Chambers dined together in the middle of August, and the publisher came away more impressed than ever, not least of all because of Chambers's enemies. Liberals who were identified with the New Deal annoyed Luce, and they were the backbone of Hiss's support:[74] Eleanor Roosevelt, Felix Frankfurter, and Dean Acheson were in Hiss's corner. Representative Mundt touched another nerve in Henry Luce when he remarked that Alger Hiss had been a charter member of the anti-Chiang brigade in Washington.[75] Lee Pressman, an alleged Communist close to the Henry Wallace campaign, made the same link in a different way when he sneered that Chambers was a "Republican exhibitionist" who had been "bought by Henry Luce."

At lunch with his editors on 20 August, Luce decided that *Time* must support Whit Chambers. *Time* concluded that Hiss and Chambers had known each other well, and no "George Crosley" had ever existed. Chambers was, the magazine believed, a truthful man saddened by the need to expose a Communist he had once revered as a friend. "Mr. Hiss represents," declared Chambers on 25 August, "the concealed enemy against which we are all fighting, and I am fighting." Like Martin Luther, the would-be martyr added, "So help me God, I could not do otherwise."[76] *Time* hurt Hiss badly, for week after week the magazine portrayed him as cold, arrogant, slippery, and conveniently amnesiac. When Hiss, after some hesitation, finally sued Chambers for libel, Luce supplied Chambers with legal counsel in the form of Harold Medina, Jr., a young attorney working for the distinguished firm retained by Time Inc.

Perhaps out of compassion for his ex-friend Hiss, perhaps out of a desire to protect what remained of his reputation and keep his job at *Time*, Whittaker Chambers had not told the whole truth. Chambers had denied that the Hiss cell had been engaged in espionage; he feared that if he implicated Hiss in spying, he too would risk indictment. Yet Chambers finally decided to go forward, in part because he feared a perjury conviction. To protect himself, he would be ready to produce some explosive documents. The secret trove consisted of illegally obtained government documents that had been microfilmed or copied, along with material in handwriting alleged to be that of Alger Hiss.[77] In a deposition given in the presence of Hiss's counsel on 16 November, Chambers produced four pages of notes and sixty-five pages of typed documents. These were copies of papers purloined from government agencies, and Chambers claimed that the handwritten notes were in Hiss's hand. "Carl," as Chambers called himself then, was supposed to deliver the documents to a Soviet agent. But Chambers always liked to have an insurance policy handy, and he still withheld microfilm rolls of other government documents. He had found a pumpkin in a strawberry patch, cut it open and cleaned it out, and then placed the five canisters of film inside.[78] Alger Hiss would face ruin if these documents turned out to be genuine.

On 2 December HUAC chief investigator Robert Stripling subpoenaed anything relevant to Hiss that Chambers might have, and he quickly obtained the precious "pumpkin papers." Developed in a great rush, the secured documents were originals or copies of documents dating from the months before Chambers broke with the CPUSA. Chambers now told a fuller story, replete with testimony incriminating Hiss and himself in espionage in 1937–1938. Material from the "Venona" decryptions, made public since the 1990s, shows that Hiss had routinely turned over secret material to his Soviet handlers, perhaps as late as 1945.[79] Chambers did not know whether he would be believed.

Harry Luce compared Chambers to Hamlet and saw him as a tragic character. But Luce thought first of his company, and the confession of espionage greatly agitated him and his courtiers.[80] Within a few days, Luce and Billings, along with their amiable hatchet-man, Roy Larsen, decided to rid themselves of Whittaker Chambers.[81] Scrambling to occupy the moral high ground, Luce and his colleagues told each other that Chambers had deceived *Time*. But did Luce really think that a self-professed Communist active in an underground cell in Washington bore no taint of espionage? This naïveté smacked of self-deception, but, as in the case of China, Harry Luce knew what he wanted to know. Luce and his colleagues decided that the company would no longer subsidize Chambers's costly legal counsel. In addition, Luce insisted that Chambers assure the public that Time Inc. had known nothing about his espionage activities. In return for his cooperation, the company would give Chambers a generous severance package. On 5 December 1948 Whittaker Chambers, now a confessed spy and liar, offered to resign his position as a senior editor at Time Inc. For almost a week, the timing and circumstances of his departure preoccupied Henry Luce and the company's top brass.

These maneuvers required a face-to-face meeting of the kind that Luce hated. Worse still, his abandonment of Chambers reeked of hypocrisy paying tribute to Cold War politics. Luce genuinely believed that the nation owed a lot to Whittaker Chambers, but he also knew that by firing him, he was sparing Time Inc. further embarrassment. By 8 December, Luce had decided to force the issue, and he asked Chambers to stop by his apartment in the Waldorf-Astoria. When Luce arrived home in the late afternoon, Clare Luce could tell that some weighty problem preoccupied him. With a harsh command, Harry made it clear that the servants were not to disturb him. He then explained to his wife that Whit Chambers would soon be arriving. Their conversation, Luce added, would not be an easy one. Sensing the importance of the encounter, Luce wanted to discuss it afterward with Clare, in what might be called a moral postmortem. She was to eavesdrop and thereby play the invisible supporting actress in a one-act drama crafted by Harry Luce. Given her flair for melodrama, Clare Luce happily complied with her husband's wish, and she produced a compelling firsthand record of the event that transpired that evening.

When Whit Chambers arrived, an agitated Harry Luce escorted him into the library. The unseen Clare, as instructed, took up her post in the living room behind a door that led to the library. What she heard caused her to remember the conversation "more vividly, perhaps, than any other" she had ever heard.[82] Harry Luce poured cocktails, lit the inevitable cigarette, coughed repeatedly, and then got to the point. He wanted Chambers's resignation. Whit Chambers wearily reminded his boss of his longstanding willingness to resign. Luce, who interrupted people with abandon, cut Chambers off and insisted that he believed Whit's testimony about Alger Hiss. And Luce again acknowledged Chambers's great contributions to *Time*, where his revelations about Communism had enlightened editors as well as readers. Luce took another drink and was clearly upset by Chambers's pensive silence. Then, to Luce's dismay, Chambers asked why Time Inc. wanted his resignation at this precise moment.

Luce's blunt answer finally broke the awkward silence: "Well, goddam it, Whit – you told me you had been a *Communist*, but Jesus, Whit, you didn't tell me you had been a *spy*!" By Clare Luce's account, Luce was highly agitated, breathing in short bursts, coughing. Like a man who must overcompensate for betraying a friend, Luce accused Chambers of embarrassing him, of never having told him that he had been a "traitor."

Thus far, the "conversation" had consisted of Luce mixing drinks, coughing, praising, hectoring, accusing. Whittaker Chambers now had his say, and as always he spoke quietly. In a sad tone worthy of a disillusioned man betrayed by a friend, he gently reprimanded Luce. Chambers recalled thinking how important it was that a man of Henry Luce's stature had employed him, for *Time* could now enlighten the country. But Luce's comments about espionage and treason had disappointed him. By failing to understand that any member of a "Communist cell" is by definition a "traitor," Luce had shown that he still did not understand the concealed enemy against whom we all must fight. Worse still, Luce stood his ground, continuing to differentiate between Marxists or Communists on the one hand, and traitors on the other.

There was nothing further to discuss. Chambers rose, walked to the door accompanied by Luce, and then made one last confession: "You know, Harry, when you took me on, I began to have some hope for America." Chambers added, "I despair for it now." Chambers's melodramatic overstatement stung Harry Luce, but the next day he was busy editing Chambers's letter of resignation. As released by Time Inc. on 10 December, the statement absolved the company of any knowledge about Chambers's espionage.[83] But the circumstances of his departure left Chambers bitter. Soon after Hiss was convicted early in 1950, some of Chambers's former colleagues at Time Inc. wanted to rehire him, albeit in an undetermined but rather menial capacity. Chambers replied with some sarcasm, but the whole exercise was pointless, because Luce also opposed such a move. He saw no good in bringing Chambers back to Rockefeller Plaza, where he would forever more be a ghostly reminder of Time Inc.'s disloyalty. Luce therefore let a colleague give Whit Chambers the bad news, so once again the witness felt betrayed. Time Inc. was, Chambers complained, turning the "knife in the wound." He told Luce, "For your many kindnesses, I am grateful; we shall not meet again."[84]

When Chambers published his compelling memoir, *Witness*, Harry Luce wanted to break with tradition and publish long excerpts from the book in *Time*. He offered a hefty $60,000 for first serial rights. With some pleasure, Chambers rejected *Time* and entered into a deal with *Life*'s declining rival, the old *Saturday Evening Post*.[85] Nevertheless, *Time* hailed *Witness* as "the best book about Communism ever written on this continent."[86] "May God reward you," wrote Clare Luce, when she praised Chambers's "brilliant book." *Life* called Chambers a prophet, although it failed to add that at a crucial time he had been without honor in his own land – Time Inc.

A Bitter Crusader

Communism in China, Luce insisted, could have been defeated had U.S. policy been "other than it was."[87] For years, Luce, like his mentor Whittaker Chambers, had believed that Communists, leftists, and gullible liberals had undermined American support for Chiang Kai-shek. Now it seemed to Luce that subversion and espionage may have played a role, too. Maybe, Luce decided, Alfred Kohlberg was right, and treason, not gullibility, explained America's feckless China policy.[88] Luce also realized that the Hiss case could hurt the Democrats and perhaps lead to the exposure of the men who were busily plotting the demise of the China he loved so much. Bitter about the defeats of Chiang and Dewey, Luce began looking for culprits and scapegoats.

On the day Whittaker Chambers resigned, Luce spoke at Washington and Lee University, where he declared that Communism was "the most horrible conspiracy ever organised against the body, mind and soul of man."[89] He then called for its exposure and destruction everywhere. A few months later, Luce told Dan Longwell that Communism was "the most monstrous cancer which ever attacked humanity." He pledged, "We shall do our best, however feebly, to combat it at all times and all places."[90] Luce intensified his corporate crusade against Communism and considered firing *Life*'s Joseph Kastner because of a Red-baiting article written by Hearst columnist George Sokolsky.[91] Watching the spectacle, John Billings ascribed this Cold War "dementia" to the Hiss case.

The optimism of 1941 had yielded to a crusading negativism, as Henry R. Luce vainly sought a sign that America was "taking a vigorous initiative in the world."[92] Instead, Luce perceived a divided United States, confused and "uncertain of itself," a nation "dissipating its power, tragically, on a false and stultifying defense." By 1949 he feared a Democratic descent into socialism, accompanied by "a dose of backwoods 'fascism' and bigtown gangsterism."[93] In China Beijing fell to the Communists a few weeks later, and large crowds applauded the entry of their new rulers.[94] U.S. Marines sailed away from Qingdao, a port that nurtured boyhood memories cherished by Harry Luce, and the American Military Mission in China went out of business at the end of January 1949. Even Henry Luce sometimes admitted that U.S. intervention could no longer save Chiang Kai-shek. Luce would finally have to face a thorny question: How could Americans salvage something from Chiang's debacle?

In articles based on leaks from the State Department, the *New York Times* told how the administration hoped to use Mao as a "gigantic" Tito, blocking Soviet expansion in East Asia.[95] In line with this thinking, some of *Time*'s sources reported that the Soviets were *not* "scheming to bring about the downfall of the national government [of China]."[96] In fact, Stalin feared that a mistrustful Mao would become a renegade like Tito, but far more powerful.[97] (Tito had defied Stalin since June 1948 and, with covert Western support, had thus far survived.) Luce, however, was unimpressed by the musings of men he blamed for the "loss" of China.[98] Instead, *Time* declared the war that Truman refused to fight: "Not since Hitler had stood on the French coast had the danger been so great."[99] But Chiang on Formosa was not Churchill, nor did Americans equate Mao with Hitler. In fact, there was a widening divide between Time Inc.'s crusade and the more pragmatic approach to China favored by its rivals.

Debating the Autopsy

In 1949 *United States News & World Report* was sixteen years old; it had a small but devoted following.[100] David Lawrence's *U.S. News* was more aggressively conservative than *Time*, but unlike *Time*, Lawrence's magazine had since 1948 run a series of clear-eyed articles that were calculated to prepare Americans for the coming debacle. These included "Troubles in U.S. Aid to China" (5 March); "Aid to China: Is It Wasted?" (21 May); and "Facts that Dim Forecasts of Big Trade with China" (18 June). *U.S. News* recalled that the United States had supplied China with $1.435 billion in aid and loans since the war, but the Nationalists had not "crushed a single Communist force nor won a single victory of real significance." Chiang's thirty-nine U.S.-trained divisions were in a state of defeat and disrepair. His armies were poorly organized and trained, and American weapons routinely wound up in Communist hands. Meanwhile, *Newsweek* (in which Luce showed no interest) was appealing to the growing number of readers who admired *Time*'s format but detested its sarcasm, omniscience, and bias. *Newsweek* was conservative, but at least it seemed to respect the ideals of journalistic fairness and objectivity.[101] As early as January 1949, the magazine recognized the "Communist state in China" as a fact.[102] *Newsweek* also described retreating Nationalist troops as a wild mob, looting and raping after they ran from the battle. Finally, *Newsweek* painted an unappealing portrait of Chiang as a failed leader awaiting his salvation in a nuclear World War III.[103] To the Luces, these attacks merited a strong response, and for the first time, they accused "traitors" of manipulating U.S. foreign policy.

Clare Boothe Luce, who had served a term as president of Kohlberg's American China Policy Association, now published her much cited essay "The Mystery of American Policy in China." In the piece, she charged that as yet unnamed "traitors in State" had wrecked U.S. foreign policy.[104] And in this same month, July 1949, Senate Republicans leaked a minority staff report, "Communists in Government." The document alleged that the government had dismissed 8,881 persons as security risks. In the State Department, Truman's Loyalty Review Board and J. Edgar Hoover's FBI had supposedly uncovered twenty-one unnamed persons suspected of spying for the Russians, forty-five alleged Communists, and one hundred eight possibly subversive officials. Americans, however, were not yet ready to accept the implications of this explosive thesis.

When polled respondents were asked in the summer about the administration's handling of the China problem, their most frequently cited responses were "very poor," "U.S. blundered," and the like, but treason was not among the accusations.[105] And only 19 percent to 26 percent of those polled by Gallup wanted to send *any* kind of aid to China; almost double those numbers believed that there was "nothing we can do." Put another way, Americans usually agreed with Luce and *Time* when they blasted the State Department for its incompetence or worse. An equal number disagreed, however, when Luce and his allies advocated more intervention in China. This discrepancy meant that attacks on the State Department were more effective than pleas for aid to China.

Dean Acheson and senior staff sensed danger and moved to ward it off. In the spring and summer of 1949, Ambassador-at-Large Philip C. Jessup, a highly regarded professor of international law at Columbia University, directed the preparation of a so-called White Paper on recent China policy. Acheson's East Asia experts worked like lawyers building a case, as they assembled diplomatic cables outlining why the Nationalists had failed. The secretary would not yet release them, *Time* learned late in May, because the State Department didn't want to "bury the nationalists until they quit breathing."[106] Ultimately, however, the "White Paper" grew into a thousand-page defense of Democratic foreign policy called *United States Relations with China With Special Reference to the Period 1944–1949*. The first part of the report traced the history of American involvement in China. The second half consisted of documents used by the staff in preparing its history. These materials included the famous suppressed Wedemeyer report on China, for Acheson no longer feared Congressional implementation of its extreme, contradictory – and now irrelevant – recommendations. But at the heart of the report lay the cables dispatched to Washington by diplomats critical of Chiang and sympathetic to the Communists. The like-minded John King Fairbank thought that it showed that "we sought to foster a Western-style society in Kuomintang [*sic*] China, but in the end found ourselves unwillingly supporting just another third-rate bureaucratic despotism."[107]

Time quickly learned that the Jessup report "flatly and brutally" wrote off Nationalist China.[108] The battle was about to enter a new phase when Acheson released the report on Friday, 5 August 1949. The next day the *New York Times*'s large headline told the story: "U.S. PUTS SOLE BLAME ON CHIANG REGIME FOR COLLAPSE, HOLDS MORE AID FUTILE."[109] Internal Chinese factors, Acheson affirmed, had caused Chiang's defeat. In an angry response, a *Time* correspondent called the "White Paper" one of "the lowest of low points in modern U.S. foreign policy, the nearest thing to bankruptcy that a great power can acknowledge."[110] Luce's flagship also labeled the report a betrayal of Chiang noteworthy for its "eerie blend of fatalism and foolishness."[111] To Luce, the "White Paper" was a white flag, further compounding America's betrayal of its mission to China. For years, he had felt that thanks to U.S. blunders or worse, his beloved Chinese had "been taken away captive into the most hideous Babylon in history."[112]

Only weeks after the appearance of the report, Thomas Dewey conferred with Secretary Acheson and made a highly surprising proposal.[113] Thinking that Chiang's retirement would result in more American aid for China, Dewey suggested that Acheson discreetly send Harry Luce to Formosa, where he could nudge the Generalissimo into exile. Nothing came of the idea, however, and soon Dewey charged, "My Government has allowed 400,000,000 more in China to be conquered by Soviet agents."[114] Meanwhile, *Time*'s correspondents counterattacked, and the "White Paper" was their target.[115] Foremost among them was Louis Banks, who supplied a steady stream of allegations – some true, but unproven: Vice-President Wallace had nurtured the nest of pro-Communists in the State Department; Chiang's adviser Lauchlin Currie had been a Communist or at least a protector of Soviet agents; Owen Lattimore was a fellow traveler; and John K. Fairbank had infiltrated Communists and leftists into the OSS. The charges against Currie and Lattimore (in part) appear to have been valid.[116]

While Lou Banks collected his evidence, the Russians exploded an atomic bomb, and *Time* recounted that for the first time, Americans would know how it felt "to live under the threat of sudden destruction – coming like a clap of thunder and a rattle of hail."[117] *Time* saw the Soviet device as a wake-up call and soon demanded the construction of the "super," or hydrogen, bomb.[118] This new anxiety only increased demands for the heads of those who had lost China. But in the face of mounting opposition, Acheson coolly pursued his dual policy. There would be no imminent recognition of the Communist regime, but through various means Acheson hoped to pry Mao out of his virtual "alliance" with Stalin.[119] As an inducement, the administration would permit American companies to engage in nonstrategic trade – copper wire, kerosene, and the like – with the Chinese Communists. But domestic critics, as well as Chinese Communist actions, combined to undermine Acheson at every turn.[120] Mao would deal with the United States only if Washington terminated all ties to the Guomindang.[121] But would even that draconian move bring about better relations? Perhaps not, for in Mao's view, the United States was a hostile power scheming to strengthen Japan and overthrow his young government. In fact, by 1949 American occupation policy in Japan was moving in a new direction, one that Luce and *Fortune* had been promoting for two years.

7

Anti-Communist Allies in Asia

MacArthur and Rhee

Henry R. Luce looked at Asia through a lens crafted by American "China hands." Thus, he was twice removed from the realities of life in places like Japan and Korea and Vietnam. It was therefore likely that *Time*'s audience would find itself acquiring a problematic, even tendentious, view of complex developments in Asian countries lying along the fringes of the young American empire.

Luce had visited Tokyo as a nine-year-old boy in the company of his missionary father. He returned in 1946 as a guest of General Douglas MacArthur, America's proconsul in Japan. On neither occasion, however, did Luce see much of Japan or its people. Like most Americans who had lived through the recent war, Luce disliked Japanese, who had spurned the Christian message. But by the spring of 1946 *Life*'s wartime "Japs" had evolved into Japanese. The Japanese portrayed by *Life* were obedient to – and even affectionate toward – their conqueror, MacArthur.[1] In a typical tribute to American-induced progress, *Life* showed Japanese women voting for the first time.[2] Overall, Time Inc.'s coverage of Japan stressed the need for an enduring American presence there. The Japanese, Luce believed, needed to be fed, demilitarized, changed, and protected. He hailed the Supreme Commander for the Allied Powers as the right man for the task. MacArthur, Luce thought, was "one of the greatest, if not the greatest" of American generals.[3] He had met the general in 1941, in 1945, and again in 1946, and each time Luce came away more impressed. His media praised MacArthur for his many achievements, which included uprooting militarism in Japan, encouraging free trade unions, and promoting the adoption of a multiparty democratic and antimilitarist constitution. MacArthur, Luce insisted, was doing something unique in history. His work, of course, might take a thousand years to complete, but in Luce's view, Japan was being turned into an ally forever bound to the United States.[4]

MacArthur liked Time Inc.'s coverage, for he shared Luce's fondness for rhetoric filled with patriotism, grandeur, and America's God-ordained call to defend far-flung ramparts of freedom.[5] As the general once put it, "Once the process of assimilation has been completed, the Japanese may be expected to adhere to, cherish and preserve this new [American] way of life."[6] However, *Fortune*'s love letter to Douglas MacArthur did strike one sour note. Luce and *Fortune* wondered how Japan would recover if the office of the SCAP broke up the *zaibatsu*, the family-controlled industrial monopolies such as Mitsui and Mitsubishi. SCAP's "crippling of the *zaibatsu* economic aristocracy" could be justified in a few cases, *Fortune* admitted, but otherwise, the magazine claimed, SCAP was stifling Japan with measures reminiscent of a New Deal gone amok. How long, *Fortune* wondered, would American taxpayers have to feed eighty million people? These doubts about SCAP policy reflected the influence of diplomat George F. Kennan, a major source for the Time Inc. media. Kennan had visited Tokyo in 1948, and he too was troubled by MacArthur's inconsistent if belated attacks on the *zaibatsu*.[7] The Japanese economy, Kennan argued, must be restored; otherwise, Tokyo might gravitate toward a Sino-Soviet bloc dominated by Russia. Japan's economy, Kennan added, would revive only if Japan secured access to the markets and raw materials of Southeast Asia.[8]

Fortune quickly became Kennan's messenger to American business executives intrigued by the Japanese market. Alerting exporters and investors to its potential, Luce and his editors urged that Japan be opened to American products and capital. More generally, *Fortune* was paving the way for the inclusion of both West Germany and Japan in an American-dominated trading and security bloc. By demanding both peace and security treaties with Japan – long before they were signed – *Fortune* influenced American business and policymaking elites. As Chiang's fortunes declined in 1947 and especially in 1948–1949, Luce and *Fortune* came to see Japan as an essential substitute for China in America's defense of the western Pacific.[9] Repeatedly, Henry Luce demanded more coverage of Japan; he often wondered whether *Time* had "met its share of this responsibility."[10]

By the winter of 1949 Luce was convinced that SCAP was failing on the economic front. In an assault that angered MacArthur, the April issue of *Fortune* attacked SCAP's "Two-Billion Dollar Failure in Japan." Sneering that MacArthur's "long suit" had "never been economics," *Fortune* condemned SCAP for having done "nothing to channel this natural [Japanese] obedience and good will toward America into productive works." SCAP replied angrily, accusing *Fortune* of misrepresentations "injurious to the position of the United States in the Far East."[11] Time Inc., however, stood by *Fortune*'s story, although its June issue did publish General MacArthur's lengthy rebuttal.[12] MacArthur artfully blamed others for the state of the Japanese economy and then boasted about the "encouraging progress" that it was now making. *Fortune*'s board, however, was unimpressed. The magazine again condemned the anti-business bureaucracy employed by SCAP. New policies in Japan, *Time* argued, could still redeem "the West's sorry record of failure and confusion in the East."[13] Although the Luce media continued to hail MacArthur as a great man (*Time* cover, 9 May 1949), their sniping at his policies irritated him. In October, for example, *Fortune* again ridiculed "SCAPitalism," an economic botch that blocked the exposure of Japan to competitive free enterprise. Once again, MacArthur's angry response made news, but *Fortune* stuck by its guns. To Luce, the near collapse of Chiang's regime and the dire situation in Korea made the creation of a resurgent, American-protected, and perhaps rearmed Japan an urgent priority. And in Luce's rather premature and heretical view, a viable South Korea was also vital to America's strategy in the region.

Troubled Korea

As early as 1942, Henry Luce and other American supporters of the missionary movement had found a Korean leader who embodied their hopes. He was Dr. Syngman Rhee, a Christian convert married to an Austrian woman. Along with Dwight Edwards, Geraldine Fitch, and other friends of Christian Asia, Luce backed Rhee's Korean Provisional Government and lobbied for the recognition of a liberated Korea as an independent state.[14] Portraying Korea as a friend of China and a victim of Japan, Rhee's supporters in the United States pointed to the day when two Christian neighbor nations – China and Korea – would enjoy the protection afforded them by American power. Roosevelt, however, feared that recognizing Rhee would antagonize more radical exile groups, so he merely agreed to support the independence of Korea "in due course."[15] Yalta and the Soviet incursion into Manchuria soon erected new barriers to the creation of what Representative Clare Luce called a "bulwark of Christian democracy" in a unified Korea. Many Koreans had responded warmly to the American Christian mission, among them a large number of Presbyterian converts. (During the Boxer Rebellion, the Luce family had found safety in Korea.)

In 1945, few Americans in government (or outside it) paid much attention to Korea. Henry Luce was an exception. The proximity of the Korean peninsula to Japan and China, and the incursion of Soviet troops into northern Korea, had provoked his interest. Hence, Luce and other friends of Rhee looked on glumly in 1945 as Russian troops occupied and plundered an already destitute northern Korea.[16] America soon found itself embroiled in a baffling situation. On paper, the Americans, along with the Soviets and the United Nations, were committed to creating a united, democratic Korea. Many Koreans saw the presence of U.S. troops in the south as a guarantor of their independent future. But did anyone really expect things to work out that smoothly? Certainly, Washington did not seem to know what to do. As *Time*'s John Walker cabled from Seoul, "Korea...stands as the first of the new problems in the Orient – the problems that suddenly confront us, without a clear background or precedent."[17] Koreans, who had cheered the arrival of U.S. troops, quickly grew disappointed with their American protectors. This aversion arose in some measure because of the ignorance of the U.S. personnel entrusted with the country's future. Upon his arrival, Lt. Gen. John R. Hodge, the American commander, described the Koreans as "the same breed of cats as the Japs."[18] His occupation forces came equipped with a geographical guide to Korea – published in 1905.[19] Despite Luce's interest in the country, *Time*'s occasional correspondents shared this widespread ignorance. One described the Koreans as displaying "extraordinary apathy and laziness," as people who had happily served as Japan's slaves.

The Allies had agreed to a temporary UN trusteeship for all of Korea, a plan that greatly disappointed Korean patriots. Worse still, the incipient Cold War had come to the Korean peninsula, and even the UN plan came to nothing. *Time* noted the "virtual breakdown in relations between the Americans and the Russians in Korea."[20] The Americans would not recognize Kim Il Sung's Communist Korean People's Republic in the north. The Soviets refused to work with the rightist groups gaining the upper hand in the south, and General Hodge employed local security personnel who once served Japan. Throughout the country, economic misery and growing political chaos and repression subverted earlier hopes. In Washington and Tokyo, however, strategic planners cared little about Korea. Nor did *Time*, despite the occasional comments by its preoccupied editor-in-chief.[21] The poor, divided country did not seem crucial to American defenses in the western Pacific.

Luce's interest in Korea intensified in direct proportion to the decline in Chiang's battered regime. Luce favored the establishment of an independent, American-guided state in southern Korea, a formula he supported early on for both western Germany and Japan.[22] Through his media – particularly after 1946 – Luce influenced policymakers as well as the public, and his advocacy contributed to the militarization of the American empire. Luce supported the authoritarian Rhee without reservation, and he worked to prevent Truman from abandoning him as he had abandoned Chiang. When Rhee visited the United States in 1947, Luce introduced the Korean dignitary to powerful Americans and cohosted a lavish dinner for him.[23] Rhee thanked Luce profusely for helping him gain the "sympathetic interest and understanding of so many influential people."[24] Suddenly, *Time* began to harp on the threat to Rhee from the north, where the Soviets were creating an army of one hundred thousand troops. The south, by contrast, was allegedly training a few "boy scouts," or a police and constabulary contingent numbering at most forty-four thousand men.[25] *Life* expressed worry about the two thousand refugees fleeing to the south each week and demanded that Truman build up and defend southern Korea.[26]

By the winter of 1947 the United States had virtually written off the UN trusteeship plan. Instead, the Truman administration intended to turn southern Korea over to a stable, more or less freely elected government acceptable to the UN. The United States would then withdraw the forty-five thousand troops stationed there.[27] MacArthur supported this withdrawal, in part because he hoped to redeploy some of those forces to Japan.[28] (Despite his later claims, MacArthur considered South Korea virtually indefensible.) Modest U.S. economic aid, Truman hoped, would then sustain the Korean economy for a few years. The South Korean forces would have to fend for themselves. Luce, however, feared that in this scenario South Korea would fall, and Japan would be threatened. Like Rhee, with whom he corresponded, Luce thought that South Korea represented a "frontline position" where Communism and democracy were locked in mortal combat.[29]

To Luce and to *Fortune*'s senior editors, South Korea might still have a bright side. If made viable with American help, that country could shine as a selling point for democratic capitalism in East Asia. Its progress and prosperity, Luce hoped, would provide a contrast with the impoverished north and would foster confidence in American ideals. Some State Department officials agreed, but the administration needed to be persuaded.[30] In pursuit of Luce's goals, *Fortune*, which reached important elements of the foreign and American business elites, became a fervent crusader for a huge $540 million Korea aid plan currently under discussion in the Congress.[31] Some progress could be cited. Elections were held in May 1948, and, thanks to a leftist boycott, Rhee's faction won a majority. The UN General Assembly promptly recognized Rhee's Republic of Korea (ROK) and authorized its rule in South Korea. In December, the world body called for the prompt withdrawal of all foreign forces from Korea. Soviet forces began to leave late in 1948, and the last U.S. occupation forces withdrew in the early summer of 1949.[32] Despite these orderly withdrawals of foreign troops, the Korean imbroglio was not winding down. In fact, it was entering a phase of full-blown crisis and war. Neither Kim Il Sung nor Rhee accepted the status quo. Their foreign backers had withdrawn, but the Cold Warriors in Washington and Moscow could still pull some strings.

The Communists and their leftist allies refused to accept Rhee's rule, and a bloody struggle ensued. In one incident in Sunchon, Communist rebels slaughtered one hundred police and five hundred civilians; government forces responded by killing everyone under suspicion.[33] American witnesses saw the pile of corpses assembled in the police compound grow and grow.[34] But despite Rhee's brutality, his Republic of Korea remained vulnerable. A small U.S. advisory group remained, but its mandate foresaw only the creation of a lightly armed ROK force of one hundred thousand men. North Korea's much larger army, by contrast, was equipped with Soviet armor and artillery.[35] Through 1948, Stalin appears to have been content with the division of Korea, but his North Korean clients were clearly more militant.[36] As a result, the simmering civil war, massive repression, and the influx of refugees from the north caused widespread unrest in the young Republic of Korea.

Dean Acheson's Department of State wished to ensure the survival of the South Korean economy after U.S. aid terminated on 30 June 1949. After much strife, the Congress had finally appropriated a mere $60 millon, an amount that would hardly buoy the sagging South Korean economy. Much more aid had failed to save Chiang in China; indeed, he had fled to Taiwan, and Mao had recently proclaimed the People's Republic of China. Stalin now had the Bomb. In East Asia, from Siberia and Manchuria and Korea to Indochina, the balance of power had shifted against the United States and its clients. In December, however, Acheson and other U.S. officials stubbornly insisted that the ROK could defend itself against a North Korean attack unless Kim received Soviet or Chinese assistance. Acheson's statement, however, skirted the key question: What would the United States do if the North Korean army, fortified by logistical and air support from Russia or China (or both), crossed the thirty-eighth parallel?

Speaking at the National Press Club on 12 January 1950, Dean Acheson failed to place the ROK within the U.S. defensive perimeter in Asia.[37] He was trying to avoid being drawn into the conflicts roiling China and Korea, but Acheson's apparent indifference doomed a $150 million aid bill proposed for South Korea.[38] Three weeks later, a much more modest aid proposal of $50 million passed. At this point, *Time*'s fears suddenly evolved into unmerited optimism. In the winter and spring of 1950, the magazine argued that the U.S. Military Assistance Group in South Korea was creating the "elements of seven [ROK] modern combat divisions."[39] Worse still, *Time* prophesied on 12 June that North Korea could not conquer the south "without heavy reinforcements."[40] But what if the north did strike? Luce and his coterie of Rhee backers could only look on in dismay. MacArthur had already decided that South Korea was more or less indefensible, and Acheson wanted the UN to handle any future Korean crisis. Stalin and Kim might reasonably conclude that if attacked, Syngman Rhee would have to fight alone.[41]

Saving French Indochina

The French, who were fighting to hold Indochina, were reaching a different conclusion. The ever hotter Cold War could only accelerate American efforts on their behalf. This expectation would not have been reasonable a few years earlier, despite growing American acquiescence in French control of Indochina.

Shortly before his death, a weary President Roosevelt commented, "I would agree to France retaining these colonies [in Indochina] with the proviso that independence was the ultimate goal." A pattern quickly emerged: The United States would support the French retention of Indochina in return for vague promises of independence.[42] True to form, France later recognized a "Free State of Vietnam," a concoction that was neither free, nor a state, nor Vietnamese. Through long years, the United States would support the French effort in Indochina. This alliance would not be a happy one, for as Time Inc.'s readers soon learned, the news from Vietnam was discouraging. On 22 October 1945 *Life*'s "Revolt in Saigon" told how "Annamites" (Vietnamese) had assassinated Lt. Col. Peter A. Dewey after mistaking the head of the OSS mission in Saigon for a French officer.[43] Like Lt. Col. Dewey, U.S. policy and its apologist Time Inc. were trapped between the designs of a colonial power and the aspirations of a subject people. The French were deploying American equipment, but *Time* still insisted that America was not fighting Vietnamese nationalism.[44] Referring to the "explosive Indo-China situation," *Time* piously advocated the creation of a semiautonomous Indochina within the French Union.

Like American policymakers, Henry R. Luce spent a lot of time searching for a non-Communist alternative to Ho Chi Minh – labeled a "Mongoloid Trotsky" in the pages of *Time*. But if forced to choose between colonialism and a Communist-led nationalism, Luce, like the U.S. government, would opt for the former. As a result, by 1947 *Time* emerged as the most influential proponent in the media of massive support for the anti-Communist cause in Indochina. Luce would stay this course for the last twenty years of his life. Before many Americans cared at all about Indochina, Luce tutored millions of his readers on the need to block the advance of Communism in Southeast Asia. By the end of 1946, the war in Indochina was raging. In covering this conflict, Time Inc. allowed ideology and propaganda to trump the cabled information available to *Time*'s editors in New York City. Correspondent Robert Sherrod soon learned this, to his dismay.

Around New Year's Day 1947, *Time*'s Bob Sherrod boarded a noisy C-47 and made the five-hour flight from Hong Kong to Vietnam. Within days, he had decided that Indochina was "the sickest part of ailing Asia today."[45] Sherrod added, "Here the revolution of the coloured man against his white masters is at its most violent." He also warned New York that Ho, who commanded vast popular support and a strong guerrilla army, would prevail in his battle against one hundred thousand French troops. However, Sherrod appended a more hopeful scenario. With some outside (American?) help, a Vietnam liberated from the French yoke would be able to govern itself and might not be hostile to the West.[46] Like Theodore H. White and John Hersey before him, however, Sherrod quickly found that his editors discarded such heretical thoughts. To Luce and his senior editors, a mere reporter was ill equipped to challenge their certainties about Indochina and its place in the looming struggle for the globe. Backed by a small army of checkers and researchers, *Time* became increasingly ardent in embracing the French cause.

Time, relying upon a much tested device, would admit that news from Indochina was a very mixed bag – before it explained away the most unpleasant facts. The magazine, for example, freely admitted that despite their tanks and planes, the French forces often found themselves isolated in besieged garrisons. Their "native" auxiliary forces were virtually worthless. The rebels shelled cities and then disappeared, only to ambush French patrols chasing them into fortified villages hidden deep within harsh mountain terrain. *Time* even alluded to the numerical superiority of War Minister Vo Nguyen Giap's Vietminh, an alarming fact in a guerrilla war.[47] Nineteen forty-seven was a very bad year for Indochina, and Henry Luce needed to come up with a response to the growing pessimism about a remote Cold War battleground.

Luce found his chosen instrument in the person of William Christian Bullitt, a presumed expert on France and, by proxy, on French Indochina. In December 1947 Bullitt published a heavily promoted article on the war for *Life* magazine. At first blush, the article seemed realistic, even heretical. Bullitt mentioned the low morale of the French troops and compared the Vietminh to the American farmers who stood their ground at Lexington and Concord. He admitted that millions of Vietnamese supported Ho, an "intelligent, completely selfless" man "endowed with great personal charm."[48] Like Luce, Bullitt knew that the French colonialists were selfish, privileged – and detested. He too hoped for

Vietnamese independence within the French Union. Then Bullitt, helped along by Luce and other editors, reached conclusions that defied his own bleak analysis. He insisted that Ho's victory would lead to "a replacement of the yoke of France by the terrible yoke of Stalin." To banish this nightmare, Bullitt advocated the creation of a U.S.-backed East Asia security pact, one calculated to save China and all of Southeast Asia. As Bullitt told a Senate committee, the United States needed to spend billions on saving Asia. Furthermore, if the French failed, "the U.S. should perhaps take a hand in the matter."

William Bullitt had outlined – and Luce had accepted – the strategy that would later involve the United States in Vietnam. In 1948, however, Americans refused to intervene militarily in China, much less in Vietnam. In the words of a scholar familiar with Indochina, "The United States had neither prepared itself to fill the vacuum, nor did it appear ready to accept the native nationalisms of various political hues which were emerging in the region."[49] In fact, government experts differed among themselves. An unidentified State Department official told his friend John Melby, "I watch the fat stew in the fire of Indochina from a distance." He added, "Sooner or later, John, we're going to do something about that place."[50] On the other side, Consul General George H. Abbott opposed the incipient alliance with France against Vietnamese nationalism. He felt that a free Vietnam, fearing China, would curry favor with the United States. Ultimately, Abbott concluded, the Vietnamese would long remember the American role during their war for independence. He feared that American policy might drive a victorious revolution into the arms of Stalin. Some support for Abbott's position could be found in the pages of *Fortune*. Written for the sophisticated business audience that Luce most respected, *Fortune* acknowledged that the Vietminh appealed to non-Communist, nationalist Vietnamese.[51] Emperor Bao Dai was a "former playboy" with "little popular support." *Fortune* even granted that Ho "could become south Asia's Tito." Soon, however, such heresies disappeared from the pages of Time Inc.'s magazines. Faced with Washington's indecision – aid to France coupled with nonintervention in Indochina – Luce and his editors decided to raise the stakes and tip the balance in favor of more direct intervention.

The situation in Indochina was dire. On paper, a "State of Vietnam" was emerging within the French Union. Led by men acceptable or beholden to France, this entity confronted an economy in shambles. Total exports were less than half what they had been in 1937.[52] Before the war, Indochina had exported 1.5 million tons of rice; in 1948 that figure shrank to about 150,000 tons. *Time* responded by following Bullitt in advocating the creation of a regional bloc supported by American dollars.[53] (In its view, "democratic American tutelage" in the Philippines was a good model for the region.)[54] And there were other good reasons for intervention: Indochina was surrounded by countries of economic and strategic importance to the West. Southeast Asia exported 97 percent of the world's natural rubber and 53 percent of its tin.[55] In addition, Luce believed, the new "Red China" must be contained along the periphery of Southeast Asia.

Communist China

The People's Republic of China (PRC) was proclaimed on 1 October 1949, and the next day the Soviet Union recognized the new state.[56] The State Department's three-person special committee on China prepared to examine the policy choices confronting the United States in East Asia. On 6–8 October the committee consulted with twenty-four China experts.[57] *Time* was highly suspicious of the resulting reports. Unlike most of the experts, it wrote off the PRC as a Soviet-style dictatorship and compared the Sino-Soviet partnership to the old Rome-Berlin Axis.[58] *Time*'s Jack Beal confirmed his editors' suspicions. Most of State's consultants Beal cabled – including John Fairbank and Owen Lattimore – favored extending eventual diplomatic recognition to the PRC. In fact, Fairbank had argued that a refusal to recognize Communist China would result in the termination of the American presence in China.[59] He also played the Soviet card, claiming that hostility toward the PRC would only "give Moscow an unearned victory."[60] Other arguments, such as the need to maintain listening posts in China, ran along similar lines.[61] George Kennan, for example, spoke in favor of a policy calculated to exacerbate tensions between Mao and Stalin.[62] Kennan appealed to James Shepley for support, but Luce, and not Shepley, made China policy at Time Inc.[63] And events in China only made him reaffirm old certitudes.

The fate of Henry Luce's beloved China philanthropies was highly uncertain throughout 1949. Some of United Service to China's sources praised the Marxist leaders as visionaries, although skeptics described them more accurately as anti-Christian and totalitarian.[64] Although the young PRC did not interfere with most USC-supported projects, it did put Madame Sun, a longtime ally of Yan'an, in charge of all relief work in China. USC endorsed the strategy of continuing its work in China, but late in 1949 B. A. Garside told Luce that the charity's situation was rapidly deteriorating.[65] At home, only five to ten thousand donors remained loyal to United Service, and one hundred seventy-five thousand former contributors donated nothing in 1949.[66] It was easy to see why. On 4 August the Yale-in-China medical college at Changsha fell into Communist hands. Worse, the director of the medical college praised the Communist regime and reassured its American friends.[67] Other optimists claimed that religious freedom still prevailed in the Christian colleges; some of them boasted that student registration was at nearly normal levels. But darker tidings soon changed the picture. Students were forced to attend mass meetings organized by the Communists; they also had to endure Marxist indoctrination.[68] Soon, an angry Harry Luce wondered why he should finance colleges that were teaching Communism.[69] In fact, the Chinese Communists were anti-Christian and xenophobic and were soon engaged in a cultural struggle against Americans. A year later, United Service to China finally closed its doors. Luce and other supporters of the missionary movement worked to reestablish Yali's Changsha campus as New Asia College in Kowloon, Hong Kong. Despite this achievement, Luce's mood grew darker. The collapse of the American mission to mainland

China left him furious at an administration that had "lost" China to a band of godless men.

With each passing day, Dean Acheson and the other men who had "lost" China became bigger targets for Luce and the China lobby. Jerome Holloway, who had served as American consul general in Shanghai, put it well when he observed, "The Republicans, having lost the '48 election, decided to win the Chinese revolution instead."[70] Within the GOP, the China bloc was growing stronger, and the bipartisan wing was diminished in strength. With Vandenberg ailing, Walter Judd, Styles Bridges, William Knowland, and their allies took the offensive and maintained their momentum for three years.[71] Henry Luce was their guide and their mouthpiece. When Acheson responded that U.S. intervention in Asia would make the country look "imperialistic," Luce exploded. "Bosh and drivel," he snarled. The Chinese people, he knew, loved Americans, and if he, Harry Luce, helped by a few good Marines, had been in charge of China policy, "China would not now be Communist."[72]

The anti-Communist consensus that Henry Luce had helped to sell to the public made possible the bipartisan foreign policy advocated by Marshall and Vandenburg – in Europe. In China, by contrast, collaboration had never been the order of the day; so the Democrats could scarcely evade some of the responsibility for Communist advances from Manchuria and mainland China to Korea and Vietnam. More grist for Luce's mill came in January 1950, with the impending announcement of a Sino-Soviet treaty. Mao was clearly no Tito; once again, Dean Acheson had failed in Asia.[73] On the other hand, politics was never far from Luce's mind, and here he spied hope. Thinking ahead, he felt that China might become a trump card in his ongoing campaign to discredit and topple Truman and Acheson. But who would play the card? Taft, Luce was certain, was unelectable. Dewey had been twice defeated, and the party was still divided between troglodyte isolationists and East Coast internationalists. Who would salvage something from the wreckage of America's policies in East Asia?

A Harder Line on Dissent

Henry Luce's anti-Communism was principled, but his commitment to the Republican cause sometimes introduced an element of expediency into the mix. Much of the time, *Time* shared the sentiments of actor Ronald Reagan when the president of the Screen Actors Guild said that he hoped that "We never are prompted by fear of Communism into compromising any of our democratic principles."[74] The Luce magazines freely criticized J. Edgar Hoover's sacrosanct FBI, and *Time* even wondered whether the FBI was a "budding Gestapo."[75] *Life* attacked Truman's loyalty boards for denying to the accused the right of cross-examination of secret witnesses.[76] *Life* also opposed the Mundt-Nixon bill, which would have effectively driven the CPUSA underground.[77] The magazine added that employers were not "obliged to fire Communists and should not concert to do so." Time Inc. wanted to identify Communists in sensitive jobs, but it would prosecute only those who had violated the Smith Act or other laws of the land.[78] In covering the Peekskill, New York, affair, where in 1949 state troopers and veterans beat up Communists and their allies in the Civil Rights Congress, *Time* condemned the riot as "misguided patriotism and senseless hooliganism."[79]

Luce rebuffed Red-hunters who complained when one of his magazines published a picture of an American eagle designed by an alleged fellow traveler. "We have not yet," Luce huffed, "adopted a policy of suppressing all news of purely artistic achievement by people who are deficient in political understanding."[80] But even as Luce and Time Inc. defended some civil liberties, they trampled others underfoot. Roy Larsen, president of Time Inc., courageously denounced violations of due process in the case of a blacklisted left-wing actress who resided in his own Fairfield County.[81] But this same Roy Larsen helped to pressure *Collier's* magazine into killing a critical essay on *Time* written by leftist media critic A. J. Liebling. Later, Larsen, working behind the scenes with the FBI, conspired to block the publication of a manuscript written by a leftist former Time Incer named Dorothy Sterling.*

The first inside story of Time Inc.'s editorial bias and operations, Sterling's proposed book was highly critical of Luce's ardent anti-Communism. Her manuscript was, however, well documented, and it profited from countless hours of interviews with former and current Time. Incers Agents and publishers invariably expressed interest; then, for reasons unclear to Dorothy Sterling, they declined to publish it. In fact, the FBI, energized by Roy Larsen, made sure that prospective publishers learned about Sterling's radical past.[†] Like Sterling, many other leftists resigned from a company where they were not wanted. For years, "progressive" ex-employees came to John Billings, who provided them with cautious letters attesting to their good work.[82] Seeing these once arrogant left-wingers beg and squirm gave him pleasure. Writing about one supplicant, Billings could not resist a smirk: "When the Revolution comes, I trust he will save me from summary execution."[83] This Cold War demanded conformity on all fronts, including sexual ones. Luce and Billings were concerned about certain rumors but finally decided that the company was free of homosexuals – except for unnamed alleged lesbians working at *Fortune*.[84]

Communism remained the great enemy, and Luce constantly worried about America's inadequate defenses. In the middle of January 1950 he rushed to Washington, where he conferred with both the secretary of national defense and the Joint Chiefs of Staff.[85] Dissatisfied with his briefings, Luce subsequently expressed his fear that the Soviets might soon sweep to the English Channel.

---

* Luce had declared in 1948 that Roy Larsen "made all idealistic projects practical and profitable" (DJSB, 15 March 1948). Behind his affable manner, however, Larsen was ever on the prowl for Communist activity directed at Time Inc. He saw this work as part of his main task – to protect the reputation of the company.
† Although she pursued a highly successful literary career, Sterling's manuscript on Time Inc. sits unread in a dusty carton in Eugene, Oregon. It bears silent witness to Time Inc.'s spotty record on the First Amendment.

Time derided Secretary Louis Johnson's $13 billion budget and other spending cuts in general as "foolish economy policies in national defense."[86] Indeed, Luce and his editors worried about atomic bombs falling on New York City. Maybe, cracked John Billings, Time Inc. should relocate to a "barn outside Indianapolis."[87] He also asked, "Is this 1939 – or 1941 all over again?" World War II–era analogies soon peppered *Time*'s pages: Munich and appeasement (Chamberlain then, Acheson now) and beleaguered islands (England then, Formosa today). In response, Luce mulled new proposals: total mobilization; higher taxes; bomb shelters. But was the public ready for such drastic measures?[88] Luce was not sure, but he had clearly tired of containment. Instead, he argued that winning the Cold War was the only way of preventing World War III. Luce began to think more about liberating Europe from Communism. He sat on the national council of the Crusade for Freedom, which was an arm of the CIA-funded National Committee for a Free Europe. Luce's longtime colleague C. D. Jackson chaired this group.[89] And Luce confidant Allen Grover joined the board of the American Committee for the Liberation of the Peoples of Russia.[90] His company's alliance with the U.S. intelligence community bothered Billings, but Luce brushed aside his concerns. In Luce's view, this new ideology of liberation would one day return the Republicans to power – and win the Cold War in Europe and Asia.

On 21 January 1950 a jury in New York found Alger Hiss guilty on two counts of perjury, and he was sentenced to serve five years in a federal prison. Right after the Hiss conviction came the arrest and confession of Klaus Emil Julius Fuchs. German-born, the Communist Fuchs had helped to build atomic bombs in both the United States and Great Britain – while betraying some of their vital secrets to the Soviet Union.[91] Luce and his colleagues in both the liberation camp and the China lobby felt vindicated. Finally, the tie between bad policy and treason had been knotted, and the Democrats stood accused. Within hours of the Hiss conviction, Senator Bridges asked whether Hiss was "representing Stalin when he stood at Roosevelt's elbow at Yalta."[92] Acheson only played into the hands of enemies like Luce and Bridges when, citing scripture, he bravely declared, "I do not intend to turn my back on Alger Hiss."[93]

The timing of recent events could not have been worse for the Truman administration. Chiang's fall, followed by charges alleging the subversion of America's foreign policy and defenses, emboldened the China lobby. Luce and his editorial allies were soon asking whether the U.S. government had been the victim of – or a partner in – an immense conspiracy. One hitherto lightweight ally now weighed in with his answer, one possibly confirmed by recent revelations about Hiss and Fuchs. Suddenly, Republicans angry about the fall of Chiang had a new, self-appointed champion. The man whose attacks on the administration would soon disrupt American life was in some measure the ugly spawn of the "Who Lost China?" craze popularized by Time Inc. Henry Luce would ultimately reject this offspring, but he could not disclaim all responsibility for his birth.

McCarthy

Time's correspondents were trained to find anecdotes that enhanced the magazine's gossipy, insider tone. Not all their vignettes were suitable for publication, but even the discards shed light on personalities covered by *Time*.

One cable that could not be printed concerned Senator Joseph R. McCarthy, Republican of Wisconsin. *Time*'s reporter wanted a memorable quotation, one worthy of a U.S. senator and former Marine captain. The *Time* man asked McCarthy whether he could recall his sentiments when the young senator-elect arrived by train at Union Station and first spied the dome of the Capitol.

Yes, McCarthy did indeed remember that day, and without hesitation he quoted the words he had uttered: "Shit! It's raining."[94]

Time had been contemptuous of Joe McCarthy since 1946, when the thirty-six-year-old former local judge and Marine ("Tail-gunner Joe") narrowly upset the veteran Robert LaFollette in the Republican primary. Chicago-based James Bell described McCarthy as a "good-looking, intellectually shallow ex-farm boy." As judge, Bell continued, his lack of intellect showed in legal opinions that "were nothing to write home about."[95] McCarthy, other sources learned, was a bachelor and a nonsmoker who was known to take a frequent drink. He was also an affable glad-hander who would drive miles to speak before a few farmers and a goat.[96] As for his performance in the Senate, *Time* dismissed McCarthy as a one-term loser. But *Time*'s stringers, having paid scant heed to the man, overlooked some of his essential characteristics. Joe McCarthy was a bully and a cynic who craved the fame that had hitherto eluded him in Washington. He would soon embrace the issue of Communist subversion in Washington – not because he believed in a cause but for base political motives. McCarthy's sudden emergence would baffle, and then tantalize, Luce and his editors.

In his search for headlines and reelection fodder, Joe McCarthy stoked fears of a hidden enemy beholden to Communist interests. Father Edmund Walsh, a dean at Georgetown University, provided him with some advice, for he knew that Senator McCarthy had already engaged in some local Red-baiting back in Wisconsin. Prodded by Walsh, McCarthy now hunted weightier game. He hoped to show that Dean Acheson had handed foreign policy – and China – over to Communists embedded in the State Department. New revelations soon fueled fears of a Soviet Union armed with atomic technology stolen with the help of American traitors. Many Americans, including Henry Luce, were ready to listen.

8

McCarthy and Korea

New Crises and Opportunities

On 9 February 1950 Joseph R. McCarthy traveled to Wheeling, West Virginia, where he made a Lincoln Day address before a Republican women's club. Waving around pieces of paper culled from his briefcase, McCarthy growled, "I have here in my hand a list of 205 [Communists] that were known to the Secretary of State . . . and who nevertheless are still working and shaping the policy of the State Department."[1] Even though McCarthy soon whittled the number of Communists down to 57, media interest intensified. Later, on the Senate floor, McCarthy revised the figure to 81. *Time*'s Washington bureau checked McCarthy's figures with John Puerifoy, the deputy undersecretary of state and the man handling security matters for Acheson. Puerifoy denied that the department harbored any Communists or fellow travelers. Relying upon the FBI, he told *Time* that the department had reviewed 16,075 cases. Two persons were found to be security risks and were terminated, and 202 others had been barred from handling classified information.[2] That made 204, close to McCarthy's fanciful figure of 205.

Puerifoy's denial did not bring the story to an end, for the Democrats referred McCarthy's charges to a subcommittee of the Senate Foreign Relations Committee, chaired by Millard Tydings. Charge and countercharge provoked lurid new headlines, which affected the thirsty Joe McCarthy like strong drink. But *Time* continued to uncover falsehoods in McCarthy's charges. His Communist number 9, for example, was David Lloyd; *Time* found that Lloyd had helped to found the anti-Communist Americans for Democratic Action. As a result of such inquiries, *Time*'s editors described McCarthy as an "irresponsible" politician.[3] And Robert A. Taft, who enjoyed a reputation for integrity, engaged in a display of hypocrisy that aggravated *Time* and *Life*. Taft insisted, "[McCarthy] has never consulted me about his course, and I have given him no advice," but the senator was less than forthright. Not only had he encouraged his colleague, but he also gave McCarthy uncorroborated data identifying purported Communists.[4] This behavior would not be cost-free, however, for *Life* early on implicated the Ohio senator and presidential candidate in McCarthy's "wild and irresponsible behavior."[5]

It was an irony of the times that amid the growing paranoia the United States was more prosperous than ever, and at peace. *Life* celebrated the flight to the green suburbs, and in town after town, new television stations came on the air. But nuclear anxieties, stories of espionage and cover-ups, and the loss of China fed fears that surfaced in various ways. A wave of flying saucer stories upset so many Americans that President Truman had to address the issue. In Washington, accusations flew more frequently than the saucers; the first post-Wheeling polls showed that about 40 percent of respondents described McCarthy's unproven charges as "a good thing for the country."[6] True, Luce and most of his colleagues were anti-McCarthy, because the senator was crude and disruptive. When arguing with his more liberal editors, however, Luce insisted that "Achesonism" and anti-anti-Communism were the sins that begat McCarthyism and were equally reprehensible.

McCarthy, the man *Time*'s correspondent had once dismissed as "midget fry," dominated the print media by late February 1950. Glowering and waving papers about, McCarthy reveled in the turmoil and the publicity. The pain of his flummoxed enemies only increased his pleasure. When rebuffed, the senator regrouped and made new charges. In fact, McCarthy was as gleeful as a child at play, especially when drunk, a frequent occurrence. When forced to modify his numbers for lack of evidence, McCarthy merely changed "Communists in the State Department" to "bad security risks." As Jack Beal wrote, "Whether McCarthy can be embarrassed at all is a question."[7] But if the Democrats screamed any louder about McCarthy being reckless, *Time* chortled, they would succeed only "in making a hero out of him." So *Time* continued to belittle McCarthy's accusations, but the "Democrats-are-soft-on-Communism" issue intrigued some of its editors, including Luce.[8] Nor was their hypocrisy lost on Washington staffers. On 8 March, *Time*'s Washington bureau advised New York that it "would be extremely unwise to write off McCarthy on the basis of the first hearing."[9]

McCarthy had moved from the minor leagues to the national stage, where *Time* was a key player. As a result, the magazine's smart-aleck tone began to irritate him. When McCarthy attacked Ambassador Philip Jessup for his ties to the Institute of Pacific Relations, Senator Tydings said, "We have some pretty important names on this list [of IPR trustees]." Tydings proceeded to mention the name of Henry R. Luce, but McCarthy quickly responded that it would be unfair to single out "the names of decent citizens who happened to be on such a list."[10] Unfair, but perhaps it would be wise to store this information for future use.

In the late spring of 1950, Gallup found that Americans, by a margin of more than five to one, opposed admitting the People's Republic of China to the UN.[11] Still, behind these numbers lay a salient fact: The gap between elites and Main Street had steadily widened. "Intelligent, well-informed Americans" surveyed for the Council on Foreign Relations favored "seeking some degree of

8.1   Vindication for *Time*: Senator Richard M. Nixon in 1950, at the time of Alger Hiss's conviction. (National Republic Collection, Hoover Institution Archives, Stanford University)

mutual toleration" between the United States and Communist China.[12] At the other end of the spectrum, many Americans neither understood nor admired the term *bipartisan*. Despite Acheson's hopes to the contrary, attacks on his China policy retained their explosive potential. Joe McCarthy, spotting a vulnerable opponent, soon labeled a professor at the Johns Hopkins University "one of the principal architects of our Far Eastern policy" and a pro-Communist.[13] Some days later, McCarthy grandly announced the discovery of the "top Russian agent" in the United States.[14] He did not identify this person, but on 23 March 1950, the name Owen Lattimore was leaked to the press. The wild charge made headlines even though their target seemed an unlikely spy: Lattimore was then director of the Walter Hines Pages School of International Affairs at the Johns Hopkins University.[15]

An expert on both China and its borderlands, Lattimore was also a popularizer.[16] He wanted to strengthen ties between "expert opinion and public opinion" and thereby influence U.S. foreign policy.[17] These goals had attracted Lattimore to the Institute of Pacific Relations, where he edited its journal, *Pacific Affairs*. Lattimore sometimes published authors whose Marxist views were openly professed. He also promoted Soviet involvement in the IPR, a policy that would later hurt him. More importantly, Lattimore met with Mao and Zhou during a brief visit to Communist Yan'an and came away impressed by the growing strength of the Chinese Communist Party.[18] Yet Lattimore remained a respected figure in Democratic circles close to the White House.

When Chiang Kai-shek asked FDR for an American political adviser, the White House recommended Owen Lattimore.[19] After serving in Chongqing in 1941–1942, Lattimore remained reasonably impressed by Chiang's patriotism.[20] Later, as director of Pacific operations for the Office of War Information, Lattimore grew more critical of both Chiang and his agents in America.[21] Subsequently, he condemned the Nationalists as corrupt and wrote off aid to Chiang as money wasted.[22] Lattimore also concluded that Mao's CCP had become "a party of moderation rather than a party of communism."[23] This was absurd, but on another point, Lattimore was on target: Yan'an, he concluded, was not taking orders from Moscow. Lattimore also condemned Chiang's government as one that was "full of crooks and militarists."[24] He heartily endorsed General Marshall's plan for a coalition government in China and favored Soviet mediation in this effort.[25] After Marshall failed, Lattimore warned Truman against all-out support for Chiang, whom he blamed for unleashing the civil war against the Communists.[26] Lattimore's writings and advice could only erode American support for Chiang.

After Beijing fell to the Communists, Owen Lattimore favored recognition of the PRC at the proper time, in order, he said, to make Communist China less dependent upon the Soviet Union.[27] He also opposed the militarization of U.S. policy in East Asia and its reliance upon allies like Syngman Rhee in South Korea.[28] Strategically, Lattimore argued, the main enemy in a big war would be Soviet Russia, not rural-based insurgents in China or Indochina.[29] The architects of Cold War conformity, however – including Time Inc. and the FBI – were suspicious of such thoughts. Jim Shepley, for example, had decided in 1948 that Lattimore and his ilk were behind the anti-Chiang propaganda circulating in America.[30]

Although the FBI's wiretaps on Lattimore revealed nothing incriminating, McCarthy would not be deterred.[31] He was receiving information from Alfred Kohlberg, who nursed an old grudge against Lattimore.[32] (Lattimore had called Kohlberg's charges against the IPR "crazy.")[33] Lattimore, moreover, supplied his enemies with plenty of ammunition, including his opinion that the Soviet model was attractive to awakening colonialized peoples in Asia.[34] In 1946, Kohlberg had escalated his attacks; he called Lattimore a Soviet intelligence operative and paid agent of Soviet propaganda.[35] He repeated his charges to various print media, among them the *New Leader*, the *New York Times*, and the *Washington Times-Herald*.[36] In response, a flip Lattimore joked about all the Russian gold weighing down his pockets.

In Joe McCarthy, Kohlberg finally found his avenging angel.[37] Lattimore, Kohlberg explained, had tried to turn China over to the Reds in 1944; homosexuals in the State Department were making sure that America withdrew from its Pacific perimeter; the appointment of Secretary Marshall in 1947 had been part of a Red conspiracy; and so on. McCarthy, armed by Kohlberg, was

8.2 Senator Joseph R. McCarthy, soon named *Time*'s "Demagogue McCarthy," 1951. (National Republic Collection, Hoover Institution Archives, Stanford University)

ready to strike. Oblivious to the danger, Lattimore was doing UN work in Afghanistan.[38]

Early on, *Time*'s Jack Beal, an apologist for Chiang, investigated McCarthy's charges against Lattimore, and he found Acheson credible when the secretary denied ever meeting him. Only twice and very briefly, Beal learned, had Lattimore been anything more than a consultant to the State Department.[39] Although McCarthy soon abandoned his wild espionage charge, the senator still insisted that (1) Lattimore was a Communist, and (2) he had helped to formulate America's China policy. Furthermore, McCarthy alleged, Lattimore had colluded with the conspirators in the *Amerasia* case.[40] But Joe McCarthy failed to document his charges, and *Life* attacked the senator for disrupting "private lives" and "government business" while shredding what remained of a bipartisan foreign policy.[41] *Time* observed that "McCarthy had said he would stand or fall on the case of Lattimore" and it "looked as if he had fallen."[42] Nevertheless, *Time* insisted that Lattimore had contributed to Chiang's fall by eroding American support for the Nationalists. This much was certainly true.

Time's slippery, opportunistic coverage enraged the man Luce called "Democrat [Tom] Griffith," *Time*'s national affairs editor, who declared himself

8.3 Owen Lattimore, often a Luce target, defies Senator McCarthy. (Library of Congress)

"ashamed" to work for Time Inc. But Luce, and not Griffith, crafted *Time*'s propaganda line: Lattimore might not be guilty, but neither was he innocent.[43] In the overheated words of Jack Beal, the professor was an accessory to "a crime so big it isn't listed as a crime and never can be proved: the conditioning of the U.S. into a frame of mind that permitted it to look complacently on an immensely important cold war defeat in Asia, that permitted it to watch the spread of danger with its instincts for alarm lulled by propaganda." "Was there," Beal asked darkly, "some unseen motive in this?"[44]

Lattimore finally confronted Joe McCarthy on 6 April 1950 in a packed hearing convened by the Tydings subcommittee. Of middling height, wearing glasses, and clad in the casual attire of the preoccupied academic, Lattimore cut an unprepossessing figure. He was unused to the klieg lights and to the noisy, smoke-filled circus where McCarthy played ringmaster.[45] But Lattimore had no intention of offering himself up as a sacrificial lamb. In his long prepared statement, the feisty professor accused McCarthy of unleashing a reign of terror, of being a fool or a knave, of shielding himself behind congressional immunity while committing libel. The witness dismissed the senator as a dummy of the China lobby, ridiculed his crazy charges, exposed Kohlberg, and stood by his statements on China policy.[46]

Jim Shepley and Jack Beal gave the round to the witness, who handled questions well. McCarthy appeared surprised, then amused, and even pleased by Lattimore's tone, but he skipped the afternoon session. There, Senator Tydings reported that the FBI had absolutely nothing on Owen Lattimore.[47] But Shepley was still wary of vindicating a man who personified the opposition to Harry Luce's China policy. McCarthy, Shepley wrote, was irresponsible and stupid; but because he was black, that did not make Lattimore white.[48] And Jack Beal's concerns only grew when admitted Communists swore that Lattimore had *not* been one of them.[49] Baited by Lattimore into dropping his immunity to a libel suit, McCarthy once again revised his charges. In the new version, Lattimore was merely "the architect of our Far Eastern policy" and a co-conspirator with the IPR against Chiang.[50] Although *Time* sadly admitted that Lattimore was – thus far – no Alger Hiss, the magazine kept the door open. Even if McCarthy had failed to expose Lattimore as a spy, he might be scaring the Reds out of the State Department.[51] Why then were *Time*'s editors and the Wisconsin senator on such poor terms?

Time magazine's unease resulted from its role as the voice of middle-class respectability. Eager to please both Main Street and Wall Street, *Time* mistrusted any kind of vulgar populism, and it had regularly ridiculed the demagoguery of HUAC's J. Parnell Thomas and Karl Mundt. Class and ethnic differences also explained *Time*'s antipathy to Joe McCarthy. His audience in places like Milwaukee was composed largely of lower-middle-class and working-class people.[52] Many of these Americans were Catholic, and often of Eastern European descent, so Roosevelt's "sell-out" of Eastern Europe at Yalta rankled them. Some of McCarthy's support also came from high school graduates adrift in a changing America whose prosperity eluded them.[53] The great organizations of the day – big government, the Republican establishment, big labor, big capital – ignored these people or derided them as "ethnics." Conspiracy – the refuge of the powerless and the envious – therefore had a strong appeal. Time Inc., by contrast, served the comfortable urban and suburban middle class, and unlike the McCarthy phenomenon, Luce's company remained largely an "Anglo-Saxon" preserve. True, people of all backgrounds read the magazine, but *Time*'s most avid subscribers remained upscale, sophisticated people, the heart of the educated middle class. Most of their letters to the editor reveal that they were not conspiracy-minded, nor were they the people once derided by Harry Luce as "flat-earth" types.

McCarthyism

In his effort to finish off Lattimore, McCarthy had found a helper in Louis Budenz, a sometime professor at Fordham University. Budenz was a reconvert to Catholicism, but he had once been a Communist and the managing editor of the *Daily Worker*.[54] Budenz was eager to make money lecturing and writing best sellers, and sensational charges could only promote his products. But how reliable was this witness, who was supposed to bury Owen Lattimore once and for all? According to the FBI, there was "no reason to believe that [Budenz] knew Lattimore."[55] McCarthy, however, countered that Budenz had named Owen Lattimore as one of a "number of Communists in the State Department."[56] When Budenz testified on 20 April, he did indeed describe Owen Lattimore as a Communist charged with infiltrating the IPR. Thereafter, Budenz continued, Lattimore propagated the myth that Chinese Communists were agrarian reformers.[57]

In response, Owen Lattimore again denied everything and made a convincing, if often wordy and confusing, case for his past defiance of the Communist Party line.[58] On 12 June *Time* agreed with Senator Margaret Chase Smith of Maine, who denounced her fellow Republican McCarthy for his "reckless abandon."[59] And on *Meet the Press*, even McCarthy admitted, "You can discredit much of what I've said" if unnamed files proved him wrong on Lattimore.[60] On the same program, panelist Frank McNaughton of *Time* exposed Louis Budenz as a highly fallible source. In response, McCarthy bobbed and weaved and dissimulated – but at times struck a nerve. He replied that it was *Time* (which he didn't "normally read"), and *not McCarthy*, that had first portrayed Lattimore as an architect of America's failed China policy. In fact, all the uproar over Lattimore appeared to have been misplaced; nothing had surfaced that had proved him to have been a spy or disloyal.[61] But if Luce was

8.4 Senator Patrick McCarran, whose investigations into the IPR found a supporter in Henry R. Luce. (Library of Congress)

right, then Lattimore was still guilty of eroding support for Chiang. In a statement reflecting a cynical contempt for constitutional rights, *Time* decided that Lattimore had "not been proved a Communist, but he had not proved that he was not one."[62] Henceforth, Luce and *Time* ridiculed both McCarthy and his enemies. At the same time, the magazine's opposition to measures of dubious constitutionality suddenly changed into support for the Mundt-Ferguson bill and for Senator Patrick McCarran's Internal Security Act.[63] By taking these positions, Luce the partisan could salve his conscience, savage his enemies, and vindicate his judgment.

Foreign Service officers fell victim, too. As one officer put it, "Some of our best people were dragged through the McCarthy grinder and had to leave the government."[64] Persecuted by loyalty boards as well as by Joe McCarthy and *Time*, dismissed, shunted aside, or exiled to minor posts outside Asia, the talented old China hands were becoming invisible. Jack Service, John Davies, and John Carter Vincent found themselves devoid of influence. Younger officers avoided the East Asia desks for fear that their careers would end before they began. At one point, a sardonic Teddy White observed that the State Department's real China experts could convene a meeting in Europe, where they served in virtual exile.[65] In 1949 and 1950 George Kennan vainly worked to ward off more attacks when he told Time Inc.'s John Osborne that the accusations were a "tragic thing for the country," for "we cannot be replaced – there are no others trained for our jobs."[66] Kennan added that the antipathy to Red China expressed by *Time*, and the demagogic populism of Joe McCarthy, would render null and void any intelligent attempt to formulate a solid foreign policy.[67] Of course, Luce saw China policy in less nuanced terms.

To Henry Luce, the first American priority in East Asia was Chiang's retention of Formosa. But Luce never thought in defensive terms, and he wanted to use that island and other points on China's periphery as launching pads for offensives culminating in the liberation of the mainland.[68] The advent of John Foster Dulles as a State Department counselor early in 1950 encouraged Luce, who spied the hand of Providence in this appointment.[69] "God bless you," Luce wrote to his friend.[70] Somehow, he hoped, Dulles would change the course of administration policy. But to Luce's horror, his friend was willing to accept the eventual entry of Communist China into the United Nations.[71] This last heresy – published in *Life*, of all places – was too much for Luce, who privately scolded Dulles for it. Without missing a beat, the supple Dulles assured Luce that he had misread the *Life* article. As he explained it, Dulles had actually made the PRC's entry into the UN dependent upon its *effective* control of China. If, he explained, America acted to bolster widespread resistance to the Communists, then the Beijing regime would not be able to fulfill that condition.[72] But Luce's hopes and fears were both exaggerated, for Dulles did not make China policy. Instead, Acheson shunted him off to work on the Japanese peace treaty, where he performed his task very well.

For the moment, no one was developing a new China policy; Dean Acheson remained fixated on NATO and the defense of Europe. This inaction in regard to East Asia was unacceptable to Luce. To him, the task at hand was critical. Until China's liberation, Luce believed, the United States and its Asian wards must at all costs maintain beachheads along Red China's long and vulnerable periphery.

MacArthur as Savior

On Sunday, 25 June 1950, Harry Luce and a few friends were enjoying lunch at his estate in Ridgefield, Connecticut. Time Inc.'s board had granted Luce his first "sabbatical," and he was eagerly anticipating several months of reading, travel, and – marvel of marvels – relaxation. But as Luce and his friends sat under the maple trees enjoying the balmy weather, they learned that North Korean forces had crossed the thirty-eighth parallel. Thus ended Luce's sabbatical leave before it began.[73]

Signs of the looming disaster were visible before that day in June: Thirty thousand Korean veterans of Mao's revolutionary war had recently returned to North Korea, where they added yet more strength to the Communists' superior forces.[74] And American diplomats and Foreign Service personnel (who often confided in local *Time* stringers and correspondents) knew that the Communist Chinese were moving more troops into Manchuria, hard by the North Korean border.[75] The Korean experts at the State Department, however, belittled North Korea's capacities, and the Central Intelligence Agency failed to foresee the invasion.[76] (A map of the Korean War appears on page 219.)

Like the administration, *Time* had no doubt that in Korea, "Moscow's guiding hand was present."[77] To some extent, this was true, but it was not the whole story. Kim Il Sung was eager to attack the south, and Mao Zedong had already decided that "the unification of Korea by peaceful means" was "not possible." As for potential dangers, it was Mao who convinced Stalin that the United States would "not enter a third world war for such a small territory"; the Soviet leader also agreed that the sooner South Korea was "liberated," the less chance there would be for "intervention."[78] On its surface, their logic was impeccable: America had not fought for Chiang's Nationalists, and Acheson had apparently written off South Korea.[79] Why, the Communists wondered, would the Americans reverse course and fight for "such a small territory"? As for Soviet policy, Stalin would support the invasion but would not enter the war. If North Korea was stymied, then China would have to bail out Kim. But Kim Il Sung and his North Korean comrades appear to have been the driving force behind the invasion. If it succeeded, they would be the big winners; but if the Americans intervened in force, then North Korea, China, and the Soviet Union would all suffer, probably in that order.

Luce and his editors wondered whether this latest Communist aggression was a prelude to a world war. But from Washington, Jim Shepley offered encouragement: "Truman," he cabled, "might be willing to make a bold move."[80] In New York an emergency meeting of the UN Security Council demanded that the North Koreans "withdraw forthwith their armed forces to the thirty-eighth parallel."[81] The president arrived back in Washington at 7:20 P.M. on Sunday, 25 June, when the news from Korea was grim. Despite divided counsel from his advisers, Truman quickly ordered that American "air and sea forces...give the [South] Korean Government troops cover and support."[82] He did so in the guise of supporting the UN, but other concerns carried greater weight. If South Korea fell, then Japan would be imperiled; Communist China would be emboldened to step up its aid to the Vietminh in Indochina and would perhaps attack Formosa.

To internationalists like Luce and Truman, the "lesson of Munich" taught that aggression appeased led to a world war.[83] So in response to the North Korean attack, the president instructed that more U.S. aid be sent to Indochina, and he strengthened American forces in the Philippines. More importantly, Truman sent elements of the Seventh Fleet to the Formosa Straits because the "occupation of Formosa by Communist forces would be a direct threat to the security of the Pacific area." In Taipei, Chiang welcomed the new crisis as the first act in the global conflict that would restore him to power on the mainland.[84]

Although Luce's relations with President Truman had been poor to nonexistent for six years, the events in Korea now mandated that he make a personal gesture. Luce was a deeply patriotic man with an ingrained respect for the office of the presidency. *Time* therefore praised Truman for having "denied Communism a rich strategic prize [Formosa] that had been in its grasp."[85] On 28 July Truman welcomed Luce and *Time*'s Roy Alexander to the White House, where they presented him with the presidential portrait that had recently appeared on *Time*'s cover.[86] Pleasantries were exchanged. But within weeks, *Time* returned to blasting Truman, and the president chortled over an article exposing Harry Luce's "private war" in China.[87] But on one point, Luce was the winner: He had steadfastly opposed America's rapid demobilization after World War II, and events in Korea vindicated him, for America clearly lacked combat-ready divisions.

The news from Seoul, the chaotic South Korean capital, remained grim. American officials spent days burning documents atop their embassy in Seoul before the Communists overran the city.[88] *Time*'s Washington staff reported that Truman had authorized air strikes on North Korean targets; and MacArthur was permitted to use "certain supporting ground units" on the crumbling Korean front.[89] Meanwhile, Rhee's troops retreated, often in disorder, and by 5 July Americans were engaged in ground combat south of the capital.[90] Even now, Luce also questioned the concept of a limited, UN-sponsored "police action" in Korea; the United States, he believed, should seek total victory.[91] Truman refused to dispatch a military mission to Formosa; worse, he requested that the Nationalist authorities "cease all air and sea operations against the mainland." And when Chiang offered to send thirty-three thousand troops to Korea, he was rebuffed. *Life* responded by demanding that the United States "reinstate Chiang Kai-shek as our full ally in the general worldwide struggle against Communism."[92] Luce responded to Truman's caution by privately denouncing that "bastard," Dean Acheson.[93] The secretary, *Time* charged, "gave Russia its opening."[94] Luce privately declared that "the State Department ought to be court-martialed."[95] "Someday," *Life* fumed, "a President of the U.S. will have to take a fighting stand against Communism somewhere west of California."[96] But later in the month, General MacArthur's journey to Taipei inspired *Life*, especially when he dispatched three squadrons of jet fighters to Formosa and encouraged Guomindang attacks on the mainland.[97] The trip riled the Truman administration, but MacArthur's appearance on Formosa paved the way for the arrival of a small military assistance group in Taipei.[98] Increased aid and greater strategic coordination were sure to follow in its wake.[99]

As in the past, information about China that undermined Luce's message rarely survived the editorial scalpel.[100] John Osborne, who had just visited Formosa, hammered the Nationalist army for its low morale, poor equipment, and general vulnerability. He also evoked the great fear permeating Formosa, where Chiang's secret police were ubiquitous and brutal.* Osborne also suggested that the first couple of China had stashed $12 million in U.S. currency in Peru. *Time*, however, was uninterested in reporting this news, and it ignored another bombshell: Former officers of the Japanese Imperial Army were training and even commanding Nationalist field units. What did appear in *Life* was John Osborne's heavily censored article "Is Formosa Next?"[101] This piece, which contradicted most of what Osborne had told Luce, presented the Nationalists as a threat to the Communist regime. Their army, *Life* wrote, "numbers half a million, and is better than any the Nationalists have ever put in the field." Not content with such faint praise, Osborne and *Life* saw a "will to fight in its ranks that is new to Chiang Kai-shek's armies." There were shortages – America's fault, of course – but *Life* concluded that MacArthur's ascendancy would right old wrongs.

At Time Inc. and in other circles, too, speculation about a wider war was rife; some reveled in it, and others feared the coming apocalypse. Senior *Time* editor Roy Alexander predicted that a general war would erupt in two years or so. New York City, he was certain, would be destroyed.[102] John Billings wrote, "We live in constant nervous dread of sudden war & sudden death." He added that this was "the great *curse* of the age."[103] Had he lived for fifty-two years, Billings asked, only to be burned alive in an atomic blast? He then breathed a sigh of relief, because he had convinced himself that his penthouse duplex at 1200 Fifth Avenue would survive an atomic bomb dropped on the city, in as much as Union Square, the presumed ground zero, lay about four miles away. And at one point, Luce naïvely thought that moving Time Inc. to Riverside Drive on the West Side would insulate it against an atomic hit. But this absurd plan had a second defect; it ignored New York City's zoning laws.[104] Roy Larsen speculated about moving Time Inc. to Chicago, and Dan Longwell traveled to

---

* Osborne warned *Time* against identifying a source critical of the regime: "We can't get the guy killed, you know."

the Southwest, where *Time* might publish in the event of an attack on New York.[105]

"We are in a new era, damn it," Luce often exclaimed in the early 1950s, and he insisted, "We are not going to end War without practicing it some more – and living with it."[106] Sadly Luce admitted that the Cold War might disfigure the world for the next "20 or 30 years."[107] But ever the visionary, he accurately foresaw a "post-Kremlin period" when the world would be "breathing at least a muted *gaudeamus* ["let us rejoice"]." To hasten that day, he longed for America's recapture of the "military initiative," and in an ominous gesture replete with nostalgic bellicosity, *Time* revived its old (1939) "Background for War" section.[108] Luce himself speculated about incinerating Russia with one thousand (or five thousand) atomic weapons. He also thought about presenting Stalin with a nuclear ultimatum. *Time*, meanwhile, informed readers that one hundred forty American cities were possible targets.

Time then explained how to survive the Bomb: Go to the basement or the center hall of one's home or to the nearest bomb shelter; turn away from the blinding flash; don't try to drive your car. *Time* said nothing about radioactivity, environmental effects, or genetic damage.[109] Colleagues like Roy Alexander vehemently objected to some of Luce's more belligerent monologues. And Jim Shepley, the resident expert on nuclear weapons, warned that the United States faced "more than an acceptable risk of losing" such a war.[110] Shepley also foresaw the day when mutual deterrence would be a fact of daily life. Luce was further disappointed when *Life*'s Ed Thompson reported that the American arsenal contained only a meager supply of nuclear weapons.[111] At the same time, Luce harbored moral scruples about launching a preventive war, so *Time* stayed its trigger finger.[112]

Henry Luce assumed that Stalin would be ready for a showdown in three years, and he advocated an expensive guns-and-butter approach to total mobilization.[113] Luce wanted to strengthen the country without unleashing the taxation and inflation that would kill the consumer boom of which *Life* had been the prophet – and beneficiary.* *Time* campaigned to increase the size of the armed forces by 636,000 men; to its joy, the Pentagon requested a supplemental appropriation of $10.5 billion.[114] Luce was pleased by a military budget that would soar to at least $50 billion per year, and he endorsed a new spate of coercive measures calculated to mobilize "our people and our resources." These proposals included federalizing the various National Guards, purging the State Department, curbing welfare programs, and registering all Communists in the United States.[115] In addition, *Life* demanded that the United States ally itself with "anti-Communists anywhere," no matter how unsavory.

---

* By the end of 1951 Time Inc.'s New York City operations employed 2,351 persons, and during the latest twelve-month period the company had hired more personnel than in any year since the war ended. Roy Larsen to David Heade, 18 February 1952, in the papers of John Shaw Billings, TLF, III, 164.

All that was lacking, Luce believed, was strong presidential leadership, a man who would lead the liberation of the world from Communism.[116] Among the tasks of the next president, he argued, would be undoing the "temporary loss of China."[117] But here Luce faced a problem: Americans feared a nuclear conflict or an expanded land war in East Asia more than they desired total victory in Korea – or China.[118] In August 1950, as UN forces gradually stabilized the Pusan perimeter, more than half of Gallup's respondents favored the idea of a mediated peace.[119] This attitude struck *Time* as pusillanimous. "If Stalin gets what [Indian Prime Minister] Nehru wants to give," scolded *Time*, "the Kremlin will have won a far bigger prize than South Korea."[120]

Luce saw the Korean debacle as a good campaign issue. This was also the sixth year of a presidential cycle, a fact that should play into the hands of the Republican opposition. And Joe McCarthy might have his uses, too: *Life* reported that "he may have been sinking into oblivion before Korea," but the senator would now be a hot issue in the elections.[121] Unless the UN and MacArthur turned things around, wrote *Time*'s Frank McNaughton, the Democrats were in big trouble.[122] And Truman's hapless China policy presented the Republicans with another opening. Although Dean Acheson had hoped to wean the PRC away from its Soviet patron, a *New York Times* headline read, "Mao's Ties With Stalin Seen as Much Stronger."[123]

Like MacArthur, Luce and his editors believed that Formosa must become a vital and *permanent* link in America's defenses.[124] But Truman had quashed MacArthur's initiatives on Formosa by early September.[125] "It is outrageous," responded Senator Bridges, "that the President has used his authority as Commander in Chief of the Armed Forces to prevent General Douglas MacArthur from expressing his views on Formosa." *Time* also suspected that Acheson was willing to appease Beijing, in effect telling the PRC, "Stay out of Korea, and you can grab Formosa later."[126] But MacArthur's prestige made it hard to defy him, so the China lobby made some progress.[127] Suddenly, *Time* learned, the Nationalists were finding it easier to buy arms through the Department of Defense.[128]

A Victory at Last?

With the front stabilized in Korea, Harry Luce finally took his long-delayed sabbatical leave.[129] In mid-July, moreover, *Time* learned that the Americans planned to counterattack in Korea, probably in the late summer or fall.[130] Public morale soared when MacArthur launched his brilliant counteroffensive at the port of Inchon. The Americans then moved rapidly inland, and the best North Korean divisions, which faced UN forces along the Pusan perimeter, were soon trapped and decimated. The once powerful enemy was reduced to a weak force of fifty thousand combatants. On 25 September *Life* excitedly published a John Osborne piece on Asian strategy.[131] The United States, *Life* argued, should prepare the Nationalist Chinese armies for "their return to the mainland of China." Unlike most of his contemporaries, Luce saw Korea as neither a police action nor a quagmire, but as one promising front in the war to liberate China.

After Inchon, MacArthur was authorized to pursue resisting North Korean forces with the understanding that only South Korean troops would approach the Chinese or Soviet frontiers. In addition, Washington warned MacArthur against continuing military operations in the north if China or the Soviet Union intervened. In October, despite threats by the Chinese Communists, MacArthur extended his offensive into North Korea and annihilated much of the retreating North Korean army. The UN, prompted by Acheson, now made it clear that forging a democratic, independent, and *unified* Korea was its war aim. With the acquiescence of MacArthur and Truman and in the face of opposition at the UN, Syngman Rhee planned to extend his government to all of North Korea.[132] Although its Washington bureau portrayed Rhee as surrounded by "yes men and old retainers," *Time* convinced many readers that the aging autocrat was a pure patriot.[133] Most importantly, he was anti-Communist.[134] In a cover story that autumn, *Time* again condemned those who would betray Rhee as they had Chiang Kai-shek.

As MacArthur's armies drew closer to the Chinese and Soviet borders, *Time's* Win Booth prematurely reported that Truman had won the Korean War. *Time* gloated that "Korea had looked like a sure thing, and it had blown up in Stalin's face."[135] Almost two-thirds of the polled public thought that the war should continue until the North Koreans surrendered, and an overwhelming majority thought that the war would soon be over.[136]

Henry Luce was already planning new counteroffensives against Mao's illegitimate state, launched from places such as French Indochina, and North Korea.

9

The Campaign for a Wider War in Asia

In the late 1940s, *Time* and its sister publications insisted that the French were fighting to save an anti-Communist bastion in a vital region – Southeast Asia. From the summer of 1949, in prose that was hard-edged and uncompromising, *Time* added a prophetic opinion:[1] The United States would have to become fully engaged in a region marked by a painful "retreat from imperialism." "If the U.S. goes into Asia," *Time* explained, then it would have to "go in with both feet, with money and authority, with the will to help Asians build their own strong, free societies and with the result of preventing them from committing national suicide under the strains of that painful process." *Time* wanted to "keep Asia's peoples in line, by offering them a better life than the Communist tempters."[2] Certainly, the situation there was grim. Sam Welles, a *Time* correspondent, visited Indochina in the autumn of 1949. He soon reported, "Ho and his [Communist Vietminh] forces can still strike almost anywhere." Welles also interviewed Acheson and reported that the administration had no coherent policy for Southeast Asia.[3] But changes were in the offing, and Time Inc. worked to accelerate the process.

Time's James Shepley and Bob Sherrod learned that the National Security Council now feared that a Communist victory in Southeast Asia would have global repercussions.[4] At the Pentagon, the Joint Chiefs of Staff agreed that Southeast Asia was "of critical strategic importance to the United States." Stalin's recognition of Ho unnerved the Department of State, as did Mao's determination to provide the Vietminh with substantial aid.[5] The United States, *Time* learned, would respond by forming an anti-Communist bloc in Southeast Asia, beginning with a massive infusion of direct aid to forces fighting the Vietminh.[6] *Time*'s Beal and McNaughton concluded, "This looks like the beginning of a bold line, weak now but foreseeably strong if assistance plans are carried through."

Misperceiving Indochina

Ho Chi Minh was a revolutionary who greatly admired the achievements of his Chinese and Soviet comrades.[7] Unlike the Communists who ran Eastern Europe, however, he was not Stalin's puppet. Ho knew that any successful insurgency must be able to draw upon the growing nationalism and desperation of the rural multitudes. His Vietminh tapped that resource, as had Tito's partisans in wartime Yugoslavia. But even when he asked for and received recognition from the heretic Marshal Tito of Yugoslavia, *Time* was unimpressed. "There is no indication at this reading that Ho is or will become an Asian Tito," its Washington bureau reported.[8] The triad of Stalin, Mao, and Ho girded *Time*'s monolithic image of Communism, one that made for a simple, powerful message: Fighting Ho meant stopping Stalin in Asia; the French struggle must be supported, even at the cost of ever deeper American involvement in Vietnam.

On 25 February 1950, *Time*'s Jim Shepley reported that the State Department favored allocating $15 million worth of military equipment to French and associated forces fighting Ho's insurgents in Indochina.[9] In March the U.S. Economic Survey Mission to Southeast Asia recommended a grant of $23.5 million in American economic assistance for the fifteen months ending 30 June 1951.[10] Shepley reported that the grand total might reach $50 million.[11] Most of this aid would be devoted to rural rehabilitation so that the West could win the allegiance of Vietnam's farmers and villagers. This emphasis reflected "lessons" learned from Chiang's failure and Mao's success.

Other assumptions inspired the interventionist mission embraced by *Time*. First, the United States, which was free of the colonialist taint, could succeed where France was failing. Second, Japan would drift out of the American orbit if it lost access to Southeast Asian markets because of Communist victories there. And third, assistance to Vietnam could alleviate the pressure on Paris so that France could contribute to the defense of Europe, as mandated by the United States.[12] Growing American assistance to the French in Indochina, Luce believed, "represented a crucial commitment by the U.S."[13]

But the situation steadily worsened. *Time* reported in March that the U.S destroyers *Stickell* and *Anderson* had steamed into Saigon Harbor, where "Communists" demonstrated and rioted against the American military presence.[14] Ominously, an unseen enemy attacked the ships with heavy mortar and machine gun fire. In the summer of 1950, *Time*'s André Laguerre toured the battlefronts of Indochina for six hectic weeks; his gripping reports made major news in both *Time* and *Life*.[15] Most Vietnamese, he admitted, were sick of a war that been raging for four years, and the French had failed to provide the village militias with adequate means of defense.[16] *Time*'s man had a close call, too. While Laguerre was in Saigon, a car raced by, and an unknown assailant tossed six grenades out of a window. One of them almost hit Laguerre, who noted that he would have liked "to have thrown it at Ho Chi Minh."[17] *Time*, however, defiantly concluded that the United States must be willing "to engage in limited military action for limited objectives."[18] Luce and his colleagues almost seemed to long for the day when Americans would replace the French as targets of an Asian nationalist or Communist movement.

Time happily observed that the staff of the U.S. legation in Saigon had grown from seven to two hundred "enthusiastic young men" who had "the right ideas."[19] *Time* hailed this expansion as proof of a "crucial commitment by the U.S." and crowed, "Washington now feels that the French position in Indo-China is a key to the entire area."[20] In August, *Time*'s editor-in-chief expressed hope that Indochina would become a turning point for the better, and not another "heartbreaking Chinese experience."[21] Always in search of a hero, Time Inc. had long sought a Vietnamese leader it could embrace: In Emperor Bao Dai, Luce had found his man. Since 1947, Luce and Time Inc. had been Bao Dai's prime propagandists in the United States. Indeed, the emperor enjoyed a better reputation at Rockefeller Plaza than he did in Vietnam. There, the Vietminh, and not Bao Dai, enjoyed, in the words of one U.S. diplomat, the "unalloyed support of the indigenous inhabitants."[22] Luce and his editors preferred to believe a high source in the State Department, who insisted that the emperor was as "ardent a nationalist as Ho."[23] Hence, Luce could take a bit of the credit – or the blame – when in March 1950 the United States recognized Bao Dai's "State of Vietnam." And in May, Secretary of State Dean Acheson fatuously claimed that the states of Indochina "now enjoy independence within the French Union."[24]

Late in May 1950, *Time* featured a lavish cover story on Bao Dai. Its caption – later borrowed by Luce's friend John F. Kennedy as the slogan for his presidency – read "The New Frontier." "The U.S.," *Time* boasted, "now has a new frontier and a new ally in the cold war." Its partner was Bao Dai's Vietnam, and the cause – freedom versus Communism – might soon require the deployment of U.S. troops, for otherwise "the U.S. might suffer another catastrophic defeat in the Far East."[25] In July *Time* celebrated the arrival of American warplanes in Indochina.[26] A few months later, *Time* reported, Emperor Bao Dai left his Riviera retreat and returned to Vietnam. He brought with him tennis rackets, cases of Scotch, guitars, and a red-headed flight attendant named Ester.[27]

Bao Dai was *Time*'s answer to Ho Chi Minh.

Promoting American Intervention

The gap between *Time*'s facts about Vietnam and its conclusions was growing wider. *Time*'s readers, for example, learned that a well-informed French officer admitted, "We can never win this fight militarily." He added, "It's just like trying to kill mosquitos with a sledge hammer."[28] This was a war of torched villages, of savage booby traps, of invisible enemies. One source told *Time* that it was like "pushing your finger into butter," for when you remove the finger, "you don't have much." *Time* itself sometimes contrasted Bao Dai's political weakness with Ho's strength on a terrain "well suited for guerrilla tactics." *Time* also knew that without the French, Bao Dai's regime would last two weeks. In sum, Vietnam was a "weak reed" upon which to lean; the U.S. alliance with Bao Dai, *Time* acknowledged, was as "ironic as anything in history," for a civil war could "only be completely won by the majority of a free people inspired by a national idea."[29] Lamely, *Time* offered suspect advice: The French should stop addressing Vietnamese men as *tu*, a form reserved for children, close friends, and pets.

But stronger American medicine was on its way to Indochina. In 1950 a Joint State–Defense Survey Mission to Southeast Asia visited the warring region. John F. Melby of the State Department, an old China hand, chaired the group, whose military contingent was led by Major General Graves B. "Bobby" Erskine.[30] On the surface, Melby and Erskine were optimistic: In a preliminary statement issued on 31 July 1950, the two men foresaw a time when the American-assisted French forces would "be able to play a very effective role in any circumstances (situation)."[31] "Much of the stigma of colonialism can be removed," Melby responded, "if . . . yellow men will be killed by yellow men rather than by white men alone."[32] He and Erskine also invented a domino theory, reasoning, "If Indo-China falls to the Viet Minh and the communists, the rest of Southeast Asia, with the exception of the Philippines and possibly Indonesia, will also fall." The Erskine survey therefore recommended that the United States provide $55 million in military aid to Indochina in 1951.[33] Within two years the United States was paying almost half the cost of the war in Vietnam. But privately, Melby was convinced that the Indochina problem was a "nightmare."[34] He bemoaned France's failure to create a viable Vietnamese state and fretted over the capture of the nationalist cause by the Vietminh.[35]

Although few American newspapers and magazines paid much attention to the jungle war, Luce's media insisted, "This [struggle] may be the ultimate political test in Asia."[36] *Life* led the way with major stories, most of which lauded the French for "keeping Indochina out of Communist hands."[37] These hands, of course, must be Soviet or Chinese, for as *Time* insisted, the "Reds [in Indochina]" probably could not win "without direct intervention by Red China."[38] But according to one well-informed source, "There is no great evidence of direct Chinese Communist participation."[39] In fact, Ho was a revolutionary nationalist who feared Chinese domination. Nevertheless, *Time* refused to see Ho as a shrewd and ruthless actor who made his own decisions.

In the autumn of 1950, the French position worsened, as the Vietminh destroyed an entire French fortification system. Ho's troops quickly forced the enemy to fall back toward the 160-mile perimeter surrounding Hanoi and Haiphong.[40] *Time* grew alarmed, for the French lacked the "will or the imagination to grant the Vietnamese anything that looked to them like real independence."[41] For the first time, Pentagon officials talked about sending American troops to Indochina. *Time* reverted to form: Independence might be a good idea – but the guns must speak first. Faced with a crisis in Indochina,

Luce and *Time* conjured up a new *deus ex machina:* Jean de Lattre de Tassigny, the French commander in Indochina, who now joined Douglas MacArthur, Bao Dai, and Chiang Kai-shek in Luce's East Asian pantheon.[42] As *Time* told the story, it was thanks to de Lattre that panic subsided and French evacuees returned to Hanoi and the Red River Delta. Perhaps all would be well, Luce thought, especially given that fresh American aid was flowing freely into Indochina.

At Rockefeller Center, a dissenting voice sounded a note of caution in regard to America's Asian adventures. Senior editor John Osborne warned in August 1950 that military means alone would not achieve victory in Asia.[43] Although he was writing about Korea, Osborne offered an uncanny prophecy of a coming Asian war in which Americans would alienate local inhabitants by destroying villages, shooting refugees, and training savage indigenous police.[44] Refugees, Osborne reported, were fleeing to the American side, along with Communist guerrillas, who were indistinguishable from other Koreans.[45] "Our men," wrote Billings, "have to shoot innocent 'gooks' for their own protection."* Although *Time* shared some of Osborne's views with its readers, Henry Luce remained convinced that a strong American policy could cleanse East Asia of Communism.[46] Five thousand brainy Americans, he believed, could solve the problem – with the help of Time Inc. on the home front.

Time and Luce were preparing Americans for a future adventure in Indochina at a time when most media ignored the place. Buoyed by reports from Korea, they looked ahead to another triumph in Vietnam.

War with China

Life's editors were exultant when they looked at pictures from MacArthur's victorious Korean front. Once again, its photographers had shown themselves to be the best in the nation. The work of Carl Mydans and David Douglas Duncan was particularly outstanding.[47] Their pictures told stories of anguish, bravery, desolation – and now, of victory. Both Duncan and Mydans won *U.S. Camera's* coveted Achievement Award for their work in Korea.

In early October, American forces crossed the thirty-eighth parallel into North Korea. *Time*, which was supposed to educate its readers, now made one of the worst in a long line of bad predictions. *Time* mocked the nervous bystanders who questioned MacArthur's move into North Korea and dismissed Red China's threat to intervene as pure "propaganda."[48] *Time* even claimed that if Mao had wished to enter the war, he would have done so when the UN forces could have been pushed "into the sea." Yet Luce's magazines were

---

* In 1999 the media reported that American soldiers had indeed panicked and shot Korean civilians. Some veterans of the events admitted that they had done so. But on 20 April 2000, the Associated Press reported that South Korean security forces had also massacred suspected spies and guerrillas trapped during the rout of Rhee's army.

ignoring omens – some of which had appeared in their own pages. In early July, *Life* had warned, "Chinese Communists have moved between 125,000 and 250,000" soldiers "to their border with North Korea."[49] *Time*'s sources indicated on 28 July and 4 August 1950 that Chinese Communist troops would enter Korea "as soon as the tide of battle" turned.[50] In August Jack Beal also learned that China's intervention in the Korean War had been pondered at a Soviet–Chinese military summit. In fact, recently released materials confirm the veracity of *Time*'s sources. These documents show that if UN forces ever moved north of the thirty-eighth parallel, the Chinese Communists would enter the war.[51]

In July Stalin had informed Zhou Enlai, "We consider it correct to concentrate immediately 9 Chinese divisions on the Chinese-Korean border for volunteer actions in North Korea in case the enemy crosses the 38th parallel." The Soviet leader promised to "try to provide air cover," and a Soviet air division arrived in the northeast in August.[52] But *Time*'s confidence, the product of euphoria multiplied by ideology, triumphed. It was not alone. Well over half of Gallup's respondents believed that the United States would have a "good" or "excellent" chance of defeating the PRC.[53] But on 10 October 1950, the Joint Chiefs of Staff again cautioned MacArthur about Chinese intervention. In the event of the PRC's entry into the war, moreover, Washington alone would decide whether the UN commander would be permitted to attack targets in Communist China.[54]

Soon thereafter, the president met MacArthur at Wake Island. Like the CIA, the general doubted that the Chinese would intervene. If they did, MacArthur assured Truman, few of their men would make it southward, and those who did would be slaughtered if they pushed on toward the thirty-eighth parallel.[55] It seemed as if the United States – which by the middle of October had suffered 4,125 dead, a few more missing, and 18,000 wounded – was on the verge of unconditional victory at a price the public could accept.[56] But in Beijing, Mao viewed MacArthur's steady march northward as a threat to Manchuria, China's industrial heartland.[57] Earlier in the year, Stalin himself warned Mao, "Japan ... will certainly lift itself up again, especially if the Americans continue their present policy."[58] Mao too believed that the United States planned to rearm Japan, China's old enemy.

Voices in the Pentagon scoffed in October at Mao's threats, which had been conveyed to the United States through intermediaries. On 30 October 1950, now "that the war was ending," *Time* looked ahead to the American-backed reconstruction of shattered Korea.[59] MacArthur had taken Pyongyang, the North Korean capital and, in defiance of orders, was pushing his troops toward the Chinese border. Supported by the public and schooled in the tradition of unconditional surrender, MacArthur would accept no substitute for victory. Luce and *Time* agreed and expressed the hope that MacArthur's triumph in Korea would lead to a wider counteroffensive against Communism in East Asia. But MacArthur's drive might result in a wider war of a different sort – one inflicted upon America by the enemy in a preemptive attack.

In late October, American troops in North Korea captured a few Chinese soldiers.[60] On 2 November Stalin learned that Soviet fighters based in Manchuria had shot down two American jets.[61] Two days later, *Time*'s Bob Sherrod reported that one battalion or regiment from each of seven Chinese divisions had moved into Korea.[62] Then *Time* scooped its rivals and reported that forty thousand Chinese soldiers from the X Corps were slowing MacArthur's offensive toward the Yalu River.[63] An alarmed MacArthur feared for the safety of his divided forces, and with good reason. The U.S. intelligence failure had been total, but the public had no sense of the catastrophe closing in on UN forces. Ignoring some of his own magazine's factual reports, Luce expressed the hope that in a few days the voters would punish the Democrats for their past bungling and credit the Republican MacArthur with the apparent victory in Korea.[64]

In a political speech delivered on 4 November, the feisty Truman said little about Korea and rather more about *Time* magazine.[65] A regular reader of a publication he despised, Truman attacked *Time* as misleading and biased. But the Republicans favored by Luce and *Time* gained twenty-eight seats in the House and five in the Senate, and in high-profile battles in Illinois and Maryland, Senator McCarthy claimed that he had caused the defeat of two leading Senate Democrats.[66] Impressed by a man whom he held in contempt, Luce wanted to have it both ways: Communism, he believed, remained "the Great Sin Against Humanity," and McCarthyism was a vulgar diversion.[67] The Communists, Luce observed, had caused massive suffering "while managing to avoid the counter-reaction of indignant horror and contempt which Hitler evoked."[68] Although he was prepared to denounce McCarthy in strong terms, Luce would have no part of a move to remove him from the Senate.[69] Luce was more eager to dislodge Dean Acheson, and *Life* again called for the secretary of state's head.[70]

Within days of the 1950 elections, UN forces in North Korea were retreating, and *Time* wrote that the entry of three hundred thousand Chinese troops into Korea might lead to disaster.[71] In the middle of November, Zhou Enlai told Stalin that China was dispatching thirty divisions to North Korea.[72] By 20 November, *Time* magazine had identified sixty thousand Chinese soldiers in Korea, with another half million awaiting orders north of the Yalu. But in its Thanksgiving issue, *Time* breathed a sigh of relief that it would soon regret. UN troops, the magazine reported, had resumed their advance; perhaps fewer Chinese than reported had entered North Korea.[73] General MacArthur took a break to engage in nonessential correspondence with Clare Luce.[74] And on 25 November, *Time*'s Washington bureau cabled good news: The war might soon be won, for the Chinese troops had apparently disappeared.[75] Wrong, and then wrong again: A crushing Chinese offensive soon sent the UN forces and their South Korean allies reeling southward. This was a land version of Pearl Harbor.

On 4 December *Time* compared the debacle to the early days of the Battle of the Bulge.[76] (Pearl Harbor or 11 September 2001 might be better analogies.) Luce returned to Time Inc. from his sabbatical leave after Allen Grover warned him that it was "unseemly" for the head of Time Inc. to do otherwise "on the eve of World War III."[77] In Washington, a jittery President Truman warned that the atomic bomb was only "one of our weapons" and indicated that under certain circumstances, MacArthur might be permitted to use it. Furthermore, the administration, and not the UN, would make the decision about the use of atomic weapons, based on reports relayed to it by the commanders in Korea. But in regard to bombing Manchuria, the United States would do so only with the approval of the United Nations. These belligerent but contradictory comments elicited panic in some quarters, and British Prime Minister Clement Attlee rushed to Washington.[78] Looking for a scapegoat, *Life* accused the British government of sinking to "its knees to the Communist aggressors of Peking."[79]

Despite Truman's inept comments, he wanted no wider war, least of all an atomic one. Holding the line in Korea remained the order of the day, and the political fallout was predictable. *Time*'s Frank McNaughton noted, "The 'get Acheson' pack howled at the heels of the Secretary of State day and night, like hungry wolves."[80] And Harry Luce was one of those wolves: With some exaggeration, Billings wrote, "Luce wants the Big War, not now perhaps but sometime." More accurately, he added that the boss was "for cracking back at the Reds wherever they try to break out."[81] For months, Luce referred incessantly to the "really miserable and horrible errors made in the recent past" and concluded, "We have to dig our way out of the consequences."[82] Even Chiang, however, rejected the idea of liberating the mainland amid a hail of nuclear bombs.[83] But he could take solace in the fact that the administration began to send more arms and ammunition to Formosa.[84]

MacArthur had promised that the war would be over by Christmas, and the advancing Chinese armies might soon redeem his pledge. The retreat of the UN forces grew more rapid during the second week of December. *Time* placed Mao Zedong on its cover, his face surrounded by a plague of red locusts. Ignoring Pearl Harbor, the magazine branded Korea the "worst defeat the U.S. had ever suffered."[85] As if it were burying the dead, *Time* mourned the final "loss of Asia to Communism." Not even MacArthur was spared as Luce and *Time* surveyed the collapse of the American mission to Asia.[86] In a shocking rebuff to its hero, *Time* told how MacArthur had "blundered and been beaten."* The general had overestimated the efficacy of air power against a technologically backward foe, the magazine admitted. *Time* then described the fighting retreat of one hundred forty thousand U.S. troops, along with their South Korean and UN allies, as leading to the "abyss of disaster."[87] John Foster Dulles invited his friend Luce to dinner, where he shocked him by uttering these defeatist words: "And the question is: shall we ask for terms?"[88] Luce's friend Joseph Kennedy called for the abandonment of Korea, as did former president Herbert Hoover,

---

* Within weeks, however, Luce the hero-worshipper was defending MacArthur against the charge that he had badly blundered. In effect, Luce repudiated *Time* when he also insisted that MacArthur's army had not suffered a great defeat. DJSB, 19 January 1951.

and Senator Taft issued an ambiguous call for withdrawal.[89] Retreat might be good politics, for Gallup published a poll[90] showing that 66 percent of surveyed Americans favored a withdrawal from Korea.*

Henry Luce, of course, hated the idea of American retreat anywhere. In response to neo-isolationism, the Luce media blasted the Hoovers and Kennedys for abandoning Korea and called for a "Grand Alliance of nations and tribes and just people against the Red Monster."[91] In Tokyo, MacArthur gravely warned against appeasement and suggested using Nationalist Chinese troops in Korea. He also wanted to impose a naval blockade of the mainland and bomb Manchurian bases and supply lines. Further, the general mused about using atomic or "cobalt" bombs as a shield in the event of a Chinese invasion of South Korea.[92] MacArthur promised a war waged by Asian boys on the ground, supported by American pilots and naval personnel. Its political appeal to Americans unnerved by massive U.S. casualties was obvious, and Taft, Luce, and other Republicans rallied to MacArthur's banner. Obligingly, *Time* insisted that "hundreds of thousands" of anti-Communist guerrillas were ready to follow Chiang into battle.[93] Senator William F. Knowland put the figure of anti-Communist Chinese partisans at one million. Against all logic, Representative Joseph Martin insisted that Chiang had eight hundred thousand troops eager to invade the mainland.[94]

Although *Time* rejected the use of atomic weapons against China, at least for the moment, it was prepared to fight a long war against the PRC.[95] The Chinese hordes, Luce believed, were "far from being invincible."[96] Coining a phrase that the Republicans would later borrow, Luce advocated "rolling back" the Iron Curtain. *Time* quickly took up the idea; *rollback* and *liberation* became its watchwords, and they would help to propel the Republicans to victory in 1952.[97] For the rest of his life, Luce was convinced that had MacArthur been allowed to proceed, it was probable that "the Communist regime in China would have fallen."[98] But what about the likely response of the Soviet Union? Once again, ideology and propaganda trumped logic.

Time and *Life* had insisted that the Russians were behind the Red Chinese intervention, but now the magazines seemed to dismiss the danger of Russian involvement in China's defense. Walter Lippmann did not. He wrote that MacArthur wanted "the Third World War now," and he wanted "to fight it in the Far East."[99] Frank McNaughton, a veteran reporter, tried to warn his editors at *Time* that thirty-five Soviet divisions based in the Far East would intervene if the United States attacked China. This decision, McNaughton concluded, would lead to World War III.[100] This catastrophe was just what the president wished to avoid. Truman was willing to fight a long war in Korea, but not on the mainland of China. The president worried about the dissipation of American strength while Western Europe remained vulnerable.[101] MacArthur dissented, arguing that the Soviets would never go to war for China.[102] Truman, however,

---

* Respondents were not asked whether they favored MacArthur's call for victory through a wider war. Had Gallup presented this alternative, the numbers in favor of withdrawal would doubtless have been lower.

was justifiably wary of the prophecies of the same man who had dismissed the Chinese danger in October. But unlike MacArthur and his followers, the administration had no formula for victory in East Asia. Restraint might make strategic sense, but fighting a war to restore a divided Korea was hardly an inspiring or popular strategy.

In late December, the U.S. Eighth Army and the X Corps escaped destruction, and by January the Chinese "volunteers" showed signs of wear. American air supremacy was taking its toll, and China's lines of communications offered the Air Force tempting targets. In fact, the war was entering a particularly delicate and dangerous stage. A massive Chinese drive toward Pusan might compel a desperate Truman to evacuate Korea – or embrace elements of MacArthur's radical strategy.

Although Western Europe was in full recovery, thanks in some measure to the Marshall Plan, Luce faulted the administration for failing to build up the West's military strength. He was wrong, however, and *Time*'s own Clay Blair explained why: Before the Korean War, the U.S. Army contained 592,000 troops; it now totaled 1,300,000.[103] The Navy had almost doubled its personnel, and so had the Air Force, and the Marine Corps had almost tripled in size. But Luce's partisan ardor acted as a blinder, and he rarely praised Truman or Acheson. Indeed, State Department officials Dean Rusk and Paul Nitze – no doves – warned the ultra-hawk John Osborne that *Life*'s denunciations of "Achesonism" could only redound to McCarthy's benefit. "What you say on that [editorial] page," they complained, "has a great effect on us and what we are trying to do here."[104] Luce, however, thought that attacking Acheson made for good politics as well as sound strategy. With Truman's favorable rating at 26 percent, 1952 promised to be a good year for the GOP.[105]

With the front stabilized in Korea, Luce saw three choices ahead: withdrawal, containment, or liberation. He favored the latter course, but if forced to choose, would opt for containment over withdrawal. So for the next two years and more, Luce campaigned for an extension of the war – if not to China, then at least to the "waist," the northern part of North Korea. But *Time*'s Clay Blair reported that General Omar Bradley, chairman of the Joint Chiefs, wanted to chew up China's best divisions, secure South Korea, and keep the war localized.[106] If the Red Chinese tried to launch a major ground offensive and used their air force in South Korea, the United States would bomb Manchurian bases and might blockade China and attack its industrial centers.[107] Luce, by contrast, wanted such action *now*. In his view, the enemy retained the initiative – thanks to Truman's supine policies. China's persecution of missionaries, including Presbyterians personally known to Luce, only heightened *Time*'s vehemence.[108]

"World War III," *Life* agreed, "*is* a possibility – this month; this year." This was all the more reason for backing MacArthur, who, said the magazine, truly understood that the non-Communist world was "fighting for its life in Asia."[109] The Pentagon establishment, however, agreed with generals Bradley and Marshall, who saw a wider war in Asia as misguided and dangerous. Public opinion, though dazzled by MacArthur's stars, supported containment and limited war. By a margin of more than seven to one, polled Americans thought that a war with Red China would redound to the benefit of Russia's designs on Europe. And in February 1951, a majority of surveyed Americans wanted to reach an agreement with Red China over Korea; an even larger percentage favored a cease-fire based on the restoration of the demarcation line at the thirty-eighth parallel.[110] A plurality or a majority of those surveyed continued to support the administration's terms for peace in Korea, even in the face of Truman's unpopularity. Many Americans blamed the war on Truman's blunders – but they wanted to contain, not extend it.

If American troops held the line somewhere near the thirty-eighth parallel, then the proponents of the wider war would lose the argument.

A Wider War in Asia?

The bad blood between General MacArthur and the Truman administration dated back to 1945. Occupation policy, proconsul MacArthur had to be reminded, was made in Washington, and not in Tokyo.[111] The man who conveyed State's objection was none other than Dean G. Acheson, secretary of state during this difficult spring of 1951. Now, an unrepentant MacArthur, despite past reprimands, again threatened to "doom Red China to the risk of imminent military collapse."[112] Truman and Acheson, who were prepared to enter into peace negotiations leading to the withdrawal of foreign forces from Korea, were furious. But MacArthur's leaked views encouraged Representative Joe Martin, who solicited the general's opinion on Korean strategy "as Commander-in-Chief of the Far Eastern Command."[113] In a reply that crassly challenged Truman, MacArthur endorsed the idea of using Chiang's troops and warned that if the United States lost the war to Communism in Asia, "the fall of Europe is inevitable." In a phrase he later employed to great popular effect, MacArthur concluded, "There is no substitute for victory."

On 5 April 1951 Republican minority leader Joe Martin released the MacArthur letter. On that same day, John Billings learned that Luce, with exquisite timing, was working to recruit MacArthur as an author. After all, Luce reasoned, the general was in Truman's doghouse and might soon welcome a career change.[114] Luce and his senior editors all assumed, however, that MacArthur would decide when to retire.* After all, Truman was *Time*'s "little man."[115] It was inconceivable that such a despised president could dismiss the great general. But Luce might have recalled that this same "little man" had dropped atomic bombs on Japan; had taken on organized labor in 1946 and 1947; had upset the Republicans and the pollsters in 1948; and had intervened in Korea with little hesitation.

---

* Luce continued to combine ideological predilections with pecuniary advantage. In retirement, MacArthur (like his enemy Truman) chose *Life* as his editorial home, and more than a decade later Time Inc. helped MacArthur write his best-selling *Reminiscences*. When he died in 1964, *Time*'s obituary conferred the rare caption "Heroes" upon the deceased MacArthur.

Early in the morning on 11 April, White House correspondents were summoned to the briefing room. With the news of MacArthur's dismissal, bedlam erupted, and the crazed reporters raced to their telephones. Washington, *Time*'s staff reported, was "torn stem from stern today."[116] So was the country. But two days later, *Time* received a sober analysis from Jim Shepley, whose words reflected his access to Marshall and the Joint Chiefs. Shepley concluded that by challenging civilian authority, "MacArthur virtually left no alternative but to relieve him."[117] Unfortunately, through intent or a blunder, MacArthur found out about the termination of his command through a press report read on the radio. He never forgave Truman for the slight and remained convinced that Secretary of Defense Marshall and General Omar Bradley had plotted against him.

Much of the country rallied to the beleaguered general's cause: More than one hundred twenty-five thousand mostly angry telegrams poured into the White House. The American people, Frank McNaughton reported, "hadn't been on such an emotional binge since the death of F.D.R."[118] *Time* called Truman "The Little Man Who Dared," and noted that "seldom had a more unpopular man fired a more popular one."[119] Joe McCarthy called Truman's action "the greatest victory the Communists could ever claim . . . ," one gained "with the aid of bourbon and benedictine" by conspirators who knew how "to get the President cheerful."[120] The real president, the senator charged, was a "sinister monster conceived in the Kremlin, and then given birth to by Acheson."[121] Representative Walter Judd called MacArthur's removal "the Kremlin's greatest victory since Yalta."[122] Senator Styles Bridges called for war with China – which he described as a "calculated risk" aimed at *preventing* World War III. (Of course, MacArthur insisted that Russia would not intervene, but as a sarcastic Jim Shepley again reminded *Time*, the general's recent credentials as a prophet were not strong.)[123]

In April 1951 MacArthur returned to the continental United States after having been overseas for nearly a generation. "War's very object," he told the awed Congress, "is victory, not prolonged indecision." After being cheered on Capitol Hill and greeted by millions in New York City, the seventy-one-year-old retired general moved into the Waldorf, where the Luces also had a suite.* *Time* blamed the administration's no-win strategy for MacArthur's demise and smelled victory in 1952.† On 24 April, shortly after the general's return to the United States, Luce visited MacArthur in his new suite at the

---

* Representative Dewey Short of Missouri reacted to MacArthur's appearance thus: He had seen "a great hunk of God in the flesh, and we heard the voice of God." Robert P. Newman, "Lethal Rhetoric: The Selling of the China Myths," *Quarterly Journal of Speech*, 2, 124. An essay written by one sixth-grader captured the mood: "We went to see the great Gen. on the twentieth of April 1951. I must say it was a big thrill! . . . As the Gen. car came by everybody roared and shouted. That was one of the biggest days of my life, if not the biggest."

† During MacArthur's triumphant tours in 1951 and 1952, he polished some of the gaudy prose that reappeared in his deeply moving farewell address at West Point in 1962: "For me, the shadows are deepening . . . The world has turned over many times since then, and those years of old have vanished, tone and tint . . . "

Waldorf.[124] Deeply moved by the Great Man, Luce returned to his office, where John Billings was bemused by the boss's "boyish susceptibility to Greatness."[125] Following its leader, *Time* became an echo chamber for MacArthur. Luce also involved himself in many MacArthur projects, from publishing his memoirs to creating a foundation in his honor.[126] Luce's adulation, however, bothered *Time*'s Washington insiders. Jim Shepley told *Time* that isolationists cheering MacArthur seemed ready for war in Asia – while they blocked Truman's military appropriations. Why go to war in Asia, MacArthur's critics wondered, when we were unready for a Soviet attack on Europe?[127]

Coached by his Republican allies, MacArthur prepared to tell a special session of the Senate Armed Services Committee his side of the story.[128] He was effective and well prepared. *Time*'s Frank McNaughton remarked that "for such a performance as this, it was, most fittingly, ascension day."[129] But Marshall and Bradley countered, arguing that a wider war with China could only weaken America as it prepared for a possible showdown with the Soviet Union in the main theater – Europe. General Bradley landed a powerful blow when he described a wider conflict in Asia as "the wrong war, against the wrong enemy [China], at the wrong time, in the wrong place."[130] Bradley also revealed that MacArthur had at one point flirted with the idea of total withdrawal from Korea; at another time he had opposed the use of Chinese Nationalist troops in Korea.

Marshall was aging, Bradley was inarticulate, and Acheson was supercilious; but as a team, they proved to be unified, effective, and, at times, brilliant. Acheson, though hated by many, effectively argued that an attack on Manchuria could unleash a "chain of events which in all likelihood would spread to general war."[131] And in this wider war, he argued, the United States would fight virtually alone. By the middle of May, Frank McNaughton warned *Time*, MacArthur's spell was rapidly dissipating. True, a plurality (39 percent) of Americans polled by Gallup supported MacArthur's call for a wider war.[132] But even this modest plurality reflected admiration for the man rather than a commitment to his strategy. Meanwhile, although American losses remained high, the front had stabilized in Korea. If containment in Asia was on trial, then a sullen nation would probably vote to acquit.

Mail coming in to the Senate favored Bradley and Marshall. Educators, who formed an important part of *Time*'s readership, supported Truman's dismissal of the general by a margin of almost two to one. Among persons listed in *Who's Who in America*, Gallup found a plurality opposed to MacArthur's strategy.[133] Because these elites consisted of the men and women for whom Luce published *Time*, Gallup's statistics demonstrated that Time Inc. might not be as influential as Truman feared or Luce hoped. When people were searching for a new, bolder strategy and Washington lagged behind, Luce's media served as a catalyst – as in 1938–1940. This time, most Americans were wary of a leap into the abyss of the wider war Luce advocated. Truman's patient global strategy, McNaughton noted, was paying dividends, and he saw "no reason to let impatience alter it in the Far East."

Luce wanted to make MacArthur *Time*'s "Man of the Year," but his editors talked him out of the idea. Once spoken of as presidential material, the old warrior became, Luce sadly admitted, a man whose impact and image were neither so "clear nor as large" as in April.[134] Although MacArthur went on a long and successful speaking tour, in fact he was "fading away." Luce realized that MacArthur seemed to be the property of the Taft Republicans and of far-right extremists like the Christian Nationalists. He abandoned any thought of a MacArthur presidency but remained an unrelenting foe of peace with Red China. Facts about the new regime only hardened his resolve.

Using sources based in Hong Kong, *Time* portrayed the PRC as a regime that had killed a million and a half people since the autumn of 1949.[135] *Time*'s Robert Neville also foresaw the coming of the disastrous communes that would later cost many more lives.[136] But *Time* continued to blunder, too. Although it admitted that the Russians could not run China the way they did Czechoslovakia, the magazine repeatedly exaggerated Russian influence.[137] Jack Beal, for example, who often relied upon Guomindang contacts, reported that Mao was no more than a puppet, and a half-dead one at that.[138] *Time* was wrong on both counts, and Mao would outlive Henry Luce by almost a decade.

Some of Luce's bitterness was the consequence of Chinese Communist attacks on him and his family. In 1950 Liu Liangmo, writing for the Shanghai newspaper *World Culture*, had published an article blasting "Henry Luce – One of the Men Behind the Scenes of American Imperialism."[139] Liu briefly discussed Luce's "most widely circulated and most influential publications" and then condemned their editor-in-chief as "one of the most wily and atrocious American propagandists." In a particularly hurtful lie, he described Luce as a man who had worked "to enslave the Chinese people."* This kind of libel only reinforced Luce's determination to bring Mao's domination of China to an end – one way or another.

Containment Prevails

John Foster Dulles was making progress on the Japanese peace treaty, and Luce was eager to help generate public support for his friend's efforts. Luce, the father of *Life*, was rather camera shy, but he made a rare appearance on television in 1951. He appeared in Time Inc.'s *Your Stake in Japan*, where he argued that Japan's reconstruction was essential to building a strong anti-Communist front in East Asia.[140] And soon, the policies advocated by Luce and *Fortune* since 1948 would become reality. A reindustrialized, rearmed Japan would form part of America's cordon around Communist China. Furthermore, there were signs that the hapless Truman administration was changing course. Frustrated by Chinese Communist obstinacy over Korea, Truman sounded more hostile

---

* Not to be outdone, *Pravda* called Henry Luce "an arch-reactionary and warmonger." *Pravda*, 7 May 1951.

to the PRC. The president finally dispatched a substantial military mission to Formosa; aid would soon flow, in the amount of $300 million.

Luce wanted to encourage this shift, so in the spring of 1951 he engineered an event that augured well for the friends of Chiang Kai-shek.[141] Its setting was to be a meeting of the China Institute in America, Inc. (CIAI). Luce had served as a board member and then president (1947) of this organization, and early in 1951 he was elected chairman of its board of trustees. Founded in 1926, the CIAI was domiciled in New York City in a "China House" purchased with funds provided by the Henry Luce Foundation. Later, the CIAI received almost half a million dollars more from this source.[142] Established to promote "educational relations between the two countries," the institute was really a cultural arm of Chiang's foreign propaganda apparatus (it had registered as a foreign agent in 1942). The institute produced a vast amount of pro-Chinese educational material. Supported by Beth Moore, Henry L. Stimson, Chinese scholar and diplomat Hu Shih, missionary Edward H. Hume, and other Luce contacts, the institute had proven to be highly effective.[143] During the latter stages of the civil war in China, for example, more than three thousand Chinese students were marooned in the United States.[144] Thanks to lobbying by Luce, Beth Moore, and Walter Judd, a federal appropriation of up to $4 million was made available to them. The China Institute administered those funds and monitored the political activities of the students.[145]

On 18 May 1951, the China Institute hosted a dinner at the Waldorf, and its agenda paid tribute to Luce as the man whom columnist Marquis Childs called "the most ardent supporter of Chiang in this country."[146] In planning the event, Luce had worked closely with John Foster Dulles, who agreed to participate in this celebration of the China Institute's twenty-fifth anniversary.[147] Eager to act as a liaison between Henry Luce and the administration he advised, Dulles suggested that the main speaker be Dean Rusk, Acheson's assistant secretary of state for Far Eastern affairs. After his guests had dined in the Twilight Lounge atop the Waldorf, Luce introduced Dean Rusk. What Rusk brought with him was a virtual peace offering to Luce and the China lobby; his gift made the front page of the *New York Times*.[148] Rusk called Red China a "colonial Russian government" and said that it was "not the government of China." Perhaps Rusk was signaling Beijing that it would be rewarded for distancing itself from Moscow, and if so, this was nothing very new. But he also implied that the West and its allies would somehow assist Chinese who were ready to revolt against the Beijing regime – and this *was* new. The *New York Times* saw the Rusk statement as a kind of repudiation of Truman's 1949 "White Paper on China," and the *Washington Post* even accused Rusk of having crossed a "diplomatic Yalu."[149] Acheson was upset with Rusk, but the assistant secretary managed to mollify him.[150]

Luce was impressed, and he subsequently did what he could to foster Rusk's career. Nevertheless, Luce, for both political and ideological reasons, continued to advocate policies that Truman was unlikely to embrace. The administration, for example, was willing to sign a truce that preserved South Korea.[151] *Time*, in its dissent, complained that a return to the old demarcation line represented a "smoldering time-bomb under the shaky structure of world peace."[152] Luce wanted to conquer most of the Korean peninsula and then attack the Communists "in their lairs" (*Time*, 14 May). But as the newsmagazine tirelessly reminded readers, despite a growing number (11,001 as of May 1951) of American dead, the administration lacked a strategy for victory in Korea.[153] *Time* went on to dismiss the young cease-fire talks over Korea as a plan to rescue Red China "from the brink of disaster" and portrayed the West as a supplicant begging for peace.[154] Unfortunately for Luce, three-quarters of the polled public favored the peace talks, and more than half supported the mutual withdrawal of UN and Communist Chinese troops from Korea.[155] Despite *Time*'s grave warnings, most surveyed Americans believed that a restored South Korea, if aided by the United States, could keep the peace in the years following an armistice.[156]

Luce remained an interventionist whom no administration could please. Here, after all, was a man who advocated "the general proposition that the U.S. must intervene in the life of nearly every country in the world for its economic and social betterment." Speaking of less fortunate nations, Luce declared that "the U.S. must work with every one of them . . . to lift them up in order that we and all men shall not go down into the pit."[157]

10

Electing Eisenhower While Fighting McCarthy

In 1952 Henry Robinson Luce, a pillar of his Presbyterian Church, almost became a Roman Catholic. China's future played a role in his near conversion.

There had been rumors for years, of course. In 1947 Corinne Thrasher, Harry's loyal secretary and a woman who detested the second Mrs. Luce, said, "There's something terribly wrong with Mr. Luce...I'm afraid he's going to turn Catholic."[1] Such fears invariably involved Harry's wife, for Clare Boothe Luce was a Catholic celebrity both in the United States and in Rome. On several occasions, she had secured private audiences with Pope Pius XII, whose "goodness" and "extraordinary sweetness" greatly impressed her.[2] In 1949 Clare Luce suggested to Pius XII that Harry was "longing in his heart – as once I did in mine – for the ineffable riches of Christ, the fullness of the Faith."[3] She asked that the pope pray for her husband's conversion. But Henry Luce, whose father had labored in the foreign mission of his beloved Presbyterian church, stubbornly persisted in his Calvinist ways. True, he made agreeable concessions to Clare – such as deeding the 7,500-acre Mepkin plantation in South Carolina to an order of Trappist monks – but he refused to leave the church of his fathers.[4] Yet by 1952, two new factors were working in favor of Clare Luce's conversion plan.

One was the Jesuit intellectual John Courtney Murray, who was Luce's theological sparring partner. Over drinks, the two men would debate everything from predestination to the American mission in the world. Committed as he was to American pluralism, Murray became a *Time* favorite.[5] Second, Luce sensed that a Republican sweep in 1952 was a distinct possibility. Within a year, he hoped, the United States would be helping to drive the godless Communists out of China altogether. So in April 1952, during Holy Week, Luce wrote an extraordinary "Declaration of Intent."[6]

Signed by Luce and John Courtney Murray and witnessed by Clare Boothe Luce, the declaration stated that

I, Henry Robinson Luce, agree that if, in the Providence of god, the Reverend John Courtney Murray, S.J., is, by the favour of the Apostolic See, named Ordinary or Vicar Apostolic of an area of China including Shantung Province, and if he shall be able to perform his apostolic ministry within this province, then, I will present myself in the Cathedral at Tsinan for admission to the Holy Roman Catholic Church by conditional baptism therein.

Yet Luce displayed some feelings of guilt, and to reconcile conversion with his reverence for a great Protestant missionary, he added, "This promise is made with all respect for the memory of the Reverend Dr. Calvin Mateer, D.D." In other words, if China were liberated from the scourge of Communism and if Father Murray was able to minister to Chinese Christians, Luce would become a Catholic. Perhaps this improbable scenario was meant to placate Clare without exposing Harry to an actual conversion. Or maybe Luce thought that his conditional pledge would somehow speed the day of China's liberation. It is certain, however, that this conversion would have strengthened Clare's church at the expense of Harry's fellow Presbyterians. But China would not be liberated in the near future, and Henry Robinson Luce died a Protestant.

Eisenhower

Luce, *Time*'s Thomas L. Matthews observed, had long since "come to the point of believing that the Republic was in danger whenever the Republicans weren't running it," and they hadn't been doing so since 1933.[7] Luce desperately wanted a winner in 1952, but the front-runner for the GOP nomination troubled him.

For a decade, *Time* had depicted Senator Robert A. Taft as hardworking but also "dull, prosy, [and] colorless."[8] And *Life*'s pictures did more damage than *Time*'s nasty prose: A high, bald pate, metal-rimmed eyeglasses, squinty eyes, all set above a parched, reluctant smile – these were the features that stood out in the magazine's portraits of Bob Taft. Put another way, Luce needed a candidate who would smile at the millions of Americans who looked at *Life* each week. This was important, for of Luce's estimated thirty-one million weekly readers, more than half read *Life*.[9] It was no wonder that Taft saw Luce as a man who took "a shot" at him whenever he got "a chance."[10] What most worried Luce, however, was Taft's isolationist record on foreign policy issues.[11] "We must not," Taft insisted early in 1951, "assume obligations by treaty or otherwise which require any extensive use of American land forces."[12] Although he usually mouthed the rhetoric of the anti-Truman China lobby, the senator had once favored recognizing the Communist Chinese if they were "willing to act like other free governments."[13] At this point, what Luce most wanted was an internationalist and a winner. Taft, he believed, was neither.

By 1952, "America's magazine" reached almost one-quarter of the reading population. One-third of middle- and upper-middle-class adults – including an astounding 44.4 percent of college-educated males – read *Life*.[14] If you owned or were paying for your own home and car, lived in a metropolitan area, and read a weekly magazine, it was probably *Life*.[15] *Life*'s competitors – *Look* (a weak look-alike), *Collier's*, which had some good writers but a declining circulation base, and the traditional, often stodgy *Saturday Evening Post* – were nearing the end of the line. *Life* was the favorite magazine of every income group but was especially popular among the wealthiest Americans, most of whom were Republicans. The consumer goods depicted in *Life* during the Depression years were now available to a generation that could afford them. "As Advertised in *Life*" became a selling point to many a retailer and manufacturer. Revenue soared, and by 1952 *Life* magazine earned $96.9 million.[16] *Life's Picture History of Western Man* and its *Picture History of World War II* had earned another $3 million in profits by the end of 1952. Luce was pleased, but he remained fixated upon finding the right candidate, a photogenic figure who would shine in *Life*.

After the war, Time Inc. treated General Dwight D. Eisenhower as if he were a national treasure slated for greater things. *Time*, for example, called him a man "hardened by war, unspoiled by fame," and early on, Luce realized that Eisenhower was politically savvy.[17] As Ike told *Time*'s Robert L. Sherrod, "You have to aim at public opinion and not only Congress."[18] C. D. Jackson, who had served in North Africa as Eisenhower's expert on psychological warfare, suggested that Luce visit Ike, the incoming president of Columbia University.[19] Impressed, Luce convinced himself that the general "had learned Republicanism along with a simple religious faith, at his mother's knees." Ike was an internationalist, one who could be further educated by the Luce media and liberal Republican newspapers such as the New York *Herald Tribune*. Eisenhower's aura of sunny optimism also dazzled Luce, who "thought it was of paramount importance that the American people should have the experience of living under a Republican administration and discovering that they were not thereby reduced to selling apples on street corners."[20] When the publisher returned from a lunch with Ike, he was invariably in a good mood.[21] Ike, however, refused to commit himself to a political career, especially after Truman sent him to build up Western Europe's defenses. But Eisenhower showed flickers of ambition; and, like Luce, he was wary of the front-runner, Bob Taft. Taft, Luce wrote, had no "style," and Ike had "a better chance of winning."[22] But while Luce nudged Eisenhower toward a bid for the presidency, he remained enmeshed in the search for the culprits who had lost China.

Luce Versus McCarthy

Senator Pat McCarran of Nevada fully justified *Time*'s adjectives, which included "pompous, vindictive and power-grabbing."[23] In his desire to outdo the young upstart McCarthy, McCarran's Subcommittee on Internal Security committed itself to the final destruction of both Owen Lattimore and the Institute of Pacific Relations. Indeed, a surprised and angry Lattimore would soon find himself condemned as the man who had *run Soviet intelligence operations in*

China. This fantasy stunned Eleanor Lattimore, who angrily dismissed such charges as "garbage." President Truman, who bore much of the blame for the plight of the State Department's China experts, believed that Lattimore, who had formerly advised him on China policy, was being "shamefully persecuted by this committee."[24] But Lattimore was not its only target. McCarran's investigators also wanted to question Time Incers about Communist infiltration of the Institute of Pacific Relations.

By hinting at a probe of *Time*, the senator tried to intimidate Luce into giving him favorable coverage, and his ploy apparently succeeded.[25] Whether by conviction or design, *Time*'s lengthy "Case Against I.P.R." praised McCarran's committee for having exposed "what looked like a powerful Communist web of propaganda and persuasion, around [Lattimore], the I.P.R. and, ultimately, around U.S. policymaking."[26] In appeasing McCarran, Luce was playing politics and settling bitter old scores with Owen Lattimore; he was also protecting Time Inc. In the case of McCarthy, however, different motives were in play. As Luce saw it, the senator from Wisconsin was crude and often ineffective; worst of all, his antics might help Taft and thereby backfire against the Republicans in 1952.[27] After declaring, "Communist infiltration of government is no longer a legitimate worry," *Life* attacked Taft for supporting an unscrupulous, indecent demagogue.[28] Luce and his editors went ahead with their plans for a special *Time* inquiry into McCarthy and his crusade.[29]

Joe McCarthy was eager to show Luce that he was not afraid of *Time*; if cornered, he would not run. When the magazine prepared to do a cover on the Wisconsin senator, its brazen target stupidly made himself available to *Time*'s reporters. The result was the first major attack leveled at McCarthy in a mass circulation organ. "Demagogue McCarthy," dated 22 October, called the senator "ham-handed," a "tramp dog," a cheap-shot artist, and a liar. *Time*'s assault enraged the senator, who accused Luce of following the line laid down by the Communist *Daily Worker*. The senator also found *Time* guilty of protecting an alleged Communist agent.[30] But Joe McCarthy appears to have been unaware of long-forgotten incidents that could have been used to embarrass Luce. In the early 1930s, the Luces' benefactress, "Auntie" Anita McCormick Blaine, had lavished much money upon the Chinese mass education movement. She insisted that those funds be disbursed by none other than Frederick V. Field, a Communist who worked for the Institute of Pacific Relations.[31] And buried in files maintained by Lattimore were scribbled notes about meetings with Luce back in 1934 at an international conference of the Institute of Pacific Relations. Lattimore lunched with Luce, whom he judged to be "a ponderous young man, verging on being a 'big man' in the American manner." Luce, Lattimore correctly observed, was "essentially humourless." He was wrong, however, when he concluded that Harry did not "take to little me, either."

In fact, Luce, with his schoolboy curiosity, thrilled to Lattimore's tales about traveling through Mongolia with nomadic caravans.[32] Inspired by the encounter, Luce began to think out loud about how he might teach Americans more about East Asia. He considered starting a new magazine, one in which the knowledgeable Owen Lattimore would play a major editorial role. "So an offer of a job *might* develop out of that," wrote Lattimore. "And wouldn't *that* be funny." Indeed, it would have been ironic had the leftist Lattimore gone to work for the young journalistic genius Luce. But this was not to be, because Luce was then preoccupied with a new project called *Life*. McCarthy's "researchers" were sloppy, and they failed to discover Luce's near alliance with the suspect Lattimore.

When Joe McCarthy complained about the *Time* cover, an amused Lattimore mocked the "Wisconsin Whimperer," and Henry A. Wallace congratulated Luce for *Time*'s "real courage" in exposing McCarthy.[33] John King Fairbank, who had once called Teddy White a whore for Harry Luce, rejoiced that the publisher had "come out rather sharply against their [McCarthy's and his allies'] procedures."[34] McCarthy then accused Luce of "prostitution of freedom of the press." Some friends thought that this latest slugfest would help Joe McCarthy: "Fact is," wrote one, "I'm tickled to death over the piece [in *Time*] – because if there is one sheet in the world *hated* by people all over the country (though they buy it) it is TIME."[35]

Joe McCarthy contacted firms that advertised in Luce's magazines, alerting them to "the viciousness of [*Time*'s] lying smear attack."[36] Implicit in the senator's message was a threat to investigate or attack companies that defied his call for a boycott. From the beginning, however, McCarthy's threats backfired, and few editorial voices came to his support. *Life* was a major player in the consumer craze, and its advertisers were not about to abandon the magazine.[37] Even the McCarthyite *New York Daily News* thought the senator had gone too far ("Low Blow, Joe"), and the liberal *New York Post* actually praised *Time* ("Joe McCarthy vs. Henry Luce").[38] *Business Week* condemned the boycott as a proposal that "would wreck the country's free press as surely as though the government took control."[39]

In attacking Time Inc., a pillar of American life, McCarthy had suffered his first political defeat since becoming a national figure. This was one of Henry Luce's finest moments, perhaps his best since the "American Century" era.

Promoting Eisenhower's Candidacy

More than ever, Luce looked forward to electing a Republican president who would deprive Joe McCarthy of the failed Asian policies that had helped to make McCarthyism possible.

While Luce battled McCarthy, John Shaw Billings observed that the editor-in-chief was "deeply in love with [Eisenhower's] candidacy." Luce expected his senior editors to convince the public of Dwight Eisenhower's virtues as a candidate; by the end of 1951, most of them had decided to back Eisenhower.[40] And in working to draft Ike, Luce collaborated with men to whom he had longstanding ties, among them Walter Judd, Henry Cabot Lodge, and Herbert Brownell. Through his work on behalf of China, Luce also knew Thomas J. Watson of IBM and Winthrop Aldrich of the Chase Manhattan Bank, men who could raise lots of money for the Eisenhower cause. But the general insisted, "I do not seek [the nomination] now, and I will not be maneuvered into appearing to seek it."[41] Lodge warned Eisenhower that unless he returned to the United States as an active candidate, Bob Taft would be nominated.

On 7 January 1952, *Life* made its urgent "Case for Ike." Eisenhower was, the magazine proclaimed, an American optimist capable of changing history for the better.[42] In Paris, Eisenhower carefully studied *Life*'s appeal and then told Luce, "You have erred grossly on the side of generosity in your estimate of my capacity." Later, the general cited "Case for Ike" as one of the factors that "helped influence" him to break his policy of "complete silence." In January Luce sailed to England on the *Queen Mary*, where he frequently conversed with Prime Minister Churchill, another admirer of Eisenhower.[43] Luce later visited Paris, where he spent two hours with Eisenhower. The infatuated publisher reveled in the "sound of the man's voice" and enjoyed "the twinkle in [Eisenhower's] brightest blue eyes."[44] Luce left Paris "under the agreeable spell of a great personality and with a sense of confidence that the Republican Party had a winner." But as John Billings noted, Eisenhower could not be nominated by "immaculate conception."[45] He would have to come home and fight for the prize, lest Taft be nominated by party regulars and loyalists.

On 6 April 1952, Eisenhower formally notified President Truman that he was resigning from the Army. Luce and his senior editors learned that the general would return home around 1 June, and after Ike landed in America, *Time* quickly decided that the people "liked what they saw."[46] But what would a President Eisenhower do about issues like Korea and Communism?

Eisenhower, Dulles, and "Liberation"

To Luce and his editors, the Korean stalemate of 1952 was a metaphor for the paralysis preventing the West from winning the Cold War.[47] *Time* tirelessly reminded readers of the toll rung up by the endless war in Korea: more than nineteen thousand dead Americans by 4 July 1952. The administration, in *Time*'s sour words, was engaging in the "limited hot pursuit of disaster."[48] But would Eisenhower, the product of Europe-firsters, be much better? Although he had visited China several times before World War II, Eisenhower had shown no particular interest in the Far East.[49] He dismissed General Douglas A. MacArthur's strategy for a wider war against China as leading to "ill-advised ventures in Korea and Formosa."[50] Although he intended to remove the restraints placed upon Chiang Kai-shek by President Truman and the Seventh Fleet, Eisenhower showed no desire to prepare the Nationalist armies for an invasion of the mainland.[51]

Perhaps Henry Luce could reeducate Eisenhower, but for the moment, Ike's shaky performance on the campaign trail called even his nomination into question. Moreover, in Texas and several other Southern states, the Taft forces had sewn up the moribund party regulars, barring pro-Eisenhower outsiders from participating. In the weeks that followed, Luce and *Time* worked to oust the contested Taft delegations.[52] In the middle of June, Luce insisted that Eisenhower denounce "the Texas steal" – in Texas. As a result, Ike went there, and as Luce suggested, he blasted the Taft clique for its methods in the South. At the Republican convention in Chicago, *Time*'s men directed General Eisenhower's campaign against Taft's "theft" of the crucial Southern delegates.[53] *Time*, meanwhile, continued its steady drumbeat: "Ike was far more likely than Taft to win in November."[54] On the floor of the convention, Eisenhower's parliamentary ploy stripped Taft of his contested Southern delegates and paved the way for Ike's victory.

Eisenhower's handlers chose Senator Richard M. Nixon of California as his running mate. The choice of Nixon was fine with Luce, because by pursuing Alger Hiss, the California congressman had helped to vindicate *Time*'s Whittaker Chambers.[55] After twenty years in the desert, Americans would, Luce expected, flock home to their old Republican Party. He rhapsodized about the "inner truth" of the convention, which *Life* described as a "victory of right over wrong."

Henry Luce hoped that Eisenhower would lead a united Republican Party to victory in 1952. In his quest for harmony in the GOP, Luce turned to John Foster Dulles, to good effect. In numerous interviews, addresses, and articles, Dulles had already performed a marvelous balancing act.[56] He assured pro-Chiang Republicans, many of whom supported Taft, that Eisenhower rejected the false choice of "either Europe or Asia." Dulles also called for a blockade of the Chinese mainland and favored "unleashing" Chiang Kai-shek.[57] Privately, however, Dulles told Eisenhower's backers that the Taft camp was neither well informed nor consistent when formulating its foreign policy principles. In the spring of 1952, Luce approached Dulles, suggesting that he write an article advocating a new, more aggressive foreign policy. With great fanfare, *Life* proceeded to publish "A Policy of Boldness."[58]

The Truman–Acheson policy of containment, Dulles argued, was too expensive and too defeatist, for in fighting bloody wars at points selected by the enemy, America would finally "drop exhausted." "A Policy of Boldness" also broadcast a clever appeal to disaffected "ethnic" Democrats, people sensitive to the charge that their party, in the Yalta agreements, had abandoned Eastern Europe to Soviet tyranny. In place of containment, Dulles suggested responding to Soviet aggression by striking "*back where it hurts, by means of our choosing*" (Dulles's italics). He failed to specify how he would retaliate, but he did call atomic bombs "effective political weapons in defense of the peace." Dulles also sought a plan to "promote liberation" of lands under Communist rule. Luce insisted that *Life* magazine had published "the embryo of a united Republican foreign policy." Even Senator Taft approved of the Dulles essay, and Eisenhower believed that Dulles's foreign policy represented a viable Republican "alternative to the Acheson policy."[59] Thanks in some measure to his article in *Life*, Dulles was chosen to write the Republican convention's foreign policy plank. The final document virtually recapitulated the Luce-prompted Dulles essay.[60]

In his quest for unity and victory after seven years of Truman, Luce convinced himself that Dulles and Eisenhower would embark upon a global crusade against Communism. His faith was misplaced. Dulles, for example, spoke of "liberation," but he had not proposed making war on China. Nor did Dulles wish to provoke "a series of bloody uprisings and reprisals" in the Soviet bloc. As for Eisenhower, did he really intend to lead America into new adventures in East Asia? Not according to a *Time* correspondent, who reported that Pentagon officials were crowing that "now MacArthur can really fade away."[61] Douglas MacArthur suggested that if elected, Ike should threaten the Chinese with a nuclear attack if they dared to move southward in Korea. A wary Eisenhower quickly rejected the plan as "impracticable."[62] Hungry for victory, Luce overlooked the creeping moderation infecting Dulles and Eisenhower.

By Labor Day, Luce, like many of candidate Eisenhower's backers, was discouraged.[63] "Ike is running like a dry creek," warned the Scripps-Howard editorial page; Luce's own editorial director ridiculed Eisenhower's "inane grin." John Billings added that the candidate looked like "an old baggy has-been in civilian clothes." The editor-in-chief complained that Eisenhower was speaking in a wooden, ineffective manner.[64] In early September, the campaign asked Time Inc. for help, and it came in the form of Charles Douglas Jackson, among others. The energetic Jackson quickly took over the hapless speech-writing shop, vastly improving the final product. Within a week of Jackson's arrival the grateful candidate thanked Luce for sending him a "God-send" named C. D., a man who had saved his sanity, "such part as is salvageable." Other Time Incers played roles in the Eisenhower crusade, too. The brilliant *Life* editor Emmet John Hughes joined Eisenhower's speech-writing team, and John Knox Jessup, the magazine's chief editorial writer, became a valued campaign consultant. Eisenhower's addresses became crisper and more effective; and his indictments of the Acheson–Truman policy in the Far East sounded like replays of *Life* editorials – which they were. Ike, for example, accused the administration of losing "700,000,000 human beings [most of them Chinese] to the Communist slave world."[65] Eisenhower also attacked Truman for his lack of a "coherent policy in Asia."[66] These sops to the China lobby and its supporters were effective.

Late in September, when Luce happily rode Eisenhower's campaign train through Ohio, he returned to Rockefeller Center aglow with confidence.[67] He also proceeded to produce some of his most biased coverage. Luce, who worked on major campaign stories with editors Max Ways, Roy Alexander, and Otto Fuerbringer, treated Adlai E. Stevenson, the Democratic candidate, as an object of ridicule. This coverage vindicated an old joke, to the effect that *Time* was even-handed during election years: Half the time it praised the Republicans, and half the time it damned the Democrats.

With each passing week, a pleased Harry Luce sensed that victory was more certain. By a huge margin, polled Americans thought that Ike, and not Stevenson, could best handle the Korean situation.[68] But Eisenhower realized that while most Americans longed for an end to the Korean War, they were not in favor of waging a bigger war against China. A plurality even thought that U.S. intervention had been a mistake in the first place.[69] Ike therefore told a cheering Illinois audience, "If there is to be a war there [in Asia], let it be Asians against Asians, with our support on the side of freedom."[70] *Life* too advocated an end to the Korean conflict; but unlike Eisenhower, the magazine wished to compel the enemy to make peace on the UN's terms.[71] The Americans, *Life* added, should also bomb Manchuria, launch amphibious assaults behind Communist lines in Korea, and impose a "selective" blockade on the Chinese coast. The resulting cease-fire, *Life* promised, would leave Syngman Rhee in control of most of the Korean peninsula, along with 80 to 90 percent of its population. After that victory, the United States and its allies in the region could decide where "choices" could be made and "the initiative recovered." This was a veiled reference to the liberation of China. But would a President Eisenhower follow Luce's volatile prescription?

Korea remained a touchy issue, but so did McCarthyism. Give-'em-hell Harry Truman, *Time* responded defensively, was himself "The Other McCarthy."[72] Though contemptuous of McCarthy, the senator's liberal critics ("muddle-heads") tended to remind Luce of the men who had betrayed Chiang Kai-shek.[73] Ultimately, Luce dismissed McCarthy as a distraction from more serious concerns.[74] When Eisenhower made a campaign appearance with McCarthy, *Time* was defensive. The general, the magazine blandly declared, had merely treated McCarthy "as the symbol of a deep sense of uneasiness among U.S. voters."[75] Luce dismissed protests against Eisenhower's collusion with McCarthy: If "the Republicans win in November," he argued, "in a year you'll be hearing very little of Senator McCarthy." Their civil liberties, Luce assured Americans, were safe.[76] Clare Luce took a different tack.[77] She praised McCarthy as a "scrapper" before chiding him for being a big-mouthed "blunderbuss."[78] But Luce bought McCarthy's basic message: Acheson, Harry Luce claimed, had been "so to speak on Stalin's payroll." And like the senator, Clare Luce also tied Stevenson to Hiss.[79] The ever elegant former editor, playwright, correspondent, and congresswoman had transformed herself into a kind of Joe McCarthy in drag.

When Eisenhower uttered the instantly famous words "I shall go to Korea," the Stevenson camp grew despondent.[80] Written by *Life*'s Emmet John Hughes, the Republican candidate's striking speech on Korea added to Eisenhower's insurmountable lead. Not taking any chances, Luce brusquely informed *Time*'s Tom Matthews that he himself would edit the preelection cover story on Dwight Eisenhower.[81] That issue of *Time* amounted to a coronation, and this time, the prodigal voters finally returned to Luce's "second church," the Republican Party. Eisenhower crushed Stevenson in suburban areas, and Ike also made inroads into the once "solid South." And to Harry's further delight, Eisenhower's landslide made it possible for the Republicans to gain narrow control of the Congress. Luce had another reason for rejoicing: With the GOP in control of the government, there would be no further talk about investigations of the China lobby, a threat that had been of some concern to him.

The "China Lobby"

Wayne Morse, a maverick Republican senator from Oregon, had for many months been demanding an inquiry into what the *New York Times* called the "loose conglomeration of persons and organizations which for various reasons are interested in China."[82] Morse provided the press with documents showing how Chiang's minions had infiltrated the American political process. He was particularly interested in the work of William J. Goodwin, who had earned thousands of dollars flacking for Chiang on Capitol Hill.[83] Working with Chen Chih-Mai, a counselor at the Chinese embassy, Goodwin schemed to influence U.S. foreign policy in favor of Chiang. The popular columnist Drew Pearson soon chimed in, accusing the Chinese Nationalists of having engaged in atomic espionage.[84] The Truman administration assembled preliminary data on various lobbyists and organizations, among them Alfred Kohlberg and the Luce-backed China Institute in America.[85]

Max Ascoli's respected *Reporter* magazine ran a series of startling pieces on the China lobby. Largely based upon research and interviews conducted by Charles Wertenbaker, a former Time Incer, the material in the *Reporter* revealed how lobbyists, embassy staffers, and American politicians conspired to help Chiang and influence U.S. foreign policy. The *Reporter* also demonstrated how the lobby relied upon the Luce media. It was all very vague and shadowy, but some of the group's activities may have been illegal. Stung by the unexpected attack, Chinese Nationalist agents struck back, accusing the *Reporter* of smearing good people. In addition, uncorroborated reports described how Guomindang agents bought newsstand copies of the magazine in order to burn them.[86] Luce had reason to fear embarrassment, but so did the Truman administration. An inquiry might expose the activities of powerful Democrats with ties to the China lobby, among them Tom Corcoran, Worth Clark, Louis Johnson, and Clark Clifford.[87] So Truman's waning administration buried the matter, but members of the lobby wondered whether it would stay buried if Stevenson were elected.

With the Republicans returning to power, Luce no longer needed to worry. President Eisenhower, who owed much to Luce and his media operations, never considered investigating the China lobby.

A Journey to East Asia

A jaunty Harry Luce came to his office the day after the election, "shaking hands and glowing happily to be on the winning side again." After twenty years in political exile, he felt vindicated by the victory to which he had contributed so much. At a lavish post-election dinner for his editors, he relished the moment. For those who accused *Time* of bias, Luce had a sarcastic answer: "I can assure you," he declared, "that among Republicans it is not generally regarded that *Time* showed any lack of objectivity."[88] Democrats and liberals demurred, and like Taft's more ardent followers, many would neither forget nor forgive Luce's role in the election of 1952. For once, those who tended to bemoan Luce's influence had been proven right.

The best post-election line was uttered when the unhappy Tom Matthews asked Luce, "Harry, now that you've got America, how do you like it?"[89] In truth, Luce liked it very much, for he expected a great deal from his friend Eisenhower. The president-elect asked Luce whether he would like an ambassadorship; but in fact, Harry would rather have been secretary of state. The only ambassadorship he coveted, Luce told Allen Grover, was the honor of representing America in a liberated China.[90] Most of all, he resolved to educate Eisenhower in the matter of China. And to boost his tutorial credentials, Luce intended to revisit East Asia and then share his wisdom with Ike and his future secretary of state John Foster Dulles, a Luce ally since 1946.

Syngman Rhee, Bao Dai of Vietnam, and Chiang Kai-shek all were eager to receive the famous publisher. Why wouldn't they be, when *Time*'s coverage in recent months had been more flattering than ever? In fact, in editing copy and writing advisory memos, Luce repeatedly ignored dissenting voices in his own camp. His aide Kip Finch, for example, had informed Luce that Nationalist Formosa was a reactionary police state incapable of retaking the mainland. Finch even argued that most mainlanders rejected the idea of "liberation" at the hands of Chiang's discredited regime. John Osborne, who had visited Formosa in the spring of 1952, echoed Finch's conclusions.[91] He worried about the influence of Chiang Ching-kuo, Chiang's son and the manager of his secret police, and longed for a democratic "third force" that would liberalize the Nationalist regime. Osborne also argued that the refurbishment of Formosa's aging, ill-equipped Nationalist forces would take at least two years. But little of the Finch and Osborne memoranda found its way into *Time*. Instead, the Chiang depicted by the magazine was a beloved Methodist and a teetotaler and nonsmoker. He commanded an army of six hundred thousand men, one-quarter of whom were prepared for the imminent war of liberation.[92] "Nowhere in the world today," added Luce, "is there a community which is living so completely for so great a purpose."[93] A *March of Time* newsfilm ("Formosa: Blueprint for a Free China") glorified Chiang's regime as a paragon of rural progress, social reform, and military preparedness.

Time Inc.'s support for Chiang's Formosa was particularly important in these years. In 1950, when the Chinese Communists consolidated their power and invaded Korea, the *New York Times* and the *Washington Post* published 247 articles and editorials about China. Two years later that number had fallen to a mere 28.[94] Into the vacuum raced *Time* and *Life* and *Fortune*, which sometimes published several China-related items in one week. In addition, the news items and even the editorials in those newspapers were usually neutral in tone, whereas Luce's publications could be counted upon to excoriate Communist

China and praise the Guomindang. Although events in Asia played prime roles in influencing public attitudes, it remained true that mass circulation publications were "capable of moving public opinion in the direction of editorial preference."[95]

Religious, educational, and humanitarian concerns worked in tandem with advocacy journalism when Luce considered his options in East Asia. Among the one million refugees from the mainland who had poured into Hong Kong were an estimated fifty thousand teachers, professionals, and scholars.[96] Some three thousand of these people were graduates of U.S. colleges, and Luce wanted to secure their talents for the West. Another factor in Luce's philanthropic effort was his desire to bolster pro-Western sentiments among the millions of overseas Chinese living in Vietnam and the Philippines. As a result of these concerns, a group called Aid Refugee Chinese Intellectuals, Inc., or ARCI, began to function in the spring of 1952. Among its major supporters were Paul G. Hoffman, Walter H. Judd, and Luce's able sister, Mrs. Beth Moore.[97] Even George C. Marshall, whom Luce privately blamed for much of China's anguish, lent his prestigious name and rich array of contacts to the ARCI operation. Luce himself donated Time Inc. stock, and the Luce Foundation supplied ARCI with $2,500 in seed money. Luce sat on ARCI's advisory board and made sure that *Life* promoted the organization. And through his longtime ties to the Rockefeller family, Luce helped ARCI tap in to the resources of the Rockefeller Foundation, then headed by his new Democratic ally, Dean Rusk.

By the time Luce toured the Far East late in 1952, ARCI had registered twenty-seven thousand refugees, thus making them eligible for assistance. The vast majority of these people would be resettled in Hong Kong or elsewhere in Asia in ethnic Chinese communities. In a parallel effort, Luce was heavily engaged in a drive to establish New Asia College. Such an institution, Luce believed, could absorb some of the refugee intellectuals from the mainland and attract favorable notice among overseas Chinese elsewhere. Luce wanted to select Formosa as the site for the college, but Hong Kong won out. This happened because some donors were wary of tying the future of New Asia College to a regime that repressed intellectual freedom.[98]

During his visit to East Asia, Luce called upon President Rhee in Seoul, and as always, the president demanded the unification of Korea and the expulsion of the Chinese armies.[99] Luce also conferred with General James Van Fleet, the American commander. Van Fleet spoke about defeating the enemy – at the acceptable risk of forty thousand more UN casualties. Like Luce, he preferred this outcome to a bloody stalemate fought against the backdrop of futile peace talks.[100] Luce echoed such views when he insisted that, given two or three more U.S. divisions, the Communist armies in Korea could "and must be" destroyed.[101] Luce maintained that at the very least, the UN should march to the "waist" of North Korea, thereby unifying most of the country.[102] He also decided that free elections in a united Korea should take precedence over the quest for an armistice.[103] In a bitter aside, Luce mocked unnamed Americans who had killed a million civilians in World War II, but would not bomb Red bases beyond the Yalu River. He certainly had his work cut out for him. Eisenhower, who had talked about free elections in a united Korea, was now willing to return to the status quo ante there, with a few minor modifications. And there was no indication that he would push Japan into an unpopular alliance with Chiang and Rhee.

Touring Vietnam

Before his frequent visits to foreign lands, Harry Luce was in the habit of reviewing old stories in *Time*. (In fact, he may have been the magazine's most gullible reader.) Referring to the bound copies that adorned his office at Rockefeller Plaza, Luce could find many articles about France's war in Indochina. At times, *Time*'s faith in technology blinded it to the strength of a nationalist movement capable of mobilizing the peasantry. But modern artillery and air power, the magazine later admitted, were stymied by the doctrine of guerrilla warfare developed by General Vo Nguyen Giap: "Our object is not to take Haiphong or Hanoi, but to start a war of attrition."[104] French dive-bombers dispersed concentrations of guerrillas, who then escaped into a world sheltered by triple-tiered jungles and impenetrable darkness.

In its search for a path to victory, *Time* convinced itself that Jean de Lattre de Tassigny, the commander in Indochina, was a "French MacArthur." In *Time*-speak, de Lattre was "impeccable from kepi to pigskin gloves" and displayed a "hawklike profile."[105] Comparing the French commander to the heroes who had once defended Verdun, *Time* sometimes came close to declaring victory in Vietnam. It would exude this same overconfidence for the next fifteen years. When de Lattre visited New York, he repaid Luce for his support. Luce booked a large room at the Union Club and hosted a gala dinner for the friendly French commander.[106] But Luce's stubborn optimism could not banish all doubts, for *Time* admitted that few Vietnamese wanted to fight on France's side. And to the magazine's regret, de Lattre soon died of cancer at age sixty-two.[107] *Time* then described the "permanent nightmare" in Indochina, and in a moment of candor, it denounced French tactics ("Maginot-mentality") and acknowledged the efficacy of Vietminh General Vo Nguyen Giap's hit-and-run tactics.[108] But France's setbacks only intensified *Time*'s demand for greater American involvement in Vietnam.

"Whether the U.S. likes it or not," opined *Time*, "the U.S. is very much in the 'dirty war' itself."[109] Naturally, *Time* was sympathetic when the French expressed their desire for a "definite U.S. promise of armed forces for Indo-China – sea and air support, not ground troops – in the event the Chinese invaded."[110] But *Life* went further in the late summer of 1951, when the magazine declared, "Of all new battlefronts where American troops may soon be fighting, Indo-China is generally considered the likeliest."[111]

In December 1952, Harry Luce made extensive notes in Indochina during his "excellent visit with jungle and delta war." As usual, he met only with high officials, including French generals, the U.S. ambassador, and the puppet prime minister of Vietnam. Yet Luce did gain some real insights into thorny problems. A visit with Emperor Bao Dai left him unimpressed. He saw that French colonialism had looted the country and left bitterness in its wake. Luce also realized that the French Union was weak and was viewed with disdain by most Vietnamese. Luce saw the gap that divided the francophile upper classes in Saigon from the peasants in the countryside. And however superficially, Luce also grasped a central fact that eluded *Time*: *All* Vietnamese patriots – presumably including those led by Ho Chi Minh – feared China. But Luce refused to delve more deeply into its implications, for his findings would have blurred *Time*'s rock-hard image of the Sino-Soviet-Vietminh monolith. As Clare Luce put it, Mao was a "servant of the power of the Kremlin," and *Life* insisted, "It's all one war, and our war, whether the front be in Europe, Korea or Indo-China."[112] Ultimately, the publisher sought security in old verities, which described Indochina as "a base in the general conflict against Communist China."[113]

Luce convinced himself that the Philippines, which he viewed as a success story inspired by American benevolence, could serve as a model for Indochina. In that country, Luce argued, "the United States blew the trumpet note which was to end colonialism."[114] He added, "We gave the gift of freedom, but they received." Ramon Magsaysay, an ambitious anti-Communist Filipino politician, had greatly impressed Luce. In fact, Time Inc., working with and subsidized by the CIA, was soon funneling illegal money into Magsaysay's campaign coffers. The funds were laundered by having the politician "write" an article for *Life*, but the essay was incoherent and had to be completely redone.[115] In subsequent years, *Time* celebrated President Ferdinand Marcos of the Philippines as an ally who was building a pro-American model for Southeast Asia.[116]

Americans, Luce concluded, must pressure the French into instituting reforms – while arming them ever more heavily. He did concede that the Vietnamese must have real independence – but not until 1960. By downplaying Ho Chi Minh's appeal to that great force called nationalism, *Time* was helping to usher in a tragedy of immense proportions. But to Luce, "U.S. determination could win the cold war in East Asia."[117] *Time* and *Life*, more than other major publications, were preparing Americans for intervention in Indochina.

An Alliance with the White House

A lunch with the affable Ike inevitably left Luce feeling chipper. "It was a wonderful experience," he would tell Billings.[118] So when Ike summoned Luce to the Commodore Hotel for a friendly lunch early in 1953, the publisher happily complied.[119] But there were jarring moments, such as when Ike demonstrated his golf swing instead of responding to Luce's entreaties regarding Asia. Eisenhower, Luce complained, refused to read and was smart but "never thoughtful." In fact, Luce did his best to ignore more serious warning signs, as when Eisenhower was noncommittal about his intentions in regard to Korea.[120]

When Luce urged Ike to visit Taiwan, the president-elect rejected that controversial bit of advice.[121] He smiled at the China lobby – but warded off its
embrace.

Other major differences were papered over: *Time* and Luce insisted that
Americans were tired of the *stalemate* in Korea, and not of the war itself.[122] In
fact, most Americans wanted to end the war without enlarging its battlefields;
Eisenhower knew this, but Luce did not. Ike also rebuffed Walter Judd, who recommended that the president-elect give a major role in Asia policy to Douglas
MacArthur. Publicly, Ike was gracious: After a lunch with MacArthur, he referred to him as "my old commander."[123] But in regard to Walter Judd's recommendation, Eisenhower explained that he could not appoint MacArthur
without "having to be to the end of time his aide." Eisenhower had long before
played that role, and he did not intend to repeat it.[124] Ike, reporters discovered, refused to be co-opted by the Asia-firsters.[125] But Luce would hear no
evil: Eisenhower and Dulles, Luce insisted, would bring about a "shift of world
power."[126]

To the dismay of some of his top editors, Luce insisted that Time Inc. express unadulterated admiration for the young administration. Although citizen
Luce would sometimes complain privately about Ike's lack of a militant policy, editor Luce rushed to make alibis for Eisenhower in his magazines. Why
not, when the new crowd in Washington included some old friends? Emmet
Hughes aided Eisenhower for a time, and the president made full use of this
talented intellectual. C. D. Jackson – crusading idealist, gossipy conspirator,
and hail-fellow-well-met – went to work as special assistant to the president
for international affairs. In his White House office, he concocted imaginative
if impractical tricks for winning the Cold War. Jackson, however, quickly discovered that Eisenhower was a cautious man, and Dulles was vain, secretive,
boring, and instinctively turf conscious.* And to his regret, Jackson found that
the new administration was loath to take on Joe McCarthy, whom Jackson
despised. Both Jackson and Hughes would leave the administration before its
first term ended, but for some time, they supplied Luce – and hence *Time* –
with inside information about foreign policy issues.† Over the next eight years,
Luce and his staff at Time Inc. would enjoy unprecedented access to the president and his administration. How sweet this was, compared with their chilly
relations with FDR and Harry Truman.

---

* Flying home from overseas before the inauguration, Jackson found himself sitting opposite Dulles.
  The secretary of state said nothing for an interminable hour. Finally, he asked Jackson a question:
  "Where do you get your shoes?" DJSB, 19 December 1952.
† C. D. Jackson briefly returned to the White House in 1958 as a speechwriter and consultant. He
  died in 1964.

PART THREE

TIME INC., EISENHOWER, AND ASIAN POLICY, 1952–1959

11

Unwelcome Moderation

Eisenhower's Caution in East Asia

Harry Luce was now in his mid-fifties, and though highly energetic, he was showing signs of wear. His hearing had steadily worsened, and his teeth showed signs of neglect. Luce smoked incessantly, ignoring medical evidence about cigarettes that *Time* itself took seriously.[1] But he was still ready to share in an unusual adventure: Early in 1953 President Eisenhower nominated Clare Boothe Luce to be ambassador to Italy. For more than three years, Harry spent almost half his time in Rome, attending receptions, touring the city, and hanging out in Time Inc.'s small bureau. Like a diligent student, Luce read everything he could about the Eternal City and even bragged, "I know more about Rome than anybody since Nero."[2] He was immensely proud of his controversial wife,[3] whose hard line against "appeasement" struck some as unfortunate in the new era that followed Stalin's death.*

Whether in Rome or New York, Harry Luce, like *Life*, believed that "the peace we sought in China cost China its freedom."[4] China, he fervently believed, remained an American responsibility. For this reason the nomination of Walter Robertson to be assistant secretary of state for Far Eastern affairs gave great satisfaction. As Jack Beal cabled from Washington, Robertson's "estimates of [Department of State] maneuvers, of personalities – and of Yalta – could not be more in line with ours than if we had written the qualifications for the job ourself."[5] Robertson, for example, thought that the cessation of military aid to Chiang in 1946 represented "stupid, blundering idiocy on the part of our government."[6] Like Luce, Robertson viewed Zhou Enlai as a "charming gentleman who would cut his grandmother's throat if he saw advantage in it," and he insisted upon the solidity of the Sino-Soviet alliance.[7] The new assistant secretary described Luce's ally Walter Judd as the "best-informed member of Congress" on the China issue.[8] Robertson would not labor alone: Karl Rankin, ambassador to Taipei, and Everett Drumright, who reported on China from his

---

* Soon, terms like "the thaw" and "peaceful coexistence" challenged the hard-line rhetoric of the late Stalin éra.

11.1   Chief Justice Fred Vinson swears in Clare Boothe Luce, ambassador to Italy, in 1953 while Secretary of State John Foster Dulles looks on. (Library of Congress)

listening post in Hong Kong, were both fervent advocates of the Nationalist cause.[9]

Time expected that Ike, Dulles, Robertson, and like-minded congressional leaders would effect a revolution in U.S. foreign policy. But Luce's hopes had again subverted his judgment. True, the new president "unleashed" Chiang, and certainly, unshackling the Nationalists boosted morale on Formosa; but Chiang would remain on his island fortress.[10] Nor would Ike join the Nationalists in a war against Beijing. In addition, Harry's son Henry Luce III ("Hank") reported that plans to bolster the Nationalist army by recruiting overseas Chinese had failed to secure Eisenhower's support.[11] Jack Beal, who enjoyed good access to Dulles, learned that the new secretary had assured America's allies – especially the cautious British – that nothing reckless would be done.[12] Harry Luce, however, gave his readers a different impression.

Luce's report "America and Asia" (*Life*, 2 March 1953) was both a profession of faith and a program for change. The striking cover revealed its author's intent: Determined Nationalist soldiers were training for The Day ("Formosa Gets Ready"). America, Luce again reminded *Life*'s readers, needed to help them, for "the Pacific Ocean is now our ocean." But Luce warned that as long as Red China existed, Japan, currently a vital American outpost, remained a precarious ally: Forced to trade with its old enemy, China, Japan might one day subvert the American strategic position in the western Pacific. But there was reason for hope. Luce mused about dislodging Manchuria from "Soviet control," although that control existed largely in his imagination. Chiang, Luce argued, ran the "best government in all Asia," one inspired by "democratic idealism." As part of his propaganda campaign, Luce at one point insisted that *Life* publish a long article by the Generalissimo himself. Although managing editor Ed Thompson thought Chiang's piece dull, editorial director John Billings growled, "Well, he's got to run it, whether he likes it or not."[13]

"Go forward, bravely, straightforwardly, gently," Luce advised America, but growing Soviet nuclear strength sometimes interrupted his reveries. As *Time* wrote in January, this was the time to talk tough to the Soviets before the Russians could "use the same terms [i.e., the H-bomb] in talking back."[14] The goal, in *Time*'s words, was to be "able to hurt the enemy more than he can hurt the U.S."[15] In fact, Luce and *Time* longed for a global victory that could be won "without total war."[16] The Kremlin's talk about "peaceful coexistence" failed to impress *Time*; and *Life* cautioned readers, "'Relaxed tensions' can be at least as dangerous as cold war."[17] Nor did cogent reports anticipating Sino-Soviet tensions impress Luce, even when they were filed by his son Hank.

In the summer of 1953, young Luce reported that Chinese industrialization worried the Soviets, who were not eager to see China become a major power.[18] (Robert Bowie, head of the State Department's policy planning staff, may have been the authority cited in Hank Luce's cable.)[19] Although Luce junior might get away with a certain show of independence, other *Time* correspondents were more careful. They typically reported, "The two communist countries are united...and it is ridiculous to think they can be divided."[20] In fact, if Russia and China were solidly united as allies, as *Time*'s editors claimed, then that made the case for a U.S. policy calculated to divide them *more*, not less, compelling.[21]

In the summer of 1953, the administration agreed to armistice terms in Korea. Communist prisoners would not be forced to return to their homelands, and Eisenhower had been prepared, as *Time* claimed, to enlarge the air war if the enemy launched major new offensives. Yet none of this was novel, for Harry Truman had also refused to accept forced repatriation, and he too had been prepared to extend the war if China moved too far south. Moreover, the armistice line drawn in 1953 closely followed the prewar demarcation between the two Koreas. Luce regretted the fact that Eisenhower had failed to reunite Korea, but *Time* helpfully decided that a "diplomatic stalemate was preferable to a military stalemate."[22] Had Harry Truman agreed to the same armistice, *Time* would have savaged him.

Thanks to its favoritism to the Republicans, *Time*'s readers came to regard the magazine as the voice of the White House. But privately, Luce complained that the Communists controlled half of Korea, thanks to the cease-fire; the French position in Indochina was crumbling; Red China seemed stronger and not weaker; and Chiang unleashed was once again tethered. Equally troubling to Luce was the fact that Prime Minister Churchill, Ike's good friend, seemed eager to engage in dialogue with the Communists. When in Luce's presence, Churchill enjoyed ridiculing China's military potential: "It takes more than 600 million pigtails to make an army!"[23] The Red Chinese, he believed, were "not a first class power."[24] Moreover, Britain had recognized Red China and Churchill was not averse to new summits with Stalin.[25] We certainly do not...want our State Department run by the British," Luce responded in September 1953.[26] He feared that Eisenhower too might show weakness.

In the words of John Billings, Luce's "affection for Eisenhower & Dulles and his duty as *Time's* editor sometimes conflict – and he squeals out loud in his personal pain."[27] But publicly, Luce remained Eisenhower's loyal ally, for as John Billings observed, meeting with Ike affected Luce "like strong liquor."[28] No more than a gentle reprimand ever surfaced, even though the president was cautious about poking "the [Soviet] animal through the bars of the cage."[29] True, *Life* once warned the White House, "If we are going to rely on these [new nuclear] weapons...we have got to be prepared to use them."[30] Ultimately, however, *Time* accepted Ike's assurance that a willingness to contemplate the use of nuclear weapons was the "greatest single responsibility of the President in this age, and I fully accept it."[31] Eisenhower's artful ambiguity probably eluded Luce.

11.2   President Eisenhower with Clare Boothe Luce, ambassador to Italy. (Library of Congress)

Shielding Eisenhower was made easier by his cultivation of Luce and his operatives. Ike was careful to praise a Luce speech when it seemed "to say exceedingly well many of the things" on his mind.[32] The president also did personal favors for Luce. For example, Ike contacted Texas oilman Sid Richardson, who agreed to raise money for Luce's pet project, the National Presbyterian Church in Washington, D.C. But favors aside, Luce was unlikely to attack Eisenhower for another reason: Time Inc.'s easy access to the administration was too valuable to risk. After twenty long years in the Democratic desert, Luce would not easily break with Ike.

Luce's admiration for his friend John Foster Dulles strengthened his ties to the administration.[33] Like Luce, Dulles was given to ruminations about the interplay between Christian morality, international politics, and power. (Luce and Dulles served together on the National Laymen's Committee of the Restoration Fund of the Presbyterian Church in the U.S.A.) Luce insisted in September 1953, "[Dulles] is the champion of the proposition that politics (including international politics) has something to do with morals and that morals have something to do with God."[34] Dulles would, *Time* had predicted, abandon the "negative policy of containment."[35] In numerous conversations with a vaguely attentive secretary of state, Harry Luce sketched out a system called "peace through law." Instead of the brutal chaos that then defined international relations, Luce would put in place an American-sponsored international law respected by all. The coming "understanding between the peoples," he hoped, would then result in a new world order.[36] American bounty and love of freedom would be exported to its grateful beneficiaries, and free men under God would work to build the Heavenly City. "Peace through law" doubtless served as a propaganda cover for the holy war against lawless Communism, but Luce, like many other internationalists, believed in it. Through his tireless efforts, "peace through law" concepts influenced the rhetoric of both the American Bar Association and the Eisenhower administration.[37] Yet doubts gnawed away at Luce.

Privately, Henry Luce suspected that the secretary was really pursuing goals that smacked of containment.[38] He also worried that Eisenhower and Dulles might "neutralize" Formosa and allow Red China to enter the UN. Public opinion polls displayed a certain ambiguity, too. By a margin of almost three to one, surveyed Americans opposed the admission of Red China to the United Nations, but most respondents also opposed abandoning the UN in the event of Beijing's entry.[39] Faced with this data, Luce and the China lobby argued ever more loudly that (1) the Chinese Communists were out to destroy the UN Charter and must not be allowed to enter the organization, and (2) Red China was run by a savage clique directed by Moscow. In October 1953, more than two hundred concerned Americans of like mind laid the foundation for the Committee of One Million Against the Admission of Communist China to the United Nations (hereafter called the Committee of One Million, or COOM).[40] Ultimately, the committee claimed that 1,037,000 Americans had signed its charter, and it boasted of having 6,000 contributors and a mailing list containing 25,000 names.[41]

The man behind the committee was Marvin Liebman, its young secretary. An ex-Communist turned anti-Communist crusader and a career publicist, Liebman organized petition drives and provided friendly newspapers with appropriate op-ed pieces. Liebman also acted as a liaison between the lobby and its favored leaders, among them Rhee, Chiang, and later, Ngo Dinh Diem. The energetic Marvin Liebman made frequent use of allies in organized labor and also in academe, where Professor Richard L. Walker (Yale, then the University of South Carolina) helped to generate anti-Communist materials supportive of friendly East Asian regimes patronized by the United States. Luce himself was a member of and contributor to COOM. *Time* could be counted upon to spread the word about the new Committee of One Million, and the committee distributed large numbers of articles culled from Luce's magazines.[42]

Eisenhower and Dulles were careful not to cross swords with the Committee of One Million, but they also worked to restrain Chiang. For this delicate task Eisenhower required a messenger who stood in the good graces of the COOM and the China lobby.[43] During the last phase of the Korean War, General James A. Van Fleet, who had commanded UN forces in Korea, had been sympathetic to South Korean calls for an all-out drive for victory.[44] Van Fleet subsequently wrote two highly publicized articles for *Life* and thereby earned the respect of both Luce and the China lobby. Because of Van Fleet's credibility, he was now in Taipei, where his task was a challenging one.[45] Van Fleet assured Chiang that Americans would "support any plan" that might enable "Free China to achieve victory in the Far East." But the general was noncommittal when Chiang tried to obtain more heavy artillery and tanks – precisely the weapons needed by the Nationalists if they were to ever retake their homeland. To avoid misunderstanding, in late May the administration sent Defense Secretary Charles E. Wilson to Taipei. "Engine Charlie" Wilson, the blunt-spoken former head of General Motors ("What's good for General Motors is good for America") warned the touchy Chiang against an overemphasis upon "military preparedness."[46] When the Generalissimo asked for the equipment needed to outfit two armored divisions, the secretary bluntly advised him to construct a modern power plant instead.

"Unleashing Chiang" and "liberation" were mere slogans – but not to Henry R. Luce.

K. C. Wu as Apostate

In the spring of 1954, Luce and the China lobby had to endure another unpleasant episode. To understand the uproar over K. C. Wu's defection from Formosa, one must go back almost a decade, to the Chinese civil war, when Luce's press praised K. C. Wu as the brilliant forty-three-year-old mayor of the hitherto ungovernable city of Shanghai.[47] Indeed, Dr. Wu Kuo-chen ("K. C." to his many American friends) had been educated in the United States. Luce praised Wu as "extremely able," a "lively person," and a "Princeton man," and called him a "very good friend."[48] According to Claire Chennault, Wu, who was later the governor of Taiwan, had "done a superb job." But he had "hurt many feelings and pocket books by insisting on land reforms, reduction of rentals, collection of taxes from [all], [and] honesty in public office."[49] Wu found that his advocacy of greater democracy provoked resistance on the part of the clique around Chiang.[50] By the spring of 1953, Wu suspected that the regime was behind a possible assassination attempt. He left the government on 10 April and never again met with Chiang.[51] He decided to gather his family and leave Formosa, but he soon ran into trouble orchestrated by Madame Chiang. At first, she apparently wanted to give him $10,000, as a way of securing his loyalty, but when Wu turned down the funds and threatened to go public with charges of tyranny and corruption, Madame relented.

In May the Wu family departed for the United States. Left behind was a fourteen-year-old son, allegedly because he would have to serve in the army before obtaining a passport. After arriving in Seattle, Wu remained reasonably silent. (Friends of the China lobby assumed that Wu was merely squabbling with Chen Cheng or other politicians around the Generalissimo.) Then the Chiangs tried to entice him back to Formosa, and when Wu refused their offers, the regime spread rumors that he had fled Formosa with a fortune in stolen money.[52] On 7 February 1954, Wu denounced Chiang's authoritarianism and called for democracy on Formosa.[53] He hoped that his old admirer, Harry Luce, would rally to his cause.

In making his case, Wu supplied Luce with many plausible details and noted that he had resigned only when an administration friendly to Chiang had come to power in Washington.[54] But when Time Inc. rejected his exposé, Wu published it in *Look* instead. Wu's charges upset Luce, who quickly mobilized his network. *Time*'s Jim Shepley spoke with Walter Robertson and Admiral Arthur Radford, both of whom expressed "unshaken confidence in the Generalissimo."[55] Claire Chennault, who had praised Wu, suddenly accused him of becoming "sour and embittered because of personal ambitions."[56] Walter Judd thought that the expatriate was perhaps a bit crazy. After all, Judd added, "totalitarian government is the only kind that has proved effective in the Far East." (What did he think of Tojo's Japan?)

Wu, once a hero to *Time*, now found himself the target of a widely cited smear campaign launched by B. A. Garside. This Luce family tool attacked Wu as vain, ambitious, and unpatriotic.[57] True to its tried and tested formula, *Time* published some of Wu's criticisms of Chiang's regime and then gave Wu's enemies the last word: The regime blamed Wu for spreading "malicious propaganda" that could only aid the Communists.[58] Time Inc. and its allies managed to sow doubts about Wu's charges and motives. Wu, who remained in the United States, faded into obscurity.

Burying the McCarthy Era

After Eisenhower took office, Luce closely monitored the purge of "Acheson-ism" at the State Department. John Carter Vincent was of particular concern to *Time* because he had been a patron of General Stilwell and a confidant of

Foreign Service officers critical of Chiang. The Loyalty Review Board of the Civil Service Commission reopened Vincent's case.[59] He was soon suspended and ordered to return home from his post in Tangier. But Acheson would not let the matter rest, and Harry Truman, in his last days in office, appointed a new review board. Friends of the China lobby were furious, and Secretary Dulles quickly revoked Truman's decision. Relying upon his security chief, Scott McLeod (whose services were supplied by Senator Styles Bridges), and beholden to Walter Judd, Dulles cleared Vincent of the disloyalty charge. He let him keep his pension but made him resign. *Time* gloated and insisted that Vincent's analyses had been "pro-communist" and "criminally negligent." In fact, John Carter Vincent was a "scapegoat," for he was being persecuted, not for having been wrong about the Communists, but for having been right about Chiang's imminent doom.[60]

In February 1953 Betty Vincent appealed to Henry Luce as a fellow patriot and Christian. Describing her husband's fate as "frightening and dangerous,"

11.3   Ambassador Luce and Secretary Dulles at the time of an audience with Pope Pius XII. (Library of Congress)

Mrs. Vincent hoped that Luce would change course and "make the end a happier one" than her "nightmares" permitted her "to believe possible." Appealing to Luce's pride in his work, Mrs. Vincent mentioned that *Time* was widely read among students at her son's prep school.[61] Luce mulled things over for a number of days and then responded. To Luce, Vincent's take on China represented apostasy.[62] He believed that millions of Chinese were dead because men like Vincent had undermined Chiang Kai-shek. Luce therefore rebuffed Mrs. Vincent. Ironically, *Life* shed a crocodile tear or two over the low morale that drained the Foreign Service of its strength. But Luce would defend embattled Foreign Service officers only if they first purged themselves of "Achesonian" ways of thought.[63] Vincent, Luce concluded, had not done so.

Overall, Time Inc.'s position on civil liberties was far shakier than it had been in the late 1940s.[64] Reversing earlier positions, Luce and his editors now viewed the mere avowal of Communism as proof of conspiracy.[65] And while Luce talked grandly about his yearning for the "clash of honest debate in all realms of thought, for . . . intellectual freedom," his editorial director Billings bragged about firing employees who invoked their Fifth Amendment privilege.[66] Even Luce's courageous opposition to McCarthy reflected an antipathy to the senator's style rather than an attack on his goals. This opposition also smacked of politics. Luce had always insisted that a Republican victory would be the best antidote to McCarthy. But even in the face of McCarthy's ever wilder charges – against Protestant clergy, U.S. Army officers, and university presidents – the president refused to engage the Wisconsin renegade.[67] In response, *Life* attacked the McCarthyite purge of books stored in libraries maintained by the U.S. Information Service, and *Time* blasted McCarthy's "junketeering gumshoes."[68] Retaliating, McCarthy again labeled *Time* a pro-Communist smear sheet, especially after it published exposés about his insider trading and influence peddling.[69] In March 1954, *Time* glumly admitted that McCarthy was "more prominent than ever before."[70]

Through his reckless behavior, however, McCarthy had managed to energize a potentially fatal coalition: It included U.S. senators, the Pentagon, some of the administration, and much of the press.[71] *Time* demanded action but fretted, "The axes that will cut down McCarthy's power will have to be a lot sharper than those in the hands of [the Department of the Army] last week."[72] Soon, however, *Time*, like most of the country, watched in fascination as the Army-McCarthy hearings, chaired by "amiable, rotund Karl Mundt," resulted in the senator's self-immolation. McCarthy – scowling, smirking, showing a sweaty face bedecked with a five-o'clock shadow, and emitting "half-stifled belches" – lurched toward his doom.

In Joe McCarthy's opinion, *Time* was one of his hangmen. He had once described an article about him as "not a bad story at all – for Time Magazine," and on another occasion, the senator had complained that a *Time* cover "made him look like a bum."[73] But *Time* now brandished a new weapon in its war against McCarthy, and it was Cold War homophobia. (This was ironic in the light of McCarthyite attacks on limp-wristed, cookie-pushing, left-wing pansies in the State Department.) In the fevered world of Joe McCarthy, upper-class leftists who betrayed their country might easily be "perverts" who eschewed morality. *Time* relished McCarthy counsel Roy Cohn's "inseparable" affection for G. David Schine, who displayed the "build and features of a junior-grade Greek god."[74] And the magazine loved the scene where Army counsel Joseph Welch responded to McCarthy's request for a definition of the word *pixie*: "Yes, I should say, Mr. Senator, that a pixie is a close relative of a fairy."[75] Homophobia thus impaled the very men – McCarthy and Cohn – who had so recently brandished it as a weapon.

As John Billings had wisely prophesied, McCarthy was "in the process of hanging himself."[76] *Life* gloated about "burying the McCarthy era once and for all," and in the autumn of 1954, the U.S. Senate censured McCarthy for unseemly conduct.[77] Although Luce later admitted that Eisenhower should have acted earlier, the "irrational nightmare" did go away, just as he had predicted.[78] Now Luce hoped that the administration would finally address the real peril staring America in the face, which he defined as follows: "The massive event in the world today is massively armed Communism – the military might of Red Russia and Red China which are neither responsive to any rule of reason nor responsive to any sentiment of decency or humanity."

Americans, Henry Luce concluded, must show a "willingness to wage war."[79]

Nation-Making?

Month after month and year after year, Time Inc. devoted more space to the war in Indochina than all of its competitors combined. The Vietnamese, *Time* asserted, were holding reasonably free elections, even in the midst of the war.[80] The Indochina war, Luce concluded in April 1953, "should be won soon."[81] Interventionist optimism was the order of the day. In his report on Asia for *Life*, Luce had decided that the United States might "have a hand in nation-making there." The war in Indochina had already cost the United States $1.5 billion, and in Luce's view, a loss there would be a "catastrophe." Given their bias, Luce and his editors typically ignored unpleasant omens.

One unidentified policymaker warned *Time*, "In Korea, we were coming to the rescue of a friendly people." But in Vietnam, "we would be moving in on the side of an unpopular foreign army struggling against a well established guerrilla force in a hostile population."[82] Against all evidence, Luce insisted that Ho Chi Minh wanted to create a *Chinese* Communist puppet state in Vietnam.[83] France, the magazine learned from one cable, was confronting a situation in which the enemy was "everywhere" and the front line was "nowhere."[84] From Saigon, another *Time* correspondent wrote about Communist Vietminh fighters who were "bypassing and ambushing [the] French but [were] refusing [to] do pitched battle anywhere."[85] In March, *Time* admitted that in the north the French controlled only a 6,000-square-mile wedge of land at the mouth of the Red River. Even there, they had to contend with forty thousand guerrillas.[86]

A cable sent to Time Inc. reported that Ho Chi Minh was deeply suspicious of the Chinese; that the court of Emperor Bao Dai was filled with men who had collaborated with the Japanese during the war; that the French did not trust their Vietnamese allies.[87] The gap between the information *Time* received and its published version of events steadily widened. Invariably, *Time* found a reason for renewed hope. The latest miracle was called the Navarre plan, after the new French commander (in *Time*-ese: "slim, trim Henri Navarre").[88] Navarre promised that he would push his men into the jungle and force the enemy to fight. France, weary of the war, would take heart if it spied the "light at the end of the tunnel" (General Navarre, 20 May 1953).[89] *Life* stressed Navarre's "taste for action."[90] The gap between Time Inc. and the truth was growing wider, even as Luce ignored public opinion. Americans, however, by margins of six to one, and even ten to one, opposed the dispatch of troops to Indochina.[91]

A Dissenting Voice on Vietnam Quashed

In the early summer of 1953, Time Inc. received a string of depressing pictures and cables from *Life* photographer David Douglas Duncan. He described an Indochina in which foreign mercenaries – but not many French or Vietnamese – were doing the real fighting. Although 577,000 soldiers and auxiliaries were officially under arms on the French side, they could not defeat a far smaller Vietminh force.[92] According to one independent Vietnamese editor who confided in Duncan, there was one great nationalist in Vietnam, "but unfortunately" he was "a communist named Ho Chi Minh." Duncan's devastating reports derided "inept French colonialism" and portrayed the French effort in Indochina as trapped in a "hopeless quagmire." He thereby coined a term that would resound for years to come.[93] Most of this material did not make it into *Time*, but to the dismay of Henry Luce, *Life* did publish a spread displaying David Duncan's version of the war in Indochina.[94]

Duncan's pictures showed languid French officers taking long siestas after having enjoyed two-hour, wine-soaked lunches. Calling Vietnam a "cesspool," Duncan argued that U.S. support for the dirty war had sullied America's image among once friendly Vietnamese. How could it be otherwise, when the Americans supplied the French with the napalm that ravaged their countryside? Duncan's heresy actually appeared in Luce's *Life*.[95] This happened because the editor-in-chief was absent in Rome. John Billings acted as editorial boss at Time Inc., and as a result he paid less heed to the complex weekly operations at *Life*.[96] Into the void moved senior editor Sidney James, who examined Duncan's gripping pictures and found them eminently publishable. In fact, James concluded that the hapless French seemed to have "a melancholy genius for living down to the worst you think or say about them." Adding an element of farce, the same issue of *Life* ran an editorial calling for *more* U.S. support in a war that was "indispensable to saving Indochina from the Communists."[97] If the French failed, *Life* implied, Americans would succeed.[98]

When the Duncan article appeared, both the French government and the American mission in Indochina were outraged. C. D. Jackson, who was working for Eisenhower, bore the brunt of the first assault: Prominent French newspapers, seconded by their government, attacked *Life*'s "slander."[99] This article, Jackson agreed, furnished "invaluable documentation to those who want to pull out." The Duncan spread, moreover, embarrassed Luce, who had just told high French officials how much he admired the new offensive spirit displayed by their army in Indochina.[100]

Donald R. Heath, U.S. ambassador to the Associated States of Indochina, also complained to Luce. Duncan, Heath protested, had portrayed the French as greedy mercenaries fighting a dirty colonial war in which "millions of American dollars [were] going down a rat-hole."[101]

The implications of the piece in *Life* outraged Luce, who referred to Duncan as a "Rover Boy" who had "fouled up basic policy."[102] Although Luce agreed that Duncan was a "great photographer," he briefly put him on the inactive list. Luce was not willing to apologize to the French Foreign Ministry, but he did agree to place a full page in *Life* at Ambassador Heath's disposal. There, the U.S. envoy told readers that France was "fighting the good fight in Indochina, the fight of the free world against Communism."[103] He concluded, "Final victory . . . is possible." *Life*, meanwhile, atoned for the heretical David Duncan piece by publishing misinformation supplied by the Department of State.[104] Paris, *Life* promised, would grant real independence to Vietnam, and the war would be won within two years.[105] (In fact, France failed to grant independence, and the war was lost less than a year later.)* Frustrated, *Time* called for an attack on Communist China, which it blamed for many of France's troubles in Indochina.[106]

At the end of September 1953, *Time* issued a prophetic warning in regard to the U.S. role in Indochina: "There is no guarantee that it will not some day have to be extended with American blood."[107]

Indochina: An American Dilemma?

Back in April, *Time*'s editors had received a dispatch containing the name of a small village near Laos called Dien Bien Phu. At first, the magazine labeled the obscure place a headquarters base for a Vietminh regiment. *Time* then went on to describe how General Navarre's paratroopers, flying in on U.S.-supplied C-47 transport planes, took the village in a "brilliant airborne attack."[108] Nor did the omniscient *Time* reject the strange strategy of General Navarre: The French held the low ground and *wanted* the enemy to surround them on the hills overlooking Dien Bien Phu. The Vietminh would then come, and, pounded

---

* Some of *Time*'s erratic or misguided reporting on Vietnam reflected its failure to assign a reporter to Hanoi on a permanent basis. For almost a decade, most of its information about the war came from sources in the Pentagon, the State Department, and Paris. Occasionally, a correspondent based in Manila or Hong Kong might visit Vietnam, a country about which he knew little.

by French air power and artillery, they would bleed to death. John Foster Dulles insisted that the Communist offensive was a sign of Ho Chi Minh's weakness in the face of the French resistance; *Time* believed him.[109]

In late January 1954, correspondent John Mecklin alluded to growing numbers of Vietminh troops around "beleaguered Dienbienphu." However, the Luce publications remained steadfast.[110] *Time* cited General Navarre's confidence in ultimate victory, but the magazine should have paid more attention to one of its inside sources. "French pilots don't like to take chances," Bedell Smith of the State Department complained.[111] The situation grew more desperate, and in February, *Time* learned that high-ranking figures at the National Security Council and in the Pentagon were musing about using nuclear weapons in Indochina.[112] There was also talk about imposing a naval blockade on China or installing a U.S. command in Indochina.[113] Later, *Time* staffers covering the Pentagon reported a rumor that American carriers had entered the Gulf of Tonkin and were ready to launch their warplanes. After encountering Soviet submarines, however, the American warships departed.*

In the late winter of 1954, the French government considered extricating itself from the war. It might, the United States learned, attend a five-power peace conference, one that included Red China. Dulles felt trapped, because he knew that at such a summit, much of Indochina might be handed over to the Communists. But would the Pengaton act to salvage the French position, or would it take over the war altogether? Luce certainly hoped so. *Time*'s Washington sources rashly predicted that the United States might send its soldiers into the jungle war.[114] But Ike was contemptuous of French tactics and worried about being tarred by their colonialist brush.[115] In fact, Eisenhower would not move into Indochina without the prior consent of a very nervous Congress.[116] Nor would he intervene without the support of Prime Minister Churchill, who wanted to test the waters at a Geneva peace conference.[117] *Time* also admitted that Eisenhower felt other "pressures against the involvement of U.S. manpower."[118] Eisenhower's "New Look" in defense strategy, which mandated cuts in the army, rendered unlikely expensive ground deployments in Southeast Asia. Intervention in Indochina meant, in the words of one *Time* correspondent, "goodbye to budget balancing and lowered taxes."[119] Jack Beal reported that the Democrats had "raised the specter of U.S. armies marching across the jungles; of the U.S. getting involved in another Korea."[120] Gallup reported that Americans opposed sending ground troops by a margin of three to one, and a majority even rejected the dispatch of "air and naval forces" to Indochina.[121] Jack Beal sadly added, "The American people want their government to keep out of fighting wars."[122]

All this was very frustrating to Luce, for the Americans were already paying 70 percent of the war's cost and had given the French three hundred sixty planes and fourteen hundred tanks.[123] Why then were the French losing the war? To Luce and his editors, the answer could be found in corrupt French colonialism.

---

* Time Inc. would soon be mourning its own casualty. The great photographer Robert Capa stepped on a land mine in the Red River Delta and died at the age of forty.

If Americans were in charge, they reasoned, things would be different. *Time* therefore bemoaned the fact that the U.S. public had "not been prepared for greater involvement."[124] C. D. Jackson thought that Time Inc. might be able to mold public opinion: "We simply must get over our complex that every little brown or black man with a tommy gun in his hand is automatically a 16-carat patriot on his way to becoming the local George Washington."[125] Time Inc., in other words, would decide who was the true Vietnamese patriot. Neither Luce nor Jackson nor *Time* was willing to confront the truth: The Vietminh prevailed against superior force because of their nationalist appeal to the rural population. This fact would not change when American commanders replaced French ones.

By early April, it was clear that Eisenhower would not deploy U.S. ground forces in Vietnam.[126] Nor would the United States bomb Vietnamese targets, as requested by the French.[127] In fact, as Dulles later admitted to *Time*, the president had given both the divided Congress and the reluctant British veto power over American intervention.[128] (One disgusted *Time* correspondent asked where you stopped the Reds – at "the Canadian border?")[129] Dulles's problems were compounded by the lack of Indochina experts in the State Department. During this era of McCarthyism, only one junior analyst had any claim to expertise on Vietnam, and he soon left for the Foreign Service. But even if senior experts had been available, would they dare tell their superiors that by demonizing Ho Chi Minh, the United States was involving itself in a war against Vietnamese nationalism, and not Chinese Marxism? *Time*'s editors continued to prepare its readers for an American mission whose very premises were flawed. Ho Chi Minh, Jack Beal insisted, was a Communist who took "his orders from Moscow."[130] *Time* brushed aside Ho's fear of long-term Chinese domination and rejected the rather stunning analogy between the peasant-based revolutions in Yugoslavia, China, and Vietnam.

Despite Eisenhower's maddening caution, Time Inc.'s wrongheaded certitude was not devoid of results. Among *Time*'s most avid readers were two American politicians with national ambitions: senators John F. Kennedy and Lyndon B. Johnson. Their pronouncement on Southeast Asia mirrored *Time*'s language, and knowing as they did what Luce had done to Acheson and Truman, they would think twice about "losing" Indochina.

By the end of April, the battle at Dien Bien Phu had entered its final days. *Time* learned that the British would not act, and in addition, "the answer [to French requests for U.S. bombings] was, sadly, no."[131] In an attempt at damage control, Dulles quickly assured *Time* and the China lobby that the situation in Southeast Asia would not lead to U.S. recognition of Red China.[132] The secretary went further, promising that in the event of a Geneva peace conference, he would not meet with Zhou Enlai "unless our automobiles collide." But *Time* was nervous. On 7 May the Dien Bien Phu fortress fell.[133] In *Time*-ese, a "torn-up world of broken stones and cluttered bunkers" was the setting for the last, heroic futility. Cabling from Hanoi, John Osborne described cities that were in the calm of a "coma," "awaiting death."[134]

One day after Dien Bien Phu fell, the nine-power peace conference convened in Geneva.[135] As Dulles scurried to find a way out of the mess created by the French, Luce's men privately reviled him for his blunders and his hesitation.[136] *Time*'s cover on Zhou ("Waging war and talking peace") was intended to warn Dulles against "appeasement" or recognition.[137] Negotiation of an Indochina cease-fire crafted by the Communist powers, *Time* feared, represented a threat to the "rest of Asia."[138] Instead of peace, Luce and *Time* wanted to forge a new coalition that would "fight off the Communists to the bloody end."

For the next few months, Dulles worked to convince such friends that others – possibly including Eisenhower – were to blame for the West's feckless stance. Had America been free to act, Dulles told *Time*, it long ago would have endorsed "self-determination" for Indochina.[139] As usual, the Luce media decided to give the Republican Dulles the benefit of the doubt: *Life*, against Luce's better judgment, praised the secretary for trying to cobble together a new anti-Communist coalition amid the wreckage in Southeast Asia.[140] *Time* and Luce now relished the idea of greater American involvement in the war. Commanded by a man like James Van Fleet, American instructors could train a "native," anti-Communist army.[141] (By 11 August 1954, 342 soldiers of the U.S. Military Assistance Advisory Group would be based in Saigon.) *Time* was also happy to learn that Pentagon sources spoke of responding to further "Chinese" aggression in Indochina by dropping A-bombs on Manchuria. There was even talk about reopening the Korean front as a way of punishing China.[142] And lest they forget, Luce reminded graduates of Occidental College, "The massive evil in the world today is . . . the military might of Red Russia and Red China."[143]

Incoming cables warned *Time*'s editors that Churchill and Eden would probably arrive in Geneva later in June; like the new French premier, Pierre Mendes-France, they desired a compromise.[144] *Time*, however, would not admit the obvious: that Chinese pressure, seconded by the Soviets, was forcing the victorious Vietminh to *scale down* their demands.[145] Beijing certainly disliked the prospect of a united, nationalist Vietnam. And Red China, some American officials believed, might release eighty-three American civilian and military prisoners in return for some kind of normalization of relations. But when asked about negotiating face-to-face with Zhou at Geneva to secure their freedom, however, Dulles replied, "No, we will not do it."[146] To strengthen Dulles's resolve, *Life* editorialized against the "Red plan to subvert and control the whole world." The magazine warned that the smooth Zhou would beguile the West, because he was "a ruthless intriguer, a conscienceless liar, a saber-toothed political assassin."[147] *Time*, referring to the "smell of peace" in the air, added that a deal with the Reds would be "like a pact with Hitler."[148]

Time moaned that "the free world" was "close to another big retreat before Communism." Reliable sources indicated that in the coming settlement, Laos and Cambodia would be neutral. The French would abandon northern Vietnam and, with it, the Red River Delta.[149] Vietnam would be temporarily divided at the seventeenth parallel, but nationwide elections would take place in two years. Limits were placed upon the presence of foreign bases and military personnel. Although the United States had neither signed nor supported the "Final Declaration," it agreed not to undermine it. In the south, a weak Vietnamese government under Emperor Bao Dai struggled to survive.

In Washington, *Time*'s staff reviled the settlement concluded on 20–21 July. Calling it "Munich, 1954," they complained that "we took a hell of a licking at Geneva."[150] C. D. Jackson, writing to Luce, argued that "the loss of Indo-China made the loss of Southeast Asia inevitable." *Time* went further and concluded that the *global* balance had shifted in "favor of Communist power."[151] And even as Dulles insisted that a new Southeast Asia Treaty Organization (SEATO) might "lead to the gain of the future," *Time* voiced skepticism.[152] But in an important cable, *Time*'s Washington staff hinted that Dulles might favor "junking a multilateral alliance in favor of U.S. guarantees to any Asian nation" that was "prepared to resist the advance of Communism."[153] Luce hoped that with the French mostly out of the way, Americans – noncolonialist, idealistic, and inspired by a can-do spirit – could do the job in Southeast Asia.

An American Dunkirk?

The polls showed that a plurality of Americans wanted to "try to win [Red China] away from Russia," and even some *Time* correspondents timidly alluded to Sino-Soviet tensions.[154] Privately, Dulles thought that the PRC was here to stay, and he continued to muse about a compromise in regard to the China seat at the UN.[155] And Eisenhower, an instinctive politician, knew that peace was good politics. More importantly, the president realized that nuclear deterrence mandated caution in addressing hot spots like the Taiwan Straits. Luce understood this reasoning – local crises could escalate into thermonuclear horrors – but he nonetheless rejected compromise in Asia. In response to perceived U.S. timidity, *Time* found solace in the belligerent words of South Korea's Syngman Rhee, who told the U.S. Congress that war against Red China was a good idea, even if Soviet Russia entered the conflict.[156] Rhee's "general argument," *Time* opined, was "difficult to dispute." Luce still mused about an attack on China by Rhee and Chiang, backed by an unspecified amount of U.S. aid. In his view, if the Soviet Union came to China's defense, so much the better. The drain upon its resources would weaken Russia as America supplied its Asian proxies with the bombs and wherewithal they required.

In a long memorandum, "Russian Atomic Power and the Lost American Revolution," Ambassador Clare Boothe Luce attacked the Geneva conference on Indochina as an American Dunkirk.[157] To the Luces, the "massive retaliation" threatened by Dulles sounded hollow. Luce wondered, "What the hell [good] does 'wide atomic lead' do us, if the other fellow has enough to destroy us, anyway?"[158] In Luce's view, reliance upon the threat of thermonuclear retaliation would only frighten our allies into seeking surrender instead of chancing annihilation.[159] In addition, fear of provoking Russia or China would make it impossible for the United States to involve itself in Third World trouble spots. In response to the new era of terror, Luce proposed spending three to five billion dollars more on the Pentagon, thus signaling, "From now on, we mean victory."[160] Luce was urging an open-ended nuclear race, a position that would later make him the foremost national advocate of bomb shelters for every family in the land.[161] Presumably, nuclear supremacy, if fortified by a defense against attack, would render "liberation" a real policy option. Luce's assumptions, however, flouted public opinion. As long as Eisenhower was in charge, people would accept containment and even the nuclear balance of terror ("deterrence").

Keeping the Pressure on Mao and Ho

On 3 September 1954, Communist artillery gunners shelled Quemoy Island, a heavily fortified Nationalist bastion. Quemoy was only four or five miles from the Chinese coast, and twelve miles from the port of Amoy; its status as a Nationalist symbol humiliated the People's Republic. Seen in this light, the bombardment and the accompanying verbal bombast were mostly propaganda. And because the fall of the offshore islands would not make a Communist invasion of Formosa any easier, some U.S. military planners viewed them as expendable.[1] Dulles, who had already committed the United States to the defense of Formosa, believed that Quemoy could hold out on its own.[2] Moreover, *Time*'s reporters knew that Red China was not preparing to attack Formosa.[3] But Luce demanded U.S. action: A proper response to the Red Chinese bombardment, he reasoned, might be a U.S.-backed blockade of the coastline opposite the islands. *Life*'s heavy artillery also shelled the British, whom Luce suspected of selling Dulles on "appeasement." "Stand by Free China!" *Life* demanded, and *Time* wanted "to find out at what special, awkward point the U.S." would begin "to care deeply."[4] "Chiang," Walter Robertson told *Time*, "is the most cooperative ally we have in the entire world."[5] Robertson, who had helped to formulate Dulles's China policy, was being used to allay Luce's concerns about administration inactivity in East Asia.

Unlike Luce, Eisenhower felt that Chiang was keeping too many of his forces on the offshore islands; if those bastions fell, Nationalist morale would plummet. The president, who knew something about amphibious landings, decided that it would be best if *Chiang* ordered a withdrawal from some of the islands.[6] At the very least, he should thin out his forces (fifty thousand men) there. And the administration wielded a big stick: Its forthcoming security pact with Formosa would not pledge the United States to defend the offshore islands. Because a friend of the China lobby would need to give Chiang the bad news, Walter Robertson, though ailing and ulcer-ridden, flew to Formosa. Dealing with the Generalissimo would not be easy, because the Chinese Communists were escalating the crisis. Americans incarcerated in the PRC received long prison sentences, and more shells crashed into Chiang's offshore fortresses.

In response to these events, Dulles created a new form of containment, one garbed in creative ambiguity. The United States would not commit itself to a war over the beleaguered islands but would defend them against any offensive that was *"primarily a preliminary movement to an all-out attack on Formosa."*[7] The secretary also foresaw a role for the UN in this crisis. Judging by the polls, Dulles, and not Luce, was right: Only 10 percent of those individuals surveyed by Gallup in October would support bombing the mainland even if the Communists invaded *Formosa*, much less Quemoy.[8] To an angry Harry Luce, an American appeal for UN intervention implied the neutralization of Formosa, followed by Red Chinese entry into the world body. Luce's reporters stoked these fears when they filed copy about "kicking Nationalist China off the Security Council."[9] But despite its suspicions, *Time*'s "Man of the Year" would be John Foster Dulles.[10] The cover story itself was classic *Time*-speak. It contained celebrations of "massive retaliation" (about which Luce had many doubts), the growth of NATO's strength in Europe, and the "101,521" miles traveled by John Foster Dulles in 1954 alone. But in return, Luce expected a firmer U.S. policy.

Time soon asked, "If neither Korea nor Indo-China nor Yikiang [Island] nor the Tachens is the place to fight the Communists, is there such a place?"[11] And *Life* went further: Its full-page editorial "Crisis of Free China" (31 January) expressed fear for the fate of Formosa itself. Chiang, in *Time*'s view, realized that the main enemy was the "Communist conspiracy directed from Moscow."[12] Citing Chinese who bemoaned the "first American double cross since the [1949] White Paper," *Life* warned, "The Administration will be criminally negligent unless it finds a way to convince all non-Communist Asians that we will not stand for [the neutralization of Formosa]."

In January 1955, Walter Robertson worked to appease *Time* by claiming that the UN ploy was a clever trap: The Reds were bound to spurn the Dulles offer and thereby lose a propaganda battle.[13] But old concerns lingered until the Red Chinese themselves, to *Time*'s delight, repudiated intervention by the Security Council.[14] Moreover, Walter Robertson again assured a skeptical *Time* that the United States would not recognize Red China. Chiang's imminent withdrawal from certain threatened islands, Robertson added, had nothing in common with Dien Bien Phu. The Tachen Islands, he pointed out, "were nothing but a man trap." Chiang's twelve thousand troops were needed elsewhere, and the United States would provide air cover for their evacuation. In effect, Chiang had been "released." From now on, he would be allowed only to retaliate; he could not initiate military action.

An alarmed Luce promptly dictated a message to Eisenhower by telephone. He blasted recent U.S. policy as the worst betrayal of China since the infamous 1949 "White Paper." And Luce told Eisenhower, "I now offer you my opinion that any slight weakening in the position and posture of the US as the forceful ally of all anti-Communists in Asia would, at this juncture, lead to disastrous consequences."[15] "You've got to defend them," Luce told the president when they discussed the offshore islands, and he said the same thing to Secretary Dulles.[16] In response, Eisenhower merely promised that the United States would not try to "dominate" the Nationalists, nor force them to undertake measures that "they would deem of serious damage to their political or military position."[17] The president agreed that Quemoy and Matsu were of value to Formosa, but he would move to defend them only if "convinced that the capture of these two places by international Communism would inevitably result in the later loss of Formosa to the free world."[18]

The Formosa resolution proposed by Eisenhower and endorsed by the Congress on 28 January 1955 authorized the use of force in the defense of Formosa and the nearby Pescadore Islands.[19] According to Jack Beal, Dulles had been willing to "publicly name Quemoy and Matsu" as part of the defensive perimeter, but Eisenhower had overruled him.[20] Luce remained suspicious, however, and *Life* was saddened by the U.S.-assisted evacuation of the Tachen Islands.[21] An unhappy Harry Luce favored air attacks, possibly even nuclear ones, against Red Chinese airfields and military bases facing the offshore islands and Formosa. But the Allies would repudiate such actions, and even *Fortune* admitted, "A Chiang who attempted to return to China under a mushroom cloud might not find himself welcome."[22] *Fortune* warned, however, that inconsistent American words and actions condemned Chiang to exile on an "Asiatic Elba" and weakened American influence throughout East Asia.

Eisenhower knew several important things that eluded Luce. In April 1955, as the Straits uproar subsided, Eisenhower mused that Chiang "might have seen the wisdom of trimming the garrison on the offshore islands down to the leanest fighting weight possible."[23] Writing to Dulles, the president expressed irritation when two heroes of the China lobby – Assistant Secretary Robertson and Admiral Arthur Radford – were themselves unable to grasp this strategic truth. Eisenhower owed much of his popularity to the Korean armistice, and most Americans were grateful that Eisenhower had avoided engaging American troops in World War III or in some ill-conceived Asian adventure. Peace and prosperity, and not "liberation," made Eisenhower's reelection in 1956 a virtual certainty. Overall, 68 percent of the public approved of the president's handling of his job, and only 18 percent disapproved.[24]

Time and Luce sought consolation in the fact that Dulles *might* choose to defend Quemoy.[25] And in the event of war, Red China would be hit.[26] *Life* hailed America's commitment to defend Formosa and listed its version of Chiang's assets: $1.5 billion in aid to Formosa since April 1951 (*Life*'s figures varied from issue to issue); Chiang's 350,000-man army along with his 75,000-man air force.[27] In April *Time*'s cover portrayed Chiang (whose name meant "Firm Rock") as a lone sentry manning the ramparts, ready for any emergency.[28] As it had repeatedly done in the past, *Life* was trying to tell Americans that Formosa, or even Quemoy, was, like Britain in 1940, a fortress resisting the common enemy. But as Gallup showed at the beginning of May, three-quarters of polled respondents favored an international conference on the "Formosa dispute" – one in which Red China and Russia participated.[29] And three weeks later, only 36 percent of Gallup's respondents endorsed a public commitment to the defense of the offshore islands.[30]

Harry Luce yearned for the time when a man like James A. Van Fleet (a "100% non-appeaser") might be in charge of China policy. As a result, he engaged Van Fleet as *Life*'s emissary to Formosa, and the retired general insisted that the offshore islands were vital to the defense of Formosa. He also threatened Red China with a hail of nuclear bombs.[31] Van Fleet, however, was not a policymaker, and his exclusion from the administration mirrored Eisenhower's suspicion of the Asia-first coalition for which Henry R. Luce was the prime media spokesman. John Osborne reported that Assistant Secretary Robertson was prepared to impose a U.S.-crafted peace plan upon Chiang and Formosa.[32] Osborne also claimed that even Walter Robertson had warned that this agreement would probably result in de facto U.S. recognition of the PRC. Egged on by Jack Jessup at *Life*, an angry Luce wondered out loud "whether Dwight David [Eisenhower] has a strategic concept and if so what it is." Luce also faulted Ike for not developing a "great policy of world leadership."[33] "The heart of today's news," he declared in May, "is that the President of the world's principal anti-Communist power hopes to come to [an] understanding with Asian Communism."[34] But Luce, a loyal Republican, nonetheless insisted that "before making [an] all out blast we should make strenuous effort to get Foster [Dulles] to explain confidentially."[35]

Discovering Diem

Peaceful coexistence in Europe had finally resulted in an Austrian state treaty, and the West German chancellor visited Moscow for the first time. Foreign Minister Molotov even toured the United States at one point appearing in Cheyenne wearing a cowboy hat.[36] There was talk of a four-power summit meeting, to be held in Geneva during the summer of 1955. An uneasy status quo prevailed in the Straits, and Zhou Enlai mused about the possibility of a *peaceful* liberation of Formosa. After "peaceful coexistence" became popular, Luce swallowed hard and publicly acknowledged, "The Spirit of Geneva was created primarily by an American President representing the American nation."[37] Ike, in *Life*'s defensive words, had not given away the store – unlike Roosevelt at Yalta.[38] Time Inc. was again playing Republican politics, but another factor kept Luce's company tethered to the administration.

Time Inc. was an arm of U.S. foreign policy. From the Philippines to Iran and Guatemala, Time Inc. fronted for the administration and worked with the CIA and other agencies in the battle against Communism. Luce liked to say, "The policy I advocate is intervention" and "interference in the internal affairs of other countries." Luce wanted to create a world in which pro-Western regimes – preferably, but not necessarily, democratic – might survive. Although Luce had once defended the right of "'people' to work out their own salvation, making their own errors and follies," he jettisoned that right when Communism was the perceived threat.[39] Such was the case in Indochina.

In 1954 and 1955, "free" South Vietnam was in terrible shape. The ravages of war, multiplied by an influx of refugees and political chaos, sapped the limited strength of the new state. *Time*'s State Department sources thought that the chances of "saving" South Vietnam were perhaps one in thirty.[40] From the beginning, however, Luce rallied to the idea that the United States must create a viable South Vietnam. Always a proponent of the great man theory of history, Luce and *Time* resolved to sell Premier Ngo Dinh Diem to the American people.

Diem was a devout Catholic, who in the early 1950s had lived in a New Jersey seminary. There, he was "discovered" by a Brooklyn congresswoman named Edna F. Kelly, who shared her highly favorable impressions with *Time*. Diem later served as an oblate, or lay member, in a Belgian monastery; his austere religiosity recommended him to the Luces and their allies in the Catholic Church. Luce's concern for Catholic refugees fleeing to the south only increased Time Inc.'s investment in Diem's regime. And another factor militated in favor of Diem's coronation by Henry Luce: The Vietnamese leader had declared, "America, and only America, at this crucial moment [1951], can resolve the dilemma inherent in the [Indochina] situation."[41] Time Inc. returned the compliment, and to *Time*, Diem was frugal and incorruptible, a staunch patriot. Above all, he was both anti-Communist (the Vietminh had killed one of his brothers) *and* independent of French influence (Diem had spurned all political offers, pending the grant of full independence to his country).[42] *Time* realized that the premier displayed authoritarian tendencies and could seem remote; but to its editors, Diem was the only alternative to Ho Chi Minh.[43] The Luce media decided that Diem could, with the right amount of American support, surmount his problems.

In the difficult year that followed the Geneva accords, Premier Diem had to contend with various military and business interests eager to keep South Vietnam divided. In the army, generals trained and paid by the French plotted against Diem, and sects variously composed of religious leaders, gangsters, and political enemies bedeviled him. In the towns and cities, four hundred fifty thousand refugees sapped the economy. Diem's access to U.S. aid enabled him to survive early challenges, but Eisenhower offered only conditional support. *Time* was unhappy about this tepid assistance, so its cover story on Ho Chi Minh explained why Diem must be supported.[44] Ho, after all, was a devious, fraudulent nationalist beholden to the Red Chinese and to Moscow.[45]

In November 1954 *Time*'s John Mecklin, who had covered Diem, made two startling prophecies. First, if the Saigon government grew stronger and attacked the Vietminh apparatus in the south (*Time* estimated that the Vietminh controlled 85 percent of the countryside),[46] the north might invade. Second, Mecklin indicated that Diem might block the nationwide elections scheduled for 1956 – even at the risk of provoking war. But 1956 seemed ages away, for in this autumn of 1954, the standoff between Ngo Dinh Diem and his generals threatened to erupt into civil war. As U.S. policymakers vacillated,

Time tried to goad Ike into action, and it chastised Pentagon officials who did "not want to get bogged down upon the Asian mainland."[47] Demanding that Asian Communism be "stemmed and turned," *Life* called for an "all-out effort in Vietnam."[48]

In March 1955, when the festering sore erupted into a major crisis, *Time* told how corrupt sects, conspiring with the French, had tried to overthrow the plucky little leader Ngo Dinh Diem. In pictures and in colorful words, *Time* contrasted the austere, pro-American Diem with the bizarre "pope" of the defeated Cao Dai sect. *Time* insisted that the Diemists now enjoyed the allegiance of half the people and were gaining on the Reds. Indeed, as the French presence receded, Diem's government assumed some of the trappings of sovereignty: control of the currency, control of the Port of Saigon, and military command. But *Time*'s inability to resist a colorful tale sometimes undermined its credibility: One of Diem's soldiers kicked over a wreath placed to honor Vietminh dead. Then a fearless young boy stepped forward and put it back.[49]

Much of *Time*'s optimism stemmed from information provided by Professor Wesley Fishel, a political scientist at Michigan State University who advised Diem on governmental organization. Fishel fed *Time* a steady series of stories, all of which depicted Diem as a wildly popular ruler hailed by "ecstatically happy" crowds.[50] Fishel's Diem loved America but lacked the requisite development experts, whom the United States needed to supply. In Washington, Jack Beal's sources now told him that Diem would not be abandoned "unless the Vietnamese themselves [were to] come forth with an acceptable alternative."[51] French forces finally withdrew from the Saigon region, and Diem began to scheme his way out of nationwide elections, which he was likely to lose. On 7 May the United States made it clear that if Ngo Dinh Diem wished to overthrow Bao Dai, the self-exiled head of state, he was free to do so. *Time* was happy, and it denounced those American officials who had stuck by the discredited emperor, whom Luce himself had introduced to the American people.[52]

"Every son, daughter and even distant admirer of the American Revolution," wrote *Life*'s editors, "should be overjoyed and learn to shout, if not to pronounce, 'Hurrah for Ngo Dinh Diem!'"[53] The Luce media routinely contrasted Diem, who read Gandhi and meditated before a picture of the Virgin, with Bao Dai, "the front man for cynicism, greed and moral bankruptcy."[54] *Time* did not blush when reporting that Diem won a plebiscite on displacing Bao Dai with 98.2 percent of the vote. The new president would soon repudiate the Geneva accord on the 1956 elections, and again *Time* cheered.[55]

With increasing vehemence, *Time* suggested that the United States needed to develop a military capability suited to contingencies like the one confronting South Vietnam. As a result, Time Inc. entered into an alliance with dissident soldiers like Matthew Ridgway, who called for an end to Eisenhower's cuts in military manpower. *Life*, for example, advocated the creation of mobile tactical forces equipped with small nuclear weapons.[56] In addition, covert action and counterinsurgency became two of *Time*'s obsessions. Colonel Edward Lansdale was already "maneuvering against the Communists" in Vietnam; *Time* fondly recalled his help in elections held in the Philippines.[57] Presumably, a flexible response – mobile ground troops, the CIA, and perhaps small atomic bombs – would facilitate a more activist policy in Southeast Asia.

A Shocking Proposal

On 9 August 1955, Henry Luce wrote an uncommonly long and carefully crafted letter to C. D. Jackson, his chief adviser on Cold War strategy.[58] The little essay, Luce explained, emerged from an attempt to "come up with a radically new 'approach' to the China question." The Luce letter showed that its author had suddenly accepted what had been unthinkable assumptions:

1. A "quick immediate military overthrow of the Red regime" was highly unlikely.
2. Some as yet undefined but "elaborate scheme of cooperation" with Beijing was desirable.

Thanks to the cables supplied by *Time*'s observers in Hong Kong and other places, Luce became convinced that China's pressing drive to industrialize would soon result in mass starvation. America, he speculated, could squeeze China ever tighter and hope that the looming catastrophe would cause the overthrow of the People's Republic. But with famine on the horizon, Luce felt uncomfortable advocating a policy that would contribute to the starvation of millions of innocent Chinese. So, with some hesitation, Luce suggested a radical formula "to avert a great human disaster in China." Improbably, the great Cold Warrior suggested that the United States approach Beijing and offer assistance. In return for this aid, the People's Republic would merely have to renounce its hostility to the United States and declare its desire to cooperate "on the fullest scale and on the fullest good faith."

Nostalgia, realism, and humanitarianism contributed in equal measure to Luce's stunning proposal. He fantasized about vaulting back to 1946 (his last visit to the mainland) and wondered "if somehow we" could "pick up the sino-American dialogue from there." The man whose refrain "Who Lost China?" had helped to terminate that dialogue threatened to change course. In 1952, he had promised to convert to Catholicism if he could return to a liberated China, the land of his birth. That vow had brought liberation no closer. Three years later, Luce was feeling old age creep up on him. Perhaps he longed to reach a compromise that would allow him to return "home." In any event, Luce momentarily abandoned the China lobby and was prepared to meet Red China more than halfway.

Luce's scheme had three major components:

First, the United States, the UN, and Red China would run a two-year experiment called the Economic Exploration. An Economic Mission would draw upon a $20 billion fund – more than the whole Marshall Plan had expended on Europe between 1948 and 1952, and perhaps $160 billion in

A.D. 2005 dollars. The Economic Exploration would raise China's standard of living and secure its economic advancement.

Second, Luce foresaw a "Political Mission," which would take the form of a commission equally composed of members appointed by Chiang and by the Communists. The commission would consult with Chinese citizens on both Formosa and the mainland as it searched for a political consensus and a modus vivendi. The body would also seek to determine what form of government the people preferred.

Third, an "International Exploration" would be directed by the UN and would "determine whether, or under what conditions, China" could be "received into the family of nations as a reliably peace-loving nation." In other words, Luce, of all people, was preparing for the admission of "Red China" into the UN – sixteen years and one big war before that event occurred.

Henry Luce had privately recognized the PRC.

Had Luce pursued his opening to Beijing, Chiang would have felt betrayed, but the publisher's apostasy would have given Eisenhower room to maneuver. The president had expressed interest in some kind of relationship with China and had privately mused about trading with the most populous country in the world. With the "spirit of Geneva" abroad in the world, why not extend it to East Asia? Zhou himself had declared his friendship for the American people and had called for negotiations and the avoidance of war. In Geneva, there were signs that long-stalled talks between the Red Chinese and the United States might bear fruit: A week before Luce wrote his letter, Beijing had released a few American prisoners.

A new policy might be very good politics at home, and Ike could win again as the man who brought peace and plenty to Asia. There is no doubt that Luce's move would have intrigued Adlai Stevenson, the likely Democratic nominee in 1956, and other politicians might have broken free of the dictates laid down by the Committee of One Million. Instead, however, Henry Luce ultimately decided to remain a loyal member of the China lobby. Upon reflection, he totally rejected a scheme that would have hurt his friends – the Chiangs, the Soongs, the Kungs, B. A. Garside, Walter Judd, and many others. Moreover, on 24 September 1955 Eisenhower suffered a massive heart attack. Luce decided that this was no time to divide the party and play into the hands of the men – Acheson, Stevenson, and Truman – who had embraced Alger Hiss and reviled Chiang Kai-shek. And the 1956 elections loomed, a fact that was sure to drive Luce into his quadrennial frenzy of partisanship.[59] The sad thing is that Luce's prophecy was correct: Within two years, millions of Chinese would be suffering and dying. And within a decade the paranoid regime – isolated by the policies of its own leadership as well as the U.S. government – would devour some of the best among its own people.

Readers of Luce's media would never have guessed that their editor-in-chief had, however briefly, contemplated a radical change of course in China policy. In *Life*'s Christmas issue, one read that Communism was "a form of Satan in action, to be resisted by all means at all times."⁶⁰ Early in the new year, *Life* published an angry editorial blaming Truman for the "loss of the Asian mainland to Communism."⁶¹ Not to be outdone, *Time* insisted, "There will never be peace – must never be peace – in Communist China."⁶² In 1956 Luce and his allies in the Committee of One Million also made sure that the two major party platforms promised to bar Red China's entry into the United Nations. The committee's point man here was a *Time* ex-correspondent, Eddie Lockett. If a problem arose, one finds Lockett noting, "visit personally with Henry Luce and get him interested."⁶³

Life's opening salvo in the presidential campaign appeared on 16 January 1956 and was provocatively titled "How Dulles Averted War." Shepley knew that John Foster Dulles tended to "moralize" and possessed a "well known extreme vanity" so that "his head was easily turned by flattery."⁶⁴ So by "stroking" the Dulles ego, Time Inc.'s Washington bureau chief, Jim Shepley, engineered a coup. Dulles granted an interview in which he bragged about having taken America to the brink of war – and then averting it by forcing the Communists to retreat. The first trip to the brink had allegedly occurred in 1953, when Eisenhower threatened to bomb China with "tactical" nuclear weapons if the Communists did not accept a compromise cease-fire in Korea. The president had mused about using tactical nuclear weapons, but Eisenhower never seriously considered launching them against either North Korean or Communist Chinese targets. And although Dulles implicitly threatened Beijing with a nuclear attack, his warning "had little or no impact on the Communists."⁶⁵ Indeed, they may not have even known about the alleged threat. Moreover, contemporary scholars tend to agree that "milder, nonnuclear persuasive diplomacy" led the Chinese to sign the armistice. In other words, despite Dulles's braggadocio, there was no nuclear "brink" in Korea in 1953.⁶⁶

Dulles, who had been the glummest of observers at Geneva, now reversed course and celebrated the division of Vietnam as a victory. In 1954, *Life* continued, Dulles had threatened Red China with a nuclear attack if it invaded Indochina. Beijing allegedly drew back, thereby saving southern Vietnam, Laos, and Cambodia. But this assertion was fiction: China itself had schemed with the West to create a divided Vietnam; a war-weakened Communist north would be dependent upon the PRC. Dulles's third trip to the brink, however, was more plausible: The administration had perhaps saved Quemoy and Matsu for Chiang by taking a "calculated risk."⁶⁷

What they read in *Life* infuriated Dulles's many critics among congressional Democrats: What, they asked, had happened to the role of the Congress in leading the nation to war? *Life*'s use of the word *brink* caused much of the trouble. The secretary had never called his diplomacy "brinkmanship," and he felt that *Life*'s captions had made him sound like a warmonger rather than the lover of peace that he was. Eisenhower, who was troubled by the uproar, tried to help Dulles. So did Luce, who accepted responsibility for *Life*'s use of the errant words.⁶⁸

One issue did provoke a brief public split between Luce and Dulles, and in this case the publisher was the "liberal." News organizations wanted to see Red China for themselves, and on 6 August 1956 Communist China finally offered visas to fifteen American correspondents. Luce hoped that the Department of State would validate their passports, for he was thinking of Time Inc.'s journalistic interests: He could not stand aloof while Americans read his rivals' publications for firsthand information about China, of all places. So *Life* angrily condemned the State Department's ban on travel to Red China, and Luce urged that Dulles change course.[69] Harry even advocated the equal treatment of Chinese reporters if Beijing acted appropriately in welcoming their U.S. counterparts.[70] But Dulles's refusal to grant visas to Chinese reporters prompted a counterveto by the PRC. The American journalists would not visit China. As a result, *Life*'s brief public split with Dulles was quickly breached. The secretary continued to do favors for Luce and vice versa. It would be 1960 before a journalist, Edgar Snow, would return to China with a validated U.S. passport.[71]

"Liberation" Abandoned

The abortive plan to exchange journalists was atypical. In 1956 Luce urged that the administration adopt a more aggressive foreign policy.[72] This recommendation, however, flew in the face of the momentous events that were roiling Russia and its satellites. Blinded by a vision of monolithic Communism, *Time*'s editors feared that the signs of liberalization in Eastern Europe might encourage those misguided Americans who sought to bring Red China out of its isolation. While drily recounting the facts surrounding Nikita Khrushchev's stunning denunciation of the dead Stalin, *Time* waited almost six weeks before acknowledging that real changes were unsettling the Communist bloc.[73] Even then, the magazine insisted that there was no sign of a "weakening of the links between Communist parties."[74] "Communism has not changed," insisted Whittaker Chambers in *Life*.[75] Time Inc. did not admit the obvious: Khrushchev's denunciation of Stalin was sure to undermine relations between Russia and China.[76]

Just before the election, *Time*'s rhetoric about "liberation" was put to the test. In Hungary, large masses of students and workers revolted against Soviet domination, and Eisenhower and NATO did little or nothing to help them. How would *Time* and *Life*, the prophets of liberation, respond? They bowed to political expediency and the nuclear reality. People wanted peace, so *Life* decided that U.S. policy had "no room for aggressive intervention," but neither did it "champion the status quo," whatever that doublespeak meant.[77] Only after Eisenhower won in a landslide did *Life* call for a "'liberation' policy" that was "more than words." But by then, the Hungarian patriots were dead or arrested, or had fled. Luce did other favors for the administration in this election year. Because Chiang's new book *Soviet Russia in China* was a diatribe against the containment policies slated to reelect Eisenhower, *Life* did not serialize it until half a year after the election.[78]

In the autumn of 1957 the PRC's promised liberalization ("let a hundred flowers bloom") began to give way to the "Great Leap Forward" into Communism. This rush into agrarian communism and small-scale industrialization was wasteful and cruel, as millions of collectivized peasants were herded into communes and other millions produced low-grade steel in backyard furnaces. Relentlessly, *Fortune* and its sister magazines exposed the fiasco, which Luce and some of his correspondents had foreseen years before.[79] Scenes from the mainland fed *Time*'s appetite for ridicule: Chinese peasants marched off to work singing "Manure Sources Are Plentiful."[80] *Time* portrayed the PRC as an "implacably and unchangingly sinister" enemy, but it also insisted that Red China was "vulnerable."[81] In the magazine's vivid image, "Mao's nightmare effort to reduce 650 million human beings to the status of draft animals" had suffered a terrible defeat.[82] *Time* lauded Formosa's alleged democratization – and then expressed approval when Chiang fudged the constitutional rules and accepted a third presidential term.[83]

But what about signs of a Sino-Soviet divorce or, at least, of a separation? Senator Henry Cabot Lodge, an expert on foreign policy and a man Luce respected, suggested in February 1955, "If there's a conflict the Chinese Reds [will] tell the Moscow Reds to go to hell." Two months later, Winston Churchill personally told Luce that there was "trouble" between the two Communist giants. He added, "There might well someday be serious conflict between Russia and China."[84] Mao's claim to be leading a large part of humanity into real Communism rankled the Soviet leadership; and one Chinese general dared to denounce the postwar Russian looting of Manchurian industrial assets. These facts should have elicited the questions that *Time* refused to ask: Would continued U.S. pressure break Beijing, or would isolation push the PRC closer to Moscow? Why would Americans adopt a hostile posture toward a Red China that was invading no one and was squabbling with the real enemy, Russia? And why worry about a PRC that was so effectively wrecking its own economy? Secretary Dulles, at least, pondered such questions.[85] But in this summer of 1958, Dulles remained wary of the China lobby, and he again denounced the idea of recognition.

Two weeks later, the Chinese Communists bombarded Quemoy and some adjacent islands.[86] People's Liberation Army forces ultimately hit the small islands with about six hundred fifty thousand shells (*Time*, 5 January 1959), but Chiang's Nationalist F-86 Sabres defeated Mao's MIG-17s. The Nationalists, who kept one-third of their ready forces on the islands, remained defiant. The U.S. Navy helped to resupply the beleaguered fortresses. Dulles again refused to rule out the use of force, and Eisenhower promised to block any Far Eastern "Munich." But Dulles also observed that the United States had made no commitment to assist Chiang if he attempted to reconquer the mainland. Clearly, the administration would settle for some kind of cease-fire, and it again suggested that Chiang thin out his garrisons on the contested islands. The Generalissimo, under pressure, did renounce the use of force in his "sacred" mission of reconquest, and in November the Communists suspended their bombardment of the islands. Although *Time* saluted Eisenhower for standing down the Communists, the truth was less to Luce's liking.[87] As Marvin Liebman, secretary and manager of the Committee of One Million, put it, American policy was intent upon "keeping the Free Chinese armed forces as purely defensive units."[88] In fact, the administration as well as the American people wanted to defuse the tiresome Straits of Formosa time-bomb.

An uneasy compromise was in the works: The Communists would observe a self-imposed cease-fire, and Chiang, prodded by the Americans, would thin out his forces on the islands. But if Chiang Kai-shek was not going to return to the mainland; if Beijing was willing to observe a cease-fire; and if Communist China was really irritated with the Soviets, might not a review of U.S. policy be in order? Luce's answer was a firm no. He still dreamed about returning to the land of his boyhood, to the vineyard where his parents had labored to win souls for Christ.[89] And after the brief turnabout in his 1955 letter to C. D. Jackson, Luce's chosen instrument remained Chiang Kai-shek, the guardian of the China that Luce knew and loved. American public opinion, however, offered Luce reason for concern.

Recognize Red China?

A huge majority of Gallup's respondents wished to turn the problems of the offshore islands *and* Formosa over to the United Nations.[90] Although polled respondents still opposed Red China's entry into the UN, a few bold liberals were calling for recognition. Articles endorsing recognition began to appear in mainstream publications, and the anti-Communist Americans for Democratic Action supported an opening to China. Harry Luce could not bring himself to admit that the United States, like the PRC and the Republic of China, might one day learn to coexist with a de facto "two Chinas" policy.[91] What really shocked Luce, however, was a report issued by the World Order Study Conference of his own Presbyterian Church. In December 1958, L. Nelson Bell, father-in-law of evangelist Billy Graham and a Presbyterian involved in the missionary movement, wrote to Harry Luce. The World Order Study, Bell explained, recommended that the United States recognize Red China and seat it in the United Nations. Luce denounced the recommendation as "prudently uncritical of Communist governments," and *Time* condemned it as a betrayal of both Formosa and the Protestant missionary movement.[92]

Once again, *Time* found solace in the fact that Catholics, at least, seemed steadfast in their opposition to the atheist tyranny. The magazine was moved by their plight in China; a year later, when Beijing put Bishop James E. Walsh on trial for conspiring against the PRC, *Time* celebrated his heroic faith. Walsh received a twenty-year sentence after being convicted of conspiracy and espionage.[93] To Luce, Walsh, and not Nelson Bell, was a figure worthy of admiration. The agitated Luce saw recognition as a betrayal of his father's missionary legacy, so he turned for support to his old friend Henry P. Van Dusen, the influential president of the Union Theological Seminary. The two men had marched together in earlier campaigns for both Britain and China, but this time Van Dusen shocked Luce by supporting the World Order Study. The time was coming, declared the theologian, when the United States would have to recognize Red China and permit its entry into the United Nations. The People's Republic, he noted, was not about to disappear, and in a cruel analogy, Van Dusen reminded Luce of another futile policy of nonrecognition: Had ignoring (1917–1933) Soviet Russia dislodged that Communist regime? Van Dusen bemoaned the fact that no one – especially Luce – was preparing the American people for the momentous change that needed to take place.[94]

Disappointed but unconvinced, Luce turned to the Committee of One Million, which quickly launched a counterattack. Editorials denouncing the study group's recommendation appeared in prominent publications, and the committee quickly found 7,437 Protestant clerics who opposed the recognition heresy.[95] But Luce's China policy was becoming more problematic, and even the world of sport could not evade the China issue. In May 1959 the International Olympic Committee withdrew its recognition of Nationalist China. Time brought change, and some of the figures who had defended the China lobby's ramparts departed. Claire Chennault, who had posed for a cigarette commercial for Camels in 1955, died of lung cancer. Walter Robertson, the China lobby's strong right arm in the administration, retired.[96] In China, as *Time* belatedly admitted in 1960, forced industrialization was being deemphasized, and the Beijing regime was making concessions to peasants who wanted to till private plots. The PRC also advocated "creative socialist distribution" (i.e., pay calculated on the basis of work accomplished) in the countryside.[97] But Red China's retreat from the excesses of the Great Leap Forward failed to impress *Time*, which refused to rethink stale policies.

The Luces were saddened by John Foster Dulles's mortal illness. Now past seventy, the secretary was dying of stomach cancer, and by April 1959, he was at death's door. Clare Luce sent a moving message to the stricken secretary, and Harry assured him "how often" he was in the Luces' "thoughts, spoken and unspoken, and always with deep affection."[98] *Time* saluted the old warrior in a two-page encomium that buried Luce's doubts and differences in a blizzard of sentimental prose.[99] After Dulles's death on 24 May 1959, *Time* captioned its obituary with a word it saved for longtime favorites: "Heroes." Saluting Dulles as "freedom's missionary," *Time* said farewell to a man who had meant much to its editor-in-chief. Years later, Luce still praised Dulles as a moralist, a great Cold Warrior, and a man of Christian faith. Forgiven were the caution, the bumbling, the inconsistencies, and the opportunism. Forgotten were the restraints placed on Chiang. Instead, Luce said of Dulles, "He ran the course, he kept the faith."[100] At least Red China would not soon receive recognition, and Alfred Kohlberg could brag to a friend in 1960, "The State Department is still dancing to the tune played by me and my associates of the China lobby."[101]

Perhaps so, but the Dulles years had signified the triumph of containment, and not the achievement of liberation, and Henry Luce knew it.[102]

In this spring of 1959 Luce was serving on a study group of the Council on Foreign Relations (CFR). At the request of Senator J. William Fulbright, chairman of the Senate Committee on Foreign Relations, Luce's panel prepared a report titled "The Nature of Foreign Policy and the Role of the United States in the World."[103] The draft document, "realist" and technocratic in spirit, disappointed Luce. Though an ardent supporter of both foreign aid and of arms exports to friends, Luce liked to link these programs to broader American ideals.[104] He argued that sound economic growth depended on "freedom," and not just on economic formulas. He also preached that the United States must offer "leadership in this emerging world civilization." Luce felt compelled to distance himself from the CFR's report, but another heresy quickly surfaced.[105] On the Hill, the Senate Foreign Relations Committee was busy studying the so-called Conlon report, which supported the admission of Red China into the UN.[106]

While Luce was fretting about the Conlon report, the Special Studies Project of the Rockefeller Brothers Fund stated that the two large Communist countries might "not always be drawn together by common interests."[107] Luce, whose father had often drawn upon the Rockefeller largesse, was a dissenting member of the fund's foreign policy panel. But despite his presence, the Special Studies Project declared that the United States should refrain from actions that might drive Red China into a closer alignment with Moscow. By contrast, *Time* would admit only that China's size and strength meant that Beijing was not a satellite but a loyal Soviet surrogate, charged with troublemaking in Asia.[108] Yet in 1957, Moscow had again rebuffed the Chinese when they requested access to missile technology.[109] People at Time Inc. knew of these rumors, but they relied upon arguments dear to Chiang and the Committee of One Million: Signs of a rift were a ruse to lull the West into surrender or appeasement.[110] In one editorial ("Bear vs. Dragon"), *Life* cautiously probed the racial and ideological aspects of the sour relationship and expressed hope that its decline might someday "cleave a path toward freedom in Asia."[111] This bit of tepid heresy provoked the ailing Alfred Kohlberg into writing an angry letter of denunciation, and *Life* became more cautious thereafter.[112]

Only in late 1959 did *Time* admit that Sino-Soviet relations had soured, but even then, the magazine wrongly insisted that discord was not likely to cause an "open breach."[113] When several hundred Soviet technicians left China and the official media of the two countries attacked each other's governments with ever more profound gusto, *Time* obstinately insisted that a Tito-like break was not in the making.[114] Rather than see the Sino-Soviet split as an opportunity for the West, the Luce media portrayed the rift as a struggle for the control of the world revolutionary movement.[115]

In the summer of 1960, Luce suggested to a Senate committee that the United States dedicate itself to *winning* the Cold War.[116] In Luce's words, making the world safe for democracy was still a worthy goal – but it first required victory in the war against Communism.[117] Luce's strategy was based upon his search for a way out of a dilemma: He feared a Soviet first strike, and in response, advocated a program designed to "bring home to every man and woman the possibility – and the virtue – of his doing something about his own self-defence."[118]

Luce embraced much of the Rand Corporation's grim report on fallout shelters, which argued that 90 million out of 180 million Americans might be shielded from nuclear annihilation.[119] Believing that fallout shelters would embolden American policymakers to win the Cold War, Luce made *Time* their prime media advocate.[120] After completing his bunkers with the help of a massive federal appropriation, Luce would be willing to risk "hot" war. For Christian reasons, he would not initiate such a war – although the distinction between risking one and starting one might be visible to him alone.[121] Predictably, the left rejected the Luce proposal, but so did President Eisenhower, who defended the administration's very modest civil defense program.[122] Instead of spending two billion more on the Pentagon, Ike thought that the United States could *cut* the defense budget by that much, unless the country made "assumptions of a dark hue."[123]

Feeling isolated and unhappy, Harry Luce had become a prime apologist for the military-industrial complex that the retiring Dwight Eisenhower was about to denounce.

Marketing Diem

On the Indochina front, Luce and his network of contacts were working hard to sell Ngo Dinh Diem to the American people and their congressional representatives. Although its commitment to Diem lacked the passion displayed in regard to Chiang, the entire China lobby had indeed taken the president of Vietnam under its wing: The Committee of One Million was particularly active in making propaganda for him. In 1957 Marvin Liebman, COOM's secretary, toured South Vietnam and met with the "father of his country." Liebman returned with a message for the committee: Diem must be supported. Liebman also hinted that Diem, if spurned, might go "neutralist." Then, working through Tom Corcoran and other China lobby insiders, the committee effectively mobilized congressional support on Ngo Dinh Diem's behalf.[124] One of its time-tested techniques involved the mass distribution of articles published by Time Inc. This made sense, given the nature of Luce's view of Vietnam.

From *Time*, Americans learned how Diem had brought "peace and stability" to South Vietnam.[125] In fact, *Time* no longer covered Diem; it celebrated him. In countless American schools, children who would be of draft age in five or ten years took weekly *Time* quizzes; if they wanted good grades, they needed to know that Ngo Dinh Diem was a great man. When these students were ready for *Time* itself (supplied to school districts at near cost by the publisher), they would learn that Communism was now on the defensive in Southeast Asia.[126] To *Time*, Diem and his family were model citizens and allies of the West. *Time* allowed that the president and his family echoed "authoritarian overtones," but the magazine invariably lauded their achievements.[127] And near the president stood Madame Ngo Dinh Nhu, who had married the president's sinister brother. Portrayed as beautiful, Western-minded, and highly independent, *Time's* Madame Nhu evolved into a kind of Asian Clare Boothe Luce.[128] But after 1950, Luce's take on Indochina reflected input from sources other than *Time*. Christopher Emmet, a foreign policy adviser to Clare Luce, observed that prominent American Catholics might, if properly instructed, embrace the anti-Communist cause in Indochina.[129] Vietnam, after all, contained two million Catholics, and Ngo Dinh Diem was no stranger to the United States. Emmet had early on suggested that the U.S. government would be wise to support the patriot Diem, and the Luces would later become two of his more important American patrons.

By 1957, Luce had become active in the American Friends of Vietnam (AFV).[130] Chaired by retired General John W. O'Daniel, who had recently been training Diem's troops, the AFV gained the support of liberals like Arthur Schlesinger, Jr., a Harvard historian who had once written important essays for *Life* and *Fortune*.[131] Christopher Emmet served on the AFV's national committee, as did Senator John F. Kennedy. With its access to military, liberal, and Catholic circles, the AFV was well qualified to introduce Diem to America's political elites. Luce himself hosted a major salute to Diem in the spring of 1957, when the visiting president was awarded the Admiral Richard E. Byrd Memorial Award for his "service to the community of freedom."[132] Diem, Luce declared, was "one of the great statesmen of Asia and of the world." The president, he added, had not merely stopped Communism; he had also shown that freedom was "worthy of every sacrifice." The AFV's main media outlet was, of course, Luce's Time Inc. Portrayed as a stalwart anti-Communist and friend of democracy, the little president emerged in the Luce press as the giant whom Ike had called a "miracle man."

In 1959 and 1960 the Luce media suddenly turned a spotlight on the backward, mountain kingdom of Laos, which abutted Vietnam.[133] Because of the proximity of Laos to China and other players in the region, *Time* tried to understand the warring factions.[134] But the old right-versus-left, Communist-versus-democrats formula did not work well in a land populated by hostile tribes and tamer elephants – and where no Diem was available. Although *Time* did its best to depict Laos as a key Cold War battleground, it finally admitted that modern weaponry might not accomplish much "in the guerrilla fighting that plagues Laos."[135] In near despair, *Time* even began to consider the wisdom of supporting a UN-supervised, neutral Laos.[136] The magazine's treatment of nearby Cambodia was more predictable. There, the popular King Norodom Sihanouk had recognized Red China and tried to steer a neutralist course in foreign policy.[137] But *Time* sensed that pro-Western pressures might eventually undermine Sihanouk and "bring about the very tragedy" that anti-Communist Thais and South Vietnamese wanted to prevent.

Confused by Laos and concerned about Cambodia, *Time* felt more secure in Saigon. Indeed, this late Eisenhower era – perhaps 1959 – marked the brightest time in *Time*'s version of South Vietnam. Though unsurprised by Ngo Dinh Diem's reelection, *Time* admired the electorate's 87 percent voter turnout.[138] Yet an ominous note cast dark shadows: Red guerrillas, probably about three to five thousand of them, had infiltrated into South Vietnam through the jungles and mountains of Cambodia and Laos.[139] In the south, they were assassinating Diemist village leaders and had already killed two American military advisers.[140] Overall, eight hundred soldiers and civilians were dying each month. Late in 1960, a clique of frustrated junior officers revolted against Diem. Although he suppressed the uprising, the president suddenly became subject to criticism from *Time*. Readers learned, for example, that Diem's "agrovilles," or fortified resettlement villages, were hated by the few peasants who populated them.[141] *Time* began to express unease about Diem's aloofness; it even admitted that thirty thousand prisoners populated his reeducation camps.[142] The president's "dictatorial ways" (Diem called his French-influenced philosophy of government "personalism") were of concern, too. Nevertheless, lacking an alternative, *Time* still clung to the fiction that Diem was the widely respected "father of his country." So its readers were ill served by editors who concealed the fact that Diem was a secretive and remote leader. If he was at all popular, it was in the minority Catholic community.

Luce's support of a failing authoritarian sounded a dreary but familiar ring. *Time* and Luce had adopted the same tone during the last years of Chiang's rule on the mainland. But as Eisenhower prepared to retire to Gettysburg, *Time* hinted at a policy option that had no analogy in China's recent civil war.

On 13 January 1961, *Time* matter-of-factly repeated a question asked by an unnamed U.S. official: Would American Marines "be prepared to stay in the jungles [of Vietnam] five, six or ten years?"[143] *Time* and Luce would do their best to make sure that the incoming Kennedy administration answered in the affirmative. Here, Luce's longstanding ties to the Kennedys promised to make his job a bit easier.

PART FOUR

TIME, LUCE, AND THE LOOMING DISASTER IN VIETNAM, 1960–1967

13

Time Inc. and Nation-Making in Vietnam

From Kennedy to Johnson

Henry Luce first met Ambassador Joseph P. Kennedy before World War II, probably in London. Luce was immediately attracted to this blunt-spoken tycoon, who radiated power and self-confidence. Moreover, Kennedy had something of the rogue about him, and this wicked streak titillated the more conventional Harry Luce. In addition, the Kennedy brood (nine children) was made for *Life*, which became a kind of "family album." And Luce's magazines, Joe Kennedy knew, could do a lot for his four sons.[1] So Kennedy cultivated Luce, and Time Inc. rarely disappointed *Life*'s favorite Democrat.[2] Even during his controversial ambassadorship to Great Britain, *Time* and *Life* rarely attacked Joe Kennedy for his isolationist views.[3] The ambassador's private criticisms of Franklin Roosevelt deepened his friendship with Luce, who soon helped Kennedy by promoting the literary career of his second son.

Young Jack Kennedy had lived in England during the appeasement era and subsequently wrote his senior thesis at Harvard College on Britain's failure to prepare for war.[4] This was a dicey political subject in the light of Joseph Kennedy's ambassadorship, but young John's lengthy paper demonstrated both skill and discretion. Joseph Kennedy decided that Jack should publish his thesis, for a quality book, he noted, "really [made] the grade with high-class people [and stood] you in good stead for years to come."[5] In July the ambassador rang Luce from London, asking whether the influential publisher would write a foreword to Jack's book. Without hesitation Luce agreed to do so.[6]

Luce's promotion of *Why England Slept* helped to make the book a best seller.* In 1946 the Luce media warmly greeted Jack Kennedy's entry into Massachusetts politics.[7] *Time* later saluted Congressman Kennedy for his "good looks, charm and an impressive war record."[8] Soon, *Life* celebrated young Senator Kennedy's marriage to Jacqueline Bouvier, and *Time* called him a "curious blend of Boston conservatism and New Deal liberalism."[9] Nor had

---

* Many of these copies were purchased and distributed by Joseph P. Kennedy.

13.1   A formal portrait of Henry Robinson Luce, editor-in-chief of Time Inc. (Library of Congress)

Kennedy's belligerent comments about the rising Red tide in the Far East gone unnoticed. The young senator, who had visited Indochina in 1951, earned *Time*'s respect when he later supported "united action by many nations" in Southeast Asia, even if it involved "some commitment of our manpower."[10]

By 1956, Luce's newsmagazine was booming Senator Kennedy as a vice-presidential candidate who possessed "looks, brains, personality, and an attractive wife."[11] By coincidence, Jack tried to gain the vice-presidential nomination while the Luces relaxed on the Riviera as guests of the Joseph Kennedys.[12] Kennedy did not win, but by 1957 *Time* took him seriously as a future presidential nominee.[13] Other ties brought the Luces and Kennedys closer together, too. When Clare Luce ran into trouble in 1959 while striving to become ambassador to Brazil, Senator Kennedy came to her aid. "I've known Mrs. Luce all my life," he commented with some exaggeration, and "I most certainly would vote for her confirmation."[14] *Time* acknowledged Kennedy's "capacity as a leader" and began to treat him as the clear front-runner for the presidential nomination in 1960.[15] And despite evidence that Jack himself may have been married once before, Luce and his editors refused to divulge untoward information about JFK's colorful private life.

On 15 July 1960 Joseph P. Kennedy was in New York City on his way to Europe. His son Jack was in Los Angeles, preparing to accept the Democratic presidential nomination. Luce was expecting the ambassador's arrival at his apartment in the Waldorf, where the two men would dine and then watch the candidate on television. Joe Kennedy appeared and was in a fine mood, but the motive for his visit was transparent: Would Time Inc. treat candidate Kennedy fairly, or would JFK undergo the fate of Adlai Stevenson?

Sprinkling his conversation with the usual profanity, Kennedy assured Luce that no son of his would be a "goddam" liberal. The publisher brushed aside Joe's assurance, however, for any Democratic candidate, Luce reasoned, would have to project a liberal image in domestic affairs. But, Luce warned, if Kennedy showed any signs of weakness "toward the anti-Communist cause," Time Inc. would "clobber him." Relieved, the elder Kennedy promised Luce, "You don't have to worry about that." Then the ambassador watched his son accept the nomination, and afterward Luce escorted him to the front door. Before leaving, Joe Kennedy told Harry Luce, "We are truly grateful for all that you have done for Jack."[16]

In return, Luce and *Time* expected that President Kennedy would intensify U.S. nation-building in South Vietnam, while working to undermine the People's Republic of China.

An Acceptable Democrat

Harry Luce admired Jack Kennedy's quick intelligence, his wit and charm, and his fondness for reading history. The senator showed respect for Luce, too – he invariably called him "Mr. Luce" – but Kennedy also liked to kid humorless Harry about his Republican politics and *Time*'s bias. And Kennedy was fortunate in another way: Luce, like many of his Republican contemporaries, admired Richard M. Nixon but did not like him. (How could the anguished Calvinist Luce warm up to a man who told him that he found the Presbyterian faith appealing – because it was "so easy"?)[17] *Life* jolted the Republican candidate when it declared that in foreign policy, "the difference between the two candidates... is narrow and the choice not easy."[18] Nixon felt betrayed by Time Inc.'s neutrality.

At *Time*, things were a bit more difficult for Kennedy. Although he was a highly innovative managing editor, Otto Fuerbringer was also a rock-ribbed Republican, and one who admired Dick Nixon. Fuerbringer had come to *Time* back in 1942, and as managing editor he upgraded the magazine by improving its design and adding essay-like think pieces. But the "Iron Chancellor" was also demanding and aloof, even arrogant, and he personified *Time*'s personality – as seen by its critics. In August, however, the managing editor suffered a "serious cerebral incident," and although Fuerbringer later recovered, Democrat Tom Griffith would run *Time* for the rest of the presidential campaign.[19] Under Griffith's direction, *Time*'s Jack Kennedy showed "New England reticence," and his energetic younger brother Bobby was a man "of brutal honesty and impeccable integrity."[20] By October readers had gained the impression that candidate Kennedy was charismatic, a quick study – and, above all, good copy. Nixon, though intelligent and well informed, came across as dour, plodding, and dull. Without hesitation, *Time* pronounced Kennedy the winner of the crucial first television debate and declared that he had demonstrated his mettle in foreign affairs during a second televised encounter with Nixon.[21] Lacking any personal rapport with Luce, the moody Nixon could do nothing to change *Time*'s mind.

The Kennedy camp was exultant: Speechwriter Arthur M. Schlesinger, Jr., boasted, "This is the best *Time* political coverage since 1936." Recalling how close the election was, the new president agreed that had *Time* cut him up, he would not be living in the White House.[22] Kennedy therefore made sure that the Luces were treated like family during the inaugural festivities. After the music stopped, however, Luce was determined to see that the new president took a hard line in regard to North Vietnam and Red China. Here he could look to a staunch ally within the new administration, for his support had helped to make Dean Rusk secretary of state.[23]

Time and JFK

John Kennedy was an avid reader, and he was convinced that *Time* influenced people at home and abroad. "My God," the president would say, "everyone reads *Time*," adding, "They really read that goddam magazine!"[24] Although a majority of Americans now (1961) took their news about world events from television, *Time* remained important, especially in the field of foreign policy.[25] The president always received an advance copy of *Time*'s forthcoming issue, which he avidly scanned for news about himself or his family. Kennedy also knew a great deal about its senior editors – when they dispatched copy to the printers, and who was up and who was down. On occasion, *Time* would infuriate him, but Kennedy never ruptured his personal ties to Luce. JFK also got along well with *Time*'s White House correspondent Hugh Sidey, who "could see him any time."[26] He would banter with Sidey, asking him about "old Lucey." Kennedy once added, "I kinda like [Luce]" and then compared him to his own, self-made father.[27] In fact, Kennedy was the luckiest Democrat in memory: *Time* rarely savaged him.

President Kennedy's inaugural address pleased Luce, who copied out one notable phrase in his own notebook: "Let every nation know, whether it wishes us well or ill, that we shall pay any price, bear any burden, meet any hardship, support any friend, oppose any foe to assure the survival and the success of liberty." In a speech to Time Inc. executives in May, Luce again cited "bear any burden," but his bellicosity transcended Jack Kennedy's vision. Either we win the Cold War by 1965, Luce warned, or "we shall ... have negotiated our own surrender."[28] He was dismayed by Kennedy's lack of resolve at the Bay of Pigs,

13.2 Editor-in-chief Luce in a typically intense moment. (Library of Congress)

and Luce made clear that *Time* intended to demand the overthrow of Communism throughout the world.[29] For his part, President Kennedy continued to mistrust Otto Fuerbringer, whom he would blame for the occasional offensive article. Once, the president even complained to *Time*'s Hugh Sidey, "You assured me [Fuerbringer] was on death's door."[30] But the relationship between Luce and JFK flourished. On a personal note, *Time* grieved over an ill friend when it described the massive stroke suffered by Joe Kennedy late in 1961.[31] Gone were the memories of his defeatism and appeasement and isolationism: What remained was a man who had "served his country ably."

In his new foreword to the 1961 reissue of *Why England Slept*, Luce decided that Kennedy's slim volume mandated a new crusade: Victory over Communism, like victory over Hitlerism, was a must.[32] The trouble was that the price of victory was high, perhaps too high for Kennedy and even for Luce: In 1961 the American Century might prevail only against the backdrop of a nuclear-poisoned planet, pockmarked by craters carved by hydrogen bombs. So despite its occasional outbursts and fears about Kennedy's toughness, Time Inc. was most often a friendly critic. JFK sometimes accused *Time* of being unfair to him or his family, but overall, Kennedy had no reason for complaint.[33] As a result of its affinity for the Kennedys, Time Inc. enjoyed good access to the new administration. In return, JFK often manipulated a pliant publishing house. Late in 1962, for example, Kennedy ordered Luce and Fuerbringer to Washington, where he made sure that they saw top-secret evidence of Soviet missile perfidy in Cuba.[34] As a result, *Time* declared that the president's defiance of the Soviets over their missile deployment showed his "resolve" at its historic best.[35]

A China Initiative Foiled

In the spring of 1961, President Kennedy pondered an initiative in regard to Red China, and once again, he involved Luce in his scheme. The president acted with his usual subtlety, inasmuch as Luce's media still took a hard line in regard to China. (Only in the autumn did *Time* finally acknowledge the global implications of the Sino-Soviet split, but even then the magazine merely cited a "new rift in an uneasy partnership." In fact, there was no longer any partnership, and Kennedy knew it.)[36] Hoping to further fracture the crumbling Sino-Soviet axis, Kennedy considered proposing a new arrangement for the China seat at the United Nations. He also intended to make some gesture, perhaps recognition, toward Outer Mongolia, a Soviet satellite wary of China.[37] Both moves would be anathema to Chiang's American friends, but it was possible that their influence upon public opinion was waning in the light of recent Soviet challenges to the West.[38] If Russia was the main enemy, as most Americans believed, then why not meet Beijing halfway? Although Americans continued to oppose Red China's entry into the UN, more than half of Gallup's respondents thought that the United States should try to improve relations with Communist China. Furthermore, a majority of Americans favored remaining in the UN if the world body admitted Beijing to membership.[39] In addition, a near majority of polled respondents was willing to send food to hungry Red China.[40]

If the popular president could get Luce on board, then the outrage of the China lobby might be checked. So Kennedy coyly asked Luce this question: What were the prospects of barring Red China from membership in the UN in the autumn of 1961? Although Kennedy was clever, Luce saw through the ploy. After surveying opinion at the State Department, he was supposed to tell the president that, sadly, it would be impossible to bar Beijing from the UN. According to this script, Kennedy could then offer a compromise acceptable to Red China, while shielding himself from assault by the China lobby by invoking the authority of Harry Luce. Luce was not a man of guile, and he seems to have overlooked the president's political motivation. So he turned for advice to former UN ambassador Henry Cabot Lodge, now a *Time* consultant. Lodge surveyed his own experts and forwarded the relevant information to Luce. The publisher later recalled telling the president that he "should waste no time in seeing that it was made perfectly clear that the United States was going to maintain its very strong stand against admission of Red China and that if a strong stand were taken right then, without any further delay, that the chances were very good that once again we would receive the necessary votes." Kennedy thanked Luce, and nothing came of his aborted initiative.[41] But Time Inc. intensified its vigilance, and as late as the summer of 1963, *Fortune* insisted against all evidence that Chiang might attack the mainland and provoke an uprising against a hated regime.[42]

An opening to China might have spared the Chinese people the catastrophe that was to befall them a few years later. And had Kennedy followed through, events in Vietnam might have taken a less bloody toll on countless lives. But in 1961 Kennedy was not ready to defy Harry Luce in regard to either China or Vietnam. Had the young president lived to serve a second term following Luce's retirement in 1964, the outcome might have been different – for China, for Vietnam, and for the United States.

Winning a Dirty Little War

In Luce's view, a fully mobilized America could win what *Life* had once (1950) called "all the dirty little wars with which the people responsible for world order are always charged."[43] Luce decided that Kennedy might understand the need for one such "dirty little war" – the revolution now engulfing Ngo Dinh Diem's South Vietnam. Crossing the jungles and mountains of chaotic Laos, North Vietnamese guerrillas were pouring into South Vietnam. By the spring of 1961, U.S. intelligence put the number of recent infiltrators at more than ten thousand.[44] Diem insisted that he "must give first priority to military measures against Viet Cong." In practice, this commitment excused the postponement of overdue reforms. In reality, nepotism and repression flourished. As a result, President Diem became increasingly unpopular among peasants, students, and younger officers.[45] How could his American patrons cope with the depressing situation?

In April *Fortune*'s Charles Murphy spied a shift in the U.S. "grand strategy."[46] Specially trained forces, Murphy reported, were needed for action in places remote from the European center stage of the Cold War. Fortunately for Americans concerned about U.S. casualties, the army might not "be called upon to carry the brunt of the fighting," provided there was "time to improve the training of our allies' armed forces." The source of these thoughts appears to have been Lt. Gen. Lionel C. McGarr, who believed that Americans in South Vietnam could train highly motivated "anti-guerrilla guerrillas" of the Army of the Republic of Vietnam (ARVN).[47] *Time* became the voice of McGarr's "can-do" Americans, and beginning in the winter of 1961, the newsmagazine honed the image of "the American guerrillas." U.S. Army Special Forces would train partisans to fight in places like South Vietnam.[48] Such soldiers, *Time* argued, were the answer in "small nations threatened with Communist infiltration." Later, *Time* boasted that "guerrilla warfare training" had become "the nation's fastest expanding field of military activity."[49] Army recruiters proudly displayed *Time* when signing up potential American guerrillas. Kennedy, of

course, would not want to be blamed for "losing" South Vietnam, so *Fortune*'s
Charlie Murphy was pleased that the president had made "South Viet-Nam
our first concern in Southeast Asia."[50] *Time* followed the line laid down by
Ambassador Frederick Nolting, who predicted that South Vietnam might veer
toward neutrality if the United States abandoned Diem.[51]

Thanks to an unwelcome, leaked request from Kennedy, Vice-President
Lyndon Johnson visited head of state Ngo Dinh Diem in May 1961.[52] Although
urging him to get closer to his people, Johnson also promised unflagging U.S.
support for the "independence and territorial integrity of Viet-Nam."[53] Diem,
Johnson claimed, was "in the vanguard of those leaders" who stood for "free-
dom on the periphery of the Communist empire in Asia." Johnson concluded,
"We must decide whether to support Diem – or let Vietnam fall."[54] *Time* ap-
proved of Johnson's hyperbole, even when he called Diem the "Churchill of
Asia" and likened him to Woodrow Wilson, FDR, and Andrew Jackson.[55]
Haunted by memories of what the "loss" of China had done to Truman,
Kennedy and Johnson feared that the fall of South Vietnam would threaten
their bid for reelection.

At the time of Johnson's visit to Vietnam, the State Department began to
"examine the diplomatic setting within which a possible commitment of U.S.
forces to Viet-Nam might be undertaken." In addition, the Joint Chiefs of Staff
recommended the deployment of U.S. troops in South Vietnam.[56] But neither
Kennedy nor Johnson – nor Diem – favored taking such a hazardous step. Nor
did Secretary of State Dean Rusk and Secretary of Defense Robert S. McNamara
wish to commit U.S. troops to South Vietnam. In a November 1961 memorandum, they emphasized that "U.S. forces could not accomplish their mission
in the midst of an apathetic or hostile population."[57] U.S. troop deployment
would further tarnish Diem's tattered nationalist credentials; only the South
Vietnamese armed forces, McNamara reasoned, could win the war.[58] Kennedy,
moreover, compared unforeseen military escalations to drinking alcohol: The
effect wears off, and before you know it, you are gulping down more and more.
Nothing was solved, and only the drinker suffered.[59]

Instead of deploying American field units, the U.S. Army intended to send
more advisers, who would "assist in training of the new Vietnamese forces."
This action would violate the Geneva accords, but *Time* dismissed the doctrine of nonintervention as irrelevant.[60] Most South Vietnamese soldiers would
not fight, North Vietnamese were infiltrating through Laos, and American instructors could not tell the difference between a Viet Cong and a Vietnamese
Ranger.[61] In South Vietnam, as one scholar has written, "the U.S. Army trained,
organized, and equipped an army more suited for a conventional, Western
battlefield than an insurgent, Asian countryside."[62] Moreover, the heightened
American presence only augmented the *nationalist* credentials of the Viet Cong,
whom *Time*, like the U.S. defense establishment, still dismissed as Communist
terrorists.[63] Few Vietnamese outside of Diem's circle saw Hanoi as the puppet
of China or Russia. American planners, however, perversely insisted that China
was the real enemy: Johnson, for example, argued that the battle against China

"must be joined in Southeast Asia." *Time* too insisted that China, and not Vietnamese nationalism, was behind Hanoi and the Viet Cong.[64] But Stanley Karnow of *Fortune* knew better. China's economic plight, he argued, along with its ever nastier conflict with Russia, made it unlikely that Beijing was spoiling for a fight in South Vietnam.[65] The roots of the problem, Karnow knew, lay in Vietnam itself.

To many farmers in South Vietnam, the Diem regime represented one more crowd of selfish, nepotist looters, alien in religion and haughty authoritarians to boot. At the State Department, therefore, planners decided to "strengthen President Diem's popular support . . . under the direction of Ambassador Nolting."[66] *Time* agreed that Diem needed to shore up his popular support – but now its editor perversely endorsed Diem's hated agrovilles, the enclosures where uprooted peasants lived in insecurity and misery.[67] Americans, according to the magazine, could bring revolutionary, modernizing developments to South Vietnam. Schools, sewers, hospitals, and roads all led via a swampy detour to Luce's American Century. "We are going to win in Viet Nam," said Attorney General Robert F. Kennedy, and *Time* believed him.[68] By 1962, however, the war was going badly.

Time became more critical of Ngo Dinh Diem's high-handed ways. Taking this criticism as betrayal, Diem's sister-in-law, Madame Nhu, wrote to *Time*, defending her government.[69] At this point, the magazine could not decide whether Madame was "Joan of Arc" or "Lucrezia Borgia," but in the months ahead, *Time* would create a new image for her in America – that of the Asian Dragon Lady: smart, ruthless, and needlessly provocative.[70] Clare Boothe Luce played a role in this transformation. She identified closely with Madame Nhu, for both were beautiful, outspoken women who survived by manipulating powerful men. Both were also given to making vitriolic comments about their enemies. When Madame Nhu's father threatened to disown his daughter after she made additional offensive remarks, Clare offered to "adopt" her. And later, Mrs. Luce advised Madame Nhu in the matter of her proposed memoirs.[71]

By February 1962, *Time* ominously expressed the view that Diem could not win his war.[72] But because the magazine insisted that "South Viet Nam must be defended at all costs," *Time* feared the domino-like effect of Diem's fall.[73] Given this logic, the magazine advocated the dispatch of more U.S. helicopters, pilots, and ground crews to South Vietnam, along with equipment suitable for amphibious warfare along its guerrilla-infested waterways. The expanded conflict, *Time* added, could "gain the U.S. invaluable experience of guerrilla warfare." So like General Giap, Ho Chi Minh, Fidel Castro, and Mao Zedong, the editors of *Time* were preparing for a Third World scenario with not one, but many Vietnams.

Promoting Intervention

Time and the *New York Times* aside, Vietnam was not a big news story during these first two years of the Kennedy administration. The Kennedys wanted

13.3   Asia-first allies since 1941: Henry R. Luce celebrates his acquisition of General Douglas MacArthur's reminiscences early in the 1960s. (Library of Congress)

to keep Vietnam out of the news, for political reasons.[74] The American advisers roaming around South Vietnam could be challenged under the Geneva agreements; and America was not at war.[75] At one point, the president agreed that it had been a mistake "to let *Life* go in and take pictures, with helicopters flying over the country, etc."[76] Time Inc. still had no bureau in Saigon. But with mounting urgency, *Time* and *Life* took the lead in explaining why the United States needed to fight in a guerrilla war on the other side of the world: Behind the Viet Cong lay Hanoi, and behind Hanoi lay Beijing or Moscow (or both). Virtually ignored by Time Inc. were the indigenous roots of many of the insurgents fighting in the south. True, Hanoi directed and supplied the National Liberation Front, but as locals, the Viet Cong mixed terror with shrewd insights into the real problems of nearby villagers.[77]

The Viet Cong struck wherever they wished, making a mockery of the words of General Paul D. Harkins (head of the Military Assistance Command in South Vietnam), who had pledged to win "the hearts and minds of the people."[78] Even *Time* sometimes wondered how U.S.-advised forces could defeat an enemy whose hit-and-run tactics, hidden supply routes, and constant reinforcements rendered it elusive and dangerous. But the magazine invariably fell back upon comforting clichés. Transfixed by misapplied "lessons of Munich," both *Time*

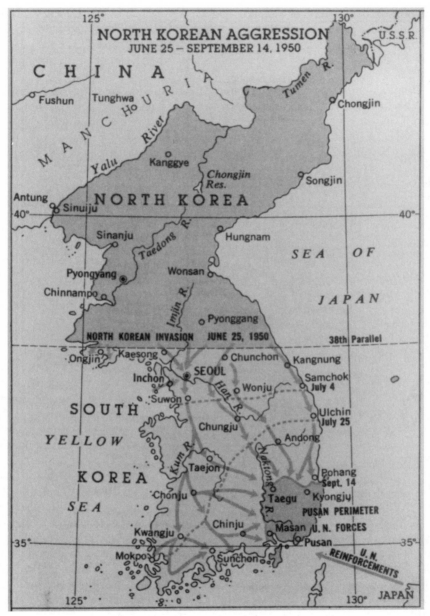

MAP 1 North Korean Aggression, June 25–September 14, 1950. (Hammond World Atlas Corporation)

and the administration insisted that "aggressors" must not be "appeased." This preconception led to a policy that one historian has aptly called a "textbook example of great-power arrogance and self-deception."[79] In effect, Luce insisted that the United States *must* intervene; and he believed that once it did so, *it could not fail.*

Despite defoliation programs, the routine torture of Viet Cong prisoners by ARVNs and government police, and ever rising Viet Cong "body counts," the State Department's status report (August 1962) emitted a gloomy tone.[80] The Viet Cong were growing more numerous, and ever bolder. The neutralization of Laos had failed to stem the flow of ex-southerners and North Vietnamese regulars into South Vietnam.[81] *Time* felt that an escalation of the American military effort was essential. The magazine reported early in 1962 that about thirty-six hundred U.S. pilots and instructors were active in South Vietnam, and that figure would soon rise to seven thousand.[82] On 20 April 1962, *Time* briefly noted that "the first [two] Americans to die in battle against the Communist Viet Cong guerrillas fell in a remote valley of South Viet Nam last week."[83] But the warning failed to deter Luce and his editors, and from this spring of 1962, *Time* prepared its readers for the deployment of U.S. combat troops.[84]

More than ten thousand U.S. advisers were in country, with four thousand more to follow, and in October 1962 *Time* mourned the twenty-seven Americans who had already died in South Vietnam.[85] Indeed, the magazine came close to admitting that some U.S. advisers – especially Huey helicopter pilots – were already engaged in combat, but the shadowy VCs (perhaps twenty-five thousand of them) often eluded them – and sometimes shot them down. Still, C. D. Jackson insisted in July 1963 that although "the reportage from Vietnam" was "pessimistic," the people in Washington "with some justification believe the retrogression has stopped."[86] Luce saw the Jackson memorandum and registered no dissent, even though the Buddhist uprising against Diem's rule was shaking the regime's flimsy foundations.

Government troops killed rioters in Hue, and in Saigon a monk, Quang Duc, immolated himself in protest in June 1963.[87] Early in August, even *Time* worried about the effect of these troubles on a war that was as "ugly and indecisive as ever."[88] *Time* also reported that Madame Nhu had joked about self-immolating Buddhists ("if they burn 30 women, we will go ahead and clap our hands").[89] To make matters worse, *Time*'s Charles Mohr interviewed the Diem family and found its members "arbitrary, puritanical, imperious and devious."[90] But was Diem still viable?[91] Ambassador Nolting was leaving his post, and the new ambassador, Luce's friend Henry Cabot Lodge, did not share his predecessor's vested interest in the South Vietnamese leader.

Without emotion, *Time* learned in September that a coup was to be staged.[92] And the fact that Diem's circle was rumored to have put out neutralist peace feelers to Hanoi would certainly make him dispensable, as far as *Time* was concerned.[93] Neutrality, Luce believed, was immoral, and it threatened the war against Communism. As *Time* noted, neutrality would make it impossible to use

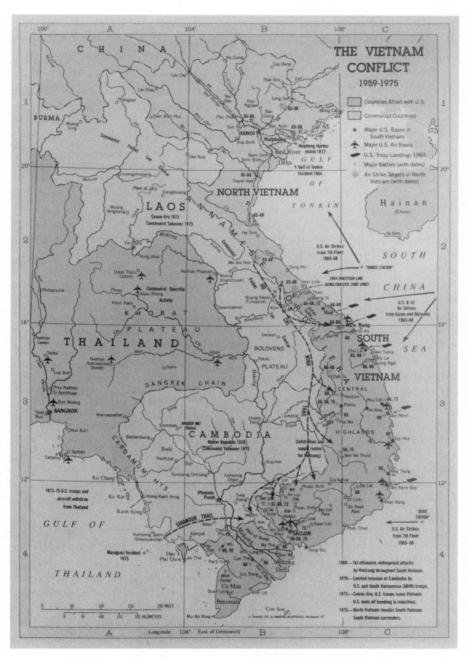

MAP 2 The Vietnam Conflict, 1959–1975. (Hammond World Atlas Corporation)

Vietnam as an experimental American battlefield in the new age of technology-driven counterinsurgency.[94] Going further, managing editor Otto Fuerbringer said that he looked forward to the day when the U.S. Seventh Fleet would "blow the hell out of [the Communists]."[95]

Dissident Voices Suppressed

American correspondents in South Vietnam, including those at *Time*, were good Cold Warriors, and they supported the goal of denying South Vietnam to the Communists. But like his colleague Charles Mohr, *Time*'s Frank McCulloch could see that the war was going badly. By the summer of 1963, after all, the United States was spending $1.5 million a day on South Vietnam, but the Communists were still fielding an estimated force of thirty-one thousand men.[96] As a result, Mohr and other American reporters, among them David Halberstam of the *New York Times*, were increasingly hostile to Diem. Mohr met with managing editor Otto Fuerbringer, and true to form, *Time* published some of Mohr's unwelcome information – only to explain it away a few sentences later.[97] By this time, Fuerbringer had long since decided that the American correspondents who gathered regularly at the bar on the eighth floor of the Caravelle Hotel in Saigon were lopsidedly anti-Diem and hence antiwar.[98]

Discontent bubbled up again when Mohr told the New York office that the war was being lost. He added that he was sick and tired of seeing *Time* print the optimistic propaganda put out by senior U.S. commanders. Fuerbringer's first impulse was to fire Mohr, but this would not be easy. Luce admired the man's reporting, if not his attitude toward Diem, and had enjoyed traveling with Mohr through India back in 1961. And Richard Clurman, the head of *Time*'s news service, had seen Vietnam for himself, and by 1963 he knew that Mohr was right. But to Luce, expressing doubts about America's Christian ally in Southeast Asia (Diem) was reminiscent of the attacks upon Chiang two decades before. Although Luce was friendly with Clurman, he also considered Fuerbringer a very good editor. Moreover, John Mecklin, former *Time* correspondent and current director of the U.S. Information Service in Vietnam, agreed with Mohr's critics.[99]

Late in September 1963, *Time* ran an article calling the American reporters in Saigon pro-Buddhist and hostile to the war effort.[100] Worse, on 11 October, *Time* condemned the antigovernment pessimism rife among the likes of David Halberstam and Neil Sheehan of the *New York Times*. Mohr was embarrassed and decided to resign. Although Luce was willing to have *Time* make an indirect apology, Fuerbringer slyly excised even that mild mea culpa. So Charlie Mohr, despite the entreaties of Dick Clurman, refused to withdraw his resignation.[101] In fact, the Mohr episode cast light on the dark side of Henry Luce's philosophy of journalism: An editor studied all the facts reported by correspondents in the field, weighed the arguments against his own values – and then told the readers who was right. The final product showed that *Time* was validating the American mission to South Vietnam – after rejecting the insights of its own journalists.

Fuerbringer and Luce failed to realize that the Buddhist troubles in South Vietnam reflected the reaction of a xenophobic society against a foreign-imposed, "forced-phase modernization." Instinctively, they criticized the Buddhists for their lack of anti-Communist passion: The Catholics, wrote *Time*, had "always seemed to be tougher anti-Communists."[102] But in backing Diem, the United States found itself fighting a war on behalf of widely despised generals and politicians who had sided with the French against their own compatriots. Buddhist activists and the Viet Cong, by contrast, represented more authentic versions of Vietnamese nationalism. Nevertheless, *Time* embraced the latest Pentagon line: that the United States could accomplish its military task within two years.[103] But the mood behind the closed doors of the State Department was more pessimistic. In the words of one of the few Foreign Service officers who knew Vietnam, "I felt there was no way we would ever win the war or that Diem could ever win."[104] Weary of Diem's arrogant incompetence, the administration and Ambassador Lodge encouraged a coup. In an act that shocked Kennedy (who had reason to fear this outcome), the two Diem brothers were murdered by military conspirators.[105]

Uncowed by his bloody debut, *Time*'s editors argued that the new strongman, General Duong Van Minh, might usher in a time of stability, democracy, and victory.[106] His biographical details, however, were not encouraging. Though currently lauded as South Vietnam's man of the hour, *Time*'s Minh had also served the discredited French Vichy regime and had fought for the French against the Vietminh. *Time* also failed to see that a regime created by men who murdered their predecessors might be inherently unstable. After a pause, the Viet Cong stepped up their attacks, and General Minh proved ineffective. In a typical week, the Viet Cong lost eighty-five weapons but captured three hundred – mostly American made. Washington no longer anticipated the gradual withdrawal of U.S. advisers within the promised two years.[107] After *Time*'s Murray Gart flew on twenty-six helicopter missions in five days and then filed depressing copy, even *Time* agreed, "The war cannot possibly be won by 1965."[108] In fact, General Minh himself wanted to negotiate a settlement with the enemy, and his American patrons soon sought an alternative to him.[109] The morass was deepening. How would Kennedy respond to the looming crisis?

Some have argued that President Kennedy was planning to withdraw from this morass in 1964 or 1965; others claim that he would never have dispatched combat forces to Vietnam. But these are unprovable contentions, for this calculating, cautious president would have thought long and hard before "losing" South Vietnam to the Communists.[110]

At home, these were very good times. The economy was strong, and a civil rights revolution promised to expand the American dream. Time Inc. itself was in grand shape: Return on investment was high, and the company now employed seven thousand seven hundred men and women. Its revenues were $400 million, and Time Inc. remained one of the best managed companies in America.[111] Never had readership been higher, and advertising revenue poured in. Luce saw an America where African Americans in the South were fighting for their civil rights, with *Time* as their ally. So despite Vietnam, Luce insisted, "The American dream has been, in so many ways, fulfilled."[112] His media continued to treat Kennedy gently, and JFK usually reciprocated. On the occasion of the gala celebrating *Time*'s fortieth birthday in 1963, President Kennedy sent a warm message gently teasing Luce about the middle-aged magazine's infrequent admissions of fallibility. Luce fully expected that the president would win reelection in 1964, and the editor-in-chief was thinking ahead with some pleasure to his long-postponed retirement.

Lyndon Johnson

Early in the afternoon on Friday, 22 November 1963, Harry Luce was in the Time-Life Building lunching with some of his senior editors. Otto Fuerbringer heard the phone ring and got up to answer it. He then stunned his colleagues by announcing that President Kennedy had been shot.[113] *Time* published a generous obituary, in which it also boasted of the late president's fascination with the magazine.[114] Luce himself recalled that Kennedy had been a man of grace, style, and intelligence. But his thoughts raced ahead to Lyndon Baines Johnson's sudden presidency. A former U.S. senator and vice-president, Johnson's relations with Time Inc. had been very good since the mid-1950s.

To Luce and his editors in those years, Lyndon Johnson was a skilled Senate majority leader who respected Ike's prerogatives in foreign policy.[115] Hardworking, moderately constructive on civil rights (at least recently), Senator Johnson was also eager to establish a national reputation. Writing to Luce, he noted, "Your publications have won...universal acceptance in the heart of America."[116] "I'd rather have one line in *Time* magazine or the *New York Times*," Johnson flattered *Time*'s Hugh Sidey, "than I would in all the other newspapers in the country."[117] Sitting in his Senate office, LBJ regaled Sidey with his political war stories, all the while gulping down large amounts of Scotch. Johnson became a coveted source, and to *Time*, that meant a protected source, for there was a side of Johnson that Luce's readers never saw: garrulous, profane, and at times sadistic, paranoid, and manipulative. Had *Time* forewarned its readers, they might not have been so confused by Johnson's later deceptions.

After Johnson's accession to the presidency, *Time*'s reporters continued to enjoy good relations with the new administration.[118] Luce set the mood for this long honeymoon. According to *Time*'s Otto Fuerbringer, Luce considered the president's "Great Society" address "the best speech of the decade."[119] Johnson's War on Poverty impressed him, too. To Luce, the new president's policies promised civil rights for African Americans, a renewal of American idealism, and, perhaps, a new era in South Vietnam. At *Fortune*, senior editor Max Ways portrayed the new president as pro-business and as a unifying figure during the tense days after 22 November.[120] Yet Vietnam loomed as a major challenge. By early March 1964, 194 Americans had died in Vietnam, but instead of looking for a way out, a defiant Secretary McNamara promised, "We shall stay for as long as it takes."[121] *Time* mused about an American takeover of the war, and Luce tried to goad Johnson into action.[122] *Time* bluntly warned readers that "the increased tempo of the fighting raised new doubts about the Saigon regime's ability to win with American advice and equipment alone."[123] When Pentagon strategists wanted to launch air attacks against Hanoi in the late spring of 1964, *Time* concurred.* In fact, its editors thought that deploying American combat forces in Vietnam "could be worth the price." Unless the United States held the line now, the magazine insisted, all of East Asia would fall, and "the U.S. would only have to fight later" (5 June 1964). Yet some of *Time*'s anecdotes told why South Vietnam was a weak link in its grand strategy.

Time depicted Saigon as a city that exuded corruption and decline.[124] And in true *Time* style, a snappy anecdote (12 March 1965) recounted the words with which one Saigon merchant hawked his wares to passing GIs: "No V.D., no V.C., Buy from Kim Chi." In the countryside, moreover, the VC ran things pretty much as they pleased, especially at night. Nevertheless, Luce and Fuerbringer stumbled defiantly forward, like two sleepwalkers. But they were doing more than endangering their credibility; *Time*, by ignoring contrary indicators, was helping to prepare gullible readers and craven politicians for a painful misadventure.

---

* From New Delhi, Ambassador Chester Bowles wrote to the president and warned him that only a land reform program could save South Vietnam. Otherwise, Bowles added, the Republic of Vietnam would go the way of Chiang Kai-shek's China. Senator Mike Mansfield (D.-Montana) also told Johnson of his fear that the United States was on the brink of turning the conflict into an unjustified American war, which would cost many American lives.

14

A Troubled Crusade in Vietnam

For twenty-five years, Henry Luce had been musing about taking early retirement so that younger men could run his sprawling company. Driven as he
was, Luce had hung on. But now, because he had already passed Time Inc.'s
mandatory retirement age of sixty-five, the editor-in-chief decided to leave the
scene. Clearly, stress and endless smoking had taken their toll. In the late 1950s,
moreover, Luce had apparently suffered a heart attack while on an airliner.
Thereafter, Luce took anticoagulants as well as dicumarol.[1]

By the early 1960s, Luce's behavior was sometimes not Luce-like. Once, a
colleague walked into Harry's office and was stunned to see him asleep on
a couch.[2] Harry had also complained to his physician about loss of potency,
probably in connection with his latest lady friend. Acting like a younger man
(or as some unkind observers said, an old fool), he engaged in a dalliance with
Jean Campbell, the young granddaughter of Lord Beaverbrook and a Time Inc.
employee. Apparently, Jean liberated that side of Luce that had always eluded
others – childlike, funny, teasing. But Campbell wanted him for herself, and
Clare would not grant a divorce.* So Clare manipulated Harry into ending an
affair that had astounded and dismayed his colleagues. Luce then, with some
sense of resignation, entered into another stage of his partnership with Clare.
Clearly, he was feeling his mortality. Luce finally resigned as editor-in-chief in
April 1964 and soon became the first and only "editorial chairman" of Time
Inc. Yet he cast a long shadow.

Luce's hand-picked successor as editor-in-chief was the trusted Hedley
Donovan, who had acquired broad executive and editorial experience at Time
Inc., especially at *Fortune*. A native of Minnesota and a World War II vet-
eran (naval intelligence), editorial director Donovan was forty-nine years old.
Thoughtful, prudent, and sometimes slow to express an opinion ("deadly

---

* Clare Luce's venomous wit remained unsurpassed. According to several contemporaries, she suggested that the Luces switch partners: Luce could marry Jean while Clare wed Jean's grandfather,
  Lord Beaverbrook – thus making Clare Harry's grandmother.

Hedley," some called him), Donovan hoped to make *Time* less predictable and more fair. In the words of Henry Grunwald, a future managing editor of *Time*, "Donovan lacked Luce's creative imagination, but he encouraged creativity."[3] Though a Vietnam hawk, he lacked both Harry Luce's theological certitude and Otto Fuerbringer's bellicosity. *Time* would change, but very slowly.

An Alliance with Lyndon Johnson

Luce's uncommon enchantment with Democrat Lyndon Johnson owed a good deal to his dismay at the putative Republican nominee. To Luce, Barry Goldwater was a throwback to Taft and the isolationists.[4] Goldwater's contempt for multilateralism and his bullheaded approach to world affairs further offended Luce, especially when the senator scoffed at terms like the "rule of law" and "world peace through law" – concepts dear to Luce. Goldwater's rejection of Johnson's pending civil rights legislation further alienated Luce. He preferred Nelson Rockefeller or William Scranton, but Goldwater won the nomination in 1964. To Luce, Lyndon Johnson was a better bet.

Luce was delighted to sit in the Oval Office while Lyndon Johnson shamelessly showed off, wheeling and dealing on the phone.[5] Indeed, this president was putting a lot of energy into winning a trophy that had eluded John Kennedy: *Life*'s editorial endorsement. Luce was amenable. In fact, this publisher, who had deeply mistrusted FDR, now reposed too much faith in the equally duplicitous LBJ. During the campaign, Johnson denied that he intended to involve America more deeply in Saigon's war. We would not, this president promised, send Americans into a war that Asian boys should be fighting. LBJ dismissed suggestions that he might bomb or invade North Vietnam and accused his opponent of advocating a wider war. The polls vindicated Johnson's strategy. When the Vietnam issue did blow up, it was in Goldwater's face. The Republican nominee, confusing stupidity with honesty, mused about defoliating South Vietnam through the use of nuclear weapons.[6] Some questioned Goldwater's sanity, and after managing editor Fuerbringer briefly flirted with the idea of backing the Arizona senator, *Time* changed course and attacked the Republican nominee as a primitive of questionable judgment.[7] Faced with the Goldwater alternative, the Luce media spared Johnson, even as *Time* excoriated the "dirty, ruthless, wandering war" in Vietnam.[8]

In August 1964, attention shifted to the Gulf of Tonkin, where Hanoi's boats had allegedly attacked two American destroyers on patrol. In retaliation, carrier-based U.S. planes struck five enemy targets. Although the facts of the case were murky, Congress's bipartisan, broadly worded Gulf of Tonkin resolution granted the president authority to use force to repel aggression in the region. Few citizens foresaw the time when the Gulf of Tonkin resolution would be cited – by both Johnson and *Time* – as a justification for an enormous American land presence in Indochina.[9] But *Time* stood by Johnson, "for the fall of South Vietnam would probably mean the Communists' overrunning all of Southeast Asia."[10]

Luce's favorite proconsul, General Douglas A. MacArthur, saw things differently. When Johnson visited the dying MacArthur in Walter Reed Hospital, the general warned him against getting "bogged down in a land war in Asia." And in 1965 General Mark Clark said virtually the same thing.[11] *Time* cited these experienced fighters of Asian wars – and quickly discarded their counsel.

China Policy: New Ambiguities

In the autumn of 1964 Luce decided to revisit East Asia. He toured Tokyo, Bangkok, and Hong Kong and came away amazed.[12] Their skyscrapers and bustling real estate markets reinforced his view that the West could remake Asia. Vietnam was foremost in Luce's mind; like *Time*, he demanded "far greater involvement" on the part of the United States in Indochina.[13] After talking to leaders in many countries, Luce came away convinced that "the Asians" were "with us in Vietnam even if they" didn't "say so in public."

In Saigon, Luce dined with *Time* correspondents Frank McCulloch and Jim Wilde, among others. In his usual monologue, Luce argued that with enough stamina, the right American proconsul could save the day in South Vietnam. But suddenly, Luce was stopped in his tracks. Wilde, who had been silent for a long time, jumped up and shouted at editorial chairman Luce. "The day that the war could be won," Wilde roared, "would be when a Vietnamese battalion with fire in its gut got out there and fought."[14] Luce was dumbfounded, but Wilde's argument had no lasting effect upon him. Like *Time*, Luce believed that South Vietnam's lack of "nationhood" only mandated greater U.S. involvement there.[15] If South Vietnamese were cowards or incompetents or patsies for the Reds, then American can-do would fix the mess.

A sentimental visit to the Chiangs only reinforced Luce's hard line. Madame was aging a bit, Luce admitted, but Chiang seemed "in fine shape physically," and Luce had "never seen him keener mentally."* Luce visited the Nationalist stronghold on the island of Quemoy and compared it to West Berlin. He also decided that recognizing Red China would mandate pulling the Seventh Fleet all the way back to Hawaii. Though acknowledging Beijing's military and economic weakness, Luce still insisted that the West had underestimated "China's capacity for subversion."[16] "China," *Time* warned, "is the real enemy in Asia, and the greatest threat anywhere to world peace."[17] The magazine concluded that action might have to be taken to curb a nuclear-armed China, but it failed to specify what kind.[18] As usual, Clare Luce went further and spoke of holding firm in Southeast Asia even if it became "necessary to wield a nuclear stick over the head of Mao Tse-tung."[19] Some of these opinions reflected information provided to the Luces by Madame Chiang Kai-shek, who believed that a nuclear-armed China would try to conquer the world.[20] Yet the Luces harbored growing uncertainties about China, and sometimes these doubts surfaced.

---

* Mme. Chiang outlived her husband by almost three decades.

Clare Boothe Luce was the fifth most admired woman in America, and her comments and articles invariably generated media interest.[21] In December 1964 she publicly admitted that the Beijing regime was "for the foreseeable future, here to stay."[22] And while threatening China with nuclear war, she also mused about trading with Beijing in order to exacerbate the Sino-Soviet rift. As for Henry Luce, he acknowledged that Taiwan was losing support in the UN. Clearly, he hoped to wean Beijing away from its warlike rhetoric and back into the family of nations. Luce told editor-in-chief Hedley Donovan that if he ever felt compelled to recognize Red China, he could do so without worrying about his former boss's reaction.[23] Time Inc. nonetheless remained loyal to its one-China policy, even though the Sino-Soviet split weakened the lobby obsessed with isolating and destroying Red China. Indeed, the problems facing the lobby coincided with the public reemergence of China experts like Luce's old nemesis, Professor John King Fairbank.[24]

Invalid Certainties and Masked Deceptions

Within the administration's councils of war, Under Secretary of State George W. Ball was a kind of in-house gadfly. Loyal and discreet, he nonetheless challenged myths about Beijing's intentions and bucked the consensus for a wider war in Indochina. In a remarkable internal memorandum that asked, "How valid are the assumptions underlying our Viet Nam policies?" Ball warned against deploying U.S. ground forces. With stunning accuracy, Ball predicted that bombing North Vietnam would make America look like "a great power raining destruction on a small power." Nor did Ball believe that Americans were equipped to fight a dirty war in remote jungles. Above all, he realized that the United States was attacking a nationalist enemy on behalf of an unworthy, unpopular ally in Saigon. Instead, Ball favored a diplomatic and political settlement, American withdrawal, and a neutral South Vietnam guaranteed by the great powers.[25] But neither Johnson's inner circle nor *Time* could accept his prescription.

Time, as often happened, continued to ignore the implications of its own facts: The magazine grudgingly admitted that Ho played off the Chinese against the Russians; Hanoi also feared a "virtual occupation" by the Chinese in the aftermath of any future U.S. air attacks.[26] Few caches of Chinese arms had showed up in South Vietnam; the most notable Soviet military assistance to Hanoi consisted of ground-to-air missiles needed for the defense of North Vietnam; Beijing was worried about North Vietnam's growing alliance with Moscow; and China was trying to avoid a clash with the United States.[27] By implication, further American pressure would only cause Ho to draw *closer* to Mao and to Moscow. But in issue after issue, *Time* reiterated its insistence that Vietnam represented a "decisive contest between the U.S. and Red China," for Red China was "the enemy."[28] So *Time* continued to ignore unwelcome reports and to mislead its readers. The magazine was providing cover for an administration bent upon deception and intervention.

In October 1964 *Life* endorsed the president, who needed no help. Nothing could stave off the defeat of the hapless, loose-lipped Goldwater, and Johnson won in a landslide. Luce almost certainly voted for Johnson; ironically, he may have been one of the few citizens who chose the president because he would take the United States more deeply into Vietnam. For unlike Luce, the public was growing uneasy about the war in the jungle; respondents polled in November 1964 now called Vietnam the number one issue, and a plurality thought that the effort there was going badly.[29] In fact, American planes were already engaged in combat missions in South Vietnam, although the administration refused to confirm this fact until late February 1965.[30] But Johnson's job ratings remained high, and only one-quarter of Americans polled that winter opposed American intervention in South Vietnam.[31]

With the election over, *Life* commissioned a special issue on Vietnam, and its people met with senior U.S. officials on 14 November 1964.[32] Their briefings provided misleading, optimistic material, which contradicted information available to the administration. When *Life* published its special on 27 November, it parroted the White House line. *Time* too remained in the dark about the president's real intentions, although it complained about his undue caution.[33] To Luce, one thing was clear: Either the United States stood by South Vietnam, or it retreated into a shell-like "Fortress America." In *Time*'s view, the war in South Vietnam, which was now costing the United States $2 billion a year, was worth it. Luce concurred, as was evident when Peter Jennings and Howard K. Smith of ABC conducted a television interview with him. Their guest was clearly trying to prepare the public for an imminent escalation of the war. Insisting that the United States interdict enemy soldiers and supplies infiltrating into South Vietnam, Luce added, "Having announced the aim [of saving South Vietnam], we have to go [on] until it is accomplished."[34] *Time* wrongly predicted that bombing Laos would slow the rate of infiltration into Vietnam.[35] Buddhists and students rioting against the U.S. presence in South Vietnam were dismissed as "hoodlums." Once again, *Time* denied the obvious: The United States was clearly at war against much of Vietnamese society. How could it be otherwise, when *Time* itself admitted that Marines near Danang could not "distinguish between the Viet Cong and the loyal South Vietnamese"?[36]

LBJ was planning to escalate in the face of a deteriorating situation, and *Time* approved when Johnson unleashed the U.S. Air Force against North Vietnam.[37] Although the president remained secretive about his long-range plans, if any existed, Johnson's bombing did hearten the public.[38] In May 1965, after weeks of the bombings, only 13 percent of Gallup's respondents favored a total withdrawal from Vietnam.[39] But would bombing Vietnamese in the north really bolster the hapless generals playing at government in Saigon? (Robert McNamara had known all along that air attacks would not terminate Hanoi's aid to the NLF. Indeed, Johnson himself had expressed doubts about the wisdom of an extended air campaign.) In fact, after the unleasing of "Rolling Thunder," the North *increased* its infiltration of the south – as *Time* itself had foreseen on 5 March 1965. Might stronger, and possibly unpopular, measures be needed, among them calling up the army reserves or dispatching a vast army to Vietnam? Certainly, the president seemed favorably inclined toward proposals for an "increased American effort" on the ground. When General Howard K. Johnson, however, indicated that victory on the ground might require the deployment of five hundred thousand U.S. troops, he stunned an administration unprepared for such figures.[40]

The most important escalation, it turned out, took place on the ground, and not in the air. Thirty-five hundred Marines landed near Danang, where the ever stronger Viet Cong threatened American air bases. By June 1965, it was clear that at least thirty thousand more U.S. troops would soon be deployed in South Vietnam. In July McNamara offered a gloomy appraisal of the war, but Johnson still refused to call up the reserves or declare a national emergency.[41] He feared provoking any one of a number of parties – Russia or China or the Congress or the American people. Hence, the president and his men hinted, evaded, and misled, and the phrase "credibility gap" entered the national vocabulary. People were confused.[42] Dumping the problem onto the lap of the UN was the course that made the most sense to a plurality of polled Americans.

Through it all, Lyndon Johnson could count on *Time*, for as presidential aide Jack Valenti told him, "Time Magazine is in thorough accord with your current foreign policy in . . . Viet Nam."[43] But even *Time* was bothered by mounting evidence of deception, and *Fortune* knew that two hundred thousand to three hundred thousand American troops might soon be fighting in Vietnam. Senior editor Charles Murphy belied administration optimism when he bluntly declared that the U.S. Army was unprepared to mount a counterinsurgency effort in the jungles of Indochina.[44] When Murphy, for example, flew over a VC-infested area at five thousand feet, he commented, "I never did see a Vietcong." And in one vaunted "allied" sweep north of Saigon, "what failed to come, for all but a few of the patrols, was Victor Charlie [the Communists]."[45]

The gap between incoming cables and final copy widened. From South Vietnam, *Time* correspondent Frank McCulloch cabled that land communications were poor and dangerous, so it was hard to tell whether a local action had succeeded or failed. Viet Cong were capturing ever more American weapons from their hapless ARVN foes. Maps that showed government control of villages became sour memories when one was fired upon from those same places a few hours later. And as always, it was hard to tell VC from civilians. Nowhere did ARVN units seem eager to engage the enemy: If the Americans liked the war so much, the South Vietnamese reasoned, let them fight it.[46] POWs told American interrogators what they wanted to hear. U.S. officers quickly learned that body counts guaranteed rapid promotions and multiple decorations. Inflated "body counts" of dead VC (sometimes including hogs or civilians) were also passed to U.S. forces by ARVNs eager to curry favor. Otto Fuerbringer and *Time* insisted, however, that the ARVN forces were growing stronger. Official briefings in Saigon (the "5 o'clock follies") or Washington were upbeat, and it would be 1967 before a senior official would have the temerity to tell the White House that the public did "not accept this evidence as sufficient," because it failed to "answer charges of Vietnamese corruption, inefficiency, and inadequate performance."[47] Americans, however, were growing skeptical. "I get a hopeless feeling when I try to get on top of things," noted Dan Rather of CBS in the spring of 1966.[48]

In Washington, dissenting voices tried to change policy. Within the administration, longtime presidential counselor Clark Clifford warned against a "quagmire" that failed to offer "a realistic hope of ultimate victory."[49] By November 1965, one hundred sixty-five thousand U.S. troops were deployed in South Vietnam, and the *New York Times* speculated about an eventual commitment of two hundred fifty thousand men.[50] Such figures proved that the South Vietnamese had effectively lost their own war. Meanwhile, the bombing and the battles were driving huge numbers of refugees from the countryside into Saigon, which was unprepared to house them.

The ascendant figure in Saigon was now Air Force General Nguyen Cao Ky, who looked and acted like a character out of the comic strip "Terry and the Pirates." Although he could not pacify the South, Ky strutted about in his black jumpsuit carrying a pearl-handled revolver, vowing to attack the north. One Johnson adviser described Ky, who admired Hitler, as "bottom of the barrel."[51] Remarkably, however, *Time* called Ky a national hero.[52] In a cover story, the magazine described him as "eloquent and honest, astute and independent, and above all, a man who cared passionately about the defense and the welfare of his nation."[53] Into 1967, the magazine admired Ky's "remarkable adaptability to the art of Asian politics."[54]

At the White House, a report from hawkish professor Henry A. Kissinger of Harvard University spread more gloom. The Viet Cong, Kissinger reported after touring Vietnam, were inspired fighters, and the Vietnamese as a people were strongly xenophobic. But Lyndon Johnson did not intend to lose a land to Communism, so the administration deceived the nervous public. When Johnson finally admitted in June 1965 that U.S. troops were fighting beside the ARVNs, *Time* glossed over Johnson's deceptions.[55] In a major feature, the magazine labeled Vietnam "the right war at the right time" and insisted that a Communist, united Vietnam would become a Chinese satellite.[56] If Vietnam fell, *Time* opined, then the United States would have to fight elsewhere in the region under worse conditions.*

Time and its sister publications deceived themselves and their readers in other ways, too. The magazine and its sister media made much of Chinese Defense Minister Lin Biao's call (1965) for wars of national liberation. *Fortune* warned of the "looming struggle with Red China that we Americans must keep in the forefront of our minds...in Vietnam."[57] But Ho's war predated Lin Biao's doctrine by nineteen years. And Chinese authorship of the concept of liberation wars hardly meant that Beijing controlled the National Liberation Front in South Vietnam. Even the fact that the PRC was admittedly "hungry" and "underdeveloped" failed to change the collective mind of *Time*'s editors.[58]

---

* Vietnam fell in 1975, and the United States fought nowhere else in the region.

Perversely, China's lack of interest in entering the war in Vietnam stimulated *Time*'s dazzling display of wrongheadedness. Its editors, confident that American power had deterred China, now concluded that the long-term application of American power could also smash the Communist version of *Vietnamese* nationalism. And tragically, *Time* seemed unimpressed by reports about Soviet missile bunkers being assembled in North Vietnam: "None...have yet turned up."[59] The war in Vietnam, *Fortune* promised, could be waged with low inflation, stable taxation, and higher productivity on all fronts.[60] But more Americans had grown skeptical.

Thanks to growing dissent at home early in 1965, *Time* switched much of its Vietnam war coverage from "The World" to "The Nation." *Time* struck back at American opponents of the war, calling them "League of Women Voters" types who wanted to graft an alien idea like democracy onto "a country that could not possibly understand the working of democracy."[61] And when respected U.S senators like Albert Gore, Sr., Ernest Gruening, Olin Johnston, and J. William Fulbright questioned the war and proposed alternative strategies, *Time* derided them as naïve men who failed to recognize the need to deter Communism in Asia.[62] When Fulbright advocated the establishment of diplomatic relations with Beijing, *Time* angrily replied that Communism was a "monolithic doctrine of belligerence based on a fanatical dream of world domination."[63] Even editor-in-chief Hedley Donovan thought this was going too far, but Fuerbringer and *Time* ignored his admonition.[64] When Senator Fulbright conducted six engrossing hearings on Vietnam, they attracted thirty million television viewers. The inquiry, which turned many educated people against the war, had, in *Time*'s perverse view, merely shown that Vietnam was "a necessary war."[65] *Time* would not admit that Communist-led peasant nationalists could deny victory to Americans in South Vietnam.

Time's Contempt for Dissenters

In 1965 *Time* was the newsmagazine of choice for serious people in the newly prosperous middle class. Well educated and committed to the work ethic, *Time*'s model postwar reader was often a suburbanite, a veteran or the wife of an ex-GI, and usually white. Many had fought in World War II or Korea; thanks to the GI Bill, they were often the first in their families to attend college. By the late 1950s, the children or "baby boomers," born to such parents were being reared on television, and this changed the equation. The gap between rich and poor and between white and black – brought home to viewers by the new medium in the early 1960s – seemed less acceptable in these days of bounty.

Other social changes made for turmoil, too. The Pill changed attitudes toward sex and made it more of a risk-free option. Drugs and random, anonymous acts of violence and mass killings became more common, and new forms of dress and music symbolized a growing revolt against conformity. Crime, welfare, and ever higher rates of illegitimate births were hotly debated social issues. The civil rights revolution in the South, which Time Inc. encouraged and helped to sustain, taught many Americans that unfinished business at home took precedence over a questionable adventure in Southeast Asia. Soon, riots in Los Angeles and other cities intensified concern about the violence at home and abroad. Anti-Communist clichés and truths seemed increasingly unreal, in part because the Soviet Union appeared to be less threatening. Moscow had signed the limited test-ban treaty and was prepared to negotiate in other areas.

The televised war in Vietnam repelled many Americans, young and not so young alike. Their own country was raining bombs down upon a distant, poor nation in the Third World. In response, more youths were evading the draft or were turning to drugs, new forms of popular music, and outrageous lifestyles. Faced with their alienation, Luce recoiled in incomprehension. *Time* lashed out at antiwar "Vietniks" who were "unshaven and unscrubbed."[66] Draft-card-burning, flag-defacing traitors – this was the thrust of *Time*'s coverage. Confused by all this alienation, Luce responded by arguing that the church was "needed to give meaning to life because it is also an Age of Meaninglessness."[67] Indeed, to this self-proclaimed "square," the dropouts and longhairs and flag-burners represented living repudiations of the middle-class conventions that Time Inc. glorified. Like some of his editors, Luce – inspired by leaks made available by Johnson and J. Edgar Hoover – thought that the Communists controlled the antiwar movement. When a mob in "patriotic South Boston" attacked draft-card burners, *Time* virtually cheered it on.[68] But despite *Time*, Americans refused to see Ho as a second Hitler, nor did they worry about a "Far Eastern Munich." Americans did not fear Red China the way they had Nazi Germany in 1940 or imperial Japan in 1942.

To the unkempt demonstrators, *Time* opposed images that might have come from World War II, the "good war" that everyone supported. The magazine lauded Bill Carpenter, a twenty-eight-year-old Medal of Honor winner, and Weldon James of Louisville, a colonel in the Marine reserves who had volunteered for duty in Vietnam.[69] Air Force pilot Robinson Risner appeared on *Time*'s 23 April 1965 cover. But somehow, what worked for the war against Hitler did not work now. Frustrated, *Time* turned its fury on people like playwright Arthur Miller, who refused a chance to visit with President Johnson during a bill-signing ceremony.[70] And when twenty-two thousand mature, neatly dressed antiwar activists, including the Reverend Martin Luther King, Jr., gathered in Washington, D.C., in November 1965, *Time*'s article bore the snide caption "To Hanoi, from Dr. Spock."[71] The United States, the magazine claimed, was winning the war, and it should not let a minority of malcontents and freaks and misguided leftists disrupt its march to victory.[72] *Time* ridiculed demonstrators who sought a "chance to feel a little martyred."[73] *Time* then cited the exuberant Vice-President Hubert H. Humphrey, who accused the Viet Cong of committing "the most unbelievable acts of terrorism the world has ever known!"[74]

Avoiding any hint of fairness, *Time* usually printed letters to the editor from readers who agreed with its attacks on the antiwar movement. But even the famously omniscient *Time* was uncertain about key facts: "How many V.C. are killed in each [air] strike is hard to say," admitted *Time*.[75] Nevertheless,

Time plunged ahead, for the point was "to keep the enemy off balance" – but readers sometimes wondered which side was off balance.[76] *Time* itself reported that the influx of thirty-two thousand U.S. troops since February had unhinged the South Vietnamese economy. Inflation, profiteering, and corruption were rife, and by 1965 formerly rice-rich South Vietnam had to import food from the United States.[77] But the magazine's bias, influence, and profitability blinded *Time* to dangers lurking ahead.

Thanks to President Johnson's penchant for secrecy, the public remained largely unaware of the details of what *Time* in November 1965 called "the scope and savagery of the war in Viet Nam."[78] The president's insistence upon personally selecting bombing targets came in for some mild criticism, although *Time* liked his intention of "fighting and winning."[79] But Marines were dying in indecisive battles, and surface-to-air (SAM) missiles (which *Time* had virtually ignored) and antiaircraft fire had brought down 121 U.S. warplanes by the middle of October 1965.[80] "A military success of some kind is urgently needed," responded *Time*. But what kind of success? A big set-piece battle against an enemy that hid in tunnels underneath impenetrable, triple-canopied jungles?

In the autumn, Otto Fuerbringer toured South Vietnam. Like Luce visiting Chiang's China in the old days, Fuerbringer came away feeling vindicated. *Time* soon hailed the increased violence in South Vietnam as "a turning point" because the United States had "averted certain defeat."[81] The magazine scoffed at the idea (recently propounded by the hawkish Charles Murphy in *Fortune*) that Americans were not trained to fight jungle-based insurgents. Whether Murphy was right was yet to be determined, but like "Rolling Thunder," the deployment of U.S. troops had bought time for Lyndon Johnson. The polls dropped Vietnam into second place – behind civil rights – on the public's list of salient issues, and a plurality of Americans favored the dispatch of yet more troops to Vietnam.[82] *Time* named General William Westmoreland, the American commander in Vietnam, "Man of the Year."[83]

Among correspondents at *Time*, the prime Vietnam enthusiast was John Steele, who covered the White House and enjoyed easy access to Johnson. Dartmouth-educated and a Washington insider, Steele took Johnson's case to the hinterland. Addressing fifteen hundred high school principals in Cleveland, Steele defended Johnson's veracity – no easy task. He argued that the United States was protecting the little guy against aggression and, in so doing, was preventing neighboring dominoes from falling. Steele claimed that the United States supported the right to self-determination of South Vietnam, even though the U.S.-backed Diem had blocked the 1956 elections. Steele also compared the U.S. adventure in Indochina to World War II's island-hopping campaign against Japan. But that war had not represented an intervention in a civil conflict; nor did Steele sound convincing when he compared Hanoi to Nazi Germany. President Johnson, however, thought that Steele had written "one of the most articulate expositions of our purposes [in Vietnam] that we have seen."[84]

Time's New York editors eagerly repeated Steele's arguments, but in Hong Kong or Saigon *Time*'s Frank McCulloch seethed when he read their final copy.[85] Far Eastern bureau chief McCulloch had been covering Vietnam since Diem's time, so he knew something about the realities in-country. So did the staff at *Time*'s burgeoning Saigon bureau, which now employed fourteen correspondents and photographers as well as ten Vietnamese helpers. (As late as 1964, *Time*'s presence had consisted of a lone stringer.)[86] Indeed, if one read between the lines in *Time*, every account of an American success showed that victory remained elusive, just like the enemy. The first battles between U.S. forces and North Vietnamese regulars were bloody but inconclusive, in what *Time* itself (26 November) called the "valleys of death." In January 1966 *Time* estimated that seven thousand new recruits – conscripts and volunteers – joined the enemy's ranks each month.[87] Readers of the magazine also learned that one *thousand* Communists a month were infiltrating into the south, while *Time* lauded the Marines for killing *forty* VC per week. Nor were the Viet Cong and their North Vietnamese comrades fleeing their American hunters; in fact, they were fighting hard. And every day or two, the VC committed a new atrocity. The bombing of the Metropole Hotel, billet for enlisted men in the U.S. Army, resulted in the death of 8 soldiers and injuries to 137 more.[88] But *Time* shrugged off these setbacks and merely conceded that pacification might take five years, and require some six hundred thousand U.S. troops.

When the American death toll passed one thousand, *Time* came up with another false analogy. If the United States could keep a large army in Europe for twenty years, then it could do so in Vietnam, too. But in Germany the United States had had many allies, and it had not been subject to daily attack by a determined, indigenous foe trying to take back his own nation.

Nation-Building in Vietnam

By the winter of 1966, *Time*'s euphoria finally dissipated, never to return; the magazine admitted that the "political war might be going sour."[89] The best that Robert S. McNamara could say was that the United States had "stopped losing the war."[90] After thirty-seven days, the latest Johnson bombing pause had produced no results; it merely allowed Hanoi to install more Soviet-made SAMs in North Vietnam. By July 1966 the North Vietnamese and their Russian patrons had shot down 303 U.S. planes. Then, in one of its worst predictions, *Time* claimed that U.S. troops in Vietnam were "inflicting the kind of losses that no enemy can sustain indefinitely."[91] *Fortune* agreed, and it saw the Republic of Vietnam as a haven for U.S. construction companies building up that country.[92] But where could one find the forty-five thousand trained instructors and engineers needed to create a viable social and economic infrastructure in the blood-drenched countryside of South Vietnam? In general, the facts about Vietnam presented by *Fortune* – inflation, warfare, rice imports – belied *Time*'s faith in the war.[93]

Time did admit that Saigon was a city awash in filth, black marketeering, and inflation. And at that very moment, demonstrators were protesting Ky's refusal to commit himself to a timetable for constitutional government.[94] But *Time* went on to dismiss the Buddhist activists as Communist dupes and still insisted that the United States could build a "sense of nationhood" in South Vietnam.[95] But like McNamara and his numbers-crunching technocrats, *Time* and *Fortune* had lost sight of a key fact: Technological mastery could never make the ARVN soldiers fight, nor could McNamara's "whiz kids" defeat Vietnamese nationalism. For the first time, in April 1966, U.S. deaths in combat outnumbered those sustained by the ARVNs.[96] The contradictions between *Time*'s faith and its facts resulted in new, dizzying, and ill-considered juxtapositions: After praising the dropping of ten million tons of bombs on North Vietnam, *Time* made two stunning admissions. First, forty-five hundred infiltrators per month were now trekking south; and political anarchy in Saigon could cost the allies the war.[97] Even *Time*'s coverage of U.S. humanitarian work in South Vietnam backfired. Stories and pictures of wounded children – it was unclear who had caused their gruesome injuries – cared for by American doctors only highlighted the horrific futility of the war.[98]

At home, a growing number of war critics did not think that the United States could win a clear victory, although Americans were not yet ready to abandon Johnson or South Vietnam.[99] A majority wanted to use more force, and not withdraw, but often those polled also endorsed negotiations through the UN. The American people exuded a confused, sour mood, one that foreshadowed growing defeatism. In response to a question about the war in Vietnam, by far the largest number (43 percent) of respondents queried by Gallup in the spring of 1966 described it as a "necessary evil."[100] By August, 62 percent of polled Americans wanted the South Vietnamese to "take on more responsibility for the fighting of the war in Vietnam." The problem was that Luce's vaunted "allies" were incapable of defending a regime that lacked legitimacy.[101]

Meanwhile, a self-pitying president flailed about. (He went to the Lincoln Memorial and declared, "He stuck it out, and so shall we!") Johnson also demanded the public's support while attacking his critics as "nervous nellies." In May 1966 a sample of Americans, when asked about the 1968 election, told pollsters that they preferred other candidates to Lyndon Johnson.[102] Luce remained a solid supporter, even though he had lost his initial enthusiasm for much of the Great Society. He also realized that "a lot of people" didn't "like" Johnson.[103] A grateful president paid little attention to Luce's carping against some of his domestic policies. Sure, Johnson told Clare Luce, *Time* had occasionally burned him, but "never on matters that seriously affected his policies."[104]

Luce still enjoyed coming to the White House. As presidential assistant Bill Moyers told his boss, "He simply wants to hear you talk about Vietnam." The distraught president would then receive Luce, who happily listened to LBJ talk on and on about Vietnam or the economy.[105] Each time, both men felt better as a result of their meeting. Reinvigorated, Luce would take to the hustings and repeat the fiction that Vietnam was the setting for a fight for freedom, where the United States was "not fighting alone." Luce added that nation-building in

South Vietnam was a success, and he told a group of advertising executives that the war concerned the "future of Asia." America, Luce insisted, must build the Pacific community – by taking the road that ran through Vietnam.

Luce continued to advocate nation-building and pacification, even after *Time* in January 1967 printed one grotesque but typical story set in the South Vietnamese countryside:

The villagers were assembled and men between 15 and 45 led off for questioning. Within three days, Ben Suc was deserted, its people and their possessions loaded aboard boats and shipped twelve miles downriver to a refugee camp until they can be permanently relocated. Shortly after they left, torches were put to their homes.

Time used this arson as proof of the "V C's rapidly shrinking sanctuaries."[106] But how many surviving Vietnamese sneaked out of those relocation camps and joined the Viet Cong? In fact, even managing editor Hedley Donovan was having doubts about all this, but the influence of Luce and the heavy hand of managing editor Otto Fuerbringer kept *Time* on course.[107] To the magazine and to Luce, it was all a matter of will, for the power "most determined to win – at any price" would prevail.

It was no wonder that President Johnson repeatedly gushed, "Without *Time* magazine on Vietnam, I don't know how I could've done it."[108] But was this a compliment – or an indictment of both *Time* and the Johnson presidency?

15

The Final Years of the Crusade in East Asia

As he reached young old age, the retired Harry Luce thought more about the past, especially about the company he had built. Ever lonely and strangely unfulfilled, Harry reached out from Phoenix to his old colleague John Shaw Billings and expressed a desire "to vault the years and find" himself in Billings's "company."[1] As signs of ill health mounted, Luce remained convinced that he, like Bertrand Russell, must "sustain alone, a weary but unyielding Atlas, the world that his own ideals have fashioned despite the trampling march of unconscious power."[2] To Luce, Vietnam was such an ideal. As *Time* insisted in December 1965, "If the *Pax Americana* is to be credible anywhere, it must be credible everywhere."[3]

We have to fight in Vietnam, Luce declared late in 1966, "because that is where Communists are fighting."[4] That the growing nihilism in the culture – drugs, assassinations, mass murders – might be related to the violence inflicted upon Vietnam eluded Luce. But his son Henry Luce III, who worked in London for the Time-Life News Service, harbored some of the doubts that troubled millions of other Americans. In a letter to his father, Hank Luce expressed worry about the mounting American casualties, the limited results of the U.S. effort, and America's lack of visible allies.[5] Even *Time* admitted in August that since January 1966 the enemy had been able to recruit ten to fifteen thousand new soldiers each month.[6] Although the U.S. forces in Vietnam might soon number 400,000, an estimated 280,000 Viet Cong and DRV regulars ensconced in the south made victory impossible. And 113,000 ARVN soldiers had deserted in 1965 alone. Vietnam, despite *Time*'s best efforts, remained a deep sinkhole. North Vietnam could clearly take a lot of punishment; *Time* responded by advocating the bombing of its power grids and irrigation dams.[7]

No Concessions to New Realities

During these turbulent years in the 1960s, the Luces spent most of their time in quiet Phoenix, although they maintained other residences back east. Having weathered the Jean Campbell storm, the Luces settled into a kind of friendly partnership. And after forty years in journalism, Luce surprised his friends by enjoying his retirement. He traveled, played golf (poorly), gave the occasional speech, and continued to busy himself with the matters that had always obsessed him: theology, the American exception, Time Inc., politics, Communism, and China. Although Luce never converted, he was greatly interested in the theological arguments of Father Pierre Teilhard de Chardin. Father John Courtney Murray remained a good friend with whom Luce often debated theology.

In November 1966 Luce again insisted that America was helping to create a new Pacific community.[8] So did *Time*, which praised what "the U.S. had already accomplished in Viet Nam."[9] Here Luce and *Time* bucked public opinion, which disapproved of Johnson's handling of the war.[10] Others were jumping ship, but Luce remained convinced that victory in Vietnam was a goal of enormous importance. Opposition to the war at home only baffled and angered him. Not comprehending the alienation that had produced the "hippies" and other bizarre phenomena, Luce slaked his curiosity by gawking at them while touring the Haight-Ashbury district in San Francisco.

LSD was the only part of the 1960s "counterculture" treated respectfully by *Time* – mainly because certain respected theologians had expressed interest in the substance.[11] The Luces actually tried it under a physician's supervision, and in the posh Hotel Pierre in New York, Luce stunned assembled guests at a gala dinner by telling them about his involvement with LSD.[12] Predictably, each of the Luces reacted differently to the drug. Its impact upon Clare, of course, was melodramatic, yielding scenes of hell and redemption. Harry Luce's experience with LSD was rather limited and conventional (he imagined himself by the sea, conducting a great symphony orchestra). His forays into the unknown ultimately left him where he had always been: the spokesman for the conventional values of Middle America, for country, church, capitalism, and party. To the end, Luce enjoyed playing bridge and reading detective stories, and he again confessed that he was "something of a square." Naturally, Luce resented the Supreme Court for banishing his God from the public schools, and he bitterly attacked a *Life* writer who had dared to compare Beat poet Allen Ginsberg to Walt Whitman.[13]

Luce's "square" nature, however, showed a more touching side in the middle of this decade of radical change. Harry had always wanted to be a regular guy, perhaps a boy growing up in a small town in Iowa. Having heard of his wish, the town officials of Oskaloosa, Iowa (pop. 11,053), called Luce in Arizona, offering him honorary citizenship. "It means a great deal to me," said a deeply touched Harry Luce, and he graciously agreed to deliver the commencement address at William Penn College.[14] In Oskaloosa Luce felt at home, more than he ever had in New York City, where, as he had once complained, no one ever introduced him "as just a nice guy." People there, Luce would moan, "don't love me."[15] In Oskaloosa, in the American heartland, Luce did feel appreciated, even loved. He talked with his admiring new friends about local agricultural concerns and enjoyed the marching band. In his speech, Luce defiantly dismissed the doubters and hippies and antiwar "Vietniks," and he reiterated his faith in God's plan for the American mission to Vietnam and China. But he knew that even on this quiet campus, young and old alike were uneasy about the truths uttered by Henry R. Luce, honorary citizen, and by mighty *Time*.

By 1966 many China experts were openly advocating the recognition of the PRC. Beijing's isolation, they believed, combined with its economic problems and its growing fear of Russia, might offer opportunities to the West. Even *Time* admitted that China's vast armed forces were poorly armed and defensive in posture.[16] Nevertheless, its editors seized on every belligerent word uttered by Beijing.[17] Lin Biao's aggressive doctrine of national liberation or guerrilla wars proved that the Communists were still dangerous. *Time* concluded, "There is probably no concession the U.S. could make that would mollify aging Mao Tse-tung's strident, frequently hysterical anti-Americanism."[18] Unconvinced by scholars like John Fairbank and his like-minded colleagues in the Association for Asian Studies, *Time* took comfort in the old clichés that Luce had hawked for years.[19]

In 1966 Mao's Great Proletarian Cultural Revolution threw his vast country into a kind of programmed chaos.[20] *Time* admitted, "Nobody knows precisely what is happening in China."* Ignorance, however, did not undermine its certainty that China remained the real enemy in East Asia.[21] Was this revolution, *Time* asked, "the horrifying death rattle of a regime that recognized the imminence of its own end?"[22] Incredibly, *Time* mused about old Chiang's reconquest of the mainland and pronounced the Generalissimo "less outdated than validated by the present."[23] In fact, Mao's destruction of his own society robbed *Time* of one of its prime reasons for staying in Vietnam: its fear of an aggressive China that must be stopped. A convulsed society hardly threatened American power. Only in the winter of 1967, after seventeen years of exaggeration, did *Time* admit that Beijing's influence in North Vietnam was ebbing.[24]

Late in 1966 *Time* began to talk about sending seven hundred fifty thousand U.S. troops to Vietnam, while President Johnson was still claiming that the war was "not an American show."[25]

The Last True Believer

In December 1966 Johnson talked about the need for an additional $9–10 billion to pay for the war. A month later, that figure rose to $15 billion – and the president still refused to ask for a tax hike.[26] At home, more and more intellectuals and Democrats, and even Republicans, questioned Johnson's war, as did many students.[27] McNamara was shouted down at Harvard and had to be escorted off campus through underground tunnels. Actually, McNamara

---

* The magazine did not realize that America's hostile policy may have played a role in fostering this ignorance.

himself had lost faith in what George Ball called "his fundamental belief – in the pure logic of numbers." Ball added that this deficit "produced much the same trauma in his soul as in a Christian's who had lost his faith in God."[28]

The majority of Americans did not want to abandon Vietnam but expected little good to come of the war. *Time* did not share such doubts, at least not publicly, and it still scolded critics of the war. If European allies, sickened by the sight of bestial acts being committed by ARVN forces, were repelled by the American-directed war, so be it.[29] If the World Council of Churches, whose liberalism dismayed Luce, denounced U.S. intervention in Vietnam, then *Time* (of all voices!) dismissed its "highly ideological tone."[30] When Harrison Salisbury of the *New York Times* revealed the massive number of civilian casualties in North Vietnam, *Time* angrily suggested that Hanoi had duped one of the more astute reporters of the day.[31] But "The Communists," *Time* admitted in November 1966, "are far from defeated"; some of its best prose hinted at the despair derided by its editors.[32] Saigon, the magazine wrote on 20 January 1967, was "a garrison without walls in a countryside alive with enemy bands." In response, Otto Fuerbringer demanded an American war on a bigger scale.

Lyndon Johnson clung to *Time* as to a lifeboat. He granted a long interview to Hugh Sidey and rambled on like a man justifying a failed investment. Maudlin, bitter, and self-pitying ("Of course we have killed some civilians, but..."), Johnson could at least be sure that *Time* would treat him and his allies in Saigon in a kind manner.[33] Addressing students in California early in 1967, Luce described South Vietnam's new constitution as a creative adaptation of Western models.[34] In his view, Saigon's march to democracy vindicated the notion that the West had something of value to say to the East. Luce called this precious commodity "liberty under the law," and he spied signs of it in Saigon, of all places. As for the East, Luce remained smugly convinced that it had "little to say or to propose to the West." His tin ear was tone deaf to the voices of Vietnamese nationalism, or to experts who advocated an opening to China. This was tragic, for Luce's obstinacy reflected an ideologically driven blindness.

During the winter of 1967 Luce expended much energy combating a heresy propounded by members of his own Presbyterian Church. Its "Consultation Study Paper on China" had the temerity to empathize with China's resentment of the Western presence. To Luce, this attitude represented a repudiation of his family's work in China. Worse, the paper advocated a dialogue with Beijing and eventual recognition, along with the PRC's admission to the United Nations. Largely due to Luce's counterattacks, the Presbyterian Church did not make an official statement on Red China.[35]

A Loss of Credibility

Time remained an editor's magazine and not an outlet for frustrated Saigon correspondents, whose facts were "corrected" by *Time*'s New York offices. So *Time* told Americans to be patient while they awaited victory in a "mean and dirty war." And the magazine continued to celebrate the achievements of

Americans killed in Vietnam, while refusing to question the cause that had cost them their lives. In the spring of 1967, *Time* ridiculed black boxer Muhammad Ali, who refused to let himself be inducted into the armed forces.[36] But while trashing Ali, *Time* saluted the thousands of African Americans serving in integrated units in Vietnam.[37] Angry and obtuse, the magazine did not want to see what the Vietnam War was doing to America, black and white alike.

The gap between reality and myth-making at *Time* had widened to the point where it recalled Luce's propaganda for the Chiang regime in 1941–1947. But *Time* had easily survived that debacle because Chiang's failure could be ascribed to a Communist conspiracy in which most Americans believed – until Vietnam. And Americans were not dying there. This war was different, not least of all because for the first time television was more important than the print media. Television presented recent pictures *of* the event, and not words strained through an ideological filter *after* the event. At first, the U.S. Army wanted to show how it was mastering the situation, so it happily permitted print and television correspondents to wander throughout South Vietnam with camera and notebook in hand. The Pentagon insisted that in a guerrilla war, the old rules regarding the release of sensitive information about casualties and the like did not apply; the enemy was everywhere and knew almost everything, so why restrict coverage? Only after the 1968 Tet offensive did the Defense Department impose restrictions upon the press – but by then Americans had seen the horrors of this American war without precedent.

Television was creating unforgettable, disturbing images of a war unlike any in American history. CBS News, in particular, was in the forefront of a new type of war coverage. Using uncensored reports from the front, CBS showed U.S. Marines burning down a village while screaming, confused civilians watched or fled in horror.[38] Walter Cronkite, who screened such reports, gained credibility, as *Time* itself admitted. Broadcasters like Cronkite were not trapped by a formula that confused facts with opinions. And even when Cronkite finally offered his editorial view that the war could not be won, he clearly separated his considered opinion from his reporting. By contrast, Time Inc.'s editors censored their own war correspondents by filtering their cables through an ideological lens. *Time*'s clever mixture of fact and opinion had made it powerful; now the same combination exploded in its face by discrediting all of its war coverage.

Time insisted into 1967 that Vietnam was a noble, "allied" enterprise in the ongoing *confrontation with Red China*. But the enterprise hardly struck Americans as noble, and the confrontation foreseen by *Time* for fifteen years had still failed to take place. (One skeptic derided *Time* for contributing "to the mystification and general hysteria about Communist China.")[39] Its misguided claims only made *Time* vulnerable to missiles hurled by its growing array of enemies; its editors received increasing numbers of angry letters from disillusioned, confused readers. Liberal critics, who had never forgiven Luce for his mistreatment of Adlai Stevenson, now berated Time Inc. for its "unfulfillment and emptiness."[40] Dwight Macdonald, former *Fortune* editor and radical critic of *Time*, came up with this formulation: The "degree of credence with which one reads any given news report [in *Time*] is always in inverse ratio to the degree of knowledge one has of the situation that is being reported on." Vietnam proved the point.

Editor-in-chief Hedley Donovan had last been in Vietnam in 1965, when he had returned to New York flush with a sense of ultimate victory. By 1967, however, Donovan no longer believed that the United States should pay any price for victory, and he had become more skeptical about the whole Vietnam enterprise. Donovan was slowly changing the tone of *Time*, and Fuerbringer had no choice but to follow orders. In 1967 *Time* grew less dismissive of antiwar activists and admitted more often that Vietnam was a "mean and dirty war."[41] In addition, Americans, *Time* complained, refused to equate the horrors of Communism with "the evil of Nazism."[42] For the first time, the newsmagazine ridiculed the phrase "hearts and minds" and showed why and how pacification programs had failed.[43]

Luce kept his promise not to interfere, but in speech after speech, he still insisted, "We are required today to assume worldwide responsibilities, but not in the sense of imperialism."[44] Like the crusader preacher in the late eleventh century, Luce was still crying out *"Deus vult, Deus vult!"* – God wills it, God wills it.

Post-Luce: *Time* in a Changed World

In February 1967 Henry R. Luce, sporting a bowler, visited Yale for Alumni Day, and he seemed to be in good spirits. Ever an ardent supporter of civil rights for blacks, Luce was looking forward to delivering an address at Morehouse College in Atlanta, which was celebrating its centennial.[45] A predominantly black institution, Morehouse was led by Dr. Benjamin E. Mays, a famous educator and community leader. Luce, who would be speaking on 23 April, would be following in the footsteps of Dr. Martin Luther King, Jr., who had given a convocation address in November. But a few longtime acquaintances noticed that Luce appeared ashen and unhealthy. He had the look of death about him, recalled one friend.[46]

In late February, while resting in Phoenix, Luce had no appetite at breakfast. This was unusual. Although he cared little about what he ate, Luce had always polished off a hearty breakfast. Then Harry began to vomit, and he spat up blood. Against his protests, Luce wound up in an ambulance headed for the hospital, but not before he had grabbed a Bible and a Perry Mason mystery. He could not sleep, and at one point headed for the bathroom, where he apparently uttered his last words. Appropriately, they were "Oh God." A nurse rushed in and found that Harry Luce had collapsed and died. The cause was coronary occlusion, and the date was 27 February 1967. The decades of compulsive chain smoking, multiplied by extreme stress, had ended Luce's life at the age of sixty-eight.

Henry Luce's body was flown for burial to Mepkin Abbey in South Carolina, the former plantation deeded by the Luces to Trappist monks back in 1949.

Luce left most of his $110 million estate to the Henry Luce Foundation, which he had established in 1936. Appropriately, the foundation was mainly engaged in financing "exchange programs between Far Eastern countries and the U.S." and in promoting "Christian education and other missionary activities."[47]

No dramatic editorial changes ensued in the weeks after Henry Luce's death, with one modest exception. In a long essay, *Time* concluded, "Without doubt the bitterness of Communist rule will profoundly change China." The magazine could only hope that "in the process," China would also "change Communism."[48] Left open but implied was a change in U.S. policy. After visiting Vietnam in 1967, Hedley Donovan came home and admitted the "possibility of being wrong."[49] His son Peter was serving in the International Volunteer Service in Vietnam and was discouraged by the course of the war. Donovan also worried about the effect of the dismal war upon American society, and he wanted to engage in dialogue not only with Hanoi but also with antiwar dissidents. Slowly, gently, Donovan began to shunt Fuerbringer aside, and the "Iron Chancellor" would soon be out of the managing editor's job. *Life* advocated a bombing pause and peace talks with Hanoi. Johnson, feeling betrayed, had tried to head off the editorial by invoking Luce's name, but he failed.

Luce was dead, and a disillusioned Robert McNamara surrendered his post at the Pentagon to Clark Clifford. The enemy's Tet offensive in February 1968 stunned *Time*, and the magazine also voiced uncertainty about the outcome of the battle at besieged Khe Sanh. Johnson would soon be driven from office. Although *Time* still warned against abandoning Southeast Asia, its reporting had grown both more objective and more troubled.[50] Within a year of Luce's death, *Time* was voicing the ultimate heresy, as it mused about "the limits of U.S. power."[51] (A few years earlier, the magazine had angrily derided Senator Fulbright for voicing similar doubts.) *Time* was backing away from giving carte blanche to every unilateral U.S. military intervention.

Time's credibility had suffered, whereas *Life*'s appeal had fallen victim to both television and growing public lack of interest in general appeal magazines.* Broader changes were in the works, too. If *Time* were to survive, it would have to become more objective, but also "cooler" – in other words, less *Time*-like. The magazine would have to stop trying to change the world and instead would need to cover it. To prosper, *Time* would have to report on unwelcome social trends with sympathy or least empathy; it would need to blend more easily into the changing society.

In 1968 Donovan replaced Fuerbringer as managing editor of *Time*. His successor was Henry A. Grunwald. A Jewish refugee from Austria, Grunwald had joined Time Inc. as an office boy back in 1944. He had risen through the editorial ranks and had long since reached senior status. By 1967, Grunwald was also turning against a war he had once supported. *Time*, now edited by a man who shared Donovan's doubts instead of Luce's certainties, changed its policy on Vietnam.[52] By the spring of 1968, *Time* advocated the phased withdrawal of U.S. forces; in their place *Time* supported the policy that would be called

---

* *Life* would suspend publication as a weekly magazine in December 1972.

"Vietnamization." And on 10 May, the magazine made a statement that would have astounded Henry Luce: "The U.S. will have to reconcile itself to the prospect that future Saigon governments will include at least some Communists." Gone was the Red Chinese bogeyman, and *Time* even considered – although it did not endorse – immediate U.S. withdrawal. As it won its battle for survival, *Time* bore less and less resemblance to Henry Luce's newsmagazine. For one thing, it no longer sounded infallible and omniscient. There was more room for debate, even in the pages of the magazine, along with the occasional admission of substantial error.

With *Time* changing, the China lobby had lost its main voice to the nation. But the once powerful bloc was growing weaker for other reasons, too. Alfred Kohlberg was long gone, as were Claire Chennault and Styles Bridges and William Knowland and Henry Luce. The PRC had not entered the Vietnam War, and most of the newly independent nations of the Third World wanted to seat Communist China in the United Nations. By 1969, China was emerging from the engineered chaos of the Cultural Revolution. To Mao, America appeared weaker, and the Soviet buildup on his northern frontier seemed more threatening. A new American administration was eager to play China off against mighty Russia, and it also hoped to secure Chinese assistance in resolving the Vietnam issue. Richard M. Nixon and his national security adviser, Henry A. Kissinger, were even preparing to abandon the president's longtime friends in the China lobby.

Nixon's early career owed everything to his alliance with Whittaker Chambers and to the who-lost-China craze launched by *Time* and its allies. Certainly, many of Luce's old allies were appalled by Nixon's opening to China. Mrs. Claire Chennault insisted that Red China still reflected "the orientation and support of its Russian origin."[53] For the rest of his life, General Albert Wedemeyer viewed Nixon's opening to China as a betrayal of "15 million loyal Chinese of the Republic of China."[54] B. A. Garside, onetime director of United China Relief and the biographer of the Reverend H. W. Luce, wrote to Nixon denouncing his act as reflective of a "beaten and cowardly people crawling into the presence of their conqueror in abject surrender."[55] Garside even called Nixon's trip "the most colossal blunder" in American history, a judgment that few have shared. After Chiang died in 1975 and Mao in 1976, the road to full diplomatic relations lay open.

But how would Henry Luce have reacted to Nixon's stunning embrace of dialogue with the PRC? Some skeptics, after all, declared that Nixon would never have gone to Beijing in 1972 if Harry Luce had been alive. It is likely that Luce would have tried to protect the interests of his friends on Taiwan. But it is also possible that he would have accompanied President Nixon to the Great Wall. Luce, after all, never believed in staying too far ahead – or too far behind – his readers. By the 1970s, the public supported the opening to China, and between 1971 and 1973, Americans, for the first time, briefly expressed a favorable view of the PRC.[56] As long as Taiwan remained secure with U.S. help, it is quite possible that a seventy-three-year-old Luce would have happily revisited a China that he had not seen since 1946. Ever the humanitarian, Luce would have wanted to help the suffering Chinese people. And his mind would have raced ahead – and looked back – as he contemplated the renewal, albeit with difficulty, of Christian work in China.

Is there evidence for this conclusion? Clare Luce hailed Nixon's opening to China as a "good thing" and supported a "civil dialogue on mutual problems" by two nations that had been enemies for too long.[57] Luce's widow even called this conversation "the greatest hope for peace we have seen since the Cold War began." As to Nixon, Clare Luce intoned a prayer: "May God go with him to Peking." More remarkably, Clare Luce told Nixon in the late spring of 1971, "I think [Henry Luce] would be ardently in favour of your present policies in respect to China."[58]

The last seven years of *Time*'s Vietnam war coverage contradicted everything that Luce had advocated between 1949 and 1967. In a sense, *Time* rejoined the nation in 1973 when it expressed "an exhausted sense of relief" that the Paris cease-fire had finally been concluded.[59]

Acknowledging the damage done to American society, *Time*, like America, longed for healing. Gone was the fervor that had led Luce into the Chinese civil war and into the Vietnamese revolution. And when South Vietnam fell in 1975, *Time*, once its greatest journalistic patron, voiced no remorse.[60] The magazine had belatedly wearied of the failed, divisive war, but the damage had been done: Television news was a national medium and more trusted, and the *New York Times*'s regional editions soon undercut *Time*'s claim to be a unique national medium. Thanks to Vietnam, *Newsweek* had for the first time challenged *Time* as an equal, for it was gaining in readership, credibility, and advertising revenue.[61] By the 1970s *Time* sold almost five million copies and claimed twenty-two million readers, but its great age of influence (ca. 1940–1966) had passed. In years to come, *Time* would be both more objective and splashier, more socially conscious and trendier. The magazine would resemble television more and would cease being the opinionated gadfly that Luce had made a great if flawed journal.

Greatness and Failure

Henry Luce, Christian, capitalist, and patriot, once observed, "My ultimate accountability had to be to my Creator."[62] Hence, Luce was very happy when he could congratulate his senior associates for helping to strike blows for "enlightenment, liberty, for God, for country."[63] Luce was an advocacy journalist and a public figure who tried to change the world.

Coming to grips with Henry Luce's place in our history produces alternating moods of admiration and despair. He coinvented the newsmagazine, and he made *Time* a powerful force in American public life. *Life* helped to get America through the Depression, and it was the prophet of the consumerism that came to dominate American life after 1947. *Fortune* elevated business journalism and explained capitalism to a wide readership. Even former *Fortune* editor Dwight

Macdonald, a radical who broke with Luce in the 1930s, admired Luce for having helped to change American attitudes toward race. Luce also, Macdonald added, had made organized labor more acceptable to the big-business executives who read *Fortune*.[64] Luce warned Americans against the seductive appeal of collectivism and socialism in the 1930s and the 1940s. *Fortune*'s Russell W. Davenport, abetted by Luce, created the presidential candidacy of Wendell L. Willkie. Luce thereby pulled the Republican Party to the center and helped to prepare it for its return to power twelve years later. His support for Republicans during a Democratic age helped to preserve the two-party system.

Newspaper journalists despised *Time* as a stale, smarmy rewrite sheet, but in 1941 the *Los Angeles Times* called it the "most powerful single element in journalism."[65] William Randolph Hearst, who detested *Time* and Luce's interventionism, nonetheless named *Time* "the world's outstanding journalistic venture to date."[66] But Luce influenced more than journalism and foreign policy: Robert M. Hutchins, president of the University of Chicago, said that Time Inc. did more to mold the American character than "the whole education system put together."[67] Luce, his media, and his wide array of contacts helped to prepare America for the global war that Luce wanted to fight. No less an expert than George Marshall declared that had it not been for *Life*, the Army would have lost six months in its campaign for rearmament.[68] No one did more than the Luce operation to turn American public opinion against Imperial Japan in the years before Pearl Harbor. And to many Americans who lived through the years of World War II, *Life* was a weekly window on a just war waged by a newly confident United States. Luce's magazines boosted morale, helped the government wage war, informed the public, and contributed to the war effort in a myriad of other ways. In gratitude for his work on behalf of China aid, the board of United China Relief declared that "without [Luce's] leadership and devotion the movement could not have gone forward."

This was Luce's heroic time, but it contained traps of his own making. More than any other American, Luce contributed to forging the heroic wartime image of Chiang Kai-shek and Madame Chiang, and of their fighting China. But Luce would pay for the illusions he foisted upon a gullible nation. Nevertheless, more than his contemporaries, Luce foresaw the extent of America's potential power and prosperity. He knew how much good the nation could do in the world. Luce was the prophet of the Marshall Plan and the Peace Corps, and it was he and *Time* that first spoke of the New Frontier and the Great Society. Long before most Americans paid attention to the Asian economy, Luce prophesied a time when American trade with Asia would be worth billions of dollars.

In the summer of 1946, Albert Wedemeyer testified to the efficacy of Luce's work in creating the anti-Communist consensus that soon dominated American life. "Several months ago," Wedemeyer told Luce, "your periodicals were the only ones presenting this view, but now other magazines and many columnists have taken up the cudgel against the materialistic and totalitarian concept of the Russians."[69] It was Luce and *Life* that made John Foster Dulles a well-known national figure. Later, Luce provided him with terms like *liberation* and *rolling back* Communism. As secretary of state, Dulles clearly played "favorites with the Luce organization" because of his need to reach its "vast and influential audience."[70]

Within a few years, politicians of all stripes were impressed by Time Inc.'s apparent influence. Before the administration was prepared for it, Luce had begun to crusade for the restoration and rearmament of Germany and Japan. He also propagated the view that Democratic blunders, and perhaps criminality, had "lost" China. And from 1950 onward, Luce's media insisted that Americans be prepared for ever greater intervention in a remote place called Vietnam. In 1950 Dorothy Sterling, a former Time Incer, argued persuasively that Luce's "American internationalism" had influenced leaders as well as the public in favor of anti-Communist interventionism.[71] In 1956 one radio program declared, "If the Luce publications decide that Chiang Kai-shek is a great man, millions of Americans feel he is a great man."[72] But goodness and real achievement remained part of Luce's legacy, too. It was Henry Luce who had administered an early defeat to the much feared Joe McCarthy when the senator threatened to destroy Time Inc. by organizing a boycott of its advertisers.

Luce's role in engineering Eisenhower's rise to power caused him to be viewed as a kind of unofficial propaganda minister for American machinations abroad. By the 1950s, liberals and leftists routinely detested *Time*'s arrogant Republican bias, and professors of journalism or rhetoric often mocked its pretentious tricks. But they insisted upon its influence and were avid readers of a magazine they despised.

Despite Luce's undoubted political influence, he did not always get his way. Only when an issue gripped the public's imagination, and the politicians failed to act, could the Luce network influence great political debates. *Time* did so when it argued for the dispatch of destroyers to Britain in July 1940; when it presented George Kennan's containment strategy to the American people in 1946; and when it attacked Joe McCarthy in 1951. Luce could influence trends and promote ideas and products and even candidates – but he could not elect Dewey, and even without Luce and his network, Eisenhower would doubtless have won the general election. Luce's campaign for bomb shelters never succeeded. In 1961, however, John F. Kennedy said that Luce's surprisingly balanced coverage in 1960 may have accounted for his narrow victory. Yet here too our conclusion must be ambiguous: That coverage illustrated Luce's influence as well as one of his flaws as a journalist: Luce liked JFK, but his longtime association with Joseph P. Kennedy accounted for Time Inc.'s favorable coverage of his second son.

Henry R. Luce was for three decades the most determined and effective journalistic advocate of what he called the irrevocable westward expansion of the American frontier. It was logical, therefore, that Luce's influence upon the public as well as policymakers reached its peak between 1941 and the middle years of the 1960s. This era, encompassing World War II and the first half of the Cold War, featured bloody encounters between the United States and various Asian adversaries, including Japan, Korea, and Vietnam.

As a result, Americans necessarily paid more attention to Asia, and Time Inc. provided them with massive amounts of relevant but often tendentious material.

Theodore H. White, who labored for *Time* in China during World War II, later claimed that "the history of the world would've been changed" had Luce covered the China story with more objectivity. "We would've avoided two wars with Asia," White told author David Halberstam. He added, "There would've been no Korean War, there would've been no Vietnam War."[73] Writing more than thirty years ago, Luce biographer W. A. Swanberg agreed, for he ascribed much of the Cold War hysteria to "a delusion foisted on Americans by Luce's anti-communism."[74] Admitting that he had abandoned "objectivity" and had "openly attacked" his subject, Swanberg's bitter book *Luce and His Empire* reflected his hostility to America's alliance with Chiang. Swanberg also loathed the Vietnam War, and he told the *New York Times* that there was "no telling how far that tragedy [in Vietnam] was prolonged, how many more thousands of men white and yellow were wasted, by the year-after-year flag-waving promotion" of *Time*.[75] Yet in damning Luce, White and Swanberg overlooked inconvenient facts: Even in regard to Asia, Time Inc. was sometimes prophetic. Early on, Luce sensed the Communist brutality of the "agrarian reformers" who would misgovern China in the name of its suffering people. He also understood that America would have a permanent presence in Asia culturally, economically, and militarily. But Luce's failed prophecies and twisted journalism must weigh more heavily in the final accounting.

As early as 1944, Luce had told his friend H. H. Kung, "Nothing would cause me greater unhappiness than if my primary [journalistic] obligations to my fellow citizens should conflict with my love for China and the friendships there which I value so highly."[76] Repeatedly, Luce put that love and those friendships above his primary obligations to his readers. If the facts were unpleasant, Luce escaped into a world protected by ideology and bias. Ultimately, he insisted upon filtering the news about Asia through a prism that distorted the truth and turned it into fantasy.

In the years after 1948, the Luce media's Asia coverage invariably sounded two powerful themes: First, Democratic blunders had betrayed and lost "our" (meaning Luce's) China. Luce's bitter question, "Who Lost China?" – asked in a thousand threatening ways over the course of a decade – changed American public opinion and affected public policy. In pounding away at who-lost-China, Luce prepared the way for Joe McCarthy. Yes, Luce quickly came to despise McCarthy, and he helped to destroy him. But he had also helped to make Joe McCarthy possible. The second great *Time* thesis on Cold War Asia argued that Communism must be stopped in Korea and Vietnam. Had Luce had his way in Korea, the United States would have fought to conquer most of North Korea between 1950 and 1953, even at the risk of unleashing a wider war against Communist China. It is impossible to say how many more lives would have been lost, or whether a nuclear war would have erupted, if Luce had had his way. But despite the claims of Swanberg and White in regard to Luce's power, the fact is that Truman and Acheson, as well as Eisenhower and Dulles, refused to follow him into that wider war.

Ironically, the "loss" of China policy redounded to Luce's benefit in building support for intervention in Vietnam. His big theme – misguided or treacherous Americans lost China – meant that he could cow politicians into drawing a line in the jungles of Vietnam. *Time*'s prose and authority swept readers along and helped to forge a shaky consensus, at least until the mid-1960s. Time Inc. had created a popular frame of mind conducive to incremental intervention, and then to large-scale war. Lyndon Johnson knew how important this was; and it was no accident that the subsequent failure of intervention badly hurt the reputations of both the failed president and his frustrated ally, *Time* magazine.

The journalism of editor-in-chief Luce on postwar China and Vietnam was often outrageous when measured against even the most minimal standards of objectivity and accuracy. Readers thought, and had a right to think, that they were getting some semblance of objective news reporting. But an examination of the "news" provided by *Time* leads to the opposite conclusion.

Luce and *Time* were mostly wrong in the 1940s about the reasons for Chiang's decline; wrong about the sources of Mao's strength; wrong in the 1950s and early 1960s about the Sino-Soviet "axis"; wrong about the Vietnamese revolution; wrong about the "dominoes" about which Luce wrote so much; wrong about Moscow's alleged control of Ho Chi Minh; and wrong about the extent of Chinese influence in Hanoi.

How can one explain the divergence between this failed journalism and the great achievements of Luce's media in an earlier time? The answer lies in Luce's darkening mood.

The Harry Luce of the American Century era (1940–1945) confidently sketched out a positive program for America in the world. Luce wanted to make the world safe not only for American democracy but also for the coming American global empire. The Cold War changed things, however, for instead of unipolar benevolence and universal peace, Luce's postwar world would have to endure bipolar tensions magnified by the threat of nuclear annihilation. In 1945–1948 the wartime Grand Alliance dissolved into the Cold War, first at Time Inc. and then in the broader society. Millions of *Time* readers needed to be reeducated. But this mission changed Luce and blurred his vision, and as he once put it, history stole the American Century from him. Luce needed a culprit, and he decided that Soviet Communism was to blame.

Luce was right about the evils of Communism, which he had seen firsthand back in 1932. But what Luce did was to portray his enemies in East Asia as *pawns of expansionist Russian Communism*. This pernicious self-deception was comforting, in that it explained away the weakness of Luce's allies in East Asia. And in reaction to global Communism, he now wanted to make the world safe, not only for democracy but also for any regime that allied itself with the American empire. This mandate meant that everyone from the Shah of Iran to Franco of Spain was a welcome partner, to be defended and excused in the interest of building an anti-Communist alliance.

Moscow, Luce insisted for too long, ran Beijing and Hanoi. His miscalculation badly affected domestic politics, as leaders scrambled to outdo each other in isolating China, even when the PRC moved away from its Soviet ally after 1957. Largely because of his China fixation, Luce then justified American involvement in a hopeless conflict against a different variety of Asian nationalism in Southeast Asia. His analytical framework made it impossible for Luce to understand post-colonialist peasant nationalism in China, much less in Vietnam. This was a crucial lapse, for as historian Michael H. Hunt has observed, "Only in China and Vietnam, where determined and experienced nationalist elites had tied their programs to the aspirations of the peasantry, did Americans lose control – and suffer two humiliating defeats as a result."[77] All concerned are still recovering from the longest war in our history, which cost the lives of more than fifty-eight thousand Americans and many more Vietnamese.

Tragically, in the case of Vietnam, Luce proved to be an effective promoter, for he knew how to provide a product that people would buy. The "sale," however, is only one part of a successful promotion. A popular textbook tells us that marketing "must be understood not in the old sense of making a sale . . . but in the new sense of *satisfying customer needs*."[78] And here Luce failed. Despite an influx of valid information available to him and his colleagues, Time Inc.'s version of events in revolutionary East Asia reached readers only after bias and ideology had rendered it fit to print. Marketed in slick packages called *Time* and *Life*, opinionated "news" was presented by Luce as fact to millions of avid readers.

Nation-Building in the American Century

Henry Luce would often say that men are sinners and must sometimes fail. Yet they must run the race, keep the faith, and strive to build the City of God. Luce ran harder than most, and he sometimes achieved greatness as a journalist, entrepreneur, and patriot. Yet the idealism that nourished young Luce in the Chinese missionary compound a century ago soured in the middle of his adult life. After 1945, disappointed but still an ardent crusader, a bitter man tried to impose his will upon stubborn, misguided human beings, among them Chinese, Vietnamese – and Americans. Idealism became degraded and turned into a militant ideology that offered explanations intended to ward off unpleasant facts.

As for American nation-making, it appears that Luce's formula works only when a shattered society – Germany and Japan are good examples – commits to rebuild and renew structures swept aside by fascism, militarism, and dictatorship. Unless a repressive society has faced trauma and defeat, and unless it can draw upon earlier capitalist, technical, and liberal models, the American Century is an export doomed to failure. If much of a society continues to embrace anti-Western ideologies, the American concepts of property, democracy, and civil order are alien grafts rejected by the host body.

In our new millennium, as we contemplate an ever more interdependent world, Luce's relentless interventionism in cultural alien lands after 1945 serves as a warning. Instantaneous dissemination of (mis)information through new technologies may tempt us to lash out at the wrong enemies, for the wrong reason. And if intervention is the product of illusions about American omnipotence or superiority, it may only alienate its supposed beneficiaries and embitter the nation in whose name it is undertaken.

The history of Henry Robinson Luce and his journalism is thus replete with inspiring achievements; but its last chapters tell a cautionary tale.

Archival Sources

Dean G. Acheson (Harry S Truman Library)
American Bureau for Medical Aid to China (Columbia University, Butler Library)
American Jewish Committee (YIVO Institute)
Hamilton Fish Armstrong (Princeton University, Seeley G. Mudd Library)
Raymond Baldwin (Connecticut State Library)
Bruce Barton (State Historical Society of Wisconsin)
Bernard M. Baruch (Princeton University, Seeley G. Mudd Library)
John Shaw Billings (University of South Carolina, South Caroliniana Library)
Margaret Bourke-White (Syracuse University, George Arents Collection)
Styles Bridges (State of New Hampshire, Division of Records Management and Archives)
William F. Buckley, Jr. (Yale University, Sterling Library)
Raymond Buell (Library of Congress, Manuscript Division)
Claire L. Chennault (Library of Congress, Manuscript Division, microfilm)
Thomas G. Corcoran (Library of Congress, Manuscript Division)
Council on Foreign Relations
Lauchlin Currie (Hoover Institution Archives)
Russell W. Davenport (Library of Congress, Manuscript Division)
Department of State (National Archives, Record Group 59)
Thomas E. Dewey (University of Rochester, Rush Rhees Library)
John Foster Dulles (Princeton University, Seeley G. Mudd Library)
Stephen Early (Franklin D. Roosevelt Library)
Ferdinand Eberstadt (Princeton University, Seeley G. Mudd Library)
Dwight D. Eisenhower (Dwight D. Eisenhower Library, and the Library of Congress, Manuscript Division)
Christopher T. Emmet (Hoover Institution Archives)
John King Fairbank (Harvard University, Pusey Library)
Fight for Freedom (Princeton University, Seeley G. Mudd Library)

Fitch Family (Harvard University, Harvard-Yenching Library)
James V. Forrestal (Princeton University, Seeley G. Mudd Library)
Paul W. Frillman (Hoover Institution Archives)
B. A. Garside (Hoover Institution Archives)
Walter Graebner (State Historical Society of Wisconsin)
R. Allen Griffin (Hoover Institution Archives)
David Halberstam (Boston University, Mugar Library)
Paul Gray Hoffman (Harry S Truman Library)
Herbert Hoover (Herbert Hoover Presidential Library)
Stanley K. Hornbeck (Hoover Institution Archives)
Institute of Pacific Relations (Columbia University, Butler Library)
Institute of Pacific Relations, San Francisco Branch (Hoover Institution Archives)
Philip Jaffe (Emory University, Woodruff Library)
Sidney James (privately held papers)
Philip Jessup (Library of Congress, Manuscript Division)
Lyndon B. Johnson (Lyndon B. Johnson Library)
Walter H. Judd (Hoover Institution Archives)
John F. Kennedy (John F. Kennedy Library)
William F. Knowland (University of California at Berkeley, Bancroft Library)
Alfred Kohlberg (Hoover Institution Archives)
Harold D. Lasswell (Yale University, Sterling Library)
A. J. Liebling (Cornell University Library)
Marvin Liebman Associates (Hoover Institution Archives)
Edward Lockett (Harry S Truman Library)
William W. Lockwood (Princeton University, Seeley G. Mudd Library)
Daniel Longwell (Columbia University, Butler Library)
Clare Boothe Luce (Library of Congress, Manuscript Division)
Henry Robinson Luce (Library of Congress, Manuscript Division)
Henry Winters Luce (Hartford Seminary Foundation)
Luce and Hamilton Collections (Library of Congress, Motion Picture, Broadcasting, and Recorded Sound Division)
Douglas MacArthur (MacArthur Archives)
Archibald MacLeish (Library of Congress, Manuscript Division)
The Nettie F. McCormick family (State Historical Society of Wisconsin)
Frank McNaughton (Harry S Truman Library)
Dwight Macdonald (Yale University, Sterling Library)
George C. Marshall (George C. Marshall Foundation)
Joseph W. Martin, Jr. (Martin Institute, Stonehill College)
John F. Melby (Harry S Truman Library)
George Fox Mott (Hoover Institution Archives)
Reinhold Niebuhr (Library of Congress, Manuscript Division)
Office of Censorship (National Archives, Record Group 216)
Office of Strategic Services (National Archives, Record Group 226)
Richard C. Patterson, Jr. (Harry S Truman Library)

Drew Pearson (Library of Congress, Manuscript Division)
Byron Price (State Historical Society of Wisconsin)
Frank Price (George C. Marshall Foundation)
Ogden R. Reid (Yale University, Butler Library)
Franklin Delano Roosevelt (Franklin D. Roosevelt Library)
Records of the Secretary of the Navy [Forrestal] (National Archives, Record Group 80)
Robert L. Sherrod (Syracuse University, Arents Collection)
Herbert Solow (Hoover Institution Archives)
T. V. Soong (Hoover Institution Archives)
Lawrence Spivak (Library of Congress, Manuscript Division)
William H. Standley (University of Southern California Libraries)
Dorothy Sterling (University of Oregon, Knight Library)
Edward R. Stettinius (University of Virginia, Alderman Library)
Joseph W. Stilwell (Hoover Institution Archives)
Henry L. Stimson (Yale University, Sterling Library [microfilm])
Anson P. Stokes (Yale University, Sterling Library)
J. Leighton Stuart (Hoover Institution Archives)
John D. Sumner (Harry S Truman Library)
W. A. Swanberg (Columbia University, Butler Library)
Robert A. Taft, Sr. (Library of Congress, Manuscript Division)
Time Inc. Archives
Time dispatches (Harvard University, Houghton Library)
Harry S Truman (Harry S Truman Library)
United Board for Christian Higher Education in China (Yale Divinity School Library)
United China Relief, Inc., and United Service to China (Princeton University, Seeley G. Mudd Library)
Freda Utley (Hoover Institution Archives)
Henry P. Van Dusen (Union Theological Seminary Library)
James Van Fleet (George C. Marshall Foundation)
Henry A. Wallace (Franklin D. Roosevelt Library [microfilm])
Edwin Watson (University of Virginia, Alderman Library)
Albert C. Wedemeyer (Hoover Institution Archives)
Allen Weinstein (Harry S Truman Library)
Theodore H. White (Harvard University, Houghton and Pusey Libraries)
Whiting Willauer (Princeton University, Seeley G. Mudd Library)
Wendell Willkie (Indiana University, Lilly Library)
Yale-in-China Association (Yale University, Sterling Library)
Yale University in World War II (Yale University, Sterling Library)

Abbreviations

The following abbreviations occur in the notes:

CBL	Clare Boothe Luce
DDEL	Dwight D. Eisenhower Library
DJSB	Diary of John Shaw Billings
FDRL	Franklin D. Roosevelt Presidential Library
FOIA	Freedom of Information Act
FRUS	Foreign Relations of the United States (Department of State)
HHPL	Herbert Hoover Presidential Library
HRL	Henry R. Luce
HSTL	Harry S Truman Library
IPR	Institute of Pacific Relations
JFKL	John F. Kennedy Presidential Library
LBJL	Lyndon Baines Johnson Presidential Library
MDLOC	Manuscript Division of the Library of Congress
NARA	National Archives and Records Administration
TD	*Time* dispatches
TLCTHW	Time-Life Correspondence, 1940–1946, of Theodore Harold White
TLF	Time-Life-Fortune papers of John Shaw Billings
UCR	United China Relief
USC	United Service to China

Notes

Introduction

1. HRL, unpublished manuscript, the papers of HRL, 86.
2. Robert E. Herzstein, *Henry R. Luce: A Political Portrait of the Man Who Created the American Century* (New York: Scribner, 1994).
3. DJSB, vol. 36, 13 May 1953–9 December 1953.
4. Notes of Daniel Longwell, 21 September 1968, transcribed by Mary Longwell, in the papers of Daniel Longwell, 69, Daniel Longwell memos on *Life*.
5. Edward K. Thompson, *A Love Affair with Life & Smithsonian* (Columbia: University of Missouri Press, 1995), p. 117.
6. Interview with John Melby, in Charles Stuart Kennedy, comp., "A China Reader: Extracts from Oral History Transcripts from the Foreign Affairs Oral History Program" (Washington, DC: Foreign Service Institute and Georgetown University, 1995), p. 6.
7. Ibid., pp. 15–16.

1. Henry Luce and China

1. The Chinese Ambassador to the acting secretary of state, 26 September 1945, in the records of the Department of State, 811.79600, Reservations, 9-2145 (RG 59, NARA).
2. Interview with Wesley Bailey, in the W. A. Swanberg collection, 18.
3. Telephone query by Mrs. Ruth Shipley, 21 September 1945, PPF 928, Luce, Henry R. (HSTL).
4. "Mr. Luce's Chungking diary October 1945," in the papers of CBL, 455.
5. Zhou Enlai to Mr. and Mrs. Luce, 17 May 1941, ibid., 101, 5.
6. Michael C. Coleman, "Presbyterian Missionary Attitudes Toward China and the Chinese, 1837–1900," *Journal of Presbyterian History*, 56:3, 193.
7. HRL to his parents, 24 December 1916, in the papers of CBL, 23, letters of HRL, pp. 351–400.
8. Coleman, "Presbyterian Missionary Attitudes," pp. 192–195.
9. Interview with Wesley Bailey, in the W. A. Swanberg collection, 18.

10. Robert T. Elson, *The World of Time Inc.: The Intimate History of a Publishing Enterprise, Volume Two 1941–1960* (New York: Atheneum, 1973), p. 146.
11. Ibid., p. 145.
12. CBL to B. A. Garside, 11 October 1945, in the papers of B. A. Garside, 2.
13. Bill Gray, cable of 27 October 1945, in the TD.
14. HRL, telegram to CBL, 9 October 1945, in the papers of CBL, 455.
15. *Time*, 12 November 1945.
16. CBL to B. A. Garside, 11 October 1945, in the papers of CBL, 2.
17. HRL to his parents, 24 December 1916, in the papers of CBL, 23, letters of HRL, pp. 351–400.
18. Interview with Wesley Bailey, in the papers of W. A. Swanberg, 18.
19. HRL, speech to Time Inc. executives, 4 May 1950, ibid., 21.
20. HRL to John S. Billings, 8 October 1945, in the TLF, II, 66; and HRL, cable to John Billings, probably 7 October 1945, in the W. A. Swanberg collection, 17, W. A. S.
21. HRL, cable to John Shaw Billings, 25 October 1945.
22. HRL to William Gray, 16 August 1945, in John K. Jessup, ed., *The Ideas of Henry Luce* (New York: Athenaeum, 1969), pp. 190–191.
23. Charles J. V. Murphy, cable of 8 October 1945, in the TD.
24. Charles J. V. Murphy, "China Reborn," *Life*, 19 November 1945.
25. *Time*, 5 November 1945.
26. *Time*, 12 November 1945.
27. John F. Melby, memorandum of conversation with General Chou En-lai, 13 November 1945, in the papers of John F. Melby, 1, China File, General – 1946 (HSTL).
28. *Time*, 19 November 1945.
29. *Time*, 26 November 1945.
30. James Shepley to Robert Low, 23 November 1945, TD.
31. "China: What Price Peace?" *Life*, 19 November 1945.
32. DJSB, 29 August 1945.
33. DJSB, 18 June 1947.
34. DJSB, 11 August 1947.
35. DJSB, 27 August and 2 September 1947.
36. DJSB, 14 February and 2 September 1947.
37. Ralph G. Martin, *Henry and Clare: An Intimate Portrait of the Luces* (New York: G.P. Putnam's Sons, 1991), pp. 246–250.
38. DJSB, 11 August 1947.
39. DJSB, 12 August 1947.
40. CBL to HRL, probably 1947, in the papers of CBL, (X), 10.
41. CBL, notes made on 10 August 1947, in the papers of CBL, (X), 10.
42. John Chamberlain, "CBL," in the papers of John Shaw Billings, TLF, I, 49.
43. DJSB, 20 February 1948.
44. Notes by Daniel Longwell, transcribed by Mary Frazer, in the papers of Daniel Longwell.
45. Thomas S. Matthews, *Name and Address: An Autobiography* (New York: Simon and Schuster, 1960), p. 247.
46. DJSB, 29 August 1951.
47. "This is the Day," 3 April 1956, in the papers of W. A. Swanberg, 19.
48. Elson, *The World of Time Inc.*, pp. 249–252.
49. DJSB, 4 August 1947.
50. DJSB, 14 September 1945.

51. Interview with Emmet John Hughes, p. 9, in the papers of David Halberstam concerning *The Powers That Be.*
52. Interview with Allen Grover, in the papers of W. A. Swanberg, 18, interviews.
53. Notes in carton two, policy folder, in the papers of Dorothy Sterling related to Time Inc.
54. DJSB, 9 July 1953.
55. John Shaw Billings, "Luce Talk – June 29, 1950," in the TLF, Ms. vol. bd. 49.
56. The papers of John Shaw Billings, scrapbook 57, p. 325; and DJSB, 11 September 1942.
57. Notes by Daniel Longwell, transcribed by Mary Frazer, in the papers of Daniel Longwell.
58. DJSB, 15 April 1947.
59. Interview with Corinne Thrasher, in the papers of W. A. Swanberg related to *Luce and His Empire.*
60. John Shaw Billings, scrapbook 57, analecta, in the papers of John Shaw Billings.
61. DJSB, 11 September 1953.
62. DJSB, 6 January 1947.
63. *New York Times*, 8 May 1948, 13, 4.
64. HRL to C. D. Jackson, 18 June 1964, in the papers of C. D. Jackson, 1931–1967, 58, Luce 1963–64, provides a glimpse of Luce at his compassionate best.
65. DJSB, 28 March 1951.
66. Interview with CBL, the papers of W. A. Swanberg, 18.
67. HRL, "Notes on Myself," 14 July 1946, in the papers of HRL.
68. DJSB, 13 June 1947.
69. HRL, memorandum of 18 March 1946, in TLF, II, 76.
70. Ernest Havemann and Patricia S. West, *They Went to College: The College Graduate in America Today* (New York: Harcourt, Brace, 1952), p. 12.
71. "Time Inc.: In 25 Years, a Publishing Empire," *Business Week*, 6 March 1948.
72. DJSB, 19 March 1944.
73. A. T. Steele, *The American People and China* (New York: McGraw-Hill, 1966), pp. 46–47.
74. Thomas G. Patterson, "If Europe, Why Not China?" *Prologue*, 13: 32.
75. "Candidate Papers of Henry Winters Luce" before the Presbyterian Board, 1896, in the papers of B. A. Garside, 2; "In the Interest of the Kingdom," in the United China Relief Collection, 65; B. A. Garside, *One Increasing Purpose: The Life of Henry Winters Luce* (London: Fleming H. Revell Co., 1948), pp. 21–28; HRL to Members of the China Colleges Committees, 15 February 1940; and the Associated Boards for Christian Colleges in China, *An Impressive Service: The Story of the Christian Colleges of China* (February 1940), in the Anita McCormick Blaine Papers, 388, folder on HRL.
76. Memorandum from Dr. Luce to Dr. Barstow, 4 February 1933, in the papers of Henry W. Luce, microfilm frame 17509.
77. Jerry Israel, " 'For God, for China and for Yale': The Open Door in Action," *American Historical Review*, 75:3 (February 1970), 805; and Paul A. Varg, *The Making of a Myth: The United States and China 1897–1912* (East Lansing: Michigan State University Press, 1968), pp. 22–28.
78. Interview with Beth Moore, in the papers of David Halberstam relevant to *The Powers That Be.*
79. "First Families of Chicago," *The Herald-Examiner*, 27 November 1932; interviews with Henry W. Luce and Elizabeth L. Moore, 22 February 1934, and 25 and

27 February 1937, in the Nettie F. McCormick Papers, 33; and Anita McCormick Blaine Papers, 389, HWL. See also Garside, *One Increasing Purpose*, pp. 113–124, and Robert T. Elson, *Time Inc.: The Intimate History of a Publishing Enterprise 1923–1941* (New York: Atheneum, 1968), p. 23, note 4.

80. Luce lunched with Rockefeller on 30 January 1907: the Nettie F. McCormick Papers, 24, Mr. and Mrs. Henry W. Luce 1906–1922. This folder contains the Luce–McCormick correspondence, including important letters from Nettie McCormick to Henry W. Luce, 14 December 1906, and to Elizabeth R. Luce, 31 January 1907. See also W. A. Swanberg, *Luce and His Empire* (New York: Charles Scribner's Sons, 1972), pp. 25–26, and Garside, *One Increasing Purpose*, p. 150.

81. Henry R. Luce, "An American Story," in Jessup, *The Ideas of Henry Luce*, pp. 376–377.

82. Interview with B. A. Garside, in the W. A. Swanberg collection, 18; HRL, "An American Story" [1950], in Jessup, *The Ideas of Henry Luce*, pp. 376–379; and Elson, *Time Inc.*, p. 27.

83. The letters of HRL 1903–1922, p. 6, in the folder "Interests and Family," in the W. A. Swanberg collection, 17; Garside, *One Increasing Purpose*, p. 27; and Elson, *Time Inc.*, pp. 29–31.

84. Swanberg, *Luce and His Empire*, pp. 31–34; and Elson, *Time Inc.*, pp. 29–31.

85. Excerpts from HRL's letters, in the W. A. Swanberg collection, 17, interests and family.

86. Swanberg, *Luce and His Empire*, pp. 34–35; and letters of HRL, #448, in the W. A. Swanberg collection, 17, interests and family.

87. *Yale Daily News*, 7 March 1917.

88. Elson, *Time Inc.*, p. 46, estimates Luce's profit as a nice $1,500. Kobler, "The First Tycoon and the Power of the Press," *Saturday Evening Post*, 6 November 1965, claims that Luce saved the fabulous sum of $4,000 from his earnings at the *News*.

89. Interview with Mrs. Maurice T. Moore, in the W. A. Swanberg collection, 18.

90. Noel F. Busch, *Briton Hadden: A Biography of the Co-Founder of Time* (New York: Farrar, Straus, 1949), chapter 1; interview with Senator William Benton, in the W. A. Swanberg collection, 18; interview with Douglas Hadden, in the papers of Dorothy Sterling; and Elson, *Time Inc.*, pp. 16–21.

91. Interview with John M. Hincks, in the W. A. Swanberg collection, 18.

92. John Shaw Billings, scrapbook #57, p. 259, in the papers of John Shaw Billings. Luce, commenting in 1948, expressed regret: "When I went to Yale, the last thing they tried to tell me was the truth – the philosophic truth." See also Morehead Patterson, ed., *History of the Class of Nineteen Hundred Twenty* (New Haven, CT: Tuttle, Morehouse and Taylor, n.d.), pp. 269–271.

93. The letters of HRL 1903–1922, p. 15, in the W. A. Swanberg collection; Swanberg, *Luce and His Empire*, p. 45; and Elson, *Time Inc.*, p. 51.

94. HRL, interview, in the Nettie F. McCormick Papers, 33; and Elson, *Time Inc.*, p. 53.

95. Dorothy Sterling, "The Luce Empire," p. 17, in the papers of Dorothy Sterling; and Jessup, *The Ideas of Henry Luce*, p. 7.

96. The Munves notes, TM IV, in the papers of A. J. Liebling; Elson, *Time Inc.*, pp. 83–90; James Baughman, *Henry R. Luce and the Rise of the American News Media* (Boston: Twayne, 1987), p. 44; and James P. Wood, *Magazines in the United States* (New York: The Ronald Press, 1956), p. 206.

97. Elson, *Time Inc.*, pp. 77–96.

98. Byron Price, "Memoirs," in the papers of Byron Price, 4, 11.

99. Baughman, *Henry R. Luce*, pp. 34–51.
100. Interview with John M. Hincks, in the W. A. Swanberg collection, 18, interview folder.
101. The Munves notes, TM IV, in the papers of A. J. Liebling; interview with John Shaw Billings (9 November 1968), in the W. A. Swanberg collection, 18, interviews; and Elson, *Time Inc.*, pp. 120–124.
102. Jessup, *The Ideas of Henry Luce*, p. 11.
103. Ibid., p. 24; HRL to Ferdinand Eberstadt, 9 December 1942, in the Ferdinand Eberstadt papers, 103; oral history interview with Eric Hodgins, Columbia University Oral History Project, p. 51; and Lloyd R. Morris, *Postscript to Yesterday* (New York: Harper & Row, 1965 [1947]), pp. 311–318.
104. Elson, *Time Inc.*, pp. 206–209.
105. Ibid., pp. 128–143; Davenport, *History of TIME INC.*, in the papers of Russell W. Davenport, 36; Davenport to Mumford, 5 February 1940, in the papers of Lewis Mumford, in Special Collections, Van Pelt Library, University of Pennsylvania; Davenport obituary, *New York Times*, 20 April 1954; Archibald MacLeish, "The First Nine Years," in Daniel Bell et al., *Writing for* Fortune (New York: Time Inc., 1980); and the Munves notes, TM IV (J. S. Martin, 3), in the papers of A. J. Liebling; Hodgins, oral history, p. 82.
106. HRL and Bourke-White, exchange of telegrams, May 1929, in the papers of Margaret Bourke-White, 24, Henry R. Luce; Margaret Bourke-White, *Portrait of Myself* (New York: Simon & Schuster, 1963), pp. 63–76; Vicki Goldberg, *Margaret Bourke-White* (New York: Harper & Row, 1986), p. 102; and Elson, *Time Inc.*, p. 136.
107. Munves notes, II, in the papers of A. J. Liebling.
108. Notes made by Mr. Luce on his trip to China, July 1932, in the W. A. Swanberg collection, 20, HRL, 1920–1932, speeches; and Charles Wertenbaker, "The China Lobby, I – The Legacy of T. V. Soong," *The Reporter*, 15 April 1952, p. 4.
109. Diary of Leslie R. Severinghaus, cited in the W. A. Swanberg collection, 18; for Luce's account of his 1932 trip, see his rough notes for a speech delivered on 17 November 1932, ibid., 20, HRL 1920–1932, speeches.
110. Swanberg, *Luce and His Empire*, p. 42.
111. HRL to his parents, 12 September 1915, in the papers of CBL, 23, the letters of HRL, pp. 251–300.
112. HRL to his parents, 19 August 1915, in the papers of CBL, 23, the letters of Henry R. Luce, pp. 251–300.
113. Interview with Max Ways, in the papers of W. A. Swanberg, 18; and Thomas Griffith, *How True: A Skeptic's Guide to Believing the News* (Boston: Little, Brown, 1974), pp. 110–111.
114. John Shaw Billings to Henry R. Luce, 20 June 1945, in the TLF, I, 59.
115. Baughman, *Henry R. Luce*, p. 172; and Dwight Macdonald, "'Time' and Henry Luce," *The Nation*, 1 May 1937, p. 501.
116. Interview with Lila Tyng, in the W. A. Swanberg collection, 18; interview with Mrs. Maurice T. Moore, ibid.; and Lila R. Hotz, premarital letters to Luce (excerpts), ibid., 17, HRL and Lila R. Hotz; 1956 Time Inc. official publicity biography of Luce, p. 5; the Munves notes, in the papers of A. J. Liebling, TM VI [Hobson, p. 2].
117. Wilfrid Sheed, *Clare Boothe Luce* (New York: E. P. Dutton, 1982), p. 38; Martin, *Henry and Clare*, chapter 3; and Sylvia J. Morris, *Rage for Fame: The Ascent of Clare Boothe Luce* (New York: Random House, 1997), pp. 44–46.

118. Sheed, *Clare Boothe Luce*, p. 22.
119. Interview with Allen Grover, 23 May 1968, the W. A. Swanberg collection, 18.
120. Interview with CBL, ibid., Swanberg, 18; Morris, *Rage for Fame*, chapter 21; Swanberg, *Luce and His Empire*, pp. 114–116; and John S. Billings, "Recollections of Time and Life and Luce," recorded in January, 1966, T73, a, b.
121. The Munves notes, TM VII, in the papers of A. J. Liebling.
122. DJSB, 29 December 1941, and 7 and 15 May 1942; and the William Benton interview, in the W. A. Swanberg collection, 18.
123. John R. Whiting and George R. Clark, "The Picture Magazines," *Harper's Magazine*, 187:1117 (June 1943); Baughman, *Henry R. Luce*, p. 90; and Goldberg, *Margaret Bourke-White*, p. 174.
124. John S. Billings, "Recollections of Time and Life and Luce," taped interviews, Billings Papers, U. of S. Carolina; Elson, *Time Inc.*, pp. 156–158; HRL to John Shaw Billings, 1 November 1933, in the TLF papers, I, 5; interview with Manfred Gottfried (19 June 1968), and with Noel F. Busch, 22 January 1969, in the W. A. Swanberg collection, 18.
125. Important documents and sources on the gestation and early history of *Life*: Letter of agreement between Time Inc. and Margaret Bourke-White, 3 September 1936, in the Margaret Bourke-White collection, 50, Time Inc. 1935–1937; Daniel Longwell to T. George Harris, 10 May 1956, ibid., 27, Longwell; Bourke-White, *Portrait of Myself*, pp. 141–149; Goldberg, *Margaret Bourke-White*, p. 178; George Eggleston to Daniel Longwell, 3 June 1937, i, in the Daniel Longwell collection, 26, miscellaneous correspondence; Loudon Wainwright, *The Great American Picture Magazine: An Insider History of* Life (New York: Knopf, 1986), p. 105; David Cort, *The Sin of Henry R. Luce: An Anatomy of Journalism* (Secaucus, NJ: Lyle Stuart, 1974), p. 115; Wilson Hicks, Speech to Managing Editors, Louisville, 1940, in the TLF papers; and Elson, *Time Inc.*, p. 305. On Luce as a self-described promoter, see William F. Buckley, Jr., "The Life and Time of Henry Luce," *Esquire* (December 1983), p. 254. On the early issues of *Life*, see Baughman, *Henry R. Luce*, p. 95; and on the company's financial problems thanks to *Life*, see Jackson Edwards, "One Every Minute: The Picture Magazines," *Scribner's Magazine*, May 1938, p. 21; *Life*, 11 April 1938; HRL, memorandum to all members of the editorial staff of *Life*, 16 May 1938, in the Margaret Bourke-White collection, 27, HRL; Wilson Hicks, *Words and Pictures: An Introduction to Photojournalism* (New York: Harper, 1952), pp. 3–59; Wainwright, *The Great American Picture Magazine*, p. 29; Edwards, "One Every Minute," p. 20; and Goldberg, *Margaret Bourke-White*, p. 174.
126. Swanberg, *Luce and His Empire*, p. 106.
127. HRL to his parents, January 1918, in the papers of CBL, 23, the letters of HRL, pp. 451–500.
128. *Time*, 30 July 1923, linked Jews to Communism, a sign of things to come in Luce's young magazine.
129. Interview with Edward L. Bernays, 13 January 1969, in the W. A. Swanberg collection, 18; Archibald MacLeish, memorandum to Henry Luce, 12 November 1935; MacLeish, memorandum to Henry Luce (with copies to Ingersoll, Hodgins, and Grover), 14 November 1935, in the papers of Archibald MacLeish, 8; and the Commission on Freedom of the Press, Series I, 27, in the Harold D. Lasswell papers, General Files. On Jewish involvement in the *Fortune* articles, see I. M. Rubinow to Mr. Waldman, 14 November 1935, files of the American Jewish Committee, 347,

11, EXO-29; and Archibald MacLeish to H. Schneiderman, 24 December 1935, and Schneiderman to MacLeish, 27 December 1935 and 2 January 1936. Random House published the *Fortune* material in book form, as *Jews in America* (New York, 1936).

130. Wainwright, *The Great American Picture Magazine*, p. 27; and Edwards, "One Every Minute."

131. HRL, address delivered on 4 December 1937, in the papers of HRL, speeches and writings file, 74; and the papers of John Shaw Billings, scrapbook 48; and Jessup, *The Ideas of Henry Luce*, pp. 101–103.

132. HRL, notes on his trip to Europe, dated 22 June 1938, in the TLF papers.

133. John S. Billings, memorandum to all writers, 12 May 1938, in the TLF papers, I, 13; *Life*, 30 May 1938; "Czechoslovakia," *Fortune*, August 1938; and Elson, *Time Inc.*, pp. 353–354.

134. Luce announced his decision on 18 November, but see also the 28 October 1938 memorandum on the subject of Goldsborough, probably by Ingersoll, with responses from Luce, in the W. A. Swanberg collection, 18; HRL, memorandum to the staff on 19 December 1938; and John S. Billings, "Recollections of Time and Life and Luce," T73, a, b.

135. *Time*, 2 January 1939.

136. Swanberg, *Luce and His Empire*, pp. 164–165; Matthews, *Name and Address*, pp. 216–22; and "Some Recollections of T. S. Matthews," Oral History Research Office of Columbia University (1958 and 1959), p. 66.

137. June H. Rhodes to Missy LeHand, 20 April 1939, PSF 3338; and June H. Rhodes file, PPF (FDRL). Luce felt that FDR had been "dull" and "uninspired": DJSB, 16 May 1939.

138. DJSB, 16 and 25 May, 22 August, and 21 September 1939.

139. Swanberg, *Luce and His Empire*, p. 172; DJSB, 9–13 April 1940.

140. HRL, cable to Time Inc., 2 May 1940, in the W. A. Swanberg collection, 18.

141. Maurice Moore to HRL, no date but probably April 1940, in the papers of CBL, 11 (X).

142. DJSB, 3, 5, and 14 September 1940.

2. Learning to Market Chiang's China

1. Isabella Van Meter, memorandum, 10 May 1940, in the TLF papers, folder Luce trips; "The Reminiscences of Andrew Heiskell," pp. 227 ff.; and Elson, *Time Inc.*, pp. 420–421.

2. The White House, log of telephone calls, 31 May 1940, in Accession No. 9786, 2, May 1940 (Memos to General Watson); and Mr. Early's press conference on 1 June 1940, scrapbook #9, in the papers of Stephen T. Early (FDRL).

3. Interview with William Benton, the W. A. Swanberg collection, 18. Also relevant is HRL, address over WABC and full Columbia network, 1 June 1940, OF 2442 (FDRL).

4. Major George Fielding Eliot, "The Defense of America," *Life*, 8 and 15 July 1940.

5. Francis P. Miller to HRL, 23 July 1940, and Luce to Miller, 25 July 1940, in the papers of Fight for Freedom, 69; Whitney H. Shepardson to HRL, 3 February 1959, in the W. A. Swanberg collection, 19.

6. Henry R. Luce, "War Diary," 27–30 July 1940, in Henry R. Luce, unpublished manuscript, Speeches and Writings File, 86, in the papers of HRL; CBL,

"The White House," in the papers of CBL, 1; and Elson, *Time Inc.*, p. 435. Knowing he would see the film in Luce's company, FDR turned down an official invitation to attend the world premiere of *The Ramparts We Watch* at Keith's Theater, 23 July 1940: OF 2442 (FDRL). The film itself was only a modest success. Critics mostly divided along political lines, with strong praise coming from a minority of outspoken interventionists.

7. Herzstein, *Henry R. Luce: A Political Portrait*, pp. 15–16.
8. Stephen Early, telegram to HRL, 5 September 1940, in the papers of Stephen Early, 10.
9. *Time*, 7 October 1940.
10. Elson, *Time Inc.*, p. 435.
11. HRL, unpublished manuscript, p. 10, in the papers of HRL, Speeches and Writings File, 86.
12. Franklin D. Roosevelt to HRL, 13 August 1923, and Luce to Roosevelt, 23 August 1923, in the papers of Franklin D. Roosevelt concerning Non-Political Affairs, Group 14, 7 (FDRL).
13. OF 2442 contains the *Time* Chile file, summary of items variously dated 31 October; 3, 11, and 15 November (FDRL); and the White House press release of 25 November 1941, with President Roosevelt's statement about *Time*'s latest transgression.
14. Luce developed this idea in various statements, the most cogent of which later appeared in a *Life*-sponsored symposium, "Pursuit of Happiness," 14 May 1948, in the papers of Russell W. Davenport, 64–65.
15. Raymond L. Buell to HRL, 23 January 1941, the papers of Raymond Leslie Buell, 15.
16. "The American Century," in the TLF, I, 21.
17. HRL, memorandum to the managing editors of *Time*, 14 June 1940, i, in the Daniel Longwell collection, Luce 1940–1947.
18. CBL to H. H. Kung, 7 July 1941, in the papers of CBL, 104, 3.
19. *Time*, 4 October 1937; *March of Time*, IV, 1 (10 September 1937); "Background for War," *Time*, 26 June 1939; and Patricia Neils, *China Images in the Life and Times of Henry Luce* (Savage, MD: Rowman and Littlefield Publishers, 1990), p. 41.
20. *Life*, 30 August 1937.
21. Archibald MacLeish to Henry R. Luce, 15 February 1936, in the papers of Archibald MacLeish, 8.
22. Vera S. Ward to Anita McC. Blaine, 12 November 1925, in the Anita McCormick Blaine Papers, McCormick Collection, 389, Henry Winters Luce; interview with B. A. Garside, 3 September 1968, the W. A. Swanberg collection, 18.
23. HRL to Wendell Willkie, 19 November 1941, with enclosure, in the Willkie mss.; Progress Report, 5 May 1941, as well as documents concerning activities later in the year, in United China Relief, Inc., and United Service to China, papers. "American Aid to China, 1941 to 1945," in the papers of HRL, 64, United Service to China.
24. Interviews with Theodore H. White and John K. Fairbank, in the papers of David Halberstam relevant to *The Powers That Be*.
25. Interview with White, III, p. 3, Halberstam notes.
26. Interview with Fairbank, Halberstam notes, p. 2; and interview with James Thomson, ibid.
27. John King Fairbank, *Chinabound: A Fifty-Year Memoir* (New York: Harper & Row, 1982), p. 156.

28. Theodore H. White to Edward C. Carter, 8 September 1938, in the papers of the Institute of Pacific Relations, B, catalogued correspondence (White, Theodore).

29. Theodore H. White, *In Search of History: A Personal Adventure* (New York: Warner Books, 1981), p. 89.

30. Stephen R. MacKinnon, *China Reporting: An Oral History of American Journalism in the 1930's and 1940's* (Berkeley: University of California Press, 1987), pp. 127–128.

31. Theodore H. White to Hollington Tong, 18 December 1939, and White to John Hersey, 24 December 1939, TLCTHW.

32. *Time*, 3 and 10 February 1941.

33. Files pertaining to Rev. Luce in the Hartford Seminar Foundation, microfilm frames 17529–17618; and H. W. Luce, "A Brief Outline of the History of Chinese Communism," in the Archives of the United Board for Christian Higher Education in China, 15, 353.

34. HRL to his parents, 29 May 1916, in the papers of CBL, 23, letters of HRL, pp. 301–350.

35. Handwritten notes of CBL, in the papers of CBL, 1; and Elson, *Time Inc.*, p. 470.

36. DJSB, 20 May 1941; Elson, *Time Inc.*, p. 471; and HRL, address to the Commonwealth Club, 5 June 1941, in the W. A. Swanberg collection.

37. HRL, address at the Books and Authors luncheon, New York, 8 April 1941.

38. Theodore White to "Bob," 22 June 1941, in the TLCTHW; interview with Theodore H. White, 2 October 1969, in the W. A. Swanberg collection; and interviews with Theodore White and John Hersey, in the papers of David Halberstam relevant to *The Powers That Be*.

39. Theodore H. White to John Hersey, 23 December 1981, in the papers of Theodore H. White.

40. *Time*, 4 August 1941.

41. HRL, 18 June 1941 speech for UCR, in the W. A. Swanberg collection, 21; and HRL, address in Buffalo, 1 July 1941, in the Willkie mss.

42. *Cue*, 26 July 1941, along with comments made by Wesley Bailey on Luce and UCR, as cited in the Time Inc.-related papers of Dorothy Sterling.

43. *Cue*, 26 July 1941, cited in the Time Inc.-related papers of Dorothy Sterling.

44. *Life*, 7 July, 4 August 1941, and 23 December 1940; and Daniel Longwell, memorandum to Ralph Paine, 21 February 1941, in the Daniel Longwell collection.

45. George C. Marshall to A. E. Eggleston, 8 July 1941, ibid., 74, 31.

46. James V. Forrestal to Daniel Longwell, 7 November 1940, in the papers of James V. Forrestal, 53; and *Time* on Forrestal, 10 August 1942.

47. Madame Chiang to CBL, 15 August and 23 October 1941, in the papers of CBL, 840.

48. Robert Sherrod to HRL, 15 November 1941, in the papers of Robert L. Sherrod, I, 14, 1940, 1941; and Forrest C. Pogue, *George C. Marshall: Ordeal and Hope* (New York: Viking Press, 1966), pp. 202–203.

49. Clare Boothe, "Destiny Crosses the Dateline," *Life*, 3 November 1941; and *Life*, 21 July 1941.

50. Sherrod, Japan, 12 June 1941, in Wendell, memorandum to Sherrod, 11 December 1941, on "U.S. Japanese Background," papers of Robert L. Sherrod, I, 9, Time Inc., 1941–1943.

51. *Life*, 26 January 1942.

52. HRL to Daniel Longwell, no date, but the context tends to place the letter in June 1941, in the Daniel Longwell collection.

53. *Time*, 8 December 1941; and DJSB, 6 December 1941.

54. John G. Winant to Cordell Hull, 26 November 1941, in FRUS, 1941, IV, 665; memorandum of conversation by Sumner Welles, 27 November 1941, in FRUS, 1941, IV, 666–667; OPNAV TO CINCAF, CINCPAC, 27 November 1941 (27337 CR 0921), Department of Defense, "Magic," IV, Appendix, A -117; and Henry L. Stimson, *On Active Service in Peace and War* (New York: Harper, 1948), pp. 389–390.

55. Bernard M. Baruch, telegram to HRL, 8 December 1941, in the papers of Bernard M. Baruch, 192; DSJB, 8 December 1941; Theodore H. White to Joseph Liebling, n.d., but probably 1949, in the TLCTHW; Elizabeth Luce to Mr. Decker, 29 December 1941, in the Archives of the United Board for Christian Higher Education in China, RG 11, 14, 337; and Elson, *Time Inc.*, pp. 483–484.

56. *Life*, 16 September 1942.

57. Elson, *The World of Time Inc.*, p. 188.

58. DJSB, 8 September 1942.

59. *Time*, 26 July 1943; and HRL, memorandum to Roy E. Larsen et al., "The Practice of Freedom: A Memorandum on the Fundamental 'Attitudes and Convictions' of Time Inc.," 23 August 1943, in the TLF, I, 29.

60. *Life*, 10 April 1944.

61. "Conversation with Henry R. Luce," Military Intelligence Division WDGS, 18 March 1942, in the records of the OSS, 16, 69, no. 14494 (RG 226, NARA); and HRL to Ed (Thompson?), 22 July 1943, in the TLF papers, I, 29.

62. HRL, address delivered in Rochester, New York, 22 April 1942, in the W. A. Swanberg collection, 21; and HRL, address at St. Thomas Church, New York, 13 December 1942, United China Relief, Inc., and United Service to China, papers, 48.

63. "Life's Reports," *Life*, 27 April 1942; and the diary of Gen. Stilwell, 21 February 1942, in the papers of Joseph W. Stilwell, 21.

64. Marshall to AMMISCA, 12 April 1942, and the exchange of letters between Chiang and Roosevelt, in the Franklin D. Roosevelt Papers, Map Room File, 10, 1 (FDRL); and Barbara Tuchman, *Stilwell and the American Experience in China, 1911–1945* (New York: Bantam Books, 1972), pp. 4–5, 164–165, and 218–219.

65. Michael Schaller, *The U.S. Crusade in China, 1938–1945* (New York: Columbia University Press, 1979), p. 89; and White, *In Search of History*, pp. 185–187.

66. The diary of General Stilwell, entry for 4 March 1942, in the papers of Joseph W. Stilwell, 21; and White, *In Search of History*, pp. 187–190.

67. HRL, address delivered in Rochester, New York, 22 April 1942, in the W. A. Swanberg collection, 21; Jessup, *The Ideas of Henry Luce*, pp. 198–201; and HRL, address at special United Nations service, New York, 13 December 1942, in the papers of United China Relief, 48; and R. L. Buell, memorandum to the Post-War Research Committee, 8 June 1942, in the papers of Raymond Leslie Buell (unprocessed).

68. Minister of Foreign Affairs, Republic of China, to HRL, 19 May 1942, in the papers of CBL, 841.

69. "A list of LIFE, TIME and FORTUNE articles of current significance on *CHINA* prepared for school use," in the papers of United China Relief, Pr, 48.

70. B. A. Garside to James L. Crider, 19 September 1945, enclosing "Five Years of United China Relief." ibid.

71. U.S. poll of 15 July 1942, cited by Hadley Cantril, *Public Opinion, 1935–1946* (Princeton, NJ: Princeton University Press, 1951), p. 369.

72. AIPO, 8 October 1943, cited in ibid., pp. 952–953.

73. Theodore H. White to Charles Wertenbaker, 19 June 1942, TLCTHW.

74. Theodore H. White to Butsy, 15 February 1944, in the TLCTHW; White's dispatches in *The Amerasia Papers: A Clue to the Catastrophe of China*, I, 358–381; and "Reasons for Censoring Theodore H. White's Article on Chinese Communist Party," in the papers of Theodore H. White, Time-Life Dispatches, series 1A.

75. HRL to T. V. Soong, 26 November 1943, in the papers of T. V. Soong, 6, HRL.

76. E. J. Kahn, Jr., *The China Hands* (New York: Viking, 1972), p. 101; Schaller, *The U.S. Crusade in China*, p. 154; and Tuchman, *Stilwell and the American Experience in China*, p. 514.

77. *Time*, 6 December 1943.

78. Walter H. Judd to HRL, 4 August 1944, in the papers of Walter H. Judd, 31, HRL.

79. Walter H. Judd to HRL, 22 May 1944, and Luce to Judd, 25 May 1944, ibid.

80. Theodore H. White to Charles Wertenbaker, no date, in the TLCTHW; White to the Board of Review of the BPR, War Department, 5 April 1944; Jack Lockhart to Time Inc. re Teddy White, 15 April 1944, in the Office of Censorship, 1107 (RG 216, NARA); the General Records of the Army Staff, Public Information Division 1924–1946, Decimal files of General Correspondence, 35 (RG 165, NARA); and ibid., Office of Censorship, Administrative Division – Service Section, 458.

81. Theodore H. White to T. and P. Durdin, 1 June 1943, in the TLCTHW.

82. "News From China," *Life*, 1 May 1944.

83. David D. Barrett, *Dixie Mission: The United States Army Observer Group in Yenan, 1944* (Berkeley, CA: Center for Chinese Studies, 1970).

84. Fairbank, *Chinabound*, p. 266.

85. *Time*, 10 July 1944.

86. *Life*, 29 March 1943.

87. Elson, *The World of Time Inc.*, p. 206.

88. John Chamberlain, *A Life with the Printed Word* (Chicago: Regenery Gateway, 1982), pp. 90–91.

89. DJSB, 13 January 1948.

90. CBL to William Schlamm, 7 January 1946, in the papers of CBL, 124, 9.

91. Theodore Draper, "The Drama of Whittaker Chambers," *New York Review of Books*, 4 December 1997, p. 22.

92. Dorothy Sterling, "The Luce Empire," chapter 10, in the Time Inc.-related papers of Dorothy Sterling.

93. Whittaker Chambers to Herbert Solow, n.d., in the papers of Herbert Solow, 1.

94. Sterling, "The Luce Empire," chapter 10.

95. Patricia Divver, "The Ideology of TIME Magazine, II, A Research Report on TIME during the Period 1936–1944" (March 1953), in the papers of John Shaw Billings, Ms. vol. bd., 66.

96. Swanberg, *Luce and His Empire*, pp. 215–216.

97. *Time*, 12 May 1941.

98. Eric Hodgins, memorandum to Gottfried et al., 9 March 1944, in the W. A. Swanberg collection, 18.

99. Interview with Max Ways, ibid.; and interview with Marjory Newlon, in the Munves notes, TM IV, in the papers of A. J. Liebling.
100. Whittaker Chambers, *Witness* (New York: Random House, 1952), pp. 496–498.
101. Ibid., p. 477.
102. Interview with Allen Grover, in the papers of David Halberstam related to *The Powers That Be* (MLBU).
103. Dorothy Sterling, "The Luce Empire," chapter 10; and see the interviews with John Barkham and Francis Brown, in the W. A. Swanberg collection, 18.
104. Chambers, *Witness*, p. 497.
105. Janice R. MacKinnon, *Agnes Smedley* (Berkeley: University of California Press, 1988), p. 287.
106. *Time*, 13 November 1944.
107. Herbert Feis, *The China Tangle* (New York: Atheneum, 1967), pp. 198–199.
108. General George C. Marshall, memorandum for the president, 3 December 1944, in the papers of Franklin D. Roosevelt, Map Room File, 165, China A-16-3 (FDRL).
109. George C. Marshall, memorandum for the president, 20 December 1944, containing Gen. Wedemeyer's letter dated 10 December 1944, ibid.
110. Wedemeyer to Soong, 31 December 1944, in the papers of T. V. Soong, 9, Albert C. Wedemeyer.
111. Chungking cable no. 23 (notation for 8 November), sent 21 November 1944, in the papers of Theodore H. White, Series 1A, Time-Life Dispatches 2, 1944, CP.
112. White, *In Search of History*, chapter 5.
113. Simon Leys, "The Art of Interpreting Nonexistent Inscriptions Written in Invisible Ink on a Blank Page," *New York Review of Books*, 11 October 1990.
114. Cable from Jim Shepley to Eleanor Welch, 1 November 1944, in the papers of Philip Jaffe, 16, 4.
115. *Time*, 13 November 1944.
116. White, *In Search of History*, p. 271.
117. Theodore H. White to Joseph Liebling, n.d., in the TLCTHW.
118. Theodore H. White to Dorothy Sterling, 31 December (ca. 1949), in the papers of Dorothy Sterling.
119. *St. Louis Post-Dispatch*, 28 October 1949.
120. Theodore H. White to Mom and Gladys, 17 January 1945, in the TLCTHW.
121. *Life* editorial, 13 November 1944.
122. Theodore H. White to John K. Fairbank, 18 February 1945, in the TLCTHW.
123. HRL to John K. Jessup, 7 December 1944, and to David Hulburd, 8 December 1944, in the TLF, I, 44.
124. "Un-American Activities," *Life*, 26 March 1945.
125. Rep. Karl Mundt to HRL, 20 January; HRL to Karl Mundt, 24 January; HRL to Gov. Raymond Baldwin, 24 January; and Baldwin to HRL, 31 January, in the papers of Gov. Raymond Baldwin, General Files 1939–1948, in RG 69:10, 17; and "Un-American Activities," *Life*, 26 March 1945.
126. *Time*, 4 December 1944.
127. William D. Leahy to George C. Marshall, 9 November 1944, in the papers of George C. Marshall, 71, 31; Schaller, *The U.S. Crusade in China*, pp. 190–195; and John Paton Davies, "The China Hands in Practice: The Personal Experience," in Paul G. Lauren, ed., *The China Hands' Legacy: Ethics and Diplomacy* (Boulder, CO: Westview Press 1987), p. 47.
128. Feis, *The China Tangle* (New York: Atheneum, 1967), p. 205, note 10.

129. *Time*, 12 March 1945; and Feis, *The China Tangle*, p. 276.
130. Theodore H. White to David Hulburd, 9 February and 18 April 1945, in the TLCTHW.
131. Frank McNaughton, cable to Don Bermingham, 2 March 1945, in the papers of Frank McNaughton.
132. DJSB, 14 May 1948; HRL to Thomas L. Matthews, 16 January 1947, TLF, II, 92; and Jessup, *The Ideas of Henry Luce*, p. 18.
133. Edward Lockett, dispatch to Robert T. Elson, 11 June 1945, TLF, I, 58.
134. HRL to Harry S. Truman, 17 April 1945, in PPF 928, Luce (HSTL).
135. Oral history interview with John S. Service, 386 (HSTL); Walter H. Judd, interviewed by Paul Hopper, Oral history interview at Columbia University, p. 77; Zbigniew Kwiecien, "An Attempt of the American Left to Influence the U.S. Far Eastern Policy – the Case of *Amerasia*, 1937–1947," *American Studies* (Warsaw), X, 35–46; Athan G. Theoharis, *The Boss: J. Edgar Hoover and the Great American Inquisition* (Philadelphia: Temple University Press, 1988), pp. 259–261; and Harvey Klehr and Ronald Radosh, *The Amerasia Spy Case: Prelude to McCarthyism* (Chapel Hill: University of North Carolina Press, 1996), especially chs. 1–4.
136. "The Chinese Communist Movement," in the papers of CBL, 509.
137. Kenneth E. Shewmaker, *Americans and Chinese Communists* (Ithaca, NY: Cornell University Press, 1971), p. 174.
138. Owen Lattimore to Harry S. Truman, 10 June and 14 July 1945, in the papers of Harry S Truman, White House Central Files, Confidential File, State Department, Correspondence, 1952, 3 (HSTL).
139. Chiang Kai-shek to HRL, 20 June 1945, ibid., 841.
140. "Leaning Over Backward in Europe," remarks of the Hon. Clare Boothe Luce (Washington, DC: U.S. Government Printing Office, 1945); *New York Journal-American*, 20 February and 18 June 1945; and *New York Herald Tribune*, 28 May 1945.
141. Alfred Kohlberg to CBL, 22 May, 4 June, and 10 July 1945, in the Alfred Kohlberg Collection, 114, Clare Boothe and Henry Robinson Luce to 1947.
142. "At Luce Ends," *New Masses*, 23 February 1943, pp. 4–5; Virginia Gardner, "Meet Mrs. Luce," ibid., 3 October 1944, pp. 6–8; and *Time*, 30 July 1945.
143. John Lewis Gaddis, *The United States and the Origins of the Cold War 1941–1947* (New York: Columbia University Press, 1972), p. 230.
144. John Billings to HRL, 18 May 1945; and Brantz Mayor to HRL, ca. 20 May 1945, TLF, I, 56.
145. Raymond L. Buell to HRL et al., 23 May 1945, containing a memorandum to Charles G. Ross, dated 21 May 1945, in the papers of Raymond Leslie Buell (unprocessed) (MDLOC).
146. John Dower, *War Without Mercy: Race and Power in the Pacific War* (New York: Pantheon Books, 1993).
147. DJSB, 25 May 1945.
148. HRL, memorandum to Davenport et al., 1 September 1943, in the papers of Russell W. Davenport, 76.

3. Bitter Victory

1. During his tour of the Pacific theater, Luce was able to enjoy a brief visit with his son Hank, who was serving in the Navy: Luce's remarks in the W. A. Swanberg collection, 21.

2. DJSB, 6 July 1945; and Elson, *The World of Time Inc.*, II, 133.
3. DJSB, 11 and 12 July 1945.
4. Daniel Longwell to *Life* writers, 11 July 1945, TLF, I, 65.
5. "The Reminiscences of Andrew Heiskell," p. 117.
6. Eric Hodgins, report on employment, 21 September 1945, in TLF, I, 65.
7. *Life*, 30 July 1945.
8. DJSB, 17 January 1948.
9. *Life*, 17 September and 19 November 1945.
10. John S. Billings to HRL, 21 August 1945, TLF, I, 64.
11. Archibald MacLeish to Nelson A. Rockefeller, 10 August 1945, in the papers of Archibald MacLeish, 19; and MacLeish to Samuel Rosenman, 8 August 1945, ibid.
12. Elson, *The World of Time Inc.*, pp. 133–134.
13. Jessup, *The Ideas of Henry Luce*, p. 297.
14. DJSB, 1 July 1953.
15. Notes of Daniel Longwell, transcribed by Mary Frazer, in the papers of Daniel Longwell.
16. DJSB, 10 August 1945.
17. *Time*, 21 September 1942.
18. Sterling, "The Luce Empire," chapter 7.
19. *"MEMORANDUM FOR U.S. EMPLOYMENT SERVICE: The News Publishing Activities of TIME Incorporated,"* TLF, I, 25.
20. "China's Race Against Time," *Fortune* (August 1945), p. 248.
21. DJSB, 24 August 1945.
22. Theodore H. White, cable to Time Inc., 11 August 1945, TLF, I, 62; HRL to Dana Tasker, 13 August 1945, ibid., 63; and John Shaw Billings, cable to Gottfried and others, 14 August 1945, ibid.
23. Theodore H. White to Dotty (Dorothy Sterling), 31 December (no year, but possibly 1949 or 1950), in the papers of Dorothy Sterling, Time-Life materials.
24. See, for example, "China's Race Against Time," *Fortune* (August 1945).
25. *Time*, 20 August 1945.
26. Feis, *The China Tangle*, pp. 365–366.
27. HRL, cable to Eleanor Welch, 27 October 1945, TLF, I, 67.
28. "Peace in Asia," *Life*, 10 September 1945.
29. The Washington Staff to David Hulburd, Jr., 24 October 1945, in the TD.
30. *Time*, 24 September 1945.
31. Bill Gray, cable of 11 November 1945, in the TD.
32. Kenneth S. Chern, "Politics of American China Policy, 1945: Roots of the Cold War in Asia," *Political Science Quarterly*, 91: 4, 635.
33. *Time*, 29 October 1945 and 21 January 1946.
34. Kahn, Jr., *The China Hands*, p. 176.
35. Staff cable, 28 November 1945, in the TD.
36. *New York Times*, 28 November 1945, 3.
37. Jack Beal, cable of 28 November 1945, in the TD.
38. Allen Grover to John Shaw Billings, 29 November 1945, in the TLF, II, 69; and Robert T. Elson to David Hulburd, 5 December 1945, in the TD.
39. *The China White Paper August 1949* (Stanford, CA: Stanford University Press, 1967, 2 vols.), I, 133, and II, 605–609.
40. Zhang Baijia, "Zhou Enlai and the Marshall Mission," in Larry I. Bland, ed., *George C. Marshall's Mediation Mission to China, December 1945-January 1947* (Lexington, VA: Marshall Foundation, 1998), p. 203.

41. Ibid., pp. 642–643.

42. Ibid.

43. *Time*, 10 December 1945.

44. John Shaw Billings to HRL, 20 March 1952, in TLF, II, 165.

45. HRL, notes for speeches, in the papers of HRL, 74; and "Digest of a Meeting, Henry R. Luce on the Present Situation in China," 6 December 1945, in the Archives of the Council on Foreign Relations, Records of Groups, XVIII, 1945, II, 46 (B).

46. Cables for Marshall, with press summaries, December 1945, in the George C. Marshall papers, 124, 40.

47. HRL to George C. Marshall, 29 November 1945, ibid., 74, 44.

48. Steven I. Levine, "International Mediation of Civil Wars: China (1945–46) and Mozambique (1990–92)," in Bland, ed., *George C. Marshall's Mission to China*, pp. 540–541.

49. "Notes on a meeting of General Marshall with the President, Mr. Byrnes, and Admiral Leahy at 3:30 P.M., Tuesday, December 11, 1945," in the George C. Marshall papers, 124, 27.

50. Zhang Suchu, "Why Marshall's Mission Failed," in Bland, ed., *George C. Marshall's Mission to China*, p. 61.

51. Ramon H. Myers, "Frustration, Fortitude, and Friendship: The Reaction of Chiang Kai-shek to the Visit of General George C. Marshall to China, December 21, 1945 to January 8, 1947," ibid., p. 153.

52. Ibid., p. 6.

53. Roger Dingman, "Lost Chance in China," *Reviews in American History*, 9 (1981), 253–254.

54. Elson, *The World of Time Inc.*, p. 149.

55. "The Reminiscences of Andrew Heiskell," pp. 6, 285.

56. James F. Byrnes to James Shepley, 28 February 1946, in the George C. Marshall papers, 123, 39.

57. Allen Grover to John Shaw Billings, 29 November 1945, in the TLF, II, 69.

58. James Shepley, cable to Don Bermingham, 17 May 1946, in the TD.

59. Theodore H. White to Charles Wertenbaker, 4 July 1951, in the papers of Theodore H. White, 8, Wertenbaker.

60. *Time*, 21 January 1946.

61. F. L. Pinney, Jr., memorandum for Admiral Leahy, 26 February 1946, in the papers of Harry S Truman, White House Central Files: Confidential File, War Department, 35 (HSTL).

62. Zhang Baijia, "Zhou Enlai," in Bland, ed., *George C. Marshall's Mission to China*, p. 218.

63. *Life*, 14 January 1946.

64. James Shepley, memorandum for the president, 28 February 1946, in the George C. Marshall papers, 124, 29.

65. HRL to George C. Marshall, 27 February 1946, in the George C. Marshall papers, 74, 44; and *Time*, 11 February 1946.

66. *Time*, 25 March 1946.

67. DJSB, entry for 29 March 1945.

68. Zhang Baijia, "Zhou Enlai," in Bland, ed., *George C. Marshall's Mission to China*, p. 211.

69. James Shepley, cable to Don Bermingham, 17 May 1946, in the TD.

70. Myers, "Frustration," in Bland, ed., *George C. Marshall's Mission to China*, p. 158.

71. Madame Chiang Kai-shek to George C. Marshall, 2 April 1946, in the George C. Marshall papers, 60, 44.
72. Cable to General Gillem, 9 April 1946; from Chiang Chung-cheng to George C. Marshall, 9 April 1946; and from CG Army Liaison Group Chungking to War Department, 10 April 1946, ibid., 124, 36.
73. Steven I. Levine, "A New Look at American Mediation in the Chinese Civil War: The Marshall Mission and Manchuria," *Diplomatic History*, III (fall 1979), 365.
74. Correspondence between CBL and Fulton J. Sheen, undated but probably 1945–1950, in the papers of CBL, (X) 31.
75. Fulton J. Sheen to CBL, 23 November 1946, in the papers of CBL, (X) 31.
76. Fulton J. Sheen to CBL, 16 February 1964, ibid., 223, 9.
77. Fulton J. Sheen, *Philosophies at War* (New York: Charles Scribner's Sons, 1944), p. 87.
78. Opening Remarks of CBL, in debate with Mr. Earl Browder, Norwalk, CT, 6 November 1946, in the papers of Drew Pearson, 682, Luce, Clare Boothe.
79. CBL, radio interview on 28 June 1946, in the Luce and Hamilton collections, LWO 7965.
80. Jessup, *The Ideas of Henry Luce*, p. 30; and Francis Cardinal Spellman, "Communism is Un-American," *The American Magazine*, 4 June 1946; CBL to Cardinal Spellman, 24 June 1946, in the papers of CBL, 124, 12; and DJSB, 18 September 1947. *Life*, 21 January 1946, contained Roger Butterfield's flattering portrait of Cardinal Spellman as both a great American and a supple diplomat.
81. HRL to John S. Billings, 8 March 1946, in the TLF, II, folder 75.
82. HRL to Wendell Willkie, 9 May 1944, in the Willkie mss.
83. HRL, memorandum to John S. Billings, 17 November 1944, TLF, I, 43.
84. John Foster Dulles to HRL, 29 January 1945, in the papers of John Foster Dulles, selected correspondence and related material, 27.
85. HRL, interviewed by Richard D. Challener, 28 July 1965, in the John Foster Dulles Oral History Project (Princeton University Library), pp. 4–5.
86. John Foster Dulles, "Thoughts on Soviet Foreign Policy and What to Do about It," *Life*, 3 and 10 June 1946.
87. DSJB, 6 and 15 March 1946; and HRL, memorandum to Roy Alexander et al., 15 March 1946, in the papers of C. D. Jackson, 1931–1967, 57.
88. Richard G. Powers, *Not Without Honor: The History of American Anticommunism* (New York: The Free Press, 1995), p. 187; and Harvey Klehr et al., *The Secret World of American Communism* (New Haven, CT: Yale University Press, 1995), pp. 16–18.
89. *Time*, 22 October 1945.
90. *Life*, 29 July 1946.
91. Jo Davidson, *Between Sittings: An Informal Biography* (New York: Dial Press, 1951), chapter 61.
92. HRL, memorandum to Mr. Billings, 14 September 1946.
93. *Newsweek*, 29 April 1946.
94. Eddie Jones, cable to David Hulburd, 13 April 1946 in the TD.
95. James Shepley, cable to Don Bermingham, 3 May 1946 in the TD. Ironically, John King Fairbank, who despised *Time* and its China policy, later concluded that American demobilization, combined with new anxieties over Europe, "did not lend support to General Marshall's efforts." Fairbank, *China Perceived: Images and Policies in Chinese-American Relations* (New York: Vintage Books, 1976), p. 113.

96. Richard Lauterbach, cable from Shanghai to Charles Wertenbaker, 18 May 1946, in the TD.
97. James Shepley, cable to Don Bermingham, 17 May 1946, in the TD.
98. Richard E. Lauterbach, *Danger from the East* (New York: Harper & Brothers, 1947), p. 263.
99. *Time*, 8 April 1946; and Ch'en Li-fu, *The Storm Clouds Clear Over China* (Stanford, CA: Hoover Institution Press, 1994), p. 186.
100. *Marshall's Mission to China December 1945-January 1947: The Report and Appended Documents* (Arlington, VA: University Publications of America, 1976, 2 vols.), II, 346.
101. Fred Gruin, cable to Charles Wertenbaker, 12 October 1946, ibid.
102. Bill Gray, cable of 1 June 1946, ibid.
103. Henry R. Luce to Theodore H. White, 12 June 1946, in the TLCTHW.
104. John K. Fairbank to Theodore H. White, 3 February 1946, TLCTHW.
105. HRL to Theodore H. White, 29 June 1946, and White to Luce, 1 August 1946, in the TLCTHW.
106. Theodore H. White and Annalee Jacoby, *Thunder Out of China* (New York: William Sloane Associates, 1946), p. 313.
107. Years later, political scientist Chalmers Johnson made a similar argument about the Communist movement and its sources of strength in *Peasant Nationalism and Communist Power: The Emergence of Revolutionary China* (Stanford, CA: Stanford University Press, 1962).
108. White and Jacoby, *Thunder Out of China*, pp. 292–294.
109. Levine, "A New Look at American Mediation," p. 367.
110. Myers, "Frustration," in Bland, ed., *George C. Marshall's Mission to China*, pp. 157–158.
111. Dick Johnston, from Shanghai to Charles Wertenbaker, cable of 28 July 1946, in the TD; and Letter to the Generalissimo from the President of the United States, 10 August 1946, in *Marshall's Mission to China*, II, 381–382.
112. HRL, memorandum for General Marshall, undated; and S. G. Chamberlain to Luce, 15 April 1946, in the George C. Marshall papers, 74, 44.
113. George C. Marshall to Under Secretary of State Acheson, 5 July 1946, ibid., 82, United Forces, China Theater, Marshall, George C.
114. Ch'en Li-fu, *Storm Clouds Clear Over China*, p. 186.
115. Ed Lockett, cable to Don Bermingham, 12 July 1946, in the TD.
116. HRL to James Forrestal, 12 August 1946, in the records of the Secretary of the Navy, James Forrestal, 1940–1947, General Correspondence, 20, 7-7-20.
117. John Leighton Stuart, *Fifty Years in China: The Memoirs of John Leighton Stuart, Missionary and Ambassador* (New York: Random House, 1954), p. 180.
118. Philip West, *Yenching University and Sino-Western Relations 1916–1952* (Cambridge, MA: Harvard University Press, 1976), pp. 161 and 186.
119. Zhang Baijia, "Zhou Enlai," in Bland, ed., *George C. Marshall's Mission to China*, pp. 226–227.
120. Stuart to the Secretary of State, 7 August 1946, in Kenneth W. Rea and John C. Brewer, eds., *The Forgotten Ambassador: The Reports of John Leighton Stuart, 1946–1949* (Boulder, CO: Westview Press, 1981), p. 9.
121. James L. Crider, telegram to Paul G. Hoffman, 29 March 1946, the papers of HRL, United Service to China 1946–47.

122. Charles Edison to C. D. Jackson, 3 November 1947, in United Service to China papers, 46, Jackson, C. D.

123. HRL to Dean Weigle, 6 April 1946, in the records of the Yale-in-China Association, III, 83, 502; Luce to A. P. Stokes, 10 May 1947 and 9 December 1947, in the papers of Anson Phelps Stokes, Series I, 116, Henry R. Luce. Even after Luce had soured on Marshall's mission to China, he trooped to Washington to solicit the general's support for his charitable work: HRL to A. P. Stokes, 27 May 1947, ibid.

124. Meeting – 14 June 1946, in the papers of United China Relief, 55.

125. B. A. Garside's *One Increasing Purpose* (1948) featured an introduction by Henry P. Van Dusen.

126. Max Ways to John Shaw Billings, 26 July 1946, in the TLF, II, 83.

127. Notes in preparation for a book on Time Inc., in the papers of Dorothy Sterling; and "China's Crisis," *Life*, 2 September 1946.

4. China on the Brink

1. Audiotape of an address by HRL at a banquet honoring Protestant missionaries, San Francisco, California, 10 September 1946, Luce and Hamilton Collections, LWO 7965 (Library of Congress).

2. Ralph W. Ward in *Life*, 13 January 1947.

3. DJSB, 19 September 1946.

4. *Time*, 16 September 1946.

5. *Time*, 30 September 1946.

6. Elson, *The World of Time Inc.*, p. 148.

7. HRL to T. L. Matthews, 27 September 1946, in the TLF, II, 88.

8. HRL, interview about John Foster Dulles, pp. 35–36.

9. Elson, *The World of Time Inc.*, pp. 148–150. Murphy long resented Luce's decision: DJSB, 16 December 1947.

10. Stephen Hartgen, "How Four U.S. Papers Covered the Chinese Communist Revolt," *Journalism Quarterly*, 56, 175–178.

11. Correspondence between Luce and Marshall in regard to the Cleveland Council, October, 1946, in the George C. Marshall papers, 74, 44.

12. John N. Thomas, *The Institute of Pacific Relations: Asian Scholars and American Politics* (Seattle: University of Washington Press, 1974), pp. 3 ff.

13. FBI file 77–55348 (on CBL), 9 September 1955, p. 3; Allen Grover, memorandum to Mr. Luce, 3 April 1951, in the papers of HRL, 45, IPR 1948–52; and Harry Price to HRL, 27 November 1939, in the papers of the Institute of Pacific Relations, 29.

14. WWL, memorandum to ECC (Carter), 5 May 1942, in the Institute of Pacific Relations collection, 176; and Edward C. Carter to HRL, 23 June 1943, ibid., 71, HRL.

15. HRL to Juan Trippe, 23 December 1943, ibid., 269, Time Inc.

16. American IPR, *Board of Trustees 1943*, ibid., 181.

17. Ibid., 369, Pacific House.

18. Edward C. Carter to HRL, 10 May 1945, ibid., 193.

19. Charles Wertenbaker, "The World of Alfred Kohlberg," *The Reporter*, 29 April 1952.

20. Thomas, *The Institute of Pacific Relations*, p. 38.

21. Correspondence in the Alfred Kohlberg file, records of the American Bureau for Medical Aid to China, 38.

22. Edward C. Carter to Lennig Sweet, 28 April 1943; Donald D. Van Slyke, proposal presented to the UCR-ABMAC conference of 7 December 1943; and Lin Yutang, telegram to Alfred Kohlberg, 23 January 1944, in the records of the American Bureau for Medical Aid to China, ibid., 38, file Kohlberg (2).

23. Alfred Kohlberg to Pearl S. Buck, 1 May 1942, with subsequent correspondence, in the papers of Alfred Kohlberg, 21, Pearl S. Buck.

24. Alfred Kohlberg to Paul G. Hoffman, HRL, and James G. Blaine, 5 April 1944, in the records of the American Bureau for Medical Aid to China, 38, Alfred Kohlberg.

25. HRL to Wendell L. Willkie, 25 August 1942, in the papers of Wendell L. Willkie.

26. James McConaughy, telegram to Alfred Kohlberg, 25 February 1944; and Kohlberg to McConaughy, 21 April 1944, in United China Relief – United Service to China, papers, 46, Alfred Kohlberg.

27. B. A. Garside to Charles Edison, 17 and 18 October 1946, ibid., 5, American China Policy Association.

28. Federal Bureau of Investigation, New York file on Alfred Kohlberg, 6 September 1945, File 97–1011; Alfred Kohlberg to D. W. Bishop, 14 December 1944, and Kohlberg to HRL, 15 December 1944, in the papers of Alfred Kohlberg, 201, Theodore H. White; Alfred Kohlberg to Pearl S. Buck, 27 December 1944, 29 January and 24 April 1945, and 6 August 1945, ibid., 21, Pearl S. Buck.

29. Unsigned memorandum to the Executive Committee of the American IPR, 7 March 1945, in the Institute of Pacific Relations collection, 10, Alfred E. Kohlberg.

30. "Resume of some salient points in attached study of I.P.R.," in the papers of United China Relief, 46.

31. Alfred Kohlberg, materials sent to Walter H. Judd, in the papers of Walter H. Judd, 164, Kohlberg, Alfred, 1944–47.

32. Wertenbaker, "Kohlberg," *The Reporter*, 29 April 1952, p. 21; and Thomas, *The Institute of Pacific Relations*, p. 40.

33. Alfred Kohlberg to Edward C. Carter, 9 November 1944, in the papers of Philip C. Jessup, A125.

34. American IPR, "An Analysis of Mr. Alfred E. Kohlberg's Charges against the Institute of Pacific Relations," no date, in the papers of HRL, 45, IPR 1944–46.

35. John K. Fairbank to Edward C. Carter, 2 December 1946, and David Rowe to Carter, 29 November 1946, in the Institute of Pacific Relations collection, 102, testimonials.

36. Alfred Kohlberg to George Sokolsky, 13 November and 4 December 1944, in the papers of Alfred Kohlberg, 160, George E. Sokolsky; the Sokolsky columns of 16 February and 16 March 1945 and 25 April 1949; and the 1946 *Congressional Record*, Appendix A4733.

37. Meeting of the Executive Committee, American IPR, 10 February 1945, in the Institute of Pacific Relations collection, 87, American Council, Executive Committee.

38. Raymond Dennett to members of the American IPR, 27 March 1945, in the papers of United China Relief, 44.

39. Minutes of the Annual Meeting of the American Council of the IPR, 15 May 1945, in the Institute of Pacific Relations collection, 87, American Council – Board.

40. Maxwell Stewart on Kohlberg's charges contained in a memorandum dated 14 June 1945, ibid., 198, Kohlberg, Alfred.

41. Raymond Dennett to the Executive Committee, 24 May 1945, in United China Relief – United Service to China, papers, 44.

42. HRL to Edward C. Carter, 16 August 1941, in the papers of HRL, 45, IPR 1933–43.

43. Edward C. Carter to HRL, 11 September 1942.

44. Douglas Auchincloss, memorandum to HRL, 7 January 1943, in the papers of HRL, 45, IPR 1933–45.

45. *Daily Worker*, 17 August 1945, in the Institute of Pacific Relations collection, 198, Kohlberg, Alfred.

46. Alfred Kohlberg to CBL, 10 July 1945, in the papers of Alfred Kohlberg, 114, Clare Boothe and Henry Robinson Luce to 1947.

47. Edward C. Carter to HRL, 1 April 1946, and Luce to Carter, 5 April 1946, in the papers of HRL, 45, IPR 1944–46.

48. Edward C. Carter to Brooks Emeny, 27 December 1946, in the Institute of Pacific Relations collection, 217, Council on World Affairs.

49. CBL, "American Military Aid to Chinese Communist Armies," remarks made in the House of Representatives, 26 July 1946 (Washington, DC: U.S. Government Printing Office, 1946).

50. "The Manchurian Manifesto," May 16, 1946, in the papers of CBL, 526, 13.

51. Christopher Emmet to Geraldine Fitch, in the papers of CBL, 461, 9; and Christopher T. Emmet, Jr., to Mrs. George A. Fitch, 27 April 1945, ibid., 461, Emmet, C. T., Jr., 1945 July–December.

52. Alfred Kohlberg to Chiang Kai-shek, 13 December 1946, in the papers of Alfred Kohlberg, 28, Generalissimo and Madame Chiang Kai-shek.

53. Charles Willoughly to CBL, 2 April 1946, in the papers of CBL, 120, 16; and James V. Forrestal to Luce, 8 December 1947, ibid., 133, 10. In 1950, *Plain Talk* evolved into *The Freeman*.

54. CBL to James V. Forrestal, 21 September 1946, and Forrestal to C. B. Luce, 24 September, in the papers of James V. Forrestal, 70.

55. Frederick V. Field to Edward C. Carter, 14 March 1946; and to Brayton Wilbur, 27 May 1946, and Field to Carter, 9 July 1946, in the Institute of Pacific Relations collection, 203, Frederick V. Field; and Edward C. Carter to Alfred Kohlberg, 26 July 1946, ibid., 198, Kohlberg, Alfred.

56. Frederick V. Field, *From Right to Left: An Autobiography* (Westport, CT: Lawrence Hill & Company, 1983), p. 127.

57. Alfred Kohlberg to HRL, 8 August 1946, in the papers of HRL, 45, IPR 1944–46.

58. Edward C. Carter to officers of the AIPR, 13 August 1946, HRL, 45, IPR 1944–46.

59. Alfred Kohlberg to John Foster Dulles, 18 July 1946, in the papers of John Foster Dulles, selected correspondence and related material, 29.

60. Alfred Kohlberg to Edward C. Carter, 9 July 1946, in the Institute of Pacific Relations San Francisco branch, 10, Kohlberg, Alfred E.

61. Alfred Kohlberg to Edward C. Carter, 26 December 1946, in the Institute of Pacific Relations collection, 205, Kohlberg, Alfred.

62. Alfred Kohlberg to HRL, 8 August 1946, in the papers of HRL, 45, IPR 1944–46.

63. HRL to Alfred Kohlberg, 9 August 1946, and to Edward C. Carter, same date, HRL, 45, IPR 1944–46.

64. Edward C. Carter to HRL, 9 August 1946, HRL, 45, IPR 1944–46.

65. Edward C. Carter to HRL, 13 August 1946, HRL, 45, IPR 1944–46.

66. Boyce P. Price to Henry R. Luce, 30 August 1946, HRL, 45, IPR 1944–46.

67. Edward C. Carter to HRL, 18 September 1946, HRL, 45, IPR 1944–46.

68. Edward C. Carter to HRL, 22 September 1946, HRL, 45, IPR 1944–46.

69. "Windows on the Pacific," biennial report of the American Council of the IPR, Inc., 1944–46, in the Institute of Pacific Relations collection, 200, American Council, Annual Report List.

70. W. A. Swanberg, *Luce and His Empire*, p. 267.

71. *The China White Paper, August 1949* (Stanford, CA: Stanford University Press, 1967) I, 176.

72. Myers, "Frustration," in Bland, ed., *The Marshall Mission*, p. 160.

73. Ibid., p. 163.

74. Poll of August 28, 1946, cited by Cantril, *Public Opinion*, p. 953.

75. Roger B. Jeans, "Last Chance for Peace: Zhang Junmai (Carson Chang) and Third-Party Mediation in the Chinese Civil War, October 1946," in Bland, ed., *The Marshall Mission*, pp. 302–303.

76. Fred Gruin, cable to Charles Wertenbaker, 12 October 1946, in the papers of Dorothy Sterling, Time-Life materials.

77. Zhang Baijia, "Zhou Enlai," in Bland, ed., *The Marshall Mission*, p. 231.

78. Charles Willoughby to CBL, 13 January (probably 1950), in the papers of CBL, 148, 8.

79. *Time*, 7 October 1946.

80. Michael Schaller, *Douglas MacArthur: The Far Eastern General* (New York: Oxford University Press, 1989), p. 159.

81. *New York Times*, 11 October 1946, and Albert C. Wedemeyer, speech delivered at the National War College, Washington, DC, 18 November 1946, in the papers of Albert C. Wedemeyer, 7. Wedemeyer modified some of Utley's more strident comments.

82. Freda Utley to CBL, 23 May 1946, in the papers of Freda Utley, 8, *Life*.

83. Freda Utley to CBL, 21 June 1946, ibid., CBL; and Utley, letter to the editor of the *New York Times*, 20 September 1946.

84. CBL to Freda Utley, 9 September 1944, in the papers of Freda Utley, 8, CBL.

85. CBL to Freda Utley, 2 July 1946, ibid.

86. Freda Utley to HRL, 3 July 1946, ibid., *Life*.

87. Robert Coughlan to Freda Utley, 17 June 1946, in Utley, *Life*.

88. Freda Utley to CBL, 21 June 1946, ibid., folder CBL; and the *Time*–Luce–Utley correspondence (October–December 1947), ibid., 12, *Time*.

89. HRL to Freda Utley, 30 January 1948; and Freda Utley to Walter H. Judd, 5 February 1948, in the papers of Walter H. Judd, 32, Utley, Freda.

90. Owen Lattimore, "Who Said the Chinese Communists Were Not Real Communists," in the Institute of Pacific Relations collection, 266, Lattimore (2).

91. Freda Utley, "America's Unrealistic View of China" (probably written after June 1948), in the papers of Freda Utley, 22, speeches and writings.

92. Albert C. Wedemeyer to George C. Marshall, 29 May 1946, in the papers of Albert C. Wedemeyer, 82, United States Forces, China theater, Marshall, George C.

93. Elson, *The World of Time Inc.*, p. 224.

94. Allen Grover to John Shaw Billings, 25 October 1946, TLF, II, 89.

95. John Robinson Beal, *With Marshall in China* (Garden City, NY: Doubleday, 1970), pp. 256–261.

96. H. H. Kung to CBL, 2 November 1946, in the papers of CBL, box 123, 3.

97. Elson, *The World of Time Inc.*, p. 150.

98. Swanberg, *Luce and His Empire*, pp. 247–249, 265.

99. Jessup, *The Ideas of Henry Luce*, p. 205, excerpted from Luce's unpublished memoir.

100. Beal, *With Marshall in China*, pp. 244–264; and Stuart, *Fifty Years in China*, p. 181. Unlike Luce, Stuart wished to "condition further aid at each stage upon evidence" that reforms were being instituted by the central government.

101. The diary of John Leighton Stuart, p. 12 in the papers of John Leighton Stuart, 1 (Hoover Institution Archives).

102. Fred Gruin, dispatch of 17 February 1947, in the TD.

103. "Farewell to Mr. Luce," *Central Daily News*, 9 November 1946 (Time Inc. Archives).

104. White, *In Search of History*, p. 335.

105. *Time*, 28 October 1946.

106. Theodore H. White to A. J. Liebling, no date but probably 1949, Munves notes, X, in the papers of A. J. Liebling.

107. John King Fairbank, "Our Chances in China," *Atlantic Monthly* (September 1946), reprinted in Fairbank, *China Perceived*, p. 15.

108. P. M. Evans, "The Long Way Home: John Fairbank and American China Policy 1941–72," *The International Journal*, 37: 589.

109. Theodore H. White to Edward Carter, 1 November 1946, in the Institute of Pacific Relations collection, catalogued correspondence M-Z.

110. *Time*, 25 November 1946.

111. HRL, address to be delivered at the annual dinner meeting of the American Association of Advertising Agencies, 18 November 1946, in the papers of Bruce Barton, box 40, Luce folder; and "The Reminiscences of Andrew Heiskell," pp. 5, 262–264.

112. *Time*, 11 November 1946.

113. Tung Pi-wu, memorandum for General Marshall, 4 December 1946, in the papers of John F. Melby, 1, China File, General – 1946.

114. Statement by the President, United States Policy Toward China, 18 December 1946, *Marshall's Mission to China*, II, 481–489.

115. Cable of 19 December 1946, in the TD.

116. Shepley to Hulburd, 19 December 1946, in the TD.

117. *Time*, 30 December 1946.

118. Styles Bridges, memorandum to Arthur Vandenberg, 7 April 1947, and Dean Acheson, memorandum to Styles Bridges, 18 April 1947, in the papers of Alfred Kohlberg, 19, Bridges, Senator Styles.

5. Cold War Strategy

1. Personal statement of General Marshall, 7 January 1947, *Marshall's Mission to China*, II, 516–521.

2. "U.S. Foreign Policy, II," *Life*, 13 January 1947.

3. DJSB, 27 February 1947.

4. Beal, *With Marshall in China*, pp. 312–313.

5. *Cleveland Plain Dealer*, 10 January 1947.

6. HRL and James F. Byrnes, Cleveland Council on World Affairs, 11 January 1947, *March of Time* radio broadcast, NBC RWB 6410 B1–2; and *New York Times*, 12 January 1947, 1, 1.

7. The Wellington Koo Memoir, B-8; the speeches at the Cleveland meeting can be read in RG 80, Forrestal, General Correspondence.

8. "Mr. Luce Comes to Town," a statement issued by the Communist Party of Cuyahoga County, 1947.

9. Notes and interviews in the papers of Dorothy Sterling related to Time Inc., MR 1, 5, 50, p. 1.

10. DJSB, 13 February 1947.

11. *Time*, 17 February 1947.

12. Robert T. Elson, *The World of Time Inc.: The Intimate History of a Publishing Enterprise, Volume Two 1941–1960* (New York: Atheneum, 1973), pp. 151–152.

13. James Shepley, dispatch of 31 January; Frank McNaughton, 15 February; and Washington staff, 19 February 1947, in the TD.

14. Interview with James Shepley, in the papers of David Halberstam, notes for *The Powers That Be*; and HRL, diary, entry for 2 March 1947, in the papers of HRL, 86.

15. Elson, *The World of Time Inc.*, p. 223.

16. James Shepley, cable to David Hulburd, 15 January 1947, in the papers of Frank McNaughton, 20.

17. James Shepley, cable to David Hulburd, 31 January 1947, ibid., 20.

18. Steven I. Levine, "A New Look at American Mediation in the Chinese Civil War: The Marshall Mission and Manchuria," *Diplomatic History* III (fall 1979), pp. 349–375.

19. "U.S. Reaches End of Line in China," *Life*, 24 February 1947.

20. *Time*, 7 April 1947.

21. *Time*, 31 March 1947; and *Life*, 7 April 1947.

22. Zhang Suchu, "Why Marshall's Mission Failed," in Bland, ed., *The Marshall Mission*, p. 54.

23. *Time*, 19 May 1941.

24. James Burnham, "Struggle for the World," *Life*, 31 March 1947.

25. "'Struggle for the World,'" *Life*, 21 April 1947.

26. DJSB, 27–28 February; 3 and 14 March 1947.

27. *Time*, 9 June 1947.

28. "Are We Prepared?" *Life*, 26 May 1947.

29. "The U.S. Surveys Its Weak Defense," *Life*, 16 June 1947.

30. DJSB, 2 September 1947.

31. Barnes (Sofia) to Secretary of State, 9 January 1947, in the records of the Department of State, 811.917 LIFE/1–847.

32. DJSB, 23 March 1948.

33. DJSB, 21 March and 4 April 1947.

34. Sterling, "The Luce Empire," chapter 9.

35. DJSB, 11 April 1947.

36. DJSB, 3 April 1947.

37. DJSB, 11, 17, and 23 November 1947, and 3 January 1948.

38. DJSB, 17 November 1947.

39. DJSB, 18 August 1948.

40. Edward C. Carter to Arthur H. Dean, 16 January 1947, in the Institute of Pacific Relations collection, 218, Dean, Arthur H.; and Alfred Kohlberg, "To my fellow members," 18 March 1947, in the papers of CBL, 126, 5.

41. Paul G. Hoffman to Edward C. Carter, 31 March 1947, in the Institute of Pacific Relations collection, 340, proxies 1947 signed. Another factor may have influenced Luce. His onetime protégé John Hersey, who had again angered Luce by publishing

Hiroshima in the *New Yorker* rather than in *Life*, was listed as a member of the AIPR's new board.

42. Edward C. Carter, memorandum to the files, 19 February 1947, ibid., 217, Carter, Edward C.

43. Edward C. Carter to Rupert Emerson, 9 April 1947, ibid., 216, Board of Trustees.

44. Edward C. Carter, First draft of IPR's answer to a few of the many inaccuracies in Mr. Kohlberg's letter of 18 March and enclosures, 28 March 1947, in the Institute of Pacific Relations San Francisco branch, 1, Edward C. Carter.

45. Frederick V. Field, "China: After the Marshall Mission," *New Masses*, 4 February 1947.

46. Allen Grover, memorandum to HRL, 3 April 1951, in the papers of HRL, 45, IPR 1948–52; and undated part of a report written by Ethel Schroeder, in the papers of C. D. Jackson, 1931–1967, A72–26.

47. Special Meeting of the American Institute of Pacific Relations, Inc., in the Institute of Pacific Relations collection, 340, Kohlberg, Alfred; and *The Christian Science Monitor*, 23 April 1947.

48. Alfred Kohlberg to CBL, 27 May 1947, in the papers of Alfred Kohlberg, 114, Clare Boothe and Henry Robinson Luce to 1947.

49. CBL to Alfred Kohlberg, 5 June 1947, ibid.

50. Alfred Kohlberg to J. Parnell Thomas, 11 June 1947, in the Right-Wing Pamphlet Collection, 775, 2.

51. Alfred Kohlberg to William C. Bullitt, 5 October 1948, in the papers of HRL, 64, United Service to China October–December 1948.

52. Kip Finch to HRL, 29 December 1948, in the papers of HRL, 45, IPR 1948–52. Kip Finch, Luce's aide, had heard this charge made a year earlier, in 1947.

53. The Wellington Koo Memoir, F-70; Alfred Kohlberg to Walter Judd, William Bullitt, and CBL, 2 April; and Kohlberg to Wang Shih-chieh, 5 April 1948, in the papers of CBL, 147, 13.

54. Edward C. Carter to Arthur H. Dean, 22 November 1947, in the Institute of Pacific Relations collection, 218, Dean, Arthur H.

55. *Time*, 2 June 1947.

56. Interview with Dr. Wu Kuo-chen, pp. 49–52, in the Chinese Oral History Project, Oral History Research Office (Columbia University).

57. *Time*, 10 and 17 February 1946.

58. Interview with Dr. Wu Kuo-chen, pp. 30 ff.

59. Interview with Dr. Wu Kuo-chen, pp. 371 ff.; and Edward W. Martin, cited in Kennedy, comp., "A China Reader," p. 6.

60. Fred Gruin, dispatch of 22 June 1947, in the TD.

61. *Time*, 7 July 1947.

62. Robert T. Elson, dispatches of 17 May and 28 June 1947, in the TD.

63. *Time*, 6 October 1947, provided readers with a map alleging that Soviets planned to take over China.

64. *Time*, 2 June 1947.

65. HRL to Luther A. Weigle, 12 February 1947, in the papers of HRL, 71, Yale-in-China Association, Rebuilding Committee, General Correspondence 1945–48.

66. John Chamberlain, "Lovett," *Life*, 30 June 1947.

67. Yale-in-China Association, minutes of board meeting held on 28 September 1947, Yale-in-China Association Printed Reports 1937–49, Yale University Library.

68. HRL to Anson P. Stokes, 27 May 1947, in the papers of Anson Phelps Stokes, I, 116, HRL.

69. Allen Grover, memorandum to HRL, 23 October 1947, in the papers of HRL, 71, Yale-in-China Association Rebuilding Committee General Correspondence 1945–48.

70. Paul V. McNutt, statement issued in September 1948, in the papers of Alfred Kohlberg, 191, United Service to China.

71. Elizabeth Luce Moore to Walter Judd, 25 April 1947, in United China Relief – United Service to China, papers, 46.

72. *Scranton Tribune*, 25 June 1947.

73. John K. Jessup, ed., *The Ideas of Henry Luce* (New York: Athenaeum, 1969), p. 17.

74. Official documentation relevant to Wedemeyer's mission appears in the papers of Robert A. Taft, Sr., 619, foreign policy – Acheson. Wedemeyer's mission also involved a brief tour of southern Korea.

75. DJSB, 10 July 1947.

76. *Time*, 28 July 1947.

77. The Wellington Koo Memoir, E-37.

78. John Leighton Stuart, *Fifty Years in China: The Memoirs of John Leighton Stuart, Missionary and Ambassador* (New York: Random House, 1954), p. 186.

79. John F. Melby to W. Walton Butterworth, 25 August 1947, in the papers of John F. Melby, 6, personal 1947; and William Stueck, *The Wedemeyer Mission: American Politics and Foreign Policy during the Cold War* (Athens: University of Georgia Press, 1984), pp. 35–40, 74.

80. Albert C. Wedemeyer, press conference, Shanghai, 14 August 1947, in the papers of Albert C. Wedemeyer, 7, interview.

81. Albert C. Wedemeyer to HRL, 6 September 1947, ibid., China-Korea Mission, 2, HRL.

82. The Wellington Koo Memoir, E-1.

83. DJSB, 11 September 1947.

84. *Time*, 15 September 1947.

85. Albert C. Wedemeyer, *Wedemeyer Reports!* (New York: Henry Holt & Company, 1958), p. 396.

86. Albert C. Wedemeyer to CBL, 7 April 1947, made available to the author by Keith Eiler, Wedemeyer's biographer.

87. Wedemeyer, *Wedemeyer Reports!* p. 391.

88. Albert C. Wedemeyer, "Report to the President on China-Korea," 19 September 1947, in the President Secretary's File (HSTL).

89. Warren I. Cohen, *America's Response to China: An Interpretive History of Sino-American Relations* (New York: Wiley, 1980), p. 196.

90. Albert C. Wedemeyer to George F. Mott, 14 August 1980, in the papers of George Fox Mott.

91. *New York Times*, 23 October 1947, 25, 3. Luce resigned the presidency in September 1948, perhaps because she was preparing herself for a high appointment in the Dewey administration.

92. Albert C. Wedemeyer to Walter F. Judd, 31 January 1976, in the papers of Walter F. Judd, 164, Wedemeyer, Albert C. 1945–1983.

93. Albert C. Wedemeyer to Herbert Hoover, 9 January 1950; and Hoover to Wedemeyer, 13 January 1950, in the papers of Albert C. Wedemeyer, 102, Hoover, Herbert C.

94. Directive for the editorial development of *Fortune*, April 1948, cited in the Munves notes, Time I, in the papers of A. J. Liebling.
95. DJSB, 18 March, 8 April, and 30 June 1947.
96. John Shaw Billings to HRL, 18 February 1947, in the TLF, II, 94; and Billings to William C. Bullitt, 21 February 1947, ibid. The money to be paid included funds for travel expenses and the like: Luce to William C. Bullitt, 3 July 1947, ibid., II, 98.
97. John S. Billings to William Gray, 27 August 1947; and Gray to Billings, 29 August 1947, ibid., 101.
98. DJSB, 17 September 1947.
99. Alfred Kohlberg to William C. Bullitt, 23 October 1947, in the papers of Alfred Kohlberg, 21, William C. Bullitt; and Kohlberg to the editor of the *New York Times*, 24 October 1947, in the papers of CBL, 126, 4. Some relevant material was leaked to the *New York Times*, presumably by Judd, 1 September, 1947, 6. See also Alfred Kohlberg to unidentified correspondent, 30 January 1947, with attached statements by Kohlberg and George C. Marshall, in the papers of Admiral William H. Standley.
100. William C. Bullitt, "Report on China," *Life*, 13 October 1947.
101. On a more petty front, Bullitt was settling an old score. He had not forgotten how Roosevelt had humiliated him when Bullitt "outed" Sumner Welles as a homosexual.
102. *Time*, 13 October 1947.
103. Laurence Salisbury, notes, no date but October 1947, in the papers of Laurence Salisbury, 2, China.
104. Alfred Kohlberg to William C. Bullitt, 17 November 1947, in the papers of Alfred Kohlberg, 21, William C. Bullitt.
105. Will Brownell and Richard N. Billings, *So Close to Greatness: A Biography of William C. Bullitt* (New York: Macmillan, 1987), p. 312; and Ronald Steel, "The Strange Case of William Bullitt," *New York Review of Books*, 29 September 1988, p. 24; and William C. Bullitt to HRL, 20 December 1947, in the papers of HRL, 1, Bullitt, William C.
106. *Time*, 13 October 1947.
107. *New York Times*, 28 October 1947, II, 3.
108. *Time*, 20 October 1947.
109. "China and U.S. Politics," *Life*, 8 December 1947.
110. Laurence Salisbury, notes, no date but September or October 1947, in the papers of Laurence Salisbury, 2, China.
111. William Benton, memorandum to Mr. Lovett, 3 September 1947, Records of the Department of State, 111.12 Benton, William, 9-347 (RG 59, NARA).
112. Harlan Cleveland to Lowell W. Rooks, 25 September 1947; Harry B. Price to HRL, 26 December 1947, enclosing a confidential "Proposal and preliminary outline for a comprehensive program of American aid to China," and a "strictly confidential" description of Chiang's response to that proposal, no date, in the Frank Price collection, 2, 51.
113. James Shepley, dispatch of 14 November 1947, in the TD.
114. *New York Times*, 12 November 1947, 1, 8.
115. Frank McNaughton to Don Bermingham, 12 November 1947, in the papers of Frank McNaughton, 12.
116. *Time*, 24 November 1947.

117. Robert T. Elson, dispatch of 19 December 1947, in the TD.
118. *The Gallup Poll*, II, 728 (9–14 April 1948).
119. DJSB, 12 March 1948.
120. *Time*, 17 May 1948.
121. *Time*, 8 March 1948.
122. *Time*, 10 May 1948.
123. DJSB, 18 April 1948.
124. *Time*, 29 March 1948.
125. HRL, Founders' Day Address at Colgate University, 24 September 1948.
126. HRL to B. A. Garside, 26 March 1948, in the papers of B. A. Garside, 2.
127. Herrymon Maurer, "The Tyrannous Decade," *Fortune* (February 1948), pp. 113 ff.
128. HRL to Henry L. Stimson, 13 November 1939, in the papers of Henry L. Stimson, roll 99, 0720.
129. HRL to Henry L. Stimson, 26 January 1947, ibid., reel 116.
130. Henry L. Stimson, "Rough notes after talk with HRL Wednesday, 20 November 1946," ibid.
131. Luce to Stimson, 23 October 1947, ibid., 118, 0625.
132. HRL to Henry L. Stimson, 15 January 1948, ibid., 119, 0076.
133. Elizabeth C. Neary to McGeorge Bundy, 29 January 1948, in the papers of Henry L. Stimson, 119, 0167.
134. HRL to Henry L. Stimson, 20 April 1948, ibid., 0665.
135. Stimson to Luce, 28 April 1948, ibid., 0644.
136. Joseph W. Stilwell, *The Stilwell Papers* (New York: William Sloane, 1948).
137. Madame Chiang Kai-shek to George C. Marshall, in the George C. Marshall papers, 60, 45.
138. *New York Times*, 22 January 1948, 1, 2; and 24 February 1948, 12, 2.
139. *New York Times*, 1, 6, and the editorial published on 5 March 1948, 20, 1–2.
140. Jack Beal and Ed Jones, cables of 12 March 1948, in the TD.
141. "China: Blunder and Bluster," *Life*, 5 April 1948.
142. "Years of Disaster," *The Reporter*, 15 April 1952, pp. 17–18.
143. "China Reconstruction," the Pirnie file, in the papers of Styles Bridges.
144. James Shepley, cable of 11 March, and Bill Gray, cable of 3 May 1948, in the TD.
145. The Wellington Koo Memoir, F-69.
146. Material on China in the papers of Robert A. Taft, Sr., 506, China 1945–49.
147. Economic Cooperation Administration, press release of 2 June 1948, in the papers of John D. Sumner, 3, China 1948–52.
148. Robert Doyle, cable of 3 September; staff cable of 29 September; and Banks, cable of 22 October 1948, in the TD.
149. James Shepley, 21 July 1948, in the TD.
150. Allen Griffin to William F. Knowland, 18 August, 30 September, and 18 October 1948, in the papers of R. Allen Griffin, 1, Knowland.
151. Bill Gray, cable of 26 May 1948, in the TD.

6. Losing China

1. *Time*, 21 June 1948.
2. Anatol Visson, cable of 19 June 1948, in the TD.
3. "G.O.P. Prepares to Name a President," *Life*, 21 June 1948.
4. DJSB, 23 March 1948.

5. DJSB, 14 April and 20 May 1948.
6. *New York Times*, 25 November 1947, 1, 6.
7. HRL to Thomas E. Dewey, 6 November, and Dewey to Luce, 8 November 1947, in the papers of Thomas E. Dewey, 5, 113, 14.
8. *New York Times*, 26 June 1948, 1, 5.
9. DJSB, 3 September 1948.
10. Kip Finch, memorandum to Mr. Luce, 25 October 1948, in the papers of HRL, 106, memos 1948–53.
11. John Shaw Billings, memorandum to HRL, 6 July 1948, in TLF, II, 114; and Ralph Paine to Luce, 27 July 1948, ibid., 115.
12. *Time*, 5 April 1948.
13. Frank McNaughton, cable of 19 March 1948, in the TD.
14. DJSB, 14 July 1948.
15. John Tebbel and Sarah Miles Watts, *The Press and the Presidency: From George Washington to Ronald Reagan* (New York: Oxford University Press, 1985), pp. 459–460.
16. Merle Miller, *Plain Speaking: An Oral Biography of Harry S. Truman* (New York: Berkley Publishing Corporation, 1973), p. 38.
17. Staff dispatch, 29 June 1948, in the TD.
18. Win Booth, cable of 25 September 1948, in the TD.
19. CBL to Charles Willoughby, 31 December 1948, in the papers of CBL, 148, 8.
20. Editorial endorsing Dewey, *Life*, 18 October 1948.
21. Roger D. Lapham to Allen Griffin, 25 October 1948, in the papers of R. Allen Griffin, 1, Lapham, Roger D.
22. Staff cable of 20 October 1948, in the TD.
23. Harry B. Price to HRL, 22 October 1948, the papers of HRL, 39, Economic Cooperation Administration.
24. *Time*, 10 January 1949.
25. Interview with Richard McCarthy, in Kennedy, comp., "A China Reader," p. 1.
26. HRL to Daniel Longwell, 16 February 1949, in the Daniel Longwell Collection, 29.
27. Sterling, "The Luce Empire," chapter 10.
28. John S. Billings to HRL, 1 December 1949, in the papers of W. A. Swanberg, 18.
29. *Life*, 8 November 1948.
30. "Disaster in China," *Life*, 22 November 1948.
31. "The Red Shadow Lengthens over China," *Life*, 29 November 1948.
32. The China lobby became highly critical of Hoffman at this point.
33. *Time*, 27 December 1948.
34. Jack Beal, cable of 22 October 1948, in the TD.
35. Frank McNaughton, reports to David Hulburd, 1 and 12 November 1948, in the papers of Frank McNaughton, 14.
36. *Time*, 22 November 1948.
37. *Time*, 3 January 1949.
38. A good example of the litany can be found in Eddie Jones, cable to Hulburd, 2 December 1948, in the papers of Dorothy Sterling related to Time Inc.
39. *Life*, 6 September 1948.
40. Typed summaries of comments from the *China Weekly Review*, in the papers of Dorothy Sterling related to Time Inc.
41. "'Life' Marches On," *Shanghai Evening Post*, 1 December 1948.

42. *Time*, 27 December 1948.
43. Elson, *The World of Time Inc.*, p. 226.
44. Larry Laybourne, cable of 19 November 1948, in the TD.
45. *Time*, 22 November 1948.
46. Patterson, "If Europe, Why Not China," pp. 30–31.
47. *Life*, 27 December 1948.
48. *Time*, 20 December 1948.
49. Interview with Leonard Bacon, in Kennedy, comp., "A China Reader," pp. 6–7.
50. *Newsweek*, 13 December 1948.
51. *Life*, 20 December 1948.
52. HRL, penciled comment to Kip Finch, 29 November 1948, in the papers of HRL\106.
53. The Wellington Koo Memoir\H-102.
54. Manfred Gottfried, "Chiang's Tragedy," *Life*, 6 December 1948.
55. Allen Griffin to William F. Knowland, 2 December 1948, in the papers of Allen Griffin\1\Knowland, William F.
56. Patterson, "If Europe, Why Not China?" pp. 35–36.
57. HRL, "Victory through Law," address to the American Bar Association and the Pennsylvania Bar Association at their joint meeting, June 1952, in the papers of W. A. Swanberg, 21.
58. Elson, *The World of Time Inc.*, pp. 236–237; and HRL to Daniel Longwell, 2 February 1950, in TLF, II, 139.
59. *Time*, 8 December 1947.
60. Allen Weinstein, *Perjury: The Hiss-Chambers Case* (New York: Knopf, 1978), p. 4 ff.
61. Elson, *The World of Time Inc.*, p. 238.
62. Whittaker Chambers, *Witness* (New York: Random House, 1952), p. 5.
63. *Time*, 28 May and 2 July 1945.
64. *Time*, 16 August 1948.
65. DJSB, 5 August 1948.
66. Notes on a conversation that took place 5 January 1949, in the papers of John Shaw Billings.
67. Westbrook Pegler, "As Pegler Sees It," *New York Journal-American*, 29 August 1948.
68. Sam Tannenhaus, *Whittaker Chambers: A Biography* (New York: Random House, 1997), p. 319.
69. DJSB, 10 March 1950.
70. DJSB, 20 August 1948.
71. Weinstein, *Perjury*, pp. 20 ff.
72. Ibid., pp. 28–31.
73. Ibid., p. 39.
74. Chambers, *Witness*, p. 616.
75. Tannenhaus, *Whittaker Chambers*, pp. 222–223.
76. *Time*, 6 September 1948.
77. Weinstein, *Perjury*, p. 173; and Tannenhaus, *Whittaker Chambers*, p. 291.
78. Ibid., p. 301.
79. John Earl Haynes and Harvey Klehr, *Venona: Decoding Soviet Espionage in America* (New Haven, CT: Yale University Press, 1999), pp. 170–171.
80. DJSB, 8 December 1948; and Elson, *The World of Time Inc.*, p. 242.
81. DJSB, 8 December 1948.

82. CBL to William F. Buckley, Jr., 4 March 1974, in the papers of William F. Buckley, Jr.

83. Elson, *The World of Time Inc.*, p. 242; Tannenhaus, *Whittaker Chambers*, pp. 318–319; and Weinstein, *Perjury*, pp. 276–277.

84. John Chamberlain, *A Life with the Printed Word* (Chicago: Regnery Gateway, 1982), p. 69; Weinstein, *Perjury*, p. 535; and Elson, *The World of Time Inc.*, p. 243.

85. DJSB, 14 and 17 February and 22 April 1950.

86. *Time*, 26 May 1952.

87. HRL to Daniel Longwell, 16 February 1949, in the Daniel Longwell Collection, 29.

88. Alfred Kohlberg, "China Via Stilwell Road," *China Monthly* (October 1948), p. 286.

89. HRL, address at Washington and Lee University, 10 December 1948, in the papers of W. A. Swanberg, 21.

90. HRL to Daniel Longwell, 16 February 1949, in the Daniel Longwell Collection, 29.

91. DJSB, 4–5 April and 9 June 1949. To Luce's credit, Kastner survived and enjoyed a long career at Time Inc.

92. HRL to Reinhold Niebuhr, 8 January 1949, in the papers of Reinhold Niebuhr, 8, Luce, Henry R.

93. Elson, *The World of Time Inc.*, p. 247.

94. Interview with Richard McCarthy, in Kennedy, comp., "A China Reader," p. 2.

95. C. L. Sulzberger, *New York Times*, 11, 15, 18, and 21 February 1949.

96. Bookman, dispatch of 25 February 1949, in the TD.

97. Brian Murray, "Stalin, the Cold War, and the Division of China: A Multi-Archival Mystery," The Cold War International History Project, Working Paper No. 12 (Woodrow Wilson International Center for Scholars, June 1995).

98. DJSB, 24 December 1948.

99. *Time*, 31 January 1949.

100. John Tebbel and Mary E. Zuckerman, *The Magazine in America, 1741–1990* (New York: Oxford University Press, 1991), p. 174.

101. Ibid., pp. 173–174.

102. *Newsweek*, 3 January 1949.

103. *Newsweek*, 21 March 1949.

104. CBL, "The Mystery of American Policy in China," *Plain Talk* (July 1949).

105. *The Gallup Poll*, II, 852–853 (19 September 1949).

106. Louis Banks, 27 May 1949, in the TD.

107. John K. Fairbank, "Toward a Dynamic Far Eastern Policy," *Far Eastern Survey* (7 September 1949), p. 210.

108. Staff dispatch of 3 August 1949, in the TD.

109. *New York Times*, 6 August 1949, 1, 6–8.

110. Louis Banks, dispatch of 6 August 1949, in the TD.

111. *Time*, 7 November 1949.

112. HRL, comments at the inauguration ceremony at Trinity University, 8 October 1952, in the papers of W. A. Swanberg, 21.

113. Memorandum of conversation with Gov. Dewey and Mr. Jessup, 21 September 1949, in the papers of Dean Acheson, 64.

114. *New York Times*, 6 November 1949, 19, 3.

115. Louis Banks, dispatch of 24 September 1949, in the TD; ACPA, press release of 25 September 1949, in the papers of the Fitch Family Archives, 19, 31.

116. Haynes and Klehr, *Venona*, pp. 146–147.

117. *Time*, 3 October 1949.

118. *Time*, 30 January 1950.

119. Mao Zedong, flush with victory, chortled, "Leighton Stuart has departed and the White Paper has arrived." He added, "Very good. Very good. Both events are worth celebrating": Yu-ming Shaw, "John Leighton Stuart and U.S.-Chinese Communist Rapprochement in 1949: Was There Another 'Lost Chance in China'?" *China Quarterly*, 89, 90–91.

120. Chen Jian, *China's Road to the Korean War: The Making of the Sino-American Confrontation* (New York: Columbia University Press, 1994), p. 21.

121. Yu-ming Shaw, "John Leighton Stuart and U.S.-Chinese Communist Rapprochement," *China Quarterly*, pp. 74–96.

7. Anti-Communist Allies in Asia

1. *Life*, 8 April 1946.

2. *Life*, 18 March and 29 April 1946.

3. ADC, memorandum to CinC, 28 June 1945, in the MacArthur Archives, RG-3, SWPA, official correspondence.

4. HRL to John Shaw Billings, 8 April 1946, in TLF, II, 78; and DJSB, 31 May 1946.

5. Correspondence re MacArthur's Fourth of July declaration in the MacArthur Archives, RG 5, SCAP, OMS.

6. Douglas MacArthur, "A Fourth of July Message," *Life*, 7 July 1947. *Life* paid MacArthur $1,000 for the brief article, but the general returned the check.

7. David A. Mayers, *George Kennan and the Dilemmas of U.S. Foreign Policy* (New York: Oxford University Press, 1988), pp. 163–167.

8. John Osborne, dispatch of 15 July 1952, in the TD; Michael Schaller, *Altered States: The United States and Japan Since the Occupation* (New York: Oxford University Press, 1997), pp. 10–20; and Bruce Cumings, "Japan and the Asian Periphery," in Melvyn P. Leffler and David S. Painter, eds., *Origins of the Cold War: An International History* (London: Routledge, 1997), pp. 224–226. In the State Department, John D. Sumner thought along similar lines: "Proposals for American Policy in the Far East," n.d., but probably the summer of 1949, in the papers of John D. Sumner, 3, China.

9. James Shepley, dispatch of 4 July 1947, in the TD; and Lester J. Foltos, "The New Pacific Barrier: America's Search for Security in the Pacific, 1945–1947," *Diplomatic History*, XIII, 3.

10. HRL to Roy Alexander et al., 27 April 1948, in the papers of C. D. Jackson, 1931–1967, 57.

11. SCAP to Henry Luce, 11 April 1949, in the MacArthur Archives, RG 5, OMS.

12. Douglas MacArthur, "General MacArthur Replies," *Fortune* (June 1949).

13. *Time*, 9 May 1949.

14. Unsigned letter to Dr. Rhee, 17 November 1942, containing a letter signed by Fitch, Edwards, and others, to Cordell Hull, in the papers of the Fitch Family Archives, 9, 69.

15. Hong-Kyu Park, "From Pearl Harbor to Cairo: America's Korean Diplomacy, 1941–1943," *Diplomatic History*, XIII, 3.

16. George Sokolsky to Robert A. Taft, Sr., 25 August 1945, in the papers of Robert A. Taft, Sr., 670, Korea 1950.

17. John Walker, cable of 23 September, and Wilfrid Fleischer, cable of 29 September 1945, in the TD.

18. "Korea," *Life*, 19 May 1947.

19. Interview with Donald S. Macdonald, in Charles S. Kennedy, comp., "A Korean Reader: Extracts from Oral History Transcripts from the Foreign Affairs Oral History Program" (Georgetown University), pp. 1–11.

20. Wilfrid Fleischer, cable of 21 June 1946, in the TD.

21. HRL, memorandum to Billings et al., 8 April 1946, in the TLF, II, 78.

22. *Time*, 14 October 1946.

23. HRL, diary for 24 February–1 March 1947, in the papers of HRL, 86.

24. Syngman Rhee to HRL, 1 March 1947, ibid., 2.

25. *Time*, 2 June 1947.

26. "Korea," *Life*, 19 May 1947.

27. John L. Gaddis, *The Long Peace* (New York: Oxford University Press, 1987), pp. 94–96; and William W. Stueck, Jr., *The Road to Confrontation: American Policy toward China and Korea, 1947–1950* (Chapel Hill: University of North Carolina Press, 1981), pp. 154–155.

28. Ibid., pp. 153–154.

29. Syngman Rhee to HRL, 1 March 1947, in the papers of HRL, 2, Rhee.

30. Stueck, *The Wedemeyer Mission*, p. 24.

31. "Korea: The U.S. Gets to Work," *Fortune* (June 1947), p. 99.

32. Eddies Jones, cable of 31 December 1948, in the TD; and Callum A. MacDonald, *Korea: The War before Vietnam* (New York: The Free Press, 1986), pp. 14–15.

33. "Revolt in Korea," *Life*, 15 November 1948.

34. Carl Mydans, cable of 2 November 1948, in the TD.

35. Interview with Everett Drumright, in Kennedy, comp., "A Korea Reader," p. 46.

36. Kathryn Weathersby, "Soviet Aims in Korea and the Origins of the Korean War, 1945–1950: New Evidence from the Soviet Archives," Cold War International History Project, Working Paper No. 8 (Woodrow Wilson International Center for Scholars, November 1993); and John Lewis Gaddis, *We Now Know: Rethinking Cold War History* (Oxford: Clarendon Press, 1998), p. 71.

37. In other comments, however, Acheson sounded amenable to possible U.S. participation in common UN action against aggression.

38. Frank McNaughton and Jack Beal, cables of 13, 20, and 26 January 1950, in the TD; *New York Times*, 31 January 1950, 2, 2; Robert M. Blum, *Drawing the Line: The Origin of the American Containment Policy in East Asia* (New York: Norton, 1982), pp. 184–186; and Gaddis, *We Now Know*, p. 72.

39. *Time*, 5 June 1950.

40. *Time*, 12 June 1950.

41. Gaddis, *We Now Know*, pp. 72–73.

42. Walter LaFeber, "Roosevelt, Churchill, and Indochina: 1942–45," *American Historical Review*, LXXX: 9 (December 1975), 1277–1295.

43. "Revolt in Saigon," *Life*, 22 October 1945.

44. *Time*, 29 October and 12 November 1945.

45. Robert Sherrod, cable of 2 January 1947, in the TD.

46. *Time*, 23 December 1946.

47. *Time*, 6 January 1947.

48. William C. Bullitt, "The Saddest War," *Life*, 29 December 1947.
49. Paul M. Kattenburg, *The Vietnam Trauma in American Foreign Policy 1945–1975* (New Brunswick, NJ: Transaction Books, 1980), p. 6.
50. Letter to John Melby, 22 January 1948, in the papers of John F. Melby, 6, personal correspondence file.
51. "Southeast Asia: A Glossary," *Fortune*, 39 (March 1949).
52. Anatole Visson, cable of 24 September 1948, in the TD.
53. "A Program for Asia," *Time*, 18 July 1949.
54. *Time*, 31 October 1949.
55. Lawrence S. Finkelstein, "American Policy in Southeast Asia" (New York: Institute of Pacific Relations, 1950), p. 3.
56. *Time*, 3 October 1949.
57. Transcript of the round table discussion held in the Department of State, 6–8 October 1949, in the papers of Philip C. Jessup, A145.
58. *Time*, 10 October and 19 December 1949. Kattenburg concludes that the "Americans needed the perception of a Sino-Soviet threat in order to mobilize... for intervention in the region," whether or not the imagined danger was grounded in reality: *The Vietnam Trauma*, pp. 22–23.
59. John K. Fairbank, "Toward a New China Policy," *Nation*, 1 January 1949; and "America and the Chinese Revolution," *New Republic*, 22 August 1949.
60. Jack Beal, dispatch of 25 November 1949, in the TD.
61. At *Time*, Robert Doyle, who had left Shanghai one step ahead of the Communists, remained a rare but ineffective advocate of recognition. He shared some of the views embraced by dissenters consulted by the Department of State: DJSB, 18 January 1950.
62. Mayers, *George Kennan*, pp. 171–175.
63. *Time*, 19 December 1949, contained a clear expression of the Luce line.
64. B. A. Garside, report to the board of directors, 28 November 1949, in the papers of HRL, 65, USC May–December 1949.
65. B. A. Garside to HRL, 12 December 1949, in United China Relief–United Service to China, papers, 48.
66. B. A. Garside to Freeman, Mrs. Moore, and Miss Petitt, in the papers of HRL, 65, USC 1950.
67. Dr. M. Y. Ling to the trustees of the Yale-in-China Association, 18 April 1950, ibid., 71, Yale-in-China Association, printed reports 1950–1955.
68. Robert J. McMullen to R. K. Veryard, n.d., ibid., 65, USC 1950.
69. DJSB, 28 June 1950.
70. Interview with Jerome Holloway, in "A China Reader," II, 1.
71. Robert Sherrod, dispatch of 23 September 1949, in the TD.
72. HRL, speech to executives at Time Inc., 4 May 1950, in the papers of W. A. Swanberg, 21.
73. Robert Doyle, "The Conqueror from the Caves," *Life*, 23 January 1950. Anne O'Hare of the *New York Times* (22 February 1950, 28, 5) shrewdly noted that Stalin seems to have treated Mao as an equal during the treaty negotiations. If Mao was no Tito, then neither was he kin to the Soviet puppets running Eastern Europe. *Time* was aware of this fact but rarely emphasized it with sufficient vigor. See also Allen S. Whiting, "China, America, and the Korean War," *Reviews in American History*, IX, 550.
74. *Time*, 3 November 1947, on Reagan.

75. *Time*, 10 November 1947, 3 January 1949, and 8 August 1949.
76. "Is There a 'Witch Hunt'?" *Life*, 12 January 1948.
77. "The Mundt-Nixon Bill," *Life*, 14 June 1948; and *Time*, 31 May 1948.
78. *Time*, 2 August 1948 and 24 October 1949.
79. *Time*, 5 September 1949. Dorothy Sterling, a credible critic of Time Inc., alleges that *Life* discarded photographs showing scenes of worse carnage at Peekskill.
80. Elson, *The World of Time Inc.*, p. 273.
81. "Television Purge Arouses Fairfield County," Bridgeport, CT *Sunday Herald*, 10 September 1950.
82. DJSB, 19 November 1952.
83. DJSB, 24 November 1952.
84. DJSB, 24 March 1950.
85. DJSB, 20 January 1950.
86. *Time*, 20 and 27 February 1950.
87. DJSB, 16 February 1950.
88. DJSB, 10 February 1950.
89. Supported by the CIA, Clay funded Radio Free Europe and Radio Free Asia. Material on the crusade can be consulted in the papers of HRL, 39, Crusade for Freedom 1950–1952.
90. Reginald Townsend to Allen Grover, 27 February 1952, in the Daniel Longwell Collection, 29.
91. *Time*, 13 February 1950.
92. Statement by Senator Styles Bridges, 21 January 1950, in the papers of Styles Bridges.
93. *Time*, 6 February 1950, in the TD.
94. Elson, *The World of Time Inc.*, p. 270.
95. James Bell, dispatch of 14 August 1946, in the TD.
96. Aldric Revell, dispatches of 31 October 1945, and 24 April and 6 August 1946, in the TD.

8. McCarthy and Korea

1. Edwin R. Bayley, *Joe McCarthy and the Press* (New York: Pantheon, 1981), pp. 18–19.
2. Cooper, dispatch of 13 February 1950, in the TD.
3. Booth, dispatch of 3 March; staff, dispatch of 8 March; Beal, dispatches of 8 and 9 March 1950, in the TD.
4. Robert A. Taft, "Senator Taft Charges," New York *Journal-American*, 19 April 1950. One such smear victim was a Puerto Rican man who had allegedly taught at City College in New York City and later worked for the State Department in Peru: Samuel E. Guidici to Robert A. Taft, Sr., in the papers of Robert A. Taft, Sr., 27 April 1950; and Taft, memorandum to Joseph R. McCarthy, 2 May 1950, in the papers of Robert A. Taft, Sr., 915, Communism 1950.
5. *Time*, 3 April 1950, and "McCarthy and the Past," *Life*, 10 April 1950.
6. David M. Oshinsky, *A Conspiracy So Immense: The World of Joe McCarthy* (New York: The Free Press, 1983), p. 158.
7. Jack Beal, dispatch of 11 March 1950, in the TD.
8. *Time*, 20 March 1950.
9. *Time*, 6 March 1950.

10. Hannifin, cable of 13 March 1950, in the TD.
11. *The Gallup Poll*, II, 924 (interviewing dates 4–9 June 1950).
12. *New York Times*, 30 March 1950, 7, 3.
13. Hannifin, dispatch of 13 March 1950, in the TD.
14. Oshinsky, *Conspiracy*, p. 136.
15. *Time*, 10 April 1950.
16. The Lattimore memoir compiled by Fujiko Isono, *China Memoirs: Chiang Kai-shek and the War Against Japan* (Tokyo: University of Tokyo Press, 1990), pp. 3–5.
17. Owen Lattimore to Ray Lyman Wilbur, 28 April 1949, in the IPR collection, 102, Mimeographed testimonials.
18. Owen Lattimore, "Working for Chiang Kai-shek," in the papers of Owen Lattimore, 49, 7.
19. Lauchlin Currie to Owen Lattimore, 14 September 1984, ibid., 5, 3.
20. Lattimore, "Working for Chiang Kai-shek," ibid., 49, 8.
21. Robert P. Newman, *Owen Lattimore and the "Loss" of China* (Berkeley: University of Calfornia Press, 1992), pp. 100–101.
22. American Forum of the Air, "What is the United States' Responsibility in China?" 9 May 1949, in the papers of Owen Lattimore, 50, 2.
23. Owen Lattimore, fourth annual Baxter Memorial Lecture, University of Omaha, 24 March 1944.
24. Owen Lattimore, memorandum to Ambassador Pauley, 28 November 1945, in the papers of Harry S Truman, President's Secretary's File (HSTL).
25. Roger D. Lapham to Robert A. Griffin, 31 March 1949, in the papers of R. Allen Griffin, 1, Lapham, Roger D.
26. Owen Lattimore, "Is Our Economic Policy in the Far East Sound?" radio discussion broadcast on 12 January 1947, in the papers of Owen Lattimore, 50, 1.
27. Owen Lattimore to John King Fairbank, 24 July 1950, in the papers of John K. Fairbank, 15, Lattimore.
28. Owen Lattimore, "Falling without being Pushed," 3 July 1949, in the papers of Owen Lattimore, 46, 3; and Lattimore, memorandum on United States Policy in the Far East, ibid., 33, 3.
29. Owen Lattimore, "New Conflicts of Power in Asia," speech at Mt. Holyoke College, summer 1948, ibid., 50, 2.
30. James Shepley, dispatch of 16 January 1948, in the TD.
31. Robert P. Newman, "Thirtieth Anniversary Calendar of Significant Events," 1979, in the papers of Owen Lattimore, 37, 1. Kohlberg also charged that leading figures in the IPR were "agents of Soviet Military Intelligence." Alfred Kohlberg to Albert C. Wedemeyer, 27 April 1949, in the papers of Albert C. Wedemeyer, 100, Office of the Chief of Staff, Kohlberg, Alfred.
32. Eugene Staley to Edward C. Carter, 1 April 1946, in the Institute of Pacific Relations, San Francisco chapter, 1, Carter, Edward C.
33. Brayton Wilbur, memorandum of conversation with Owen D. Lattimore, 8 January 1945; and Galen Fisher to Alfred Kohlberg, 8 January 1945, in the Institute of Pacific Relations collection, 10, Alfred E. Kohlberg.
34. Alfred Kohlberg to Edward C. Carter, 9 July 1946, ibid., 205, Kohlberg, Alfred.
35. Alfred Kohlberg to Owen Lattimore, 4 October; Edward C. Carter to Kohlberg, 8 October and 24 October; and Kohlberg to Carter, 26 December 1946, ibid.
36. "The Institute of Pacific Relations and the American Far-Eastern Policy," *New Leader*, 15 December 1945; Frank Waldrop, "How Come?" *Washington*

Times-Herald, 6 June 1946; and Alfred Kohlberg to the editor, *New York Times*, 27 October 1947, in the papers of CBL, 126, 4.

37. Alfred Kohlberg to Joseph R. McCarthy, 6 June 1950, in the papers of Alfred Kohlberg, 124, McCarthy folders.
38. Owen Lattimore, "Working for Chiang Kai-shek," in the papers of Owen Lattimore, 49, 9; and Isono, *China Memoirs*.
39. Anspacher, dispatch of 27 March 1950, in the TD.
40. *Time*, 12 and 26 June 1950.
41. "The Battle of Loyalties," *Life*, 10 April 1950.
42. *Time*, 3 April 1950.
43. DJSB, 17 April 1950.
44. Jack Beal, dispatch of 7 April 1950, in the TD.
45. John King Fairbank, *Chinabound: A Fifty-Year Memoir* (New York: Harper & Row, 1982), p. 335.
46. Statement of Owen Lattimore before Subcommittee, Senate Foreign Relations Committee, 6 April 1950, in the papers of Owen Lattimore, 33, 3.
47. FBI reports on interviews with Owen Lattimore, ibid., folder 7.
48. James Shepley, memorandum to Robert T. Elson, 7 April 1950, in the TD; Jack Beal, dispatch of 7 April, ibid.; Newman, *Owen Lattimore*, pp. 253–258; and Oshinksy, *Conspiracy*, pp. 147–149. Lattimore gives his account of the 6 April testimony in *Ordeal by Slander* (Boston: Little, Brown and Company, 1950).
49. Jack Beal, dispatch of 28 April 1950, in the TD.
50. Speech by Joseph R. McCarthy, *New York Herald Tribune*, 9 April 1950, p. 32.
51. *Time*, 10 April 1950.
52. Jack Beal, dispatch of 6 May 1950, in the TD.
53. Charles J. V. Murphy, "McCarthy and the Businessmen," *Fortune*, 49 (April 1954), and "Texas Business and Joe McCarthy," ibid. (May 1954).
54. Biographical information on Budenz in the papers of Alfred Kohlberg, 21, Louis Budenz 1947–1953.
55. Newman, *Owen Lattimore*, p. 276.
56. Joseph R. McCarthy to Alfred Kohlberg, 14 and 29 March 1950, in the papers of Alfred Kohlberg, 124, McCarthy.
57. Oshinsky, *Conspiracy*, pp. 150–151.
58. Lattimore had allegedly supported Finland when the Soviets attacked that neutral country. And according to Lattimore, a Czech official whom he had befriended before the Soviet takeover in Prague was imprisoned for having associated with the "American agent, Lattimore": Owen Lattimore, page by page comment on the Kutler manuscript, December 1981, in the papers of Owen Lattimore, 37, 1.
59. *Time*, 12 June 1950.
60. Transcript of *Meet the Press*, 21 April 1950, in the papers of Lawrence Spivak, A32, radio transcripts, Sen. Joseph McCarthy.
61. Haynes and Klehr, *Venona*, pp. 142–148. Lattimore, unlike Lauchlin Currie and Harry Dexter White, is not mentioned in the decrypted messages.
62. *Time*, 1 May 1950.
63. *Time*, 21 August 1950.
64. Interview with John A. Lacey, in "A China Reader," p. 11.
65. Theodore H. White to Charles Wertenbaker, n.d., in the papers of Theodore H. White, 8, Wertenbaker.
66. John Osborne to HRL, 31 March 1950, in the TLF, II, 145.

67. John Osborne, 14 July 1952, in the TD. Osborne cited a speech delivered on 22 August 1949, when Kennan was trying to formulate guidelines for a new policy in regard to the Far East.
68. *Time*, 22 May 1950.
69. David R. Kepley, *The Collapse of the Middle Way: Senate Republicans and the Bipartisan Foreign Policy, 1948–1952* (New York: Greenwood Press, 1988), p. 77.
70. HRL to John Foster Dulles, 25 March and 12 April 1950, in the papers of John Foster Dulles, selected correspondence and related materials, 48.
71. John Foster Dulles, "How to Take the Offensive for Peace," *Life*, 24 April 1950.
72. HRL to John Foster Dulles, 21 April; and Dulles to Luce 24 April 1950, in the papers of John Foster Dulles, selected correspondence and related material, 48.
73. Henry R. Luce, unpublished manuscript, p. 33, in the papers of HRL, 86.
74. Philip West, "Interpreting the Korean War," *American Historical Review*, 94, 1 (February 1989), 90.
75. Interview with Philip Manhard, in "A China Reader," p. 20.
76. Gaddis, *We Now Know*, p. 75.
77. *Time*, 3 July 1950.
78. 12 May 1950, ciphered telegram, Shtykov to Vyshinsky re meeting with Kim Il Sung, Cold War International History Project *Bulletin*, 39; and Stalin to Soviet ambassador in Pyongyang, 1 July 1950, ibid., 40.
79. Gaddis, *We Now Know*, p. 74.
80. James Shepley, cable of 26 June 1950, in the TD.
81. Resolution Adopted by the Security Council, 25 June 1950, in the Department of State, "United States Policy in the Korean Crisis," p. 16.
82. Statement by the President, 27 June 1950, "United States Policy," p. 18; *New York Times*, 28 June 1950, 1, 6–8; Gaddis, *The Long Peace*, pp. 96–97; and David McCullough, *Truman* (New York: Simon & Schuster, 1992), pp. 780 ff.
83. Frank Ninkovich, *The Wilsonian Century: U.S. Foreign Policy since 1900* (Chicago: University of Chicago Press, 1999), p. 177.
84. Nancy B. Tucker, *Patterns in the Dust* (New York: Columbia University Press, 1983), p. 198.
85. Gaddis, *The Long Peace*, p. 87; and *Time*, 10 July 1950.
86. Presidential Appointments File, Daily Sheets, 1950 – 16–31 July, in the President's Secretary's File, 94 (HSTL); and DJSB, 28 July 1950.
87. Luce file–cross reference sheet on *The Reporter* dated 10 August 1950, PPF 928 (HSTL).
88. Interview with Donald Macdonald, in "A Korean Reader," p. 55.
89. Jack Beal, cable of 30 June 1950, in the TD.
90. Frank McNaughton, cable of 30 June 1950, in the TD; and interview with William F. Knowland, Eisenhower Administration Project (Columbia University, Oral History Research Office, 1962–1972), p. 49.
91. HRL, unpublished memoir, pp. 33–34, in the papers of HRL, 86.
92. "A Mighty Job," *Life*, 10 July 1950.
93. DSJB, 27 June 1950.
94. *Time*, 10 July 1950.
95. HRL to Max Ways, 21 July 1950, in the TLF, II, 45.
96. "A Mighty Job," *Life*, 10 July 1950.

97. Cohen, *America's Response to China*, p. 209.
98. Interview with Ralph Kartosh, in "A China Reader," II, 2.
99. *New York Times*, 1 August 1950, 4, 3.
100. John Osborne to HRL, 18 July 1950, in the papers of CBL, (X)ll.
101. *Life*, 8 July 1950.
102. DJSB, 7 July 1950.
103. DJSB, 8 August 1950.
104. DJSB, 6 February 1951.
105. DJSB, 28 July and 17 August 1950; and 3 January 1951.
106. HRL to Edward K. Thompson, 11 August 1950, in the TLF, III, 145.
107. DJSB, 27 July 1951.
108. *Time*, 24 July 1950.
109. *Time*, 2 October 1950.
110. James Shepley, cable of 7 September 1950, in the TD. Shepley, however, expressed no *moral* scruples against preventive war.
111. DJSB, 11 August 1950.
112. DJSB, 1 September 1950.
113. HRL, memorandum to Mr. Billings et al., 27 July 1950, in the Daniel Longwell Collection, 16.
114. James Shepley, cable of 9 September 1950, in the TD.
115. HRL to Thomas S. Matthews, 6 September 1950, in the TLF, III, 147; and "Program for America," *Life*, 14 August 1950.
116. HRL, memorandum to John Shaw Billings, 20 July 1950, in the TLF, III, 144.
117. "A Mighty Job," *Life*, 10 July 1950.
118. The polls asking questions about Red China's admission to the UN showed consistent public opposition, often by margins of better than two to one: *The Gallup Poll*, II, 1010 (interviewing dates 3–8 August 1951).
119. Ibid., II, 937 (interviewing dates 20–25 August 1950).
120. *Time*, 24 July 1950.
121. Ernest Havemann, "War and Politics," *Life*, 28 August 1950.
122. Frank McNaughton, cable of 18 August 1950, in the TD.
123. *New York Times*, 27 August 1950, 5, 1–2.
124. *Time*, 4 September 1950.
125. "Fighting for What?" *Life*, 4 September 1950; and "A Babel of Voices on Foreign Policy," *Life*, 11 September 1950.
126. *Time*, 11 September 1950.
127. Frank McNaughton, cable of 28 August 1950, in the TD; and *Time*, 4 September 1950.
128. Staff dispatch of 2 August 1950, in the TD.
129. HRL to his staff, 8 September 1950, Records of the Yale-in-China Association, III, 83, 503.
130. James Shepley, cable to Don Bermingham and Larry Laybourne (and shown to Luce and Billings), 12 July 1950, in the TLF, III, 154.
131. John Osborne, "His Plan," *Life*, 25 September 1950.
132. Win Booth, cable of 29 September 1950, in the TD.
133. Anatol Visson, cable of 6 October 1950, in the TD.
134. *Time*, 6 November 1950.
135. *Time*, 9 October 1950.
136. *The Gallup Poll*, II, 942–43 (17–22 September 1950).

9. The Campaign for a Wider War in Asia

1. "A Program for Asia," *Time*, 18 July 1949.
2. *Time*, 10 October 1949.
3. Sam Welles, undated memorandum but December 1949, in the papers of Dorothy Sterling related to Time Inc.
4. John Lewis Gaddis, *The Long Peace*, pp. 89–94.
5. Gaddis, *We Now Know*, pp. 160–162.
6. *Time*, 10 April 1950.
7. Gaddis, *We Now Know*, p. 159.
8. Anspacher, dispatch of 24 February 1950, in the TD.
9. James Shepley, dispatch of 25 February 1950, in the TD.
10. Report No. 1 of the United States Economic Survey Mission to Southeast Asia, "Needs for United States Economic and Technical Aid in Cambodia, Laos, and Vietnam" (Washington, DC: May 1950).
11. James Shepley, dispatch of 11 May 1950, in the TD.
12. Thomas McCormick, "Crisis, Commitment, and Counterrevolution, 1945–1952," in Grace Sevy, ed., *The American Experience in Vietnam: A Reader* (Norman: University of Oklahoma Press, 1989), p. 20.
13. *Time*, 22 May 1950
14. *Time*, 27 March 1950.
15. *Time*, 31 July 1950.
16. *Time*, 21 August 1950.
17. *Time*, 28 August 1950.
18. *Time*, 27 March 1950.
19. *Time*, 28 August 1950.
20. *Time*, 22 May 1950.
21. *Time*, 28 August 1950.
22. This was the opinion of an experienced diplomat: Speech delivered by William S. B. Lacy before the Institute of Public Affairs, University of Virginia, 11 July 1950.
23. Anspacher, dispatch of 24 March 1950, in the TD.
24. Statement by Dean G. Acheson, 8 May 1950, cited by Marvin E. Gettleman, ed., *Vietnam, History, Documents, and Opinions on a Major World Crisis* (Greenwich, CT: Fawcett Publications, Inc., 1965), p. 89.
25. *Time*, 29 May 1950.
26. *Time*, 10 July 1950.
27. *Time*, 11 December 1950.
28. *Time*, 10 April 1950.
29. *Time*, 10 July 1950.
30. "Major General Graves B. Erskine," USMC, in the papers of John F. Melby, 11, press 1950.
31. Statement by John F. Melby and Graves B. Erskine, 31 July 1950, ibid.
32. Melby complained to Acheson that the French perversely refused to train Vietnamese cadres. John F. Melby to Dean G. Acheson, 28 September 1950, ibid., 12.
33. Foreign Military Assistance Coordinating Committee, Area Report on the Joint State-Defense Survey Mission to Southeast Asia, 22 November 1950, ibid., 9, Southeast Asia file, MDAP, 1950.

34. Interview with John Melby, in Charles S. Kennedy, comp., "A Vietnam Reader: Extracts from Oral History Transcripts from the Foreign Affairs Oral History Program" (Georgetown University), I, pp. 1–7.
35. John F. Melby, Memorandum to FMACC [Final Report of Joint MDAP Survey Mission to Southeast Asia], 6 December 1950, in the papers of John F. Melby, 11, press 1950.
36. *Time*, 10 July 1950.
37. Andre Laguerre, "The Gamble in Indo-China," *Life*, 28 August 1950.
38. *Time*, October 9, 1950.
39. Anatole Visson, cable of 22 September 1950, in the TD.
40. *Time*, 23 October 1950 and 27 November 1950 (Eric Gibbs).
41. *Time*, 11 December 1951.
42. *Time*, 22 January 1951.
43. Osborne's warning was ironic, because this shrill hawk was soon prepared to launch World War III with a preemptive strike against China or Russia.
44. *Time*, 21 August 1950; and John Osborne, "Report from the Orient: Guns Are Not Enough," *Life*, 21 August 1950.
45. DJSB, 9 August 1950.
46. HRL, memorandum to Roy Alexander et al., 5 April 1950, including his memorandum "American Policy in Asia," in the TLF, II, 142.
47. Tom Maloney, ed., *U.S. Camera Annual 1951, American-International* (New York: U.S. Camera Publishing Corporation, 1951), pp. 7–9.
48. *Time*, 9 October 1950.
49. John Osborne, "Is Formosa Next?" *Life*, 8 July 1950.
50. Shea, cable of 28 July, and Beal, cable of 4 August 1950, in the TD.
51. Chen Jian, *China's Road to the Korean War*, pp. 137–145, and *Mao's China and the Cold War* (Chapel Hill: University of North Carolina Press, 2001), pp. 52–55.
52. 5 July 1950, Filippov (Stalin) to Zhou En lai (via Soviet ambassador), Cold War International History Project *Bulletin*, p. 43; and Chen, *China's Road to the Korean War*, p. 156.
53. *The Gallup Poll*, II, 940 (interviewing date 20–25 August 1950).
54. John E. Wilz, "Truman and MacArthur: The Wake Island Meeting," *Military Affairs* (December 1978), 169–176.
55. Elson, *The World of Time Inc.*, p. 289.
56. Clay Blair, cable of 28 October 1950, in the TD.
57. Chen, *China's Road to the Korean War*, pp. 159–166.
58. Cited by Gaddis, *We Now Know*, p. 72.
59. *Time*, 30 October 1950.
60. MacDonald, *Korea: The War Before Vietnam*, p. 63.
61. S. E. Zakharov to Stalin, 2 November 1950, in the Cold War International History Project, *Bulletin*, p. 48.
62. Robert Sherrod, cable of 4 November 1950, in the TD.
63. *Time*, 6 November 1950; Elson, *The World of Time Inc.*, p. 289; and staff cable of 8 November 1950, in the TD.
64. DJSB, 10 October 1950.
65. Win Booth, cable of 5 November 1950, in the TD.
66. Ronald J. Caridi, *The Korean War and American Politics: The Republican Party as a Case Study* (Philadelphia: University of Pennsylvania Press, 1969), pp. 96–97.

67. HRL, memorandum to John Billings, 19 August 1952, in the TLF, III, 167; and DJSB, 22 August 1952.
68. HRL to Roy Alexander, 2 August 1951, in the TLF, III, 159.
69. William Benton to W.A. Swanberg, 9 January 1970, in Ms Coll Swanberg, catalogued correspondence; and Benton to Eleanor Roosevelt, 28 September 1951, in the papers of William Benton, 4, General 1951.
70. "The Elections and Asia," *Life*, 20 November 1950.
71. *Time*, 13 November 1950.
72. Zhou En-lai to Stalin, 16 November 1950, Cold War International History Project *Bulletin*, p. 49.
73. *Time*, 27 November 1950.
74. CBL, telegram to Douglas MacArthur, 24 November; and MacArthur to Luce, 25 November 1950, in the papers of Douglas MacArthur, RG-5, SCAP, Office of Military Security, Luce, Clare Boothe.
75. Anatol Visson and Robert Sherrod, cables of 25 November 1950, in the TD.
76. *Time*, 4 December 1950.
77. DJSB, 4 December 1950.
78. Darby, cable of 1 December 1950, in the TD.
79. "Yardstick from Tokyo," *Life*, 4 December 1950.
80. Frank McNaughton, cable of 9 December 1950, in the TD.
81. DJSB, 5 December 1950.
82. HRL to Christopher Emmet, Jr., 7 May 1951, in the papers of Christopher T. Emmet, 86, Luce, Henry.
83. Interview with Chiang Kai-shek, *U.S. News & World Report*, 15 December 1950, p. 17.
84. *New York Times*, 7 January 1951, 1, 7.
85. *Time*, 11 December 1950.
86. DJSB, 15 December 1950.
87. *Time*, 1 January 1951.
88. Elson, *The World of Time Inc.*, pp. 289–290.
89. Caridi, *Korean War and American Politics*, p. 119.
90. *The Gallup Poll*, II, 960 (interviewing dates 1–5 January 1951).
91. HRL to John Osborne, 18 December 1950, in the TLF, III, 151.
92. MacDonald, *Korea: The War before Vietnam*, p. 69; and *Newsweek*, 20 April 1964.
93. *Time*, 26 March 1951.
94. *New York Times*, 13 February, 24, 5; and 18 February 1951, 22, 4.
95. *Time*, 18 December 1950.
96. HRL, memorandum of 15 February 1951 ("Notes on the State of the Nation and the State of the World"), in the papers of W. A. Swanberg, 19.
97. The Luce–Billings exchange on rollback appears in the TLF, III, 153; and *Time*, 29 January 1951.
98. HRL, unpublished memoir, p. 43.
99. The Lippmann statement of 10 April 1951 appears in the papers of Robert A. Taft, Sr., 628, Foreign Policy.
100. McNaughton, cable of 1 December 1950, in the TD.
101. Gaddis, *The Long Peace*, pp. 170–171.
102. *Time*, 17 April 1964.
103. Clay Blair, cable of 24 March 1951, in the TD.

104. Elson, *The World of Time Inc.*, p. 293.
105. *Time*, 19 March 1951.
106. Clay Blair, dispatch of 9 March 1951, in the TD.
107. Jack Beal and Clay Blair, cable of 24 March 1951, in the TD; and Gaddis, *The Long Peace*, pp. 100–101.
108. *New York Times*, 30 May 1951, 14, 4.
109. "MacArthur on the Spot," *Life*, 9 April 1951.
110. *The Gallup Poll*, II, 968–969 (4–9 February 1951).
111. Frank McNaughton, cable of 21 September 1945, in the TD.
112. *Time*, 2 April 1951; and Caridi, *Korean War and American Politics*, p. 144.
113. Joseph W. Martin, Jr., to Douglas A. MacArthur, 8 March 1951, and MacArthur to Martin, 20 March 1951, in Barton J. Bernstein and Allen J. Matusow, *The Truman Administration* (New York: Harper, 1966), pp. 454–455.
114. DJSB, 5 April 1951.
115. Darby, cable of 1 March 1951, in the TD, provided anecdotal data illustrating Truman's unpopularity.
116. Frank McNaughton, cable of 7 April; staff cable and McConaughy cable of 11 April, in the TD.
117. James Shepley, cable of 13 April 1951, in the TD.
118. Frank McNaughton, cable of 14 April 1951, in the TD.
119. *Time*, 23 April 1951.
120. McConaughy, cable of 12 April 1951, in the TD.
121. Caridi, *Korean War and American Politics*, p. 152.
122. Remarks of Hon. Walter H. Judd, *Congressional Record*, 11 April 1951, p. 1.
123. James Shepley, cable of 20 April 1951, in the TD.
124. John Billings, notes of 25 April 1951, in the papers of John Shaw Billings, TLF, III, 156; and HRL to Thomas S. Matthews, ibid., 155.
125. DJSB, 24 April 1951.
126. Orville C. Sanborn, "Proposal for a Publicly Supported Staff for General MacArthur," and HRL to MacArthur, 11 June 1951, in RG-5, SCAP, Time.
127. James Shepley and Frank McNaughton, cables of 20 April, in the TD.
128. *Newsweek*, 7 May 1951.
129. Frank McNaughton, cable of 4 May 1951, in the TD.
130. Staff, cable of 16 May 1951, in the TD.
131. *New York Times*, 2 June 1951, 1, 8; and 6 June 1951, 14, 3.
132. *The Gallup Poll*, II, 989 (19–24 May 1951).
133. Ibid., 983 (16 and 18 May 1951).
134. Elson, *The World of Time Inc.*, p. 301.
135. *Time*, 18 June 1951, with Zhou Enlai on the cover.
136. Robert Neville, "Rise of the Red Star," *Life*, 31 December 1951.
137. *Time*, 13 August 1951.
138. Jack Beal, cable of 4 May 1951.
139. John S. Potter translated the article and sent his version to Luce; see the papers of W. A. Swanberg, 19.
140. *Your Stake in Japan*, in TLF, 52.
141. *New York Times*, 23 April 1951, 24, 1–2; and "How the Peace Was Made: A Revealing Report by the Architect of the Treaty," *Life*, 17 September 1951.
142. Relevant papers are contained in the papers of HRL, 44, Henry Luce Foundation 1936–1962.

143. Roswell L. Gilpatric to Kip Finch, 1 October 1948, in the papers of HRL, 44, Henry Luce Foundation 1936–1962.
144. *New York Times*, 11 February 1949, 18, 8.
145. Kip Finch to HRL, 28 December 1948, in the papers of HRL, 30, China Institute 1948–49.
146. On the Waldorf dinner, see ibid., 33, China Institute 1951.
147. DJSB, 16 May 1951.
148. *New York Times*, 19 May 1951, 1, 7.
149. *New York Times*, 19 May 1951, 14, 2; and Jack Beal, cable of 26 May 1951, in the TD.
150. Thomas J. Schoenbaum, *Waging Peace and War: Dean Rusk in the Truman, Kennedy, and Johnson Years* (New York: Simon & Schuster, 1988), pp. 222–225.
151. Mayers, *George Kennan*, p. 186.
152. *Time*, 11 June 1951.
153. *Time*, 14 May 1951.
154. *Time*, 16 July 1951.
155. *The Gallup Poll*, II, 998 (8–13 July 1951).
156. Ibid., 1002.
157. HRL, "Freedom and Order," speech of 26 June 1951, before the Buffalo Chamber of Commerce.

10. Electing Eisenhower While Fighting McCarthy

1. DJSB, 19 August 1947.
2. CBL on the *Tex and Jinx* show, WNBC, 8 January 1950, in the Luce and Hamilton Collections, LWO 7965.
3. CBL to Pope Pius XII, Easter Sunday 1949, in the papers of CBL, X10.
4. DJSB, 25 April 1949.
5. Among other examples: *Time*'s cover on Murray, 12 December 1960.
6. Henry Luce, "Declaration of Intent," in the papers of CBL, [X] ll.
7. Matthews, *Name and Address*, p. 274.
8. *Time*, 29 January 1940.
9. Lillian to W. A. Swanberg, in the papers of W. A. Swanberg, 19.
10. James T. Patterson, *Mr. Republican: A Biography of Robert A. Taft* (Boston: Houghton Mifflin Company, 1972), pp. 205 and 531.
11. Allen Grover to Andre Laguerre, 17 January 1952, in the TLF, III, 163; and HRL to Thomas S. Matthews, 4 June 1952, ibid., 166.
12. Taft's speech of 5 January 1951, cited by Caridi, *The Korean War and American Politics*, p. 138.
13. Robert A. Taft to Lewis Hoskins, 17 January 1950, in the papers of Robert A. Taft, Sr., 917, Foreign Policy 1950; and ibid., 296, Campaign Miscellany Formosa 1949–1950.
14. Crossley, Inc., *National Study of Magazine Audiences 1952* (Cowles Magazines: 1952).
15. Alfred Politz Research, Inc., "A Study of the Household Accumulative Audience" (Time Inc.: 1952).
16. Elson, *The World of Time Inc.*, p. 321.
17. *Time*, 13 September 1943; "General Ike," *Life*, 25 June 1945; and *Time*, 2 July 1945.

18. Oral history interview with Robert L. Sherrod (Oral History Research Office, Columbia University, 1973), p. 10.
19. C. D. Jackson to HRL, 19 November 1947, in the papers of C. D. Jackson, 1931–1967, 57.
20. HRL, memorandum to *Time* archives, 27 July 1964, in the papers of HRL, 86.
21. DJSB, 9 October 1950.
22. DJSB, 18 January 1952; and Elson, *The World of Time Inc.*, p. 307.
23. *Time*, 20 March 1950.
24. Memorandum for the Attorney-General from the President, 5 July 1952, in the papers of Harry S Truman, White House Central Files: Confidential File, State Department, Correspondence, 1952, 43 (HSTL).
25. Allen Grover to HRL, 4 April 1951, in the papers of HRL, 45, IPR 1948–52.
26. *Time*, 10 March 1952.
27. *Time*, 22 October 1951.
28. "Taft and McCarthy," *Life*, 1 October 1951.
29. Alfred Kohlberg to HRL, 19 September, and Luce to Kohlberg, 27 September 1951, in the papers of Alfred Kohlberg, 124, McCarthy.
30. Joe McCarthy to HRL, 31 October 1951, ibid.; and Bayley, *Joe McCarthy and the Press*, pp. 169–170.
31. Gift Information 1909–1926, in the papers of Anita McCormick Blaine, 16.
32. Owen Lattimore, diary, 16 and 20 August 1934, in the papers of Owen Lattimore, 57, 2.
33. Owen Lattimore, statement before the Subcommittee on Internal Security of the Senate Judiciary Committee, 26 February 1952, p. 35 of the transcript; and Henry A. Wallace to Henry R. Luce, date uncertain but probably October 1951, in the Henry A. Wallace papers at the University of Iowa, 48.
34. John K. Fairbank to Theodore H. White, 11 October 1951, in the papers of John King Fairbank, 21, White.
35. Burton Rascoe to Alfred Kohlberg, 21 October 1951, in the papers of Freda Utley, 3, American China Policy Association.
36. *New York Times*, 22 February 1952, 11, 1; and *New York Times*, 29 January 1952.
37. "The Reminiscences of Andrew Heiskell," pp. 4, 179.
38. "Joe McCarthy vs. Henry Luce," *New York Post*, 30 January 1952.
39. William Evjue, 10 February 1952, on WIBA, Madison, WI, cited by Radio Reports, Inc.
40. DJSB, 28 December 1951.
41. Oral history interview with Walter H. Judd (Columbia University Oral History Office), p. 83.
42. "The Ike Boom," *Life*, 31 March 1952.
43. Dwight D. Eisenhower to Philip Young, 11 February 1952, and Eisenhower's diary entry of the same date, in Louis Galambos, ed., *The Papers of Dwight David Eisenhower* (Baltimore: The Johns Hopkins University Press, 1970), XIII, 970–971; and Stephen E. Ambrose, *Eisenhower, Volume One: Soldier General of the Army President-Elect 1890–1952* (New York: Simon and Schuster, 1983), p. 523.
44. HRL, memorandum to the *Time* Archives, 27 July 1964.
45. John Billings, TLF, III, 159.
46. *Time*, 16 June 1952.
47. "Our Korean Strategy," *Life*, 11 February 1952.
48. *Time*, 23 June 1952.

49. Oral history interview with Dwight D. Eisenhower, in the Eisenhower Administration Project (Oral History Research Office, Columbia University), pp. 45–51.
50. Stephen E. Ambrose, *Eisenhower*, I, 533.
51. Elson, *The World of Time Inc.*, p. 307.
52. DJSB, entries for 16, 19, 24, and 27 June 1952; and *Time*, 9 June 1952.
53. DJSB, 6 June 1952. In 1932, *Time* had assigned two men to the party's convention.
54. *Time*, 30 June 1952.
55. A good example appears in McConaughy, cable of 13 June 1952, in the TD.
56. Glasgow, cable of 11 July 1952, in the TD.
57. Walter H. Judd, "Confidential interview – John Foster Dulles – January 4, 1952," in the papers of Walter H. Judd, 199, United States State Department. See also "Notes on Overseas Writers luncheon talk, 31 January 1952, by John Foster Dulles (off the record, background only)," in the papers of Alfred Kohlberg, 56, John Foster Dulles. Privately, Dulles admitted that Chiang had "very little future on the mainland of China." Foreign Service officers conversant with China shared Dulles's negative view of Chiang's future: Interview with Jerome Holloway, in Charles Stuart Kennedy, "A China Reader," II, 2–4. See also, Wellington Koo to Dulles, 12 May 1952, in the papers of John Foster Dulles, selected correspondence and related material, 61.
58. John Foster Dulles, "A Policy of Boldness," *Life*, 19 May 1952.
59. Elson, *The World of Time Inc.*, p. 306; *Time*, 9 June 1952, praised Taft for abandoning isolationism. See also "Ike's 'Great Crusade,'" *Life*, 21 July 1952.
60. Although two veteran politicians were nominally in charge of writing the foreign policy plank, Dulles supplied the prose and the ideas.
61. Hobbing, cable of 12 July 1952, in the TD.
62. Interview with James Hagerty, I, 55 (Columbia Oral History Project).
63. DJSB, 25 and 29 August, and 3 and 12 September 1952.
64. DJSB, 15 October 1952; and HRL, memorandum to Billings, Ways, and Thompson, 29 August 1952, in the papers of Daniel Longwell, 29.
65. David L. Anderson, "China Policy and Presidential Politics, 1952," *Presidential Studies Quarterly*, 10 (winter 1980), 82.
66. *Time*, 6 October 1952.
67. DJSB, 24 September 1952.
68. *The Gallup Poll*, II, 1052 (2 February–5 March and 10–15 August 1952).
69. Ibid., 1102 (9–14 October 1952).
70. Darby, cable of 4 October 1952, in the TD.
71. "An End to the Korean War," *Life*, 15 September 1952.
72. *Time*, 1 September 1952; and HRL to Thomas L. Matthews, 23 August 1952, in the TLF, III, 168. Privately, however, Luce expressed respect for the feisty president, whom he considered the season's premier campaigner. "I personally think Harry Truman is terrific," wrote Luce to Max Ways, 3 October 1952, in the papers of W. A. Swanberg, 19.
73. HRL to John S. Billings, 8 March 1954, in the TLF, III, 197.
74. HRL to Billings et al., 27 February and 8 March 1954, in the papers of W. A. Swanberg, 19.
75. *Time*, 1 and 22 September, and 13 October 1952.
76. "Our Civil Liberties Safe," *San Antonio News*, 8 October 1952.
77. *Tex and Jinx* on WNBC, 8 June 1950, in the Luce and Hamilton Collections, LWO 7965; and CBL, n.d. but 1952, speech on Communism, RXA 9168.

78. CBL, speech delivered on the eve of the 1952 elections, in the Luce and Hamilton Collections, LWO 7965.

79. CBL, "The Blind Traitor in High Places," radio broadcast of 26 October 1952, in the MacGregor Collection, LWO 12827 R4BB.

80. Emmet John Hughes, *The Ordeal of Power: A Political Memoir of the Eisenhower Years* (New York: Atheneum, 1963), p. 34; and Ambrose, *Eisenhower*, I, 569.

81. DJSB, 27 October 1952.

82. *New York Times*, 30 April 1950, IV, 7, 3.

83. *New York Times*, 11 April 1952.

84. Drew Pearson, *Washington Post*, 6 May 1952.

85. "Persons and Organizations Known to be Engaged in or to Have Been Engaged in Propaganda and Lobbying Activities on Behalf of the Chinese Nationalist government with the Financial Support of that Government," 31 August 1951, in the papers of Harry S Truman, President's Secretary's Files (HSTL).

86. Philip Horton to Theodore H. White, 7 April 1952, in the papers of Theodore H. White, 10, *Reporter*.

87. Alfred Kohlberg to Wayne Morse, 26 November 1951, in the papers of Thomas G. Corcoran, 110, China Lobby.

88. HRL, remarks at the *Time* editorial dinner, the Union Club, New York City, 14 November 1952, in the papers of W. A. Swanberg, 21.

89. Matthews, *Name and Address*, p. 273.

90. Interview with Allen Grover, in the papers of W. A. Swanberg, 18, interviews.

91. John Osborne, memorandum to HRL, 4 April 1952, in the papers of HRL, 30, China-Formosa Report.

92. *Time*, 28 July 1952.

93. *Journal-Courier* (New Haven), 16 December 1952.

94. Tsan-Kuo Chang, *The Press and China Policy: The Illusion of Sino-American Relations, 1950–1984* (Norwood, NJ: Ablex Publishing Corporation, 1992), pp. 92 and 184.

95. Ibid., p. 246.

96. "Memorandum on the Chinese Refugee Intellectuals, Students, Technicians, and Professionals in Hongkong," in the papers of Harry S Truman, Psychological Strategy Board, 5, 091 (HSTL).

97. ARCI organizational materials (1951–52) in the papers of Walter H. Judd, 31, HRL, and ibid., 166, 2; the papers of HRL, 25, Aid Refugee Chinese Intellectuals Misc. March–August 1952; and the *New York Times*, 20 April 1952, 2, 2.

98. Records of the Yale-in-China Association, III, 83, 503.

99. Syngman Rhee to HRL, 1 December 1952, in the papers of HRL, 2, Rhee, Syngman.

100. Elson, *The World of Time Inc.*, pp. 370–371.

101. DJSB, 22 December 1952; and HRL, report on his Far Eastern tour, 22 December 1952, in the papers of W. A. Swanberg, 17, W. A. S.; and Luce to John S. Billings, 16 January 1953, in the TLF, III, 175.

102. Staff cable of 8 April 1953, in the TD, reads like a report intended to please the home office and Luce himself.

103. HRL, "America and the World – 1953," in the papers of W. A. Swanberg, 19.

104. *Time*, 16 April 1951.

105. *Time*, 24 September 1951.

106. DJSB, 24 September 1951.

107. *Time*, 21 January 1952.
108. *Time*, 3 and 10 November and 1 December 1952.
109. *Time*, 24 September 1951.
110. *Time*, 21 January 1952. The false rumor of a possible Chinese invasion appeared in other places, too: *U.S. News & World Report*, 7 March 1952.
111. "De Lattre and His Message," *Life*, 24 September 1951.
112. CBL, "St. Francis Xavier – Then and Now," 10th annual Jesuit mission dinner, 6 November 1952, in the papers of CBL, 685, 19; and "Indo-China is in Danger," *Life*, 21 January 1952.
113. HRL to John S. Billings, 22 December 1952, in the papers of W. A. Swanberg, 17, W. A. S.; and HRL on Indochina, in the TLF, III, 175.
114. HRL, "America and Asia," ibid.
115. Memoranda relating to these endeavors can be found in the papers of W. A. Swanberg, 19.
116. *Time*, 21 October 1966.
117. HRL, memorandum "1953 in Asia," in the papers of W. A. Swanberg, 19.
118. DJSB, 6–8 January 1953.
119. Dwight D. Eisenhower to HRL, 5 January 1953, in the papers of CBL, 21, 2.
120. John Osborne, dispatch of 12 December 1952, in the TD.
121. HRL to Dwight D. Eisenhower, 10 November 1952, in Eisenhower, Dwight D., Papers as President of the United States, 1953–1961 (Ann Whitman File), Administration Series, 25 (DDEL).
122. *Time*, 24 November 1952.
123. Darby, dispatch of 19 December 1952, in the TD.
124. Interview with Walter H. Judd in the Eisenhower Project, p. 103.
125. Interview with Robert L. Sherrod in the Eisenhower Project, p. 26.
126. DJSB, 16 and 27 February and 20 March 1953.

11. Unwelcome Moderation

1. *Time*, 30 November 1953.
2. Interview with Roy Alexander, in the papers of W. A. Swanberg, 18, interviews.
3. For a negative appraisal of her ambassadorship, see Claire Sterling and Max Ascoli, "The Lady of Villa Taverna," *The Reporter*, 23 February 1956.
4. "A Truce With the Bear?" *Life*, 27 April 1953.
5. John Beal, cable of 20 March 1953, in the TD; and the interview with John Holdridge, in "A China Reader," p. 9.
6. "The Reminiscences of Walter S. Robertson," Eisenhower Administration Project (Oral History Research Office, Columbia University, 1970), p. 19.
7. Interview with Paul Kreisberg, in "A China Reader," II, 16; and "The Reminiscences of Walter S. Robertson," p. 131.
8. Ibid., p. 165.
9. Interview with Larue R. Lutkins, in "A China Reader," II, 3–5; and Nancy B. Tucker, "A House Divided: The United States, the Department of State, and China," in Warren Cohen and Akira Iriye, eds., *The Great Powers in East Asia* (New York: Columbia University Press, 1990), pp. 36–37.
10. Beal and Blair, dispatch of 31 January, and staff dispatches of 4 and 18 February 1953, in the TD.

11. Hank Luce, cable of 28 February 1953, in the TD.
12. McConaughy, cable of 13 February, and Beal, cable of 14 February 1953, in the TD.
13. DJSB, 17 March 1953.
14. *Time*, 19 January 1953.
15. *Time*, 30 March 1953.
16. Elson, *The World of Time Inc.*, p. 368.
17. "A Truce With the Bear?" *Life*, 27 April 1953.
18. Hank Luce, cable of 1 August 1953, in the TD.
19. Interview with Robert R. Bowie, in "A China Reader," II, 1.
20. Lambert, cable of 29 April 1954, in the TD.
21. *Time*, 16 and 23 March 1953.
22. Henry R. Luce, Interview in the John Foster Dulles Oral History Project, Seeley G. Mudd Manuscript Library, Princeton University, p. 22; and *Time*, 12 October 1953.
23. "Churchill Speaking," 14–17 April 1955, unidentified notes (possibly made by Emmet John Hughes or CBL), in the papers of C. D. Jackson, 32, Churchill.
24. Ibid.
25. DJSB, 15 and 21 May 1953; HRL to John S. Billings, 18 July 1953, in the TLF, III, 185; Andre Laguerre to Time Inc., 22 May 1953, ibid., 183.
26. HRL to Roy Alexander, 5 September 1953, ibid., 188.
27. DJSB, 5 September 1953.
28. DJSB, 5 October 1953.
29. Gaddis, *The Long Peace*, pp. 123 and 177.
30. "The President and the Bomb," *Life*, 19 October 1953.
31. Luce's unpublished memoir, p. 52.
32. Dwight D. Eisenhower to John Crider, 5 May 1953, in the Dwight D. Eisenhower Library Central files, PPF, 953 (DDEL).
33. "The Reminiscences of Andrew Heiskell," pp. 245 ff. and p. 562; and CBL, Columbia Oral History Project, p. 92.
34. HRL, memorandum on Dulles, 18 September 1953, in the papers of W. A. Swanberg, 19.
35. *Time*, 1 December 1952 and 23 March 1953.
36. HRL, address at the Dayton Art Institute, 12 June 1943, in the papers of W. A. Swanberg, 21.
37. HRL, interview in the John Foster Dulles Oral History Project, pp. 12–13.
38. David Mayers, "Eisenhower's Containment Policy and the Major Communist Powers, 1953–1956," *International History Review*, V: 1 (February 1983), 61.
39. *The Gallup Poll*, II, 1153–1154 (6 July 1953).
40. Stanley D. Bachrack, *The Committee of One Million: "China Lobby" Politics, 1953–1971* (New York: Columbia University Press, 1976).
41. John O'Kearney, "Lobby of a Million Ghosts," *The Nation*, 23 January 1960, p. 76.
42. *Time*, 30 August 1954.
43. The correspondence between Van Fleet and *Life* can be consulted in his papers, 13, 38–39.
44. Correspondence between James A. Van Fleet and Syngman Rhee, 22 April–30 May 1953, ibid., 18.
45. "Record of [Conversations] Between President Chiang Kai-shek and General James A. Van Fleet, Special Envoy of President Eisenhower," 13, 16, 24, and 28 May 1954, ibid., 27–29, 33–34.

46. "Record of Conversations between President Chiang Kai-shek and U.S. Secretary of Defense Charles E. Wilson, 20–21 May 1954," ibid., 30–32.

47. *Life*, 21 July 1947; and William Gray, cable of 2 June 1947, in the TD.

48. Luce comments in the papers of HRL, 39, ECA.

49. Claire Chennault to Thomas Corcoran, 14 February 1950, in the papers of Thomas G. Corcoran, 105, C. L. Chennault, Personal.

50. Interview with Dr. Wu Kuo-chen, Columbia University, Chinese Oral History Project, pp. 164–185.

51. Jack Beal, cable of 20 March 1953, in the TD.

52. Interview with Dr. Wu Kuo-chen, pp. 282–293.

53. Wu did not mention the fact that Chiang's police held ten thousand to twelve thousand political prisoners incommunicado.

54. K. C. Wu to HRL, 20 February 1954, in the papers of TLF, III, 196.

55. HRL to John S. Billings, 18 March 1954, ibid., 198; and James Shepley to Billings, 22 March 1954, ibid., 199.

56. Interview with Eddie Lockett, n.d., tape 5, p. 1, in the papers of Thomas G. Corcoran, 107, C. L. Chennault.

57. B. A. Garside, "An Analysis of the Charges by K. C. Wu," in the papers of B. A. Garside, 4.

58. *Time*, 22 March 1954.

59. Ben L. Martin, "The New 'Old China Hands': Shaping a Specialty," *Asian Affairs: An American Review*, 3 (November–December 1975), 126. Material related to the Vincent case can be consulted in the papers of John Carter Vincent, 1924–1953, HUG (B), V462.10, BRD (Harvard University Archives).

60. Gary May, *China Scapegoat: The Diplomatic Ordeal of John Carter Vincent* (Washington, DC: New Republic Books, 1979), pp. 268ff.

61. *Time* covered the final stages of the Vincent affair in its issues of 29 December 1952 and 12 January and 16 March 1953.

62. Gary May, "The 'New China Hands' and the Rape of the China Service," *Reviews in American History*, 4 (March 1976), 120–127.

63. HRL to John Shaw Billings, 14 July 1953, in the TLF, III, 185.

64. "Heretics or Conspirators?" *Life*, 21 May 1956; and *Life*, 22 December 1952.

65. "That Campus Witch Hunt," *Life*, 9 March 1953.

66. HRL to James Linen, 4 February 1953, the papers of W. A. Swanberg, 19; DJSB, 8 May 1953; and "The Fifth Amendment," *Time*, 5 September 1955.

67. *Time*, 13 and 20 July and 3 August 1953.

68. "Books, Words and Deeds," *Life*, 29 June 1953; and *Time*, 12 October 1953.

69. *Time*, 12 January 1953.

70. *Time*, 8 March 1954.

71. *Time*, 1 March 1954.

72. *Time*, 8 March 1954.

73. Cable from the Washington staff to Larry Laybourne, 24 March 1954, in the TLF, III, 199.

74. *Time*, 22 March 1954.

75. *Time*, 10 May 1954.

76. John S. Billings, cable to HRL, 12 March 1954, in the papers of W. A. Swanberg, 19.

77. "The McCarthy Issue Stands," *Life*, 22 March 1954; *Time*, 29 November and 13 December 1954; and "Time for an End," *Life*, 13 December 1954.

78. HRL, unpublished memoir, p. 54, in the papers of HRL, 86.

79. HRL, commencement address at Occidental College, in the papers of HRL, 76, 13 June 1954.

80. Visson, cable of 30 January 1953, in the TD.

81. HRL, address at the Madison Avenue Presbyterian Church, 6 April 1953, in the papers of W. A. Swanberg, 21.

82. Jim Shepley, cable of 30 April 1954, in the TD.

83. HRL to John S. Billings, 5 August 1953, in the TLF, III, 187.

84. Lucien Bodard, cable of 20 June 1953, in the TD.

85. Dowling, cable of 19 April 1953, in the TD.

86. *Time*, 2 March 1953.

87. Dowling, cable of 23 July 1953, in the TLF, III, 186.

88. *Time*, 28 September 1953.

89. John S. Bowman, ed., *The World Almanac of the Vietnam War* (New York: World Almanac, 1985), p. 35.

90. "Indochina, France and the U.S.," *Life*, 3 August 1953.

91. *The Gallup Poll*, II, 1146 and 1170–71 (5 June and 18 September 1953).

92. Dowling, cables to Time-Life, 8, 11, 21, and 23 July 1953, TLF, III, 184–185.

93. Elson, *The World of Time Inc.*, pp. 374–375.

94. David Douglas Duncan, "The Year of the Snake," *Life*, 3 August 1953.

95. HRL to Sidney James, 13 August 1953, in the private papers of Sidney James. I am grateful to the late Mr. James for granting me access to his collection of *Life*-related papers.

96. John S. Billings, cable to HRL, TLF, III, 187. Billings thought that Duncan suffered "from self-righteous standards of right and wrong."

97. "Indochina, France and the U.S.," *Life*, 3 August 1953.

98. T. George Harris, 11 February 1954, in the TD.

99. C. D. Jackson to John S. Billings, 3 August 1953, TLF, III, 187.

100. Sidney L. James, *Press Pass: The Journalist's Tale* (Laguna Hills, CA: Aegean Park Press, 1994), pp. 192–193.

101. Donald R. Heath to HRL, 12 August 1953, TLF, III, 187.

102. HRL to John S. Billings, 14 August 1953, ibid.

103. Donald R. Heath, *Life*, 21 September 1953.

104. "New Hope for Indochina," *Life*, 21 September 1953.

105. *Time*, 10 August and 28 September 1953.

106. *Time*, 15 February 1954.

107. *Time*, 28 September 1953.

108. *Time*, 21 December 1953.

109. Staff cable of 30 December 1953, in the TD.

110. *Life*, 14 December 1953; and *Time*, 1 February 1954.

111. *Time*, 1 March 1954; and staff cable of 21 April 1954, in the TD.

112. Clay Blair, cable of 19 February 1954, in the TD.

113. *Time*, 15 February 1954.

114. Staff cable of 3 February 1954, in the TD.

115. John Steele, cable of 17 April 1954, in the TD. Nixon later voiced the same opinion to a group of editors: *Time*, 26 April 1954. See also Stephen E. Ambrose, *Nixon: The Education of a Politician 1913–1962* (New York: Simon and Schuster, 1987), pp. 342–347; and Dwight D. Eisenhower to Alfred M. Gruenther, 26 April 1954, in the diaries of Dwight D. Eisenhower 1953–61, frames 00081–84.

116. George Herring and Richard Immerman, "Eisenhower, Dulles, and Dienbienphu," in Andrew Rotter, ed., *The Light at the End of the Tunnel* (New York: St. Martin's Press, 1991), pp. 81–85.
117. Interview with James Hagerty, I, 112 ff., in the Eisenhower Administration Project, Oral History Research Office (Columbia University).
118. T. George Harris, 11 February 1954, in the TD.
119. John Steele, cable of 10 April 1954, in the TD.
120. Jack Beal, cable of 13 March 1954, in the TD.
121. *The Gallup Poll*, II, 1235–1236 (17 May 1954).
122. Jack Beal, cable of 8 July 1954, in the TD.
123. *Time*, 15 March 1954.
124. Harris, cable of 28 February 1954, in the TD.
125. C. D. Jackson, memorandum to HRL, 11 August 1954, in the papers of C. D. Jackson, 1931–1967, 57, Time Inc. 1953–54.
126. *Time*, 5 April 1954; and "Verdun Stand in Vietnam," *Life*, 5 April 1954.
127. Dwight D. Eisenhower to Alfred M. Gruenther, 26 April 1954, in the diaries of Dwight D. Eisenhower 1953–61, frames 00081–84.
128. Larry Laybourne, cable of 16 June 1954, in the TD.
129. Shepley, cable of 30 April 1954; and Darby, cable of 1 May 1954, in the TD.
130. Beal–Lambert, cable of 5 November 1954, in the TD.
131. *Time*, 3 May 1954.
132. Staff cable of 3 March 1954, in the TD; and see David Mayers, "Eisenhower's Containment Policy and the Major Communist Powers, 1953–1956," p. 67.
133. *Time*, and "Heroism: Futile Without Unity," *Life*, both 17 May 1954.
134. John Osborne, cable of 27 June 1954, in the TD.
135. Lambert, cable of 29 April 1954, in the TD.
136. McConaughy, cable of 15 May 1954, in the TD.
137. *Time*, 10 May 1954.
138. Lambert, cable of 28 May 1954, in the TD.
139. Staff cable of 16 June 1954, in the TD.
140. "Dulles, Geneva and History," *Life*, 3 May 1954.
141. *Time*, 14 June 1954.
142. Berger, cable of 11 June 1954, in the TD.
143. HRL, commencement address at Occidental College, Los Angeles, CA, 13 June 1954, in the papers of HRL, 76.
144. Staff cable of 16 June 1954, in the TD.
145. Jack Beal, cable of 2 July 1954, in the TD; and Gaddis, *We Now Know*, p. 163.
146. Interview with Paul Kreisberg, in "A China Reader," II, 9.
147. "Behind the Face of China," *Life*, 14 June 1954; and *Life*, 28 June 1954.
148. *Time*, 19 July 1954.
149. *Time*, 21 June 1954.
150. Staff cable of 20 July, and Jack Beal, cable of 23 July 1954, in the TD.
151. C. D. Jackson, memorandum to HRL, 27 July 1954, in the papers of C. D. Jackson, 1931–1967, 57, Time Inc. 1953–54; and *Time*, 2 August 1954.
152. *Time*, 26 July 1954; and *Life*, 2 August 1954.
153. Staff cable of 24 August 1954, in the TD.
154. *The Gallup Poll*, II, 1260 (13 August 1954); and Beal and Lambert, cable of 14 October 1954, in the TD.

155. Nancy Tucker, "A House Divided," in Cohen and Iriye, *The Great Powers in East Asia*, pp. 42–43.
156. *Time* 23 August 1954.
157. CBL, memorandum, 12 August 1954, in the papers of the Eisenhower Administration, 25, Luce, C. (2) (DDEL).
158. HRL to Jim Shepley et al., 6 August 1954, in the papers of C. D. Jackson, 1931–1967 A72–26, 57.
159. Jim Shepley, cable of 3 September 1954, in the TD.
160. Unsigned and undated memo ("Preface"), in the papers of C. D. Jackson, 1931–1967 A 72–26, 57.
161. *New York Times*, 12 January 1958, 72, 5.

12. Keeping the Pressure on Mao and Ho

1. Bennett C. Rushkoff, "Eisenhower, Dulles and the Quemoy-Matsu Crisis, 1954–1955," *Political Science Quarterly*, 96, 3, 466–468.
2. Blair, cable of 19 November 1954, in the TD.
3. Lambert, cable of 20 August 1954, in the TD.
4. *Life*, 27 September 1954; and *Time*, 20 September 1954.
5. Jack Beal, cable of 15 October 1954, in the TD.
6. Interview with John Holdridge, in "A China Reader," p. 13.
7. Rushkoff, "Eisenhower," 473. When Eisenhower later looked back, he mentioned the need to defend Formosa and omitted any reference to saving Quemoy: Interview with Dwight D. Eisenhower, in the Eisenhower Administration Project (Oral History Research Office, Columbia University, 1967), p. 53.
8. *The Gallup Poll*, II, 1273 (6 October 1954).
9. McConaughy, cable of 28 January 1955, in the TD.
10. *Time*, 3 January 1955.
11. *Time*, 31 January 1955.
12. *Time*, 18 April 1955.
13. Lambert–McConaughy, cable of 21 January 1955, in the TD.
14. *Time*, 14 February 1955.
15. HRL to Dwight D. Eisenhower, over the phone via dictation, 22 January 1955, in Eisenhower, Dwight D., Papers as President of the United States, 1953–1961 (Ann Whitman File), Administration Series, 25.
16. HRL, interview, p. 9, I, in the John Foster Dulles Oral History Project, Seeley G. Mudd Manuscript Library, Princeton University.
17. Dwight D. Eisenhower to HRL, 24 January 1955, in the papers of CBL, 2, Eisenhower.
18. Dwight D. Eisenhower to Lewis W. Douglas, 29 March 1955, in the diaries of Dwight D. Eisenhower 1953–1961, reel 6, frames 00005–8.
19. John Steele, cable of 28 January 1955, in the TD.
20. Jack Beal, cable of 4 February 1955, in the TD.
21. *Life*, 4 April 1955.
22. Charles J. V. Murphy, "*The* Crisis in the Cold War," *Fortune*, 51 (June 1955), 96 ff.
23. Dwight D. Eisenhower to John Foster Dulles, 26 April 1955, in the diaries of Dwight D. Eisenhower 1953–1961, reel 6, frames 150–151.
24. *The Gallup Poll*, II, 1320 (27 March 1955) and 1330 (6 May 1955).
25. Larry Laybourne, cable of 8 February 1955, in the TD; and *Time*, 14 March 1955.

26. This optimistic approach reflected information supplied by Jack Beal, 4 February 1955, in the TD.

27. "Faces of the Formosa Crisis," *Life*, 7 February 1955.

28. *Time*, 18 April 1955.

29. *The Gallup Poll*, II, 1329 (1 May 1955).

30. Ibid., 1333 (20 May 1955).

31. HRL to CBL, 2 February 1955, in the papers of CBL, 21, correspondence with HRL 1954–55; and *Life*, 18 April 1955.

32. John Osborne, cable to Henry Luce, 27 April 1955, in the papers of C. D. Jackson, 1931–1967, 32, *Time*, Chiang.

33. HRL, cable to C. D. Jackson, 29 April 1955, ibid., 58.

34. Emmet J. Hughes, memorandum of 13 May 1955, ibid.

35. John K. Jessup, cable to HRL, 27 April, ibid., and HRL, cable to Jessup, n.d., but probably 28 April 1955, ibid.

36. *Time*, 27 June 1955.

37. HRL, address titled "The Public Philosophy and the Spirit of Geneva," delivered at St. Louis University, 16 November 1955, in the papers of the Eisenhower Administration, Whitman File, 25, Luce, H. (2) (DDEL); and *Time*, 1 August 1955.

38. *Life*, 1 August 1955.

39. HRL to CBL, 23 April 1958, in the papers of CBL, 21, correspondence with HRL 1958.

40. Beal–Lambert, cable of 4 November 1954, in the TD.

41. Jack Beal, cable of 17 March 1955, in the TD.

42. *Time*, 28 June 1954.

43. Lambert, cable of 29 October 1954, in the TD.

44. Staff cable of 2 November 1954, in the TD.

45. *Time*, 22 November 1954.

46. Ibid.

47. John Mecklin, cable of 11 November 1954, in the TD; and *Time*, 8 November and 27 December 1954.

48. *Life*, 10 January 1955.

49. *Time*, 28 February 1955.

50. Eugene Segal, cable of 20 March 1955, in the TD.

51. Jack Beal, cable of 15 April 1955, in the TD.

52. *Time*, 16 May 1955.

53. *Life*, 16 May 1955.

54. *Time*, 19 October and 7 November 1955.

55. *Time*, 19 March 1956.

56. *Life*, 25 July 1955.

57. *Time*, 4 April 1955.

58. HRL to C. D. Jackson, 9 August 1955, in the papers of C. D. Jackson, 1931–1967, 58, Time Inc., Luce 1955 (2).

59. HRL, memorandum to Roy Alexander et al., 20 October 1955, ibid.

60. John K. Jessup, "The World, the Flesh and the Devil," *Life*, 26 December 1955.

61. *Life*, 23 January 1956.

62. *Time*, 5 March 1956.

63. Edward Lockett to Thomas Corcoran, 24 January 1956, in the papers of Thomas G. Corcoran, 70, Lockett, Edward.

64. Shepley, Columbia oral history project, pp. 10–11.

65. Richard H. Immerman, *John Foster Dulles: Piety, Pragmatism, and Power in U.S. Foreign Policy* (Wilmington, DE: Scholarly Resources, 1999), p. 72.

66. Roger Dingman, "Atomic Diplomacy During the Korean War," *International Security*, XIII: 3, 85; Rosemary J. Foot, "Nuclear Coercion and the Ending of the Korean Conflict," ibid., 111; and Shu Guang Zhang, *Deterrence and Strategic Culture: Chinese-American Confrontations, 1949–1958* (Ithaca, NY: Cornell University Press, 1992), pp. 125–126.

67. Department of State, press release No. 26, 17 January 1956, in the papers of John Foster Dulles, 105.

68. Dwight D. Eisenhower, telephone call to John Foster Dulles, 19 January 1956, in the papers of the Eisenhower administration, Dulles, John Foster, 1951–1959, telephone calls, Series A67-28, 11 (DDEL); James Shepley, Columbia oral history project, p. 5; *New York Times*, 22 January 1956, 4, 1; *Time*, 23 and 30 January 1956; and draft statements by the editor-in-chief of *Life*, 20 January 1956, in the papers of CBL, 23, 18. Ambassador Luce reviewed her husband's statement and approved it.

69. *Life*, 20 August 1956.

70. HRL to John Foster Dulles, 21 February 1957, in the papers of John Foster Dulles, selected correspondence and related material, 118; and *The Gallup Poll*, II, 1495 (30 June 1957).

71. *Time*, 25 July 1960.

72. C. D. Jackson to HRL, 23 January 1956, in the papers of C. D. Jackson, 1931–1967, 58; and *Life*, 9 January 1956.

73. *Time*, 27 February and 26 March 1956, displayed almost no feel for the implications of Khrushchev's speech. Its first insights appeared in print on 16 April.

74. *Time*, 30 April 1956.

75. Whittaker Chambers in *Life*, 30 April 1956.

76. Gaddis, *We Now Know*, p. 212.

77. *Life*, 5 November 1956.

78. HRL to Chiang Kai-shek, 18 August 1956 and 21 May 1957, in the papers of C. D. Jackson, 1931–1967, 32.

79. John Davenport, "China Passes a Dividend," *Fortune*, 56 (September 1957), p. 151.

80. *Time*, 9 March 1959.

81. *Time*, 5 January 1959.

82. *Time*, 10 August 1959.

83. *Time*, 29 February 1959.

84. The Washington staff, cable of 8 February 1955, in the TD; and "Churchill Speaking," Notes based on conversations held in April 1955, in the papers of C. D. Jackson, 1931–1967, 32, Churchill.

85. Interview with Joseph Mendenhall, in Charles S. Kennedy, comp., "A Vietnam Reader" (Foreign Affairs Oral History Program, Georgetown University), I, 3.

86. Marshall Green, "Evolution of U.S.-China Policy 1956–1973: Memoirs of an Insider" (Association for Diplomatic Studies, Foreign Affairs Oral History Program, Georgetown University), p. 7.

87. "A Classic Cold-War Campaign," *Time*, 29 December 1958, 5 January 1959.

88. Marvin Liebman, confidential report to the steering committee on his 1957 Far Eastern tour, in the papers of Thomas G. Corcoran, 120, Committee of One Million.

89. HRL to Beth [Moore] and Henry [Luce], June 1959, in the papers of HRL, 44, Henry Luce Foundation 1936–1962. Luce did not send this letter.

90. *The Gallup Poll*, II, 1569 (26 September 1958).
91. HRL, comments at a staff luncheon, 9 June 1960, in the papers of W. A. Swanberg.
92. *Time*, 5 January 1959.
93. *Time*, 28 March 1960.
94. L. Nelson Bell to HRL, 20 December 1958; HRL to Henry P. Van Dusen, 6 February 1959, and Van Dusen to HRL, 16 February 1959, in the papers of Henry P. Van Dusen.
95. Materials on the World Study Group in the papers of HRL, 37, Committee of One Million 1956–64.
96. *Time*, 13 April 1959.
97. *Time*, 24 March and 26 December 1960.
98. HRL to John Foster Dulles, n.d., in the papers of John Foster Dulles, selected correspondence and related material, 141.
99. "A Record Clear and Strong For All to See," *Time*, 27 April 1959.
100. HRL, unpublished manuscript, pp. 82–85.
101. Alfred Kohlberg to A. L. Hart, Jr., 17 March 1960, in the papers of Marvin Liebman Associates, 29, Alfred Kohlberg.
102. William F. Buckley, Jr., comments at a testimonial dinner for Alfred Kohlberg, 26 January 1960, in the papers of Alfred Kohlberg, 21, Wm. F. Buckley, Jr.
103. "Ad Hoc Group," in the papers of HRL, 38, Council on Foreign Relations 1959.
104. Luce worked with the Committee to Strengthen the Frontiers of Freedom, which Vannevar Bush chaired. The group was formed to support Eisenhower's foreign aid programs: The papers of HRL, 37, Committee.
105. HRL to Henry M. Wriston (chair of the study group), 3 November 1959, ibid., 38, Council on Foreign Relations 1959.
106. Alfred Kohlberg to J. William Fulbright, 20 November, and Chow Ching-wen to Van Fleet, 24 December 1959, in the papers of James Van Fleet, 9, 8.
107. *New York Times*, 8 December 1959, 1, 6.
108. *Time*, 13 June 1955.
109. Green, "Evolution of U.S.-China Policy 1956–1973," p. 6.
110. Interview with Marshall Green and Ambassador Manhard, in "A China Reader," p. 25.
111. *Life*, 7 December 1959.
112. Alfred Kohlberg to the Editors of *Life*, 3 December 1959, in the papers of Alfred Kohlberg, 110, Life Magazine 1955 to 1957.
113. *Time*, 12 October 1959.
114. *Time*, 22 August 1960.
115. *Time*, 21 November 1960.
116. *New York Times*, 29 June 1960, 4, 5.
117. HRL, testimony before the Senate Subcommittee on National Policy Machinery, 28 June 1960, ibid.
118. HRL, address on Founder's Day at the University of Pennsylvania, 10 January 1958, in the papers of W. A. Swanberg, 22, 1957–58.
119. The Rand Corporation, "Report on a Study of Non-Military Defense," 1 July 1958, in the papers of HRL, 38, Council on Foreign Relations.
120. Cover story in *Time*, 20 October 1961. The magazine had criticized both the Eisenhower and the Kennedy administrations for their lack "of any provision for nuclear fallout shelters, which would cut casualties by millions" (7 April 1961).

121. HRL to Dwight D. Eisenhower, 2 July 1960, in the papers of C. D. Jackson, 1931–1967, 58.
122. "Mr. Luce's Cold War," *The Nation*, 9 July 1960, p. 22.
123. Dwight D. Eisenhower to HRL, 6 July 1960, in the papers of HRL, 2, Eisenhower.
124. Marvin Liebman to Thomas G. Corcoran, 29 October 1957, in the papers of Thomas G. Corcoran, 120, Committee of One Million.
125. *Time*, 11 February 1957.
126. *Time*, 9 February 1959.
127. *Time*, 9 February 1959.
128. "Dainty Emancipator," *Time*, 26 January 1959.
129. Christopher Emmet to CBL, 4 April 1951, in the papers of CBL, 188, 10. Emmet did not identify Diem by name, but he almost certainly was referring to him.
130. Joseph G. Morgan, *The Vietnam Lobby: The American Friends of Vietnam, 1955–1975* (Chapel Hill: University of North Carolina Press, 1997).
131. Material on the AFV can be consulted in the papers of HRL, 26, American Friends of Vietnam.
132. HRL to Mr. and Mrs. Ogden Reid, 24 April 1957, in the papers of Ogden R. Reid, Part Two, *Herald Tribune*, Selected Correspondence and Subject Files 1955–58, Group No. 755, II, 35.
133. "Laos: The Unloaded Pistol," *Time*, 21 September 1959.
134. *Time*, 27 April 1959.
135. *Time*, 21 September 1959.
136. *Time*, 13 January 1961.
137. *Time*, 16 March 1959.
138. *Time*, 14 September 1959.
139. *Time*, 2 May 1960.
140. *Time*, 20 July 1959.
141. *Time*, 2 May 1960.
142. *Time*, 11 July 1960.
143. *Time*, 13 January 1961.

13. Time Inc. and Nation-Making in Vietnam

1. HRL, Oral History Interview, p. 7 (JFKL); Baughman, *Henry R. Luce*, p. 101; W. A. Swanberg, *Luce and His Empire* (New York: Charles Scribner's Sons, 1972), p. 154; and Michael R. Beschloss, *Kennedy and Roosevelt: The Uneasy Alliance* (New York: Harper & Row, 1987), p. 109. *Time*, 18 September 1939, devoted some kind words to young Jack Kennedy, after he had debriefed American survivors of the torpedoed British passenger liner *Athenia*.
2. "The Reminiscences of Andrew Heiskell," p. 253.
3. *Life*, 11 October, 22 November, and 20 December 1937.
4. The diary of John F. Kennedy, European trip 7, 1, 1937–9, 3, 37, and undated (but 1939 or early 1940) letters to his mother and father, in John F. Kennedy, Personal Papers, Early Years; and John F. Kennedy, "Appeasement at Munich (the Inevitable Result of the Slowness of Conversion of the British Democracy to a Rearmament Policy)," honors thesis at Harvard, 15 March 1940, ibid., Harvard Records 1935–1940.
5. James MacGregor Burns, *John Kennedy: A Political Profile* (New York: Harcourt, Brace & Company, 1959), p. 44; and David Nunnerly, *President Kennedy and Britain* (New York: St. Martin's Press, 1972), pp. 15–24.

6. Oral history interview with HRL, 11 November 1965, by John F. Steele, pp. 1–9 (JFKL). Two decades later, when Luce was asked why he had written the foreword, he answered "Joe": Interview with William Benton, p. 3, in the papers of W. A. Swanberg, 18, interviews.

7. "We Agree, Mr. Kennedy" appeared in *Life* on 25 August 1952, when the Republicans were desperately fighting to prevent Representative Kennedy from winning one of their Senate seats. The magazine endorsed Kennedy's call for a special session of Congress for the purpose of passing a new set of price controls.

8. *Time*, 18 August and 29 September 1952.

9. *Time*, 11 January 1954.

10. Lambert, cable of 1 April 1954, in the TD.

11. *Time*, 6 August 1956.

12. HRL, unpublished manuscript, p. 102.

13. *Time*, 2 September and 18 November 1957.

14. Interview with CBL (Oral History Collection, Columbia University), p. 61.

15. *Time*, 26 October 1959.

16. Oral history interview with HRL, 11 November 1965, for the John F. Kennedy Library, pp. 11–12; and HRL, unpublished manuscript, p. 101.

17. Interview with Otto Fuerbringer, p. 3, in the papers of David Halberstam related to *The Powers That Be*.

18. "A President for the '60s," *Life*, 17 October; and "A President for the '60s," *Life*, II, 24 October 1960.

19. Thomas Griffith, *How True: A Skeptic's Guide to Believing the News* (Boston: Little, Brown, 1974), pp. 106–108.

20. *Time*, 3 and 10 October 1960.

21. *Time*, 17 October 1960.

22. Stanley Hyman, *The Lives of William Benton* (Chicago: University of Chicago Press, 1969), pp. 538–539.

23. Interview with Otto Fuerbringer, p. 3, in the papers of David Halberstam related to *The Powers That Be*.

24. John Steele, dispatch Wash 52, NYK, p. 2, in the TD.

25. BDM Corporation, "A Study of Strategic Lessons Learned in Vietnam," IV, 3–3 (LBJL).

26. Interview with Hugh Sidey, p. 6, in the papers of David Halberstam related to *The Powers That Be*.

27. Ibid., p. 10.

28. HRL, address to Time Inc. executives, New York City, 15 May 1961, in the papers of C. D. Jackson, 58, Luce 1961–62.

29. CBL, Oral History Collection, Columbia University, pp. 88–89.

30. Interview with Hugh Sidey, p. 6, in the papers of David Halberstam related to *The Powers That Be*.

31. *Time*, 29 December 1961.

32. HRL, "Foreword to the 1961 Edition," in the papers of HRL, 86; and *Time*, 13 October 1961.

33. Interview with Hugh Sidey, p. 7, in the papers of David Halberstam concerning *The Powers That Be*.

34. Interview with John Steele, p. 5, ibid.

35. *Time*, 2 November 1962.

36. *Time*, 3 November 1961.

37. Interview with Lutkins, in "A China Reader," II, 9.

38. Thomas Corcoran to George Yeh, in the papers of Thomas G. Corcoran, 88, Yeh, George.
39. *The Gallup Poll*, II, 1710–1711 (19 and 24 March 1961).
40. Ibid., 1773 (27 June 1962).
41. Oral History Interview with HRL, pp. 29–30 (JFKL).
42. Duncan Norton-Taylor, "The Sword at the Belly of Red China," *Fortune* (July 1963), pp. 150 ff.
43. "Questions from Korea," *Life*, 7 August 1950.
44. South Vietnam, Background, 26 April 1961, Lyndon Baines Johnson, VP Security, 27 April – Vietnam (III) (LBJL).
45. "Growing Criticism of Diem Regime," IWR 12 May 1960, in the papers of Lyndon Baines Johnson, VP Security, File, 10, 27 April – Vietnam (III) (LBJL).
46. Charles J. V. Murphy, "Grand Strategy: Is a Shift in the Making?" *Fortune* (April 1961), pp. 115 ff.
47. Lt. General Lionel C. McGarr, Information, Guidance and Instructions to MAAG Advisory Personnel, 10 November 1960, Program for South Vietnam (LBJL).
48. *Time*, 10 March 1961.
49. *Time*, 24 May 1963.
50. Horace Busby, memorandum to the Vice-President, 26 April 1961, in the papers of Lyndon Baines Johnson, VP Security, 1, 8 (LBJL).
51. Ambassador Nolting, cable to Alexis Johnson, 15 May 1961, ibid., 1, 9.
52. John M. Newman, *JFK and Vietnam* (New York: Warner Books, 1992), pp. 67–74.
53. Joint Communique, in the papers of Lyndon Baines Johnson, President 1963–69, VP Security, 1, 9 (LBJL).
54. Vice-President Johnson to President Kennedy, 23 May 1961, ibid., folder 11; and "MAAG response to Vice President Johnson's request for a statement of the requirements to save Vietnam from Communist aggression," n.d. but after 12 May 1961, in Lyndon Baines Johnson, VP Security, 10, 27 April – Vietnam (II) (LBJL).
55. *Time*, 2 June 1961.
56. JCS to CINCPAC, May 1961, in the papers of Lyndon Baines Johnson, VP Security, 10, Program for South Vietnam (LBJL).
57. Robert S. McNamara, *In Retrospect: The Tragedy and Lessons of Vietnam* (New York: New York Times Books, 1995), p. 39.
58. George W. Ball, *The Past Has Another Pattern* (New York: W. W. Norton & Company, 1982), pp. 365–368; Ball, "Kennedy Up Close," *New York Review of Books*, 3 February 1994, pp. 17–19; and Warren I. Cohen, *America in the Age of Soviet Power 1945–1991* (Cambridge: Cambridge University Press, 1993), p. 156.
59. George Herring, *America's Longest War: The United States and Vietnam, 1950–1975* (New York: McGraw-Hill, 1996), p. 92.
60. *Time*, 19 May 1961.
61. "Night War in the Jungle," *Time*, 29 September 1961.
62. David Toczek, "And They Made It in Their Image," a paper delivered at a symposium on the "American Military Experience in Asia, 1898–1998," Madison, WI, 24–25 October 1998.
63. *Time*, 4 August 1961. Thirty years would pass before Robert McNamara publicly admitted that his team "totally underestimated the nationalist aspect of Ho Chi Minh's movement.": McNamara, *In Retrospect*, p. 33.
64. *Time*, 3 April 1964; the same line had surfaced even earlier, in the issue of 13 September 1963.

65. Stanley Karnow, "How Communist Economics Failed in China," *Fortune* (July 1963), pp. 155 ff.
66. Department of State, "Presidential Program for Vietnam," 23 May 1961, in the papers of Lyndon Baines Johnson, VP Security, 1, Vice-Presidential Visit # 12, Southeast Asia (LBJL).
67. *Time*, 4 August 1961.
68. *Time*, 11 May 1962.
69. *Time*, 26 January 1962.
70. *Time*, 23 March 1962.
71. CBL to Madame Nhu, 24 February 1964, and related material in the papers of CBL, 223, 1.
72. *Time*, 9 February 1962.
73. *Time*, 4 August 1961.
74. BDM Corporation, "A Study of the Strategic Lessons Learned in Vietnam," IV, 3–10 (LBJL).
75. Herring, *America's Longest War*, p. 96.
76. Telcon, Ball and Johnson, 14 February 1962, in the papers of George W. Ball, 7 (LBJL).
77. Frances FitzGerald, *Fire in the Lake: The Americans and the Vietnamese in Vietnam* (New York: Vintage Books, 1989), chapter 4.
78. *Time*, 11 May 1962.
79. Cohen, *America in the Age of Soviet Power*, p. 147.
80. Department of State, Task Force Southeast Asia, "Status Report on Southeast Asia," 8 August 1962, in the papers of Lyndon Baines Johnson, VP Security, Visit #13 (LBJL); and *Time*, 21 September 1962.
81. Interview with Paul Gardner, "A Laotian Reader," Extracts from Oral History Transcripts from the Foreign Affairs Oral History Program, compiled by Charles Stuart Kennedy (Foreign Service Institute and Georgetown University, 1995), pp. 3–4.
82. *Time*, 23 February 1962.
83. *Time*, 2 July 1962.
84. *Time*, 8 June 1962.
85. *Time*, 19 October 1962.
86. C. D. Jackson, memorandum to John Steele, 5 July 1963, in the papers of HRL, 76, *Time* Sp-Sz.
87. *Time*, 21 June 1963.
88. *Time*, 9 August 1963.
89. *Time*, 16 August 1963.
90. *Time*, cover on Madame Nhu, 9 August 1963.
91. *Time*, 30 August 1963.
92. *Time*, 6 and 20 September 1963.
93. Interview with Robert H. Miller, in "A Vietnam Reader," I, 2–3; and Herring, *America's Longest War*, p. 112.
94. *Time*, 9 August 1963.
95. David Halberstam, *The Powers That Be* (New York: Dell, 1980), p. 639.
96. *Time*, 20 September 1963.
97. Interview with Charles Mohr, p. 1, in the papers of David Halberstam related to *The Powers That Be*.
98. William Prochnau, *Once Upon a Distant War* (New York: Times Books, 1995), pp. 356–357.

99. BDM Corporation, "A Study of Strategic Lessons Learned in Vietnam," IV, 3–12 (LBJL).
100. *Time*, 20 September 1963.
101. Prochnau, *Once Upon a Distant War*, pp. 425 ff.
102. *Time*, 25 December 1964.
103. *Time*, 11 October 1963.
104. Interview with Paul M. Kattenburg, in "A Vietnam Reader," I, 3–5.
105. McNamara, *In Retrospect*, p. 84.
106. *Time*, 8 November 1963.
107. *Time*, 29 November 1963.
108. *Time*, 20 December 1963.
109. Cohen, *America in the Age of Soviet Power*, p. 162.
110. McNamara, *In Retrospect*, p. 96, claims that Kennedy would have pulled out, and Newman, *JFK and Vietnam*, p. 457, argues that Kennedy would never have deployed combat troops in South Vietnam.
111. Hedley Donovan, *Right Places, Right Times* (New York: Henry Holt, 1989), p. 249.
112. HRL, address to the 34th National Business Conference, Harvard University, 6 June 1964, in the papers of W. A. Swanberg, 22, 1964.
113. Henry Grunwald, *One Man's America: A Journalist's Search for the Heart of His Country* (New York: Doubleday, 1997), p. 292.
114. *Time*, 29 November 1963.
115. *Life*, 20 January 1958.
116. Lyndon B. Johnson to HRL, 24 August 1955, in the papers of Lyndon Baines Johnson, Subject File, 101, Public Information, Press, National [Luce, Henry R. 1955–67] (LBJL).
117. Oral History Interview with Hugh Sidey, 22 July 1971, p. 1 (LBJL).
118. Interview with John Steele, p. 5, in the papers of David Halberstam related to *The Powers That Be*.
119. Interview with Otto Fuerbringer, p. 2, in the papers of David Halberstam related to *The Powers That Be*.
120. Max Ways, "The Two Lyndon Johnsons," *Fortune* (January 1964), pp. 80 ff.
121. *Time*, 7 February and 13 March 1964.
122. *Time*, 20 March 1964.
123. *Time*, 24 April 1964.
124. *Time*, 23 October 1964.

14. A Troubled Crusade in Vietnam

1. H. W. Caldwell, To Whom it May Concern, 1 April 1959, in the papers of CBL, 22, 8.
2. "The Reminiscences of Andrew Heiskell," pp. 5, 255.
3. Grunwald, *One Man's America*, p. 353.
4. CBL, memcon of Sherman Adams, 18 June 1957, in the papers of CBL, 719, political activities. *Time*, 22 April 1957, early on took a dim view of Goldwater.
5. Interview with CBL, in the papers of W. A. Swanberg, 18, interviews.
6. *Time*, 25 September 1964.
7. *Time*, 9 October 1964.
8. *Time*, 7 August 1964.

9. McNamara, *In Retrospect*, p. 142.
10. *Time*, 7 August 1964.
11. *Time*, 19 February and 2 July 1965.
12. HRL, "The Rim of Asia," in the papers of HRL, 86.
13. *Time*, 26 February 1965.
14. Oral History Interview with Frank McCulloch, 13 May 1980, p. 36 (LBJL).
15. *Time*, 7 August 1964.
16. HRL, luncheon address on 14 October 1964, LWO 5746 R 47 (Library of Congress).
17. *Time*, 26 February 1965. Much of the American press agreed with this appraisal of the Chinese threat. Typical examples can be found in "Who is the Real Enemy in Vietnam?" *U.S. News & World Report*, 1 June 1964, and "Is Red China a 'Paper Tiger'?" *U.S. News & World Report*, 19 October 1964.
18. *Time*, 13 November 1964.
19. CBL, commencement address at St. John's University, 14 June 1964, in the papers of CBL, 691.
20. Madame Chiang Kai-shek to CBL, 31 January 1964, in the papers of CBL, 220, 3.
21. *The Gallup Poll*, III, 1915 (1 January 1965).
22. CBL, "The Crisis in the United Nations," address on 10 December 1964, in the papers of CBL, 692, 13.
23. Donovan, *Right Places, Right Times*, p. 213.
24. Ben L. Martin, "The New 'Old China Hands': Reshaping American Opinion," *Asian Affairs: An American Review* (January–February 1976), pp. 192–195; and P. M. Evans, "The Long Way Home: John Fairbank and American China Policy 1941–72," *International Journal*, 37, 584–605.
25. George W. Ball, "How Valid Are the Assumptions Underlying Our Viet Nam Policies?" in the papers of Lyndon Baines Johnson, President 1963–69, NSF, Country File, Vietnam, 222, Vietnam 10, 64 (LBJL); Stanley Karnow, *Vietnam* (New York: Penguin Books, 1984), pp. 404–405; and George W. Ball, *The Past Has Another Pattern*, pp. 380–381.
26. *Time*, 16 April 1965.
27. Interview with John Holdridge, in "A China Reader," p. 18.
28. Charles J. V. Murphy, "Traveler to the Pacific Wars," *Fortune* (August 1965), pp. 133 ff.
29. *The Gallup Poll*, II, 1908–1909 (18 and 29 November 1964).
30. "U.S. Admits Shift in Vietnam Stand," *New York Times*, 25 February 1965.
31. *The Gallup Poll*, II, 1921–1922 (31 January and 3 February 1965).
32. William M. Hammond, *Public Affairs: The Military and the Media, 1962–1968* [*United States Army in Vietnam*] (Washington, DC: Center of Military History, United States Army, 1988), pp. 108–111.
33. *Time*, 1 January 1965.
34. *Issues and Answers*, 24 January 1965, p. 12.
35. *Time*, 22 January 1965.
36. *Time*, 26 March 1965.
37. *The Gallup Poll*, II, 1925 (16 February 1965).
38. *The Gallup Poll*, II, 1929 (12 March 1965).
39. Ibid., 1939 (16 May 1965).
40. McNamara, *In Retrospect*, pp. 165 and 177.
41. "Summary Notes of 553rd NSC Meeting," 27 July 1965, in the papers of Lyndon Baines Johnson, President 1963–1969, NSC Meetings, 1 (LBJL).

42. *The Gallup Poll*, II, 1958 (29 August 1965).
43. Jack Valenti, memorandum for the President, 12 May 1965, White House Central Files, Name File, Steele, John L. (LBJL).
44. Charles J. V. Murphy, "Traveler to the Pacific Wars," *Fortune* (August 1965), p. 250.
45. *Time*, 24 September 1965.
46. Oral History interview with McCulloch, pp. 7–39 (LBJL).
47. Philip Habib, memorandum to Harold Kaplan, 26 September 1967, in NSF, Vietnam, 7E(1)a (LBJL).
48. *Time*, 10 June 1966.
49. Clark Clifford to Lyndon B. Johnson, 17 May 1965, Reference File Vietnam, 1 (LBJL).
50. Theodore Draper, *Abuse of Power* (New York: Viking Press, 1967), pp. 68–83; and *New York Times*, 4 July 1965, 6, 1.
51. McNamara, *In Retrospect*, p. 186.
52. *Time*, 22 October 1965.
53. *Time*, 18 February 1966.
54. *Time*, 3 February 1967.
55. *Time*, 18 June 1965.
56. *Time*, 14 May 1965.
57. Murphy, "Traveler," p. 252.
58. "Communism Today: A Refresher Course," *Time*, 6 August 1965.
59. *Time*, 16 April 1965.
60. Gilbert Burck, "Guns, Butter, and Then-Some Economy," *Fortune* (October 1965), pp. 119 ff.
61. *Time*, 1 January 1965.
62. *Time*, 9 July 1965.
63. *Time*, 5 June 1964 and 18 February 1966.
64. Donovan, *Right Places, Right Times*, p. 359.
65. *Time*, 18 and 25 February 1966.
66. *Time*, 16 April and 21 May 1965.
67. HRL, notes and clippings 1966, in the papers of HRL, 86.
68. *Time*, 8 April 1966.
69. *Time*, 22 April 1966.
70. *Time*, 8 October 1965.
71. *Time*, 3 December 1965.
72. "The Vietniks: Self-Defeating Dissent," *Time*, 29 October 1965.
73. *Time*, 21 May 1965.
74. *Time*, 28 May 1965.
75. *Time*, 16 July 1965.
76. *Time*, 10 September 1965.
77. *Time*, 9 July 1965.
78. *Time*, 5 November 1965.
79. *Time*, 3 September 1965.
80. *Time*, 29 October 1965.
81. *Time*, 22 October 1965.
82. *The Gallup Poll*, II, 1966 and 1971 (13 October and 21 November 1965).
83. *Time*, 1 January 1966.

84. John Steele, address to the Magazine Showcase, National Association of Secondary-School Principals, Cleveland, OH, 5 February 1966; and Bill Moyers to John Steele, 16 February 1966, in the papers of Lyndon B. Johnson, Presidential, Central Files, General, SP, ND19, CO312, Steele, John (LBJL).
85. "The Reminiscences of Andrew Heiskell," 11, 547.
86. *Time*, 17 June 1966.
87. *Time*, 7 January 1966.
88. *Time*, 24 December 1965.
89. *Time*, 18 February 1966.
90. *Time*, 28 January 1966.
91. *Time*, 24 June 1966.
92. John Mecklin, "Building by the Billion in Vietnam," *Fortune* (September 1966), pp. 113 ff.
93. Edmund K. Faltermeyer, "The Surprising Assets of South Vietnam's Economy," *Fortune* (March 1966), pp. 111 ff.
94. *Time*, 8 April 1966.
95. *Time*, 18 February and 1 April 1966.
96. *Time*, 22 April 1966.
97. *Time*, 15 and 29 April 1966.
98. *Time*, 19 August 1966.
99. *The Gallup Poll*, II, 2010 (3 June 1966).
100. Ibid., 1998–1999 and 2009 (30 March and 1 April, and 25 May 1966).
101. Ibid., 2026 (9 September 1966).
102. *Time*, 17 June 1966.
103. HRL, unpublished manuscript, p. 35.
104. Interview with Lyndon B. Johnson, 2 June 1966, in the papers of CBL, 719, political activities.
105. Bill Moyers, memorandum to the president, 1 September 1966; and HRL to Lyndon B. Johnson, 6 September 1966, in the papers of Lyndon B. Johnson, Presidential, Executive, Central Files, BE5 PR 8–1/L* (LBJL).
106. *Time*, 20 January 1967.
107. *Time*, 3 February 1967.
108. Interview with Hugh Sidey, p. 9, in the papers of David Halberstam concerning *The Powers That Be*.

15. The Final Years of the Crusade in East Asia

1. HRL to John S. Billings, 13 February 1967, Billings collection, scrapbook 40.
2. HRL, notes and clippings 1966, in the papers of HRL, 86.
3. *Time*, 24 December 1965.
4. Tom Johnson, memorandum for the president, 12 October 1967, in the White House Central Files, Executive, SP, ND19, Co312 (LBJL).
5. Henry Luce III to HRL, 1 October 1966, in the papers of CBL, 15, 6.
6. *Time*, 19 August 1966.
7. *Time*, 15 July 1966.
8. HRL, address at the Syracuse University School of Journalism, 13 November 1966, in the private papers of Sidney James.
9. "America's Permanent Stake in Asia," *Time*, 23 September 1966.

10. Gallup polls, in the Office Files of Fred Panzer, 182, Vietnam (LBJL).

11. *Time*, 25 October 1963, "LSD," 17 June 1966.

12. "The Reminiscences of Andrew Heiskell," pp. 5, 265.

13. Curtis Prendergast with Geoffrey Colvin, *The World of Time Inc.: The Intimate History of a Changing Enterprise, Volume Three: 1960–1980* (New York: Atheneum, 1986), p. 199.

14. HRL, comments, in T 8515 (LOC); the papers of HRL, 73, YMCA Mahaska Center; and HRL, William Penn College commencement address, 30 May 1966, in the papers of W. A. Swanberg, 22, 1965–67.

15. DJSB, 28 November 1951.

16. "What the U.S. Knows About Red China," *Time*, 20 May 1966.

17. *Time*, 20 May 1966.

18. *Time*, 18 March 1966.

19. *Time*, 8 April 1966; and "On Understanding Asia," *Time*, 1 July 1966.

20. *Time*, 17 June and 12 August 1966, failed to grasp the enormity of the revolution unleashed by Mao.

21. "Letter from the Publisher," *Time*, 13 January 1967.

22. *Time*, 2 September 1966. Charles J. V. Murphy, "Red China's Sinking Revolution," *Fortune* (November 1966), pp. 135 ff., predicted the imminent demise of the Communist regime.

23. *Time*, 27 January 1967.

24. *Time*, 24 February 1967.

25. *Time*, 4 November 1966.

26. *Time*, 13 January 1967.

27. *Time*, 18 November 1966.

28. George Ball, "The Rationalist in Power," *New York Review of Books*, 22 April 1993, p. 36.

29. *Time*, 19 August 1966.

30. *Time*, 5 August 1966.

31. *Time*, 6 January 1967.

32. *Time*, 11 November 1966.

33. Meeting of the president with Hugh Sidey of *Time* magazine, 8 February 1967, in the papers of Lyndon B. Johnson, President 1963–69, Meeting Notes, 3 (LBJL).

34. HRL, address at the University of California at Santa Barbara, 1 February 1967, in the papers of HRL, 82.

35. China Consultation Study Paper, 14 January 1967, distributed by Clifford Earle on 3 February; William Henderson to HRL, 24 February; and HRL to Clifford Earle, in the papers of HRL, 55, Presbyterian Study Paper.

36. *Time*, 5 May 1967.

37. *Time*, 26 May 1967.

38. *Time*, 14 October 1966.

39. Joseph Epstein, "Henry Luce and His Time," *Commentary* (November 1967), pp. 35 and 42.

40. James Wechsler, "Of Henry Luce," *New York Post*, 14 January 1965. The classic attack on *Time* for its mauling of Stevenson was written by Ben H. Bagdikian: "TIME The Weekly Newsmagazine," *The New Republic*, 23 February 1959.

41. *Time*, 6 January 1967.

42. "The Morality of War," *Time*, 20 January 1967.

43. *Time*, 3 February 1967.
44. HRL, 17 May 1966, in John K. Jessup, ed., *The Ideas of Henry Luce* (New York: Athenaeum, 1969), p. 142.
45. Correspondence regarding Luce's Morehouse College commitment can be consulted in the papers of HRL, 76.
46. Swanberg, *Luce and His Empire*, p. 480.
47. *Time*, 17 March 1967.
48. "The Mind of China," *Time*, 17 March 1967.
49. Donovan, *Right Places, Right Time*, p. 363.
50. *Time*, 8 March 1968.
51. *Time*, 16 February 1968.
52. *Time*, 12 April 1968. On the changes at the magazine, see Richard Pollak, "*Time* After Luce," *Harper's Magazine* (July 1969), pp. 42 ff.
53. Anna Chennault to Herbert Mitgang, 19 April 1971, in the papers of Thomas G. Corcoran, 110, China lobby.
54. Albert C. Wedemeyer to George Fox Mott, 14 August 1980, in the papers of George Fox Mott.
55. B. A. Garside to Richard M. Nixon, 15 July 1971, in the papers of B. A. Garside, 4.
56. Michael Y. M. Kau et al., "Public Opinion and Our China Policy," *Asian Affairs: An American Review*, 5 (January–February 1978), 135.
57. CBL, "Speculations on Sino-American Relations," Honolulu, Hawaii, 5 October 1971, in the papers of CBL, 694.
58. CBL to Richard M. Nixon, 15 June 1971, ibid., 231, 16.
59. *Time*, 5 February 1973.
60. *Time*, 7 and 14 April 1975.
61. "The Reminiscences of Andrew Heiskell," pp. 585 ff.
62. Hedley Donovan, *Right Places, Right Time*, p. 212.
63. HRL, speech to Time Inc. executives, 4 May 1950, in the TLF, II, 142.
64. Dwight Macdonald to Henry Luce III, 23 October 1972, in the papers of Dwight Macdonald, 29, 756.
65. *The Los Angeles Times*: Elson, *Time Inc.*, pp. 460–461. This appraisal appeared in 1941.
66. Bill Rich to HRL, 15 January 1942, in the papers of CBL, 841.
67. John Kobler, *Luce: His Time, Life, and Fortune* (Garden City, NY: Doubleday, 1968), p. 2.
68. *Life*, 14 and 21 August 1939; George C. Marshall to Daniel Longwell, 19 July 1940, in the Daniel Longwell Collection, 69; and C. D. Jackson, memorandum to Edward K. Thompson, 19 August 1940, ibid.
69. Albert C. Wedemeyer to HRL, 2 July 1946, from the papers of Albert C. Wedemeyer, and provided to the author by Dr. Keith Eiler.
70. Lincoln White to Mr. Berding, 24 July 1957, Office Memorandum, Department of State, in the papers of John Foster Dulles, selected correspondence and related material, 118.
71. Sterling, "The Luce Empire," chapter 6, p. 8.
72. "This Is the Day," 3 April 1956, in the papers of W. A. Swanberg, 19.
73. Interview with Teddy White, p. 5, in the papers of David Halberstam concerning *The Powers That Be*.
74. John K. Jessup, "Wrong Niche," *The New Republic*, 30 September 1972, p. 27.

75. W. A. Swanberg, letter to the editor of *New York Times Book Review*, 22 August 1988.
76. HRL, cable to H. H. Kung, March 3, 1944, in the papers of Lauchlin Currie, 5.
77. Michael H. Hunt, *Ideology and U.S. Foreign Policy* (New Haven, CT: Yale University Press, 1987), p. 169.
78. Philip Kotler and Gary Armstrong, *Principles of Marketing* (Englewood Cliffs, NJ: Prentice-Hall, 1996), p. 5.

Index